To David,

with admiration.

Bob

Solomon's Knot

KAUFFMAN FOUNDATION SERIES ON
Innovation and Entrepreneurship

Boulevard of Broken Dreams: Why Public Efforts to Boost Entrepreneurship and Venture Capital Have Failed—and What to Do about It, by Josh Lerner

The Invention of Enterprise: Entrepreneurship from Ancient Mesopotamia to Modern Times, edited by David S. Landes, Joel Mokyr, and William J. Baumol

The Venturesome Economy: How Innovation Sustains Prosperity in a More Connected World, by Amar Bhidé

The Microtheory of Innovative Entrepreneurship, by William J. Baumol

Solomon's Knot

How Law Can End the Poverty of Nations

Robert D. Cooter
Hans-Bernd Schäfer

PRINCETON UNIVERSITY PRESS
PRINCETON AND OXFORD

Copyright © 2012 by Princeton University Press

Published by Princeton University Press, 41 William Street, Princeton, New Jersey 08540

In the United Kingdom: Princeton University Press, 6 Oxford Street, Woodstock, Oxford-shire OX20 1TW

press.princeton.edu

Library of Congress Cataloging-in-Publication Data

Cooter, Robert.
  Solomon's knot : how law can end the poverty of nations / Robert D. Cooter, Hans-Bernd Schäfer.
      p. cm.—(Kauffman Foundation Series on Innovation and Entrepreneurship)
   Includes bibliographical references and index.
   ISBN 978-0-691-14792-5 (hardcover : alk. paper)   1. Law and economics.   2. Poverty.
3. Law—Economic aspects.   4. Economic development.   I. Schäfer, Hans-Bernd.
II. Title.   III. Series.
   K487.E3C668   2011
   343'.07—dc23

                                                                        2011034413

British Library Cataloging-in-Publication Data is available

Published in collaboration with the Ewing Marion Kauffman Foundation and the Berkley Center for Entrepreneurial Studies, New York University

This book has been composed in Scala and Futura
Printed on acid-free paper. ∞
Printed in the United States of America

10 9 8 7 6 5 4 3 2 1

Robert Cooter's Dedication

A common dedication reads,

"To ____, without whom this book would have been
   impossible."

During our marriage, my wife and I grew up together.
   Because of her, I became myself. Hence

"To Blair, without whom I would have been impossible."

. . .

Hans-Bernd Schäfer's Dedication

Für meine Tochter Anna mit den kleinen festen Schritten

Contents

Preface	ix
Acknowledgments	xiii

Chapter 1
It's about the Economy   1

Chapter 2
The Economic Future of the World   13

Chapter 3
The Double Trust Dilemma of Development   27

Chapter 4
Make or Take   39

Chapter 5
The Property Principle for Innovation   50

Chapter 6
Keeping What You Make—Property Law   64

Chapter 7
Doing What You Say—Contracts   82

Chapter 8
Giving Credit to Credit—Finance and Banking   101

Chapter 9
Financing Secrets—Corporations   123

Chapter 10
Hold or Fold—Financial Distress   142

Chapter 11
Termites in the Foundation—Corruption   159

Chapter 12
Poverty Is Dangerous—Accidents and Liability   179

Chapter 13
Academic Scribblers and Defunct Economists   193

Chapter 14
How the Many Overcome the Few   211

Chapter 15
Legalize Freedom—Conclusion   223

Notes   229
Bibliography   299
Index   313

Preface

How do you become the richest woman in China? Shang Yin, the eldest of a soldier's eight children, opened a printing shop in the 1980s when she was in her twenties. As China moved to a market economy, demand swelled for printed products used by new industries. A short supply of paper bottlenecked Shang Yin's business, until she made the discovery of her life: ships left Chinese harbors for the United States filled with cargo, and they returned almost empty. (The United States imports bulky goods from China to fill stores like Walmart, and exports intangible services like computer programs, Hollywood movies, and banking services.) Shang Yin had discovered a new market, and she reorganized her business to exploit this opportunity. She started buying scrap paper in the United States and shipping it back to China. Business burgeoned at her company, Nine Dragons Paper Industries, and some observers now count her as China's richest woman.

When a developing country has many entrepreneurs like Shang Yin, a cascade of innovations in markets and organizations lifts productivity, wages, and profits. Innovations in markets and organizations combine ideas and capital in bold ventures with big risks and opportunities. The central claim of this book is that sustained growth in developing countries occurs through innovations in markets and organizations by entrepreneurs; developing innovations poses a problem of trust between innovators with ideas and investors with capital (the "double trust dilemma"); and the best solutions require law.

In Shakespeare's *Twelfth Night*, a shipwreck separates brother and sister, who each conclude falsely that the other died. Reunification of Sebastian and Viola at play's end resolves confusion and causes rejoicing (but not by everyone). Similarly, economics began as a close relative to law, but their methodologies diverged in the twentieth century. When the subjects lost communication with each other, some scholars in one subject thought the other subject had died intellectually. In the last quarter of the twentieth century, however, a powerful scholarly movement brought these subjects back together.[1] Reunification of law and economics has resolved confusion and caused rejoicing (but not by everyone). With law and economics reunified, now is the time to explain some causes and cures of the poverty of nations.

These pages avoid economics jargon and technical law. Educated generalists can understand them by thinking hard and not shrinking from numbers. Besides inclusiveness, sticking to ordinary language has another big advantage: it spans disciplines. Specialists in law will encounter simple explanations of unfamiliar economic theories, and specialists in economics will encounter simple explanations of unfamiliar legal theories.

Given the importance of law and economics, readers might suppose that our newly reunified multidiscipline is concerned especially with growth. This supposition is wrong. Economic efficiency distinguishes between growth and efficiency. Increasing efficiency requires reshuffling resources from less-productive to more-productive uses, like shifting a horse and plough to a more fertile field. The theory of allocative efficiency is older, more elegant, and better confirmed empirically than growth theory. The emerging subject of law and economics has focused on traditional economic theory, not the relatively new subject of growth theory.[2] Innovation is the source of sustained growth, and the economic theory of innovation is underdeveloped, especially concerning entrepreneurship. Here is where law can repay its recent intellectual debts to economics. This book, we hope, is a down payment.

How much understanding of national poverty can law and economics deliver? No one predicted that outsourcing of services and computer software would drive so much of India's economic growth, but we can now understand the reasons for this success. Like evolution in the natural world, innovation is unpredictable looking forward and understandable looking backward. Since innovation is foreseen imperfectly, mystery necessarily clings to economic growth. Law and economics can explain how laws promote development, but they cannot predict the innovations that entrepreneurs will make.

Acknowledgments

Four institutions helped Bob Cooter and Hans-Bernd Schäfer cross a continent and an ocean to work together on this book: the Berkeley Law and Economics Program, the Hamburg Institute of Law and Economics, the Humbolt Foundation, and the Center for Contract Law at Columbia University Law School. The Humboldt Forschungspreis awarded to Cooter allowed him to visit Schäfer at the Hamburg Institute of Law and Economics. The Center for Contract Law at Columbia University Law School gave Cooter a semester as a visitor to focus on this manuscript. We also thank Bob Litan and Carl Schramm of the Kauffman Foundation for institutional support. For research and editorial assistance, we thank Zhang Wei, Ida Ng, Ursula Vogeler, Frank Müller-Langer, Sönke Häseler, and Axel Moeller.

For the best feast, each guest should contribute a dish. Many guests contributed to our feast of scholarship. Throughout the project, Blair Dean Cooter fixed our lame prose. We would like to thank the participants in two manuscript conferences devoted to this book, which were organized by Paul Edwards of the Mercatus Center at George Mason University and Henry Butler of the Searle Center (then at Northwestern University, now at George Mason University). As we neared completion, Ben Wittes of the Brookings Institution gave us remarkably penetrating comments that led to fundamental improvements in the manuscript, and Jack Rummel's line editing saved us from many errors and irregularities.

As this book draws on years of work and thought, so we would first like to thank those who taught us law and economics over the years. Bob Cooter thanks George Richardson for introducing him to microeconomics; Ken Arrow for teaching him the beauty of economic theory; Richard Musgrave who encouraged his interest in the unrecognized field of law and economics; Albert Hirschman who introduced him to economic development; and Mel Eisenberg who taught him to think like a lawyer. Bob also thanks Wolfgang Fikentscher and Robert K. Thomas for many evenings of discussion and meditation on this book's themes, and Peter Hacker and John Rawls for instruction on how to think about what is important.

Hans-Bernd Schäfer thanks Willy Kraus, who introduced him to development economics and Claus Ott, who taught him law and how to think about law over many years. He also thanks Hein Kötz, with whom he discussed many of the legal matters of the book and many other projects at hundreds of lunches, which now span more than two decades.

For useful comments on this manuscript, we would like to thank the following: Susan Rose Ackerman, John Armour, Robert Atiah, Pranab Bardhan, Jochen Bigus, Gisèle Behrens, Henry Butler, Lloyd Cohen, Paul Edwards, Thomas Eger, Merritt Fox, Manfred Holler, D. Bruce Johnson, Ed Kitch, Timur Kuran, Gregory Lablanc, Robert Litan, Curtis Milhaupt, Douglas North, Mancur Olson, Franceso Parisi, Geoffrey Parker, Svetozar Pejovich, Katharina Pistor, Christa Randzio Plath, Ned Phelps, Angara Raja, Flavia Santinoni Vera, Bruno Meyerhof Salama, Heike Schweitzer, Eric Talley, Carl Schramm, Michael Trebilcock, Stefan Voigt, and Georg von Wangenheim.

Earlier versions of the core ideas found in chapters 1–3 were presented in the Mason Ladd Lecture delivered at the Florida State University College of Law in January 2005. These were also presented in the articles "Innovation, Information, and the Poverty of Nations: The 2005 Ladd Lecture," *Florida State University Law Review* 33: 373–394, and "Escaping Poverty: Law and Growth—keynote address," *Southwestern Journal of Law and Trade in the Americas* 101 (2006): 181–187.

Solomon's Knot

Chapter 1
It's about the Economy

A grand master asks the tournament organizers to pay him by placing one penny on the first white square of a chess board, two pennies on the second white square, four on the third white square, proceeding until all thirty-two white squares are covered. The initial penny would double in value thirty-one times, resulting in more than $21 million being laid on the last white square. Growth compounds faster than the mind can grasp. Compounded over a century, 2 percent annual growth increases wealth more than seven times, which is roughly the growth rate of the United States in the previous century, and 10 percent annual growth increases wealth almost fourteen thousand times, which is roughly the growth rate of China in the last thirty years.

From the perspective of two centuries, the wealth of the richest countries has risen above the poorest like Mount Everest rising above the Ganges Plain. The gap in wealth opened because the richest countries grew richer, not because the poorer countries grew poorer. Most poor countries today are somewhat richer relative to their past and much poorer relative to the rich countries of the contemporary world. One scholar estimated income per capita for fifty-six countries in 1820.[1] He found that the richest countries in the sample had income per capita of approximately $1,800 and the poorest had $400, for a ratio of 4½:1. We repeated this same exercise for 2003 and found the richest countries had income per capita of approximately $25,000 and the poorest countries had approximately $500, for a ratio of 50:1.

The question of whether growth is faster in rich or poor nations will determine whether living standards in the world converge or diverge. If poor nations grow faster than rich nations, the gap between them will close surprisingly quickly. The lifting of so many Asians out of poverty in the late twentieth century, especially by rapid growth in China and India after 1980, is one of history's triumphs. Conversely, if rich nations grow faster than poor nations, the gap between them will widen surprisingly quickly. Income per capita declined in sub-Saharan Africa by roughly 20 percent between 1970 and 1990, which is one of history's failures. Growth has resumed in Africa, but not at a rate that will overtake rich countries.

How does an economy grow? Through business ventures.[2] A bold ship's captain in seventeenth-century England proposes to investors in a port town that they finance a voyage to Asia for spices.[3] The voyage is inherently risky. Weather is uncertain and channels are uncharted. The Dutch prey on English ships, the English prey on Dutch ships, and other pirates prey on both of them. If, however, the captain returns to the English port with a cargo of spices, they will be worth a fortune. The ship's captain must convince the investors that he can do it. He needs a large ship outfitted for two to five years of travel. To convince them, he discloses secrets about how to get to Asia and what to do when he arrives. The captain must trust the investors with his secrets, and the investors must trust the captain with the ship and its supplies.

This is a *double trust dilemma*. To solve it, the captain and the investors form a new kind of firm invented in the seventeenth century for the spice voyages: a joint stock company.[4] The participants—investors, captain, and crew—are legally entitled to shares of the hoped-for cargo. Some participants have larger shares than others, depending on their contributions. With these legal arrangements, the investors stand to gain more from the success of the voyage than by selling the captain's secrets. Similarly, the captain stands to gain more from the success of the voyage than by stealing the ship and its cargo. Self-interest enforces the commitment of the parties to the voyage.

Unlike so many other ships that sail for Asia, this one returns safely after two years. The townspeople spot the vessel sailing toward the harbor and the investors rush to the dock to keep watch over the cargo. They immediately hold a meeting of shareholders called a "general court." It divides the cargo among the shareholders, they leave the dock with their spices, and the company dissolves.

Similarly, an engineer in Silicon Valley in 1985 has an idea for a new computer technology. The engineer cannot patent the idea until he develops it. Developing it requires more money than the engineer can risk personally. He drafts a business plan and meets with a small group of investors. The engineer fears that the investors will steal his idea, and the investors fear that the engineer will steal their money. Besides the fear of betrayal, developing the idea is inherently risky—it might fail or someone else might patent the idea first. If the innovation succeeds, however, it will be worth a fortune.

The engineer cautiously explains his idea to the small group of investors, who accept his invitation to incorporate and appoint him as chief executive. They distribute shares of stock among themselves according to their contributions, and the shareholders elect a board of directors that carefully balances their interests. With this legal arrangement, self-interest causes the investors to keep the engineer's secrets and the engineer to use the money as promised. Unlike so many other start-ups, this one succeeds after five years and the firm acquires a valuable patent. The engineer and the investors subsequently dissolve the company by selling it for a lot of money to a large, established firm.

Seventeenth-century spice voyages and twentieth-century technology start-ups involve secrets, up-front investment, high risk, and high return. Many business ventures have these characteristics in muted form. To grow quickly, a business venture must combine new ideas and capital. An ancient motif on this book's cover depicts two interlinking rings called "Solomon's knot." Sailors particularly favored this kind of knot for strength and durability. Like the two rings, King Solomon held together two Jewish kingdoms, according to the Bible. Similarly, ideas and capital must unite to develop innovations and grow the economy.

In every country, growth occurs through innovative ventures, but the form of innovation differs. Innovations in Silicon Valley usually have a technological basis, such as new computer chips or programs that were previously unknown to the world. Technological innovation often requires research universities and similar institutions found especially in developed countries. The relative weakness of research universities and similar institutions in developing countries today limits their capacity for technological innovation. Technology mostly flows from developed countries to developing countries through international trade, investment, and educational exchanges. The flow hastened in the last century when major wars abated, communism collapsed, and tariffs and transportation costs fell.

Instead of improving technology, many innovations improve organizations and markets.[5] Philip Knight began the Nike Corporation by making running shoes with soles formed on the family waffle iron and selling them out of the trunk of his car in 1972. In 2006 the company reported $15 billion in worldwide sales of sports equipment and clothing. Knight obviously discovered something new, but what was it? The business of Nike is research and marketing. It thinks up new products, contracts with other firms to make them, and then markets them through extensive advertising. Nike does not manufacture anything. Its main facility in Beaverton, Oregon, is a "campus," not a factory. Instead of manufacturing, it contracts with foreign companies to make the goods that it sells. This new organizational form has spread dramatically in the United States as more and more companies "outsource" manufacturing and focus on research and marketing. Other examples of recent innovations in markets and organizations in the United States include debit cards, hostile takeovers, networks of innovators, and team production (imported from Japan).

Innovation in developing countries mostly takes the form of improving organizations and finding new markets, especially by taking organizations and markets that originate in developed countries and adapting them to local conditions. Before buying edible oil, African consumers smell and taste it to assure themselves of freshness, which requires selling it in open containers. Closed containers, however, have many advantages, including lower shipping and storage costs. Bhimji Depar

Shah figured out how to sell oil in closed containers and retain the trust of African consumers. He started an edible oil company in Thika, Kenya, in 1991 that developed into a business empire. The company's homepage reads: "Integrity is what all our people value and uphold ruthlessly which enables trust leading to empowerment." Selecting reliable salespeople and dispersing trustworthy workers around Africa required innovation in organization like Phil Knight accomplished at the Nike Corporation.

Besides new organizations, adaptations often create new contracts. The textile business in Bangladesh relies on two new contracts: bonds for warehousing and back-to-back letters of credit.[6] Bonded warehouses protect producers against theft or fraud in the chain of distribution, and letters of credit protect buyers against theft or fraud at the point of sale.

In business, adaptation is creative and risky. The adapter has an idea that is new to a developing country. Proving its worth in the marketplace requires risky investment. The investment often goes to building an organization embedding the new idea. The innovator must trust the investor not to steal his organization, and the investor must trust the innovator not to steal his money. If the adaptation succeeds, it attracts competitors, who diffuse the idea and reduce the innovator's profits. Adaptation in developing countries thus faces many of the same obstacles as invention in developed countries.

Instead of adaptation, some people imagine that developing countries can grow by imitation that is mechanical and safe. If growth were this simple, poor countries would already be rich. In poor and rich countries alike, new business ventures mostly fail and the investors lose their money, whereas a few succeed spectacularly and drive growth. Picking out the adaptation that will succeed in Africa is just as hard as picking out the invention that will succeed in Silicon Valley.

Nations are poor because their economies fail to innovate and grow. An economy can fail to grow because of military invasion as in Poland in 1939, or isolation as in the New Guinea Highlands in 1920, or civil war as in Somalia in 2000, or natural disaster as with the Sahara Desert's encroachment on farms, or a bursting financial bubble as in the United

States in 1929 and 2008. In recent decades, however, many countries have enjoyed benign conditions for growth—peace, open economies, no natural disasters, no bursting bubbles. With these background conditions satisfied, law has big effects on growth. Good law engages business energy and advances the economy, whereas bad law suppresses business energy and retards growth.

Sustained growth in developing countries occurs through innovations in markets and organizations, innovation poses a problem of trust between innovators with ideas and financiers with capital, and the best solutions are necessarily legal. Nonexistent, weak, or underenforced laws hobble economies, as some examples illustrate.[7]

> *African Diamonds:* Diamond miners in central Africa use hand tools to dig in a riverbed under the guard of teenage soldiers with Kalashnikov rifles. The miners sell the diamonds to a military officer at a small fraction of world market prices. The diamonds subsequently pass through various intermediaries until they reach Europe. Finally a courier arrives at the central railway station in Antwerp, walks quickly to one of the nearby gem shops where the merchant examines the diamonds and pays in cash, and the courier leaves the city by train within an hour.

In central Africa, producing and transporting diamonds in recent years occurred in conditions that approached anarchy. Central Africa produced few diamonds and got paid much less than the world price for them. If anarchy were replaced by secure property rights, central African nations could produce diamonds with better technology, export them through the regular channels of trade, and receive the world price. And the profits would not go to thugs who commit unspeakable cruelties and heinous abuses of human rights.

> *Moscow Security:* A man opens a small shop selling household goods in Moscow in 1992. A month later three young men visit him with copies of his bank records. Using these numbers, the men

calculate a monthly fee that he must pay them to "protect his shop from hooligans." If he does not pay, they will destroy his shop. The shopkeeper pays and his business succeeds.

Unlike diamond thieves, Moscow criminals who sell security do not want to take everything from their clients. Selling protection presupposes something to protect. In this example, the Moscow criminals impose a "security tax" that leaves room for the shopkeeper to succeed. When organized criminals provide security, however, the "tax" is much higher than when a successful state provides it. (Not to mention the dangers of competing "protectors.") When providing security, the Moscow criminals burden business more heavily than a successful state. Security is a "natural monopoly," which means that states can provide it more cheaply and reliably than private parties. Private security of property is better than anarchy but worse than effective state law.

Indonesian Textiles: In Jakarta in 1987, a businessman manufactures cloth, makes the cloth into dresses, hand-decorates them, and exports the finished product. The entire process occurs inside a single factory where cotton and silk come in the door and decorated dresses go out the door. Managers in the factory are mostly relatives of the owner. Rural households outside Jakarta would do the hand-decorations at lower wages than factory workers in the city. The businessman, however, is unwilling to leave the dresses in rural households in exchange for a promise to decorate them.

The Indonesian businessman in this example gathers everyone needed to produce a particular product into a single factory, where his relatives can monitor them. In countries with weak legal institutions, economic cooperation usually involves people with personal ties, especially relatives and friends. Most people, however, do not have enough relatives and friends to achieve the scale of activity required for affluence. Weak contract law can keep trade local and organizations small. Property and contract law lower the cost of monitoring and extend cooperation to strangers, which facilitates dispersed production, larger organizations, and wider markets.

> *Mexican Loan:* A poor man in Mexico City needs a loan to buy a refrigerator for storing food that he sells on the street. Before loaning the money, the lender needs security against the debtor's failure to repay. The legal process for repossessing the refrigerator from a defaulting debtor is too slow and unreliable. Instead, the lender requires the borrower to provide telephone numbers and addresses of his family, friends, and business associates. If the borrower falls behind in payments, the lender will use the borrower's family and friends to pressure him to repay the loan, and, if necessary, the lender will use their influence to repossess the refrigerator.

The impracticality of collecting debts through courts plagues businesses in poor countries. Mexican debtors often gain by stringing out the legal process because courts assess low interest rates on delays in collecting court judgments. High-cost debt collection can dry up loans to small businesses like the Mexican street vendor. In this example, however, the parties found a way around debt collection through the courts: rely on family and friends. One of Mexico's richest businessmen, Ricardo Salinas, began to build his fortune by figuring out how to collect debts from poor people who buy consumer durables, so household appliances became available to more people.

A different kind of financial problem known as the "soft-budget constraint" exists in countries with a socialist tradition:

> *Chinese Steel:* In 2000, the government privatizes a steel company in northern China by creating stock and divides it three ways. 33 percent is sold to the public who can resell freely ("tradable" shares), 47 percent is allocated to the government, and 20 percent is allocated to insiders who cannot sell ("nontradable" shares). After privatization, the steel company keeps losing money. Its managers, who have political influence, pressure a state bank to finance its losses by buying its bonds, which are commercially unsound.

From China to the Czech Republic, partly privatized companies subsist on soft government loans. In the case of China, their voracious appetite for cash crowded out the bonds of profitable companies in the 2000s that are the engine of China's growth. If the government hardened the soft budget constraint, the bond market would finance growth more effectively.

In some circumstances, every country softens the budget constraint of firms, as shown by the response of the United States to the financial crisis of 2008. The U.S. government committed to loaning or giving over $700 billion to financial institutions. Direct beneficiaries included former business associates of the program's administrator, Secretary of the Treasury Henry Paulson, who earlier had profited vastly from dismantling the regulations protecting against a financial crisis.[8] In spite of the unsavory character of these loans, most U.S. economists endorsed them as necessary to avoid a depression resembling 1929.

A final example contrasts loans and stock markets.

> *Ecuadorian Stocks:* A family owns a successful shrimp farm in the coastal mangrove swamps on the Gulf of Guayaquil. To grow faster in the 1990s, the business needs more capital, either from borrowing money or selling stock. If the family sells stock, investors will receive dividends when shrimp prices rise, and nothing when shrimp prices fall. If the family gets a loan, the lender must receive periodic payments, regardless of whether shrimp prices rise or fall. The small size of the Ecuadorian stock market precludes selling stock, and the family regards a loan as too risky, so it foregoes outside finance and grows more slowly.

Why are stock markets so small in countries like Ecuador? When you invest in a company that you do not control, you run the risk that insiders will appropriate your investment. Investment in stocks makes the problem especially hard to solve. Stocks entitle their owners to a share of profits, but a company's managers can hide profits. A stock market cannot flourish unless corporate and securities laws effectively protect noncontrolling investors. Compared to stocks, loans and bonds reduce the problem of protecting outsiders against insiders. Loans and bonds entitle the lenders to repayment according to a fixed schedule. Monitoring repayment is relatively easier for courts and other legal officials with the will to protect lenders. The credit market can flourish under conditions where the stock market languishes. However, borrowing is more risky for an entrepreneur than selling stocks, so weak stock markets dampen investment and slow the pace of innovation, as illustrated by the Ecuadorian shrimp farm.

As the examples suggest, this book tells the story of how insecure property, unenforceable contracts, uncollectable debts, financial chicanery, and other legal problems stifle business ventures and cause national poverty. Why care so much about wealth? Wealth is a means, not an end like happiness, goodness, holiness, beauty, love, knowledge, or self-fulfillment.[9] Philosophers and priests warn that treating means as ends perverts values. Does our study risk making growth into a fetish like falling in love with a shoe? Is the nation that wins the growth race like the winner of the pie-eating contest whose prize is another pie?

To get perspective on wealth, consider what it can and cannot do. Wealth can buy goods like hamburgers, penicillin, houses, books, theater tickets, shingles, tractors, word processors, movies, and insurance. They are means to ends approved by almost everyone, such as nutrition, health, comfort, enjoyment, education, culture, and travel. They are also means to ends that many people criticize, such as obesity, idleness, wastefulness, dissipation, display, and domination. Like most of economics, this book is more concerned with making wealth than using it wisely. Wealth matters to people. Almost everyone would prefer the wealth of Belgium to the poverty of Bangladesh. Individuals struggle mightily to increase personal wealth, and governments pursue national wealth to secure their popularity and power. The study of economic growth concerns how people can get more of what they want, whereas ethics includes the study of what people ought to want.

The measurement of wealth by economists reflects this fact. All goods sold in markets have prices. The market price of a good reflects how much people want it, regardless of whether they want it for good or bad ends. Multiply the market price times the quantity of each good that a nation produces, sum these numbers, and you have a measure of national income. Thus economists combine heterogeneous goods into a single measure of national income such as gross domestic product (GDP). Since Adam Smith, national income has been identified with the wealth of a nation.[10]

Economists also use this approach to value innovations. Shingles repel rain better than thatch, a tractor plows faster than a digging stick, a word processor corrects errors more easily than a typewriter, a moving picture entertains more than a zoetrope, penicillin cures infections better than sulfa drugs, and insurance provides more security than gold bricks. Almost everyone counts changes like these as improvements that enrich a nation, but by how much? When innovators make better goods, the additional amount that people are willing to pay for them measures the innovation's market value. Summing these increments measures growth in wealth based on market prices.

Economic measures of wealth like GDP measure the wealth of a nation too narrowly, because market prices fail to measure the value of goods not sold in markets, such as national parks, safe streets, clean rivers, public health, and graceful buildings. The same is true for non-market "bads" such as strip-mall ugliness, congestion, global warming, global dimming, high blood pressure, stupid television shows, bad architecture, litter, and intimidating thugs. A comprehensive measure of wealth or national income takes account of the nonmarket goods that people would be willing to buy if markets could sell them. Compared to GDP, more comprehensive measures of wealth that incorporate nonmarket goods reflect more accurately the quality of life and the causes of human welfare.[11]

Explaining law's effect on growth requires data to compare economic performance in different legal jurisdictions. Comparative data are abundant on narrow measures of wealth such as GDP and scarce on inclusive measures of the quality of life. This book mostly cites data on GDP that is readily available although not ideal, and we rarely cite data on the quality of life that is ideal but not readily available. We would prefer inclusive measures of wealth that encompass nonmarket goods, but we must work with the data that we have. Fortunately, the most fundamental principles for business ventures and growth are much the same regardless of wealth's measures, so more inclusive measures of growth are unlikely to change this book's conclusions.

Instead of measuring wealth comprehensively, economics could go directly to one of its ends—say, happiness. Does more wealth cause more happiness? Songwriters disagree: Barrett Strong sang, "Money don't get everything it's true / What it don't get I can't use,"and the Beatles replied, "Money can't buy me love."[12] Using statistics instead of songs, economists have examined the connection between money and happiness. Economists survey people for self-reported happiness: "Is your overall satisfaction with your life high, medium, or low?" In comparisons of nations, people report a *little* more happiness on average in richer countries than in poorer countries, but not a lot more. Similarly, within a nation, people with more money report a little more happiness on average than those with less money. On the individual level, increasing someone's wealth immediately causes a large increase in self-reported happiness, but the wealthier person's happiness soon falls back almost to its former level.[13]

This book explains how better law can promote innovation and increase a nation's wealth. It does not explain what people ought to use their wealth for or how wealth can promote happiness. People want more wealth and understanding how law can give it to them is an appropriate subject of study. The goal of increasing wealth is a more appropriate goal for particular bodies of business law like patents and financial contracts than the goal of improving individual values or increasing happiness. Law for the economy should be designed mostly to maximize wealth, not improve tastes or increase happiness.

A single phrase from the 1992 U.S. presidential campaign of Bill Clinton famously summarizes our approach in this book: "It's the economy, stupid."

Chapter 2
The Economic Future of the World

Before discussing the best laws for growth, let's compare how countries have grown. The world's patterns of growth and decline will provide the background for understanding the legal causes of growth. Angus Maddison heroically attempted to measure the wealth of nations over millennia.[1] He calculated that Egypt was the richest country in the world two thousand years ago, with a per capita income 50 percent higher than in other countries of the Roman Empire, China, or India. In the year 1000 CE Iran and Iraq under the Abbasids were the economically most advanced countries with a per capita income about 50 percent higher than in Europe or Asia. By 1500 Italy had the lead with a per capita income 50 percent higher than in the rest of Western Europe, double that of Asia, and three times that of Africa. In 1820 Western Europe and the United States had the highest income, twice as much as in Eastern Europe, Latin America, and Asia, and three times as much as in Africa.

Moving forward to more reliable data, the fastest growing nations surged ahead of the laggards, creating a gap between rich and poor nations without historical precedent. In the year 1900 the per capita income of the richest nations was around $4,000 in today's dollars, which was six times higher than in the poorest nations. In 2003 the world' richest countries had a per capita income of $24,000 dollars, which was forty times higher than the poorest nations.

Besides widening the gap between rich and poor, accelerating economic growth also changed the identities of rich and poor countries. A comparison of four nations—South Korea, Mexico, Turkey, and Senegal—shows how dramatically income rankings can change over a period of fifty years. In 1950 South Korea's income per capita was slightly lower than the other three countries, although all of them were similarly poor. By 2003, South Korea's income per capita had increased more than 900 percent, Mexico's and Turkey's increased by more than 300 percent, and Senegal had declined slightly. In 2008 South Korea's income per capita was more than twice as high as the second in the group (Mexico), and ten times higher than the last in the group (Senegal).

Many other nations also changed their ranking by wealth. To illustrate, in 1870 Argentina's per capita income was 33 percent higher than Sweden's, yet by 2004 Argentina's per capita income had dropped to 43 percent of Sweden's. In the same period, Argentina's per capita income fell from 82 percent to 33 percent of that of the United States.[2]

The gap in wealth between the richest and poorest nations is much larger today than ever before in history. This gap opened because some countries grew rich quickly while other countries stagnated. The poor countries mostly did not get poorer. Also, economic growth by one country does not usually cause economic decline by another country. Today, some poor countries are surging ahead and changing the ranking of countries by wealth, and others are languishing.[3]

If the economies of poor nations grow faster than rich ones, peoples will mingle and merge through trade, travel, and talk. Convergent growth unites the human family, like Europe's common market united peoples separated by centuries of warfare. Conversely, if rich nations grow faster than poor ones, their ways of life will separate and sympathy will attenuate, as between affluent citizens and shabby illegal immigrants in modern cities. Divergent growth undermines the common sense of humanity and separates the families of man.[4] The surprising power of compound growth will determine whether humanity is one or two.

In recent years, do countries that start poor tend to grow slower and fall farther behind countries that start rich, or do countries that start

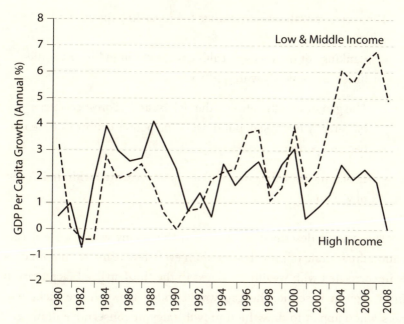

Figure 2.1 Annual Percentage Growth of Gross Domestic Product (GDP) Per Capita
Calculated from World Bank, *World Development Indicators 2009*

poor tend to grow faster and overtake countries that start rich? Figure 2.1 depicts the percentage growth rate of income per capita (GDP) for high-income countries from 1980 to 2008, and also for low- and middle-income countries.[5] Like two ballroom dancers, the two curves move up and down together, which shows that all nations are part of a world economy. Economic growth by one group of countries apparently does not cause economic decline by the other group, or else the curves would move in opposite directions. For the first half of the period, the relatively rich countries grew faster, causing living standards to diverge. More recently, the relatively poor countries grew faster, causing living standards to converge. Over the full period, there is no clear tendency for poor countries to grow faster or slower than rich countries. Nor is there a tendency for the rich to get richer by making the poor get poorer.

Three generalizations summarize the preceding discussion:

- Rankings of nations by wealth change through history, sometimes dramatically within fifty years.

- The gap in wealth between the richest and poorest countries
  has greatly increased, but most of the poorer countries have not
  become poorer.

- Economic growth across nations is uncorrelated with their level
  of wealth.

The pattern described by these generalizations would arise if each
nation drew a rate of growth at random every few years. A random draw
is uncorrelated with wealth, as stated in the third stylized fact. Starting
from a given baseline, the gap would widen between the lucky winners who happen to draw high growth rates in consecutive draws and
the unlucky losers who happen to draw low growth rates in consecutive
draws, as stated in the second stylized fact. Since growth compounds so
fast, the rankings of nations would change through history, as stated in
the first stylized fact.

In reality, however, the pattern does not seem random, as shown by
the recent history of the world's regions. Sub-Saharan Africa enjoyed
substantial growth in per capita income in the late 1960s and early 1970s.
From the mid 1970s, sub-Saharan Africa suffered twenty years of decline
in income per capita—a decline of more than 20 percent between 1975
and 1995.[6] (As usual, some countries in a region go against its trends.)
After the mid 1990s, income resumed increasing (see figure 2.2).[7]

Politics and law might explain the observed pattern in economic
growth for sub-Saharan Africa. Colonies in sub-Saharan Africa became
independent countries in a process that concluded in the 1960s. After
the euphoria of freedom subsided, unresolved ethnic and political conflicts too often devolved into anarchy or civil war. Besides ethnic strife,
the newly independent countries apparently suffered increasing corruption and decreasing competence in administration.[8] These factors
caused a sharp decline in protection of property and enforcement of

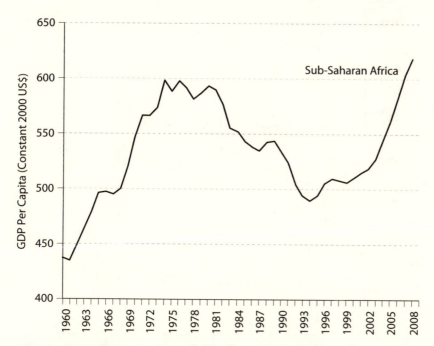

Figure 2.2. Gross Domestic Product (GDP) Per Capita in Sub-Saharan Africa Calculated from World Bank, *World Development Indicators 2009*

contracts in the 1960s and 1970s. The situation gradually improved in the 1990s.

Central planning, which is the organizing principle of communist economies, collapsed in Eastern Europe after 1989. Two groups of countries responded differently to these traumatic events. Figure 2.3 divides the countries of Eastern Europe into the eight that became members of the European Union in 2004, and the twelve that did not join the EU.[9] In the aftermath of communism's collapse, income per capita declined from 1990 to 1994 in both groups of countries. The countries that joined the EU, however, recovered in the mid 1990s and grew steadily. By 1995 their income achieved its former level before communism's collapse, and then increased by roughly 25 percent from 1994 to 2008. The twelve non-EU economies, however, remained stagnant during the second half of the 1990s. On average, income per capita in 2008 had not recovered to its level in 1990. In the case of Russia, income per capita apparently declined by

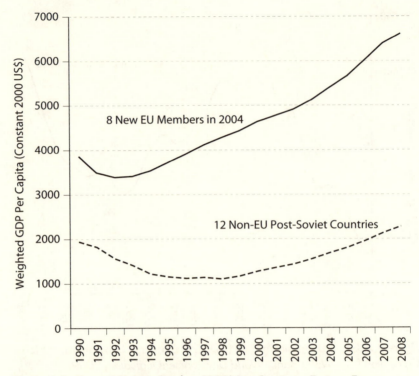

Figure 2.3. Gross Domestic Product (GDP) Per Capita in Eastern Europe (population-weighted averages)
Source: World Bank, *World Development Indicators 2009*

42 percent from 1990 to 1998.[10] After 2000, this group of countries recovered and now are they regaining the level enjoyed in 1988 under communism.[11]

Changes in law might explain the economic pattern in Eastern Europe.[12] Under communism, state planning displaced markets, nationalized industries dwarfed private ownership, and public law crowded out private law. Even so, stable bureaucracies gave officials economic power somewhat like property rights, and political bargains created obligations resembling contracts.[13] Communism's collapse after 1989 destabilized these arrangements and production declined as these countries struggled to introduce a market economy. Ten countries committed to a path to full membership in the European Union.[14] The EU imposed timetables and gave tactical support for reducing state corruption, creating independent courts, and enforcing civil law. Improvements in the law of property, contracts, and business contributed to vibrant economic growth.

By comparison, the formerly communist countries in Europe that did not join the EU made less progress toward reducing corruption, creating independent courts, and enforcing property and contract rights.[15] The same is true of the non-European countries that formerly belonged to the Soviet Union.[16] Some observers describe the result as "gangster capitalism." In any case, their economic recovery was delayed and did not carry as far. They began to recover after 2000, partly because of improvements in state administration and civil law, among other factors.[17] These changes contributed to the pattern of economic growth depicted in figure 2.3.

The Latin American region enjoyed robust growth in income per capita from 1965 until roughly 1980. Then growth paused or declined, like Eastern Europe although milder in form. In the 1990s, income per capita resumed its upward path at a modest pace. See figure 2.4.

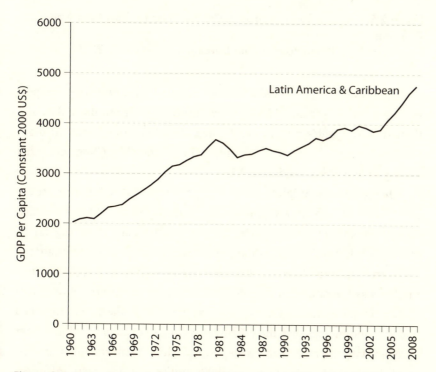

Figure 2.4. Gross Domestic Product (GDP) Per Capita in Latin America and the Caribbean
Source: World Bank, *World Development Indicators 2009*

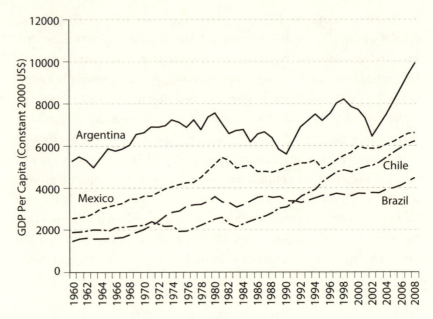

Figure 2.5. Gross Domestic Product (GDP) Per Capita in Four Latin American Countries
Calculated from World Bank, *World Development Indicators 2009*

The downturn in the 1980s and recovery in the 1990s were steepest in Argentina. Brazil and Mexico grew impressively until the 1980s, and then slowed. Chile's growth accelerated after 1985 and remained high. (In each region of the world, exceptional countries like Chile contradict the regional pattern; see figure 2.5).

Changes in law might explain this pattern in Latin America. In the late 1970s and early 1980s, almost all countries in Latin America ended state ownership of key industries (privatization), reduced the regulation of private business (deregulation), and removed barriers to international trade (free trade) and finance (free movement of financial capital).[18] The market was liberalized in a context of weak state protection of investors and competitors. Liberalization and privatization in the 1990s produced worse economic performance than Latin America had enjoyed in earlier decades, with the remarkable exception of Chile. More stability returned to finance and property law in the 1990s and economic growth resumed. These events resemble a milder form of Russia's transition to markets with weak institutions.

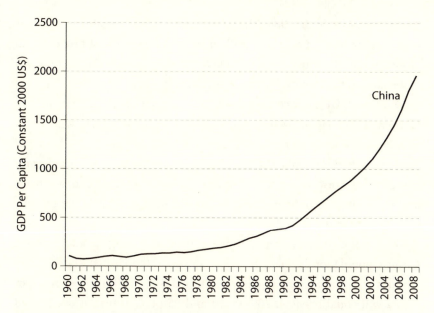

Figure 2.6. Gross Domestic Product (GDP) Per Capita in China
Source: Calculated from World Bank, *World Development Report 2009*

Roughly 20 percent of the world's population lives in China. Until the mid-1980s, income per capita was low and stagnant. From the mid 1980s through 2008 China enjoyed spectacular growth without pause, as depicted in figure 2.6. China's performance in lifting so many people out of poverty in the last twenty years has no historical parallel. Sustained growth of roughly 9 percent per year has drastically reduced absolute poverty from 25 percent to less than 5 percent of the population, and increased life expectancy from sixty-four to over seventy years.[19]

China's pattern of growth tracks massive changes in law. After the communist revolution triumphed in 1949, the state followed the Russian model of replacing markets with state administration. Officials acquired powers somewhat resembling property rights, and economic bargains among officials somewhat resembled contracts. In the 1960s, however, China's Cultural Revolution attacked the state bureaucracy and the remains of the private sector. Security of property and the enforcement of contracts collapsed, as did the economy. Subsequently, the reforms under Deng Xiaoping in the 1980s dissolved the agricultural communes and restored private businesses. Also in the 1980s, the Communist Party, the state bureaucracy, and business networks dramatically increased protection of property and enforcement of contracts. In the 1980s, China replaced state-led growth with state-protected growth, with spectacular results.

China's GDP surpassed that of Russia, Italy, France, Britain, and Germany, and Japan. Many people cannot imagine China with more economic influence in the world than the United States, but China will soon surpass the United States in national income if recent trends continue.[20] The world is becoming multipolar in economics and business, and the change is happening faster than people, especially Americans, can comprehend.

National income per capita roughly measures living standards. Since China's population is 4 to 5 times greater than the United States, when China's national income equals the United States, China's income per capita will equal between 20 percent and 25 percent that of the United States. If current growth rates continue—which is not at all certain—China's economic influence will catch up with the United States faster than its living standards.

India, whose population is smaller than China's but growing faster, suffered slow growth in income per capita until the 1980s, when growth increased significantly, as figure 2.7 depicts. The result is a remarkable achievement by historical standards, although less than China's. India started higher than China in 1965 and ended significantly lower in 2008.

Roughly 30 percent of the world's population lives in China and India. The economic performance of these two economies accounts for much of the world's progress in lifting people out of poverty in recent decades.

The pattern in India looks like a milder form of the pattern in China, with similar causes. After India gained independence from Britain in 1947, state planning gradually crowded out markets, and public law gradually crowded out private law. By 1980 India had a state-led economy like China, but it never devolved into the chaos of China's Cultural Revolution. India remained a democratic state with independent courts and good written laws of property and contracts. After 1980, India gradually dismantled state planning and took many small steps toward privatization, deregulation, and free trade. As the state withdrew its economic

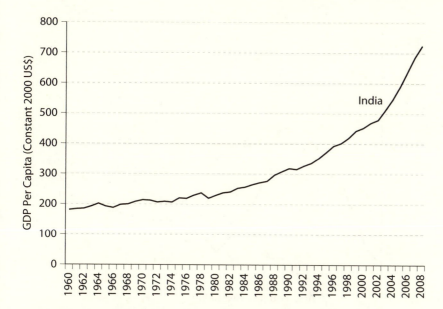

Figure 2.7. Gross Domestic Product (GDP) Per Capita in India
Source: World Bank, *World Development Indicators 2009*

controls, private property and freedom of contract strengthened. The country enjoyed high growth rates for more than twenty years.

The economic performance of the Arab countries differs dramatically depending on whether or not they have abundant oil. In the Arab oil countries, income per capita rose in the 1970s, declined in the early 1980s, stabilized, and then rose again after the late 1990s. This is exactly the pattern of world oil prices. In the Arab oil countries, changes in the world price of oil overwhelm other effects on the economy, including changes in law.

In contrast, the Arab countries whose economies are not based on oil production have far less income per capita than the Arab oil countries. Income per capita in the Arab nonoil countries increased moderately from the mid 1970s, almost at a constant absolute rate per year. (A constant growth in absolute income implies a falling *percentage* growth, just like 5 centimeters is a smaller percentage growth for a teenager than a toddler.)[21]

To depict the Arab oil countries and nonoil countries on the same graph, figure 2.8 uses a convention: it assigns the value "100" to both groups of countries in the baseline year of 1983, even though "100"

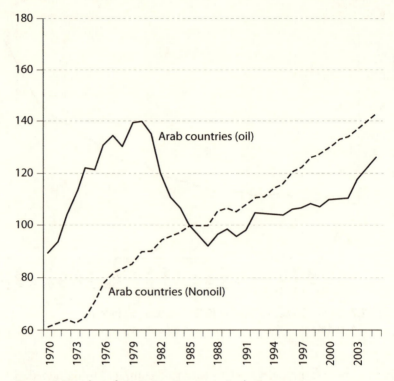

Figure 2.8. Index of GNP Per Capita in Arab Countries
Calculated from World Bank, *World Development Indicators 2007*

represents a much higher absolute value for the oil countries than for the
nonoil countries. All changes are measured against this baseline year of
1983. As depicted in figure 2.8, income per capita in the Arab oil countries fluctuated in a pattern corresponding to world oil prices, whereas it
grew at a moderate rate in the Arab nonoil countries.

In the Arab countries without oil, trends in law might help to explain
growth. Former colonies such as Algeria and dependencies such as Jordan gained their independence in a process similar to sub-Saharan Africa
that concluded in the 1950s and 1960s. The fully independent countries
pursued socialist policies that increased the power of state administrators
over the economy. Inefficiency and corruption caused weak protection of
property rights and unreliable enforcement of contracts, which undoubt-
edly hampered economic growth. Until 2011, the regional history lacked

abrupt changes in law that might reveal its effects in aggregate economic data. The overthrow of long-ruling dictators in 2011 brings new hopes and fears, and these changes will bring new data in the future about how law affects growth.

The following stylized facts summarize the economic performance of the world's regions and its two largest nations:

- Incomes declined in Africa in the 1980s and resumed growing after the mid 1990s.

- After 1990 incomes declined in central and eastern Europe, and then recovered in the middle of the decade, with faster growth in the eight countries that joined the EU than in the twelve that did not join.

- Income growth paused in Latin America in the 1980s and growth resumed in the 1990s.

- After 1980, economic growth accelerated in China and India and remained at spectacularly high levels by historical standards.

- The Arab nonoil countries experienced moderate growth since the 1970s, whereas world oil prices overwhelmed other considerations for the Arab oil countries.

Dramatic events recently demarcated new eras in developing countries—decolonization in Africa, the collapse of communism in Eastern Europe, expansion of the European Union, privatization and liberalization in Latin America, dissolution of the communes and restoration of private business in China, and dismantling central planning in India. These events caused seismic changes in the protection of property, enforcement of contracts, and effectiveness of business law. The pattern of events suggests that countries surged ahead where improved laws effectively supported innovative business ventures, and countries lagged where law failed to provide this support.

This is an astronaut's view of law and economic development. Like oxygen in the stratosphere, data are too thin for tight proofs of the highest generalizations about law and growth. (Some of our law school colleagues are uncomfortable with generalizing from imperfect data, although they are comfortable with generalizing from no data at all.) After questions are narrowed, however, statistical proofs become possible.[22] Subsequent chapters discuss many small studies that aggregate to large conclusions.

Chapter 3
The Double Trust Dilemma of Development

Economies grow when business ventures develop innovations, which requires combining new ideas and capital. Combining them confronts a dilemma illustrated by this letter sent to a Boston investment bank: "I know how your bank can make $10 million. If you give me $1 million, I will tell you." The bank does not want to pay for information without first determining its worth, and the innovator fears to disclose information to the bank without first getting paid. The obstacle to financing innovation is that an investor cannot evaluate an idea until after he knows what it is, and after its disclosure he has little reason to pay for it.[1]

To give another example, a Berkeley mathematician named Richard Niles invented bibliographic software called EndNote that many professors use on their computers. In the early stage of development, he hoped and feared receiving a call from Microsoft. Microsoft would ask for an explanation of EndNote. Once Microsoft understood EndNote, it might buy the company and make him rich, or it might develop its own version of his program and bankrupt him. Niles eventually got a call from Microsoft, which he answered with trembling, but Microsoft was merely trying to sell him its office software. Niles did get his reward later when a large publisher, Thompson, bought EndNote.

To develop an innovation, the innovator must trust the investor not to steal his idea, and the investor must trust the innovator not to steal his capital. This is the *double trust dilemma of innovation*—a new name for an underdeveloped idea that draws from a rich economics literature.[2] Distrust obstructs innovation regardless of whether it involves a new market such as insurance in Swaziland, a new organization such as an assembly line in Sichuan, or a new technology such as a faster computer chip in Silicon Valley. Like courting lovers, an innovator and an investor approach each other warily because the stakes are high.

The double trust dilemma has some workable solutions for binding the two parties together, as depicted by Solomon's knot. To secure peace in the past between two rival kings, each one gave a valuable hostage to the other. Thus in the fifth century, King Geiserich of the Vandals gave his son as hostage to King Theoderich of the Visigoths, who reciprocated by giving his daughter as hostage.[3] Hostage exchange works best when each side values cooperation more than its hostage. For example, King Geiserich presumably valued getting his own son back alive more than he valued killing the daughter of King Theoderich, and vice versa for King Theoderich.

Establishing trust between parties in a modern business transaction sometimes resembles exchanging hostages. When a buyer in Argentina contracts to purchase machine tools from a seller in Germany, the buyer fears that the seller will keep the money without delivering the machines, and the seller fears that the buyer will keep the machines without paying the money. Contract law and banking institutions offer a solution to this problem: the buyer deposits the purchase price at an international bank ("letter of credit"), and the bank releases the money to the seller on presentation of documents proving that the seller delivered the goods to the designated place. The system works because the Argentine buyer values the machine tools more than their purchase price, the German seller values the purchase price more than the machine tools, and each one can get what he wants only by doing what the contract says.

Like the exchange of hostages between King Theoderich and King Geiserich, or international trade between the German seller and the Argentine buyer, developing an innovation involves reciprocal risks between innovator and financier. In effect, the financier's money and the innovator's ideas are a double bond to guarantee their cooperation. The double bond is effective as long as each side believes that collaborating to develop the innovation is more profitable than any alternative use of the secrets and the money. This is true regardless of whether the innovation concerns a new market, organization, or technology.

Three stages in an innovation's life cycle illustrate three ways that the innovator and financier can establish trust. First, someone has a new idea and obtains capital to develop it. The innovator may form a new firm or work inside an established firm. In the first stage, only a few people in the innovator's inner circle understand the innovation. At this point, the innovation's economic value has not been established. The innovator often has to persuade the investor of its value. Second, the innovator develops the innovation sufficiently to prove its value in the market. When the innovation succeeds economically, the innovator's organization enjoys exceptional profits, and it expands faster than its competitors. Third, competitors observe the innovator's success and try to learn what the innovator knows. As competitors emulate the innovator, the innovator's profits fall and its growth slows. (Economic evolution emulates the most fit through profit detection, whereas biological evolution eliminates the least fit through natural selection.)

The three stages in an innovation's life cycle correspond to three phases of finance in Silicon Valley. Each stage secures trust between innovator and financier in a different way. According to a popular quip, initial funding for start-up firms comes from "the 3 Fs": family, friends, and fools. Family and friends have confidence in the innovator, not the innovation. This confidence inspires family and friends to invest without understanding the innovation's market value. The first stage is *relational finance*—investment motivated by personal relationships. In addition, a few fools may invest who think that they can evaluate an innovation without understanding it.

Most innovators have too few personal relationships with wealthy people to finance an innovation's full development, so they must eventually turn to strangers. The second stage of funding comes from "venture capitalists" who are not family, friends, or fools. Unlike relational finance, venture capital is a form of *private finance*. Finance is private because it comes from a small group of investors with expertise in evaluating undeveloped innovations.

The creative people who found a company often manage it badly. When the founders prove to be bad managers, the venture capitalists must replace them with good managers. In these circumstances, the venture capitalists seize the firm to increase its profitability. Alternatively, where the founders prove to be competent managers, venture capitalists may seize the firm to avoid sharing profits with the founders. Venture capitalists sometimes want to remove *good* managers who have large claims to the firm's future profits. Founders and venture capitalists have good reasons for distrusting each other. The initials "v.c." stand for "venture capitalists" and also "vulture capitalists."

Conversely, Silicon Valley innovators sometimes expropriate the investments of their financiers. Thus John P. Rogers convinced some prominent California investors to give him $340 million for a high-tech start-up named Pay By Touch that would "transform how America pays its bills" by using "biometric authentication technology" (e.g., fingerprints). In 2008 the company went bankrupt, and investors contend in lawsuits that Rogers burned through $8 million per month without producing anything of value.[4]

Innovators and venture capitalists use various legal devices to overcome their mutual distrust. The founders often commit to performance goals in exchange for financing from venture capitalists. If the founders fail to meet the stated goals, they lose their investment and their jobs. Specifically, the venture capitalists hold preferred shares of stock and the founders hold common shares. The financing contract may say that preferred shareholders can demand repayment of their investment after three years. Such a contract reassures the venture capitalists that the founders will do their utmost to perform as promised. The contract also reassures the founders that the venture capitalists will keep the firm's secrets.

Corporate governance provides another device to solve the double trust problem in Silicon Valley. The firm's bylaws may stipulate that common shareholders (founders) and preferred shareholders (venture capitalists) appoint an equal number of directors to the company's board, plus an independent director accepted by both sides. If the founders and venture capitalists disagree, the independent director holds the decisive vote. Thus the independent director will decide whether or not the venture capitalists can replace the founders with new management.

In the third stage, a successful start-up sells itself to the public. The start-up may sell directly to the public through an initial public offering of its stock, or it may sell indirectly when a publicly traded company acquires it. In order to sell stock to the public in the United States, a firm must comply with disclosure rules of the Securities Exchange Commission. Brokers disseminate the firm's disclosed information to potential investors. Many people understand the innovation sufficiently to decide whether or not to invest in its further development. Because investors in stock markets are a large group of people, we describe the third stage as *public finance*.[5]

When finance becomes public, the innovator has fewer secrets and less scope to appropriate the investor's money, so the double trust dilemma ameliorates. As the double trust dilemma disappears, public finance approaches the economist's ideal of a "competitive equilibrium." In a competitive equilibrium, no one has valuable private information and everyone earns the same profit rate ("ordinary rate of return"). Like pure contentment, a perfectly competitive equilibrium is approached and never quite reached.

Each stage of finance—relational, private, public—requires different bodies of law to solve the double trust dilemma. Any business venture requires the protection of the firm's property from predators. Without effective property protection, people fear the theft of their wealth, so they hoard instead of investing. Resources flow from makers of wealth to its protectors. Hoodlums, mafias, cheating accountants, Ponzi artists, conniving state regulators, and thieving politicians steal wealth. Families, clans, and gangs can protect property, but an effective state is much more reliable. State protection of property is the legal foundation for investment in the future.

All forms of business ventures require protection of the firm's property from outside predators, but relational finance can get by without much more legal support from the state. When law makes their property secure against outsiders, the firm's members can work together by relying on relationships, not formal contracts. In the first stage, many new firms rely heavily on personal relationships for finance. Effective property protection and strong relationships make participants in a start-up firm believe that they will enjoy future rewards from current investments of money and time.

As development proceeds, the start-up firm enters its second stage where further development requires finance by strangers, not relatives or close friends. Relationships among strangers are too thin for informal mechanisms to carry the burden of enforcing promises. To cooperate in high-stakes ventures, strangers need formal contracts with effective enforcement. As with property rights, the state can enforce contracts much more reliably than clans or gangs. In the second stage, the business venture relies mostly on formal contracts with state enforcement. Enforceable contracts enable investors to retain substantial control over how firms use their money. Contract law underpins markets for loans, bonds, and direct foreign investment.[6]

Some firms in all countries, and all firms in some countries, never go beyond private finance. (We'll say much more about this later.) In Silicon Valley, however, many firms go to the third stage in which the business venture raises capital from public markets. The business venture may raise money directly by selling its own stock to the public ("initial public offering"), or the company may proceed indirectly by selling itself to a larger firm that sells stock and bonds to the public ("acquisition by a public company").

Members of the general public who buy stocks or bonds have no control over how the firm uses their money. Instead, their money comes under the control of the firm's managers and board of directors. These insiders have many opportunities to appropriate outsiders' investments. For example, insiders use accounting tricks to convert profits into salaries, thus depriving stockholders of their dividends. If public investors don't like the firm's policies, their recourse is to sell their securities ("exit"). Protecting outsiders from insiders in public companies requires more than securing property and enforcing contracts. For public finance, the additional protection comes from the law of securities, corporations, and bankruptcy, which we call "business law."

In sum, establishing trust between innovators and investors requires law, especially the law of property, contracts, and business organizations.

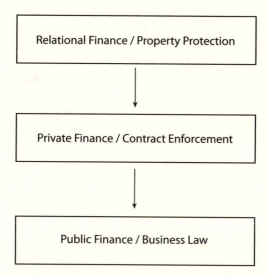

Figure 3.1. Legal Basis for Three Forms of Finance

Relational finance requires property protection, private finance requires contract enforcement, and public finance requires business law to protect outside investors, as depicted in figure 3.1. The progression requires more intensive use of law. The law's effectiveness determines the firm's ability to expand from relational to private to public finance. (Figure 3.1 is a useful simplification, although it does not show how bodies of law complement each other, which we discuss later.)

Biologists sometimes say, "Ontogeny recapitulates phylogeny," which means that the development of a single organism from birth to maturity somehow resembles the evolution of the entire species.[7] Similarly, the three stages of finance for a start-up in Silicon Valley resemble three stages of historical evolution in capital markets for countries. The industrial revolution in England, which was the world's first, went through these stages. In the early eighteenth century, inventors mostly relied on their personal assets and loans from family and friends (relational finance). As industrialization proceeded, loans from wealthy investors and banks became available more readily to new industries. Finance of industrial companies by sales of stocks and bonds to the general public

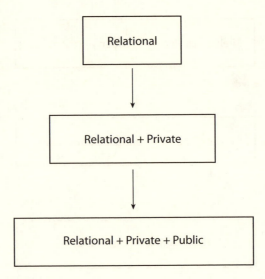

Figure 3.2. Stages in Development of Finance

came later. Public financing of industrial companies originally concerned infrastructure like canals, docks, and railways, where private business and the state intertwine. As the law became more reliable, public finance spread to manufacturing firms.[8] Figure 3.2 depicts the evolution of finance in these three stages.

Today the poorest countries have weak capital markets, so businessmen mostly borrow from family and friends. Starting from a condition of lawlessness, imposition of secure property rights can cause a spurt of growth based mostly on relational finance, as in China's new industries after the 1980s. Some peoples, notably the Chinese and the Jews, have family networks that extend business relationships beyond the usual boundaries. However, the conditions of trust among relatives do not reach the scale of modern businesses. Relational finance keeps business small and local. No modern country became wealthy by relying exclusively on relational finance.

To increase the scale of business, an economy must augment relational finance with private finance, especially bank loans. In countries where banks dominate, an elite of wealthy insiders often lend to business ventures based on private information. Thus bank finance in some developing countries performs a similar role to venture finance in Silicon Valley.

As countries become affluent, they increasingly augment private finance with public finance, which means selling stocks and bonds to the general public. Stocks and bonds compete with banks and wealthy individuals to finance economic growth.

The expansion of finance supplements earlier forms without replacing them. All three forms of finance—relational, private and public—remain important in the richest countries. The extent of public finance varies significantly among countries, including rich countries. Japan and northern Italy have achieved affluence mostly through relational and private finance, with relatively little public finance, whereas the United States and Great Britain rely mostly on public finance for mature industries. Germany appears to be shifting from the former to the latter.[9]

Expanding the basis of finance requires effective law that controls behavior, not aspirational law that expresses lofty ideals. What makes a law effective? Not just writing it down. Written law in a poor country often resembles written law in a rich country. Property and contract law-on-the-books in India and Nigeria resemble English common law, and property and contract law-on-the-books in Peru resemble the Spanish civil code. Writing down a law, however, does not make it effective. The written laws are less effective in India, Nigeria, and Peru than in England or Spain.

A law's effectiveness comes from society and the state. Many laws are obligations backed by sanctions. These obligations are as effective as the sanctions that support them. When potential injurers foresee a legal sanction, they usually obey the law.[10] The sanction can come from society, as when people threaten to shun their relatives or damage reputations, or it can come from the state, as when one person threatens to sue the other for breach of contract.

Are social sanctions sufficient to make laws effective without state enforcement? Instead of speculating about the "state of nature" from his room in London, Bronislaw Malinowski traveled to the Trobriand Islands in 1914 and observed how people resolve their disputes. He found that when one person harmed another, Trobriand Islanders used social pressure to force the injurer's family to compensate the victim's family.[11] Facts like these persuaded anthropologists that law is much older than the state.

As in the Trobriand Islands in 1914, social sanctions remain important in modern societies. Social sanctions are flexible and cheap, so the victims of wrongdoing in business rely on them first. When a businessman breaches a contract, for example, the victim may stop trading with the injurer (refusal to deal), break promises owed to the injurer (retaliatory breach), sully the injurer's reputation (reputational sanctions), and ask others not to deal with the injurer (boycott).

Nonstate organizations can improve the efficiency of social sanctions. Thus most uncut diamonds are traded without written contracts in a small number of exchanges in cities like Manhattan and Antwerp. The diamond exchanges have merchant courts to resolve disputes without relying on state sanctions. Banishment from the exchange, which ruins a diamond dealer's livelihood, is the ultimate punishment.[12] By making information easier to obtain, the Internet has increased the effectiveness of reputational sanctions, especially by posting buyers' evaluations of sellers' goods. Reputational sanctions on the Internet are so efficient that strangers buy antiques online without examining them. The Internet suggests that, instead of decreasing over time, people may rely more on social sanctions in the future.

The effectiveness of social sanctions depends on the stakes. Social sanctions suffice to prevent wrongdoing in repeated transactions with low stakes, but not in one-time transactions with high stakes. For big deals, social sanctions are insufficient to secure trust, except within tight families. In big deals, people need the state behind contracts much like diplomats need an army behind foreign policy. When buying a car or selling a house, ordinarily moral people can be ruthless, and professional car dealers and real estate agents are notoriously sleazy. Business ventures often resemble buying a house—a big deal with high stakes. Without judges or bureaucrats to threaten wrongdoers, many business ventures never launch.

The victim of a broken contract may file a civil complaint against the injurer and threaten to sue for compensatory damages. Like the head lion's roar, a credible threat of litigation usually resolves conflict. To be credible, the plaintiff must stand to gain more in damages from the court than his costs of litigating. Keeping litigation costs down thus increases the credibility of threats to litigate. When courts resolve routine business disputes efficiently, the parties usually settle out of court on terms favoring the party who would win in court. In contrast, inefficient or corrupt courts decrease the credibility of threats to sue and prevent the party who should win in court from extracting a favorable settlement out of court.

Besides social and court sanctions, civil servants in the state bureaucracy apply administrative sanctions, such as revoking permits, applying regulations, investigating violations, or imposing fines. Autocratic states especially rely on administrative sanctions to protect citizens. Thus the state bureaucracy in contemporary China, and the Communist Party that stands behind it,[13] protect the sources of economic growth by guaranteeing most property rights and enforcing many contracts. Imagine a land dispute involving an industrial enterprise in Guangzhou that wants to expand by taking land from a farm. To mediate the dispute, the parties first appeal to powerful private persons. If private mediation fails, they might turn next to a local official in the city government. If one of them rejects the local official's decision, the next appeal might go to a Communist Party official in Beijing. Many observers believe that the threat of social and state sanctions in such a chain of events deters much wrongdoing. Protection of property rights and enforcement of contracts in China is much better than in the past. However, most observers believe that China's bureaucracy performs these tasks far worse than courts in its richer neighbors like Japan or Singapore.

In developed and developing countries, new business ventures begin with secrecy, risk, and high profit expectations, and all three decrease as the venture matures. Sea routes from Europe to Asia were eventually mapped and secured, trade between them became commonplace, and middle-class Europeans could buy spices. In Silicon Valley, competitors work around patents and ferret out secrets, thus converting today's technological breakthroughs into tomorrow's commodities. However, an innovative economy never settles into a permanent condition without secrecy, risk, or extraordinary profits. Combining new ideas with capital is the immediate cause of economic innovation, which is this chapter's subject, not remote causes like demography, geography, education, factor mobilization, health, culture, religion, world prices, interest rates, inflation, regulations, and tariffs. Uniting ideas and capital in a business venture requires the law of property, contracts, and business. To prosper where law is weak, businesses must deal through relationships and self-enforcing private contracts. When laws, courts, and state bureaucracies improve, finance expands from relational to private, and from private to public, so more ideas combine with more capital to grow the economy faster.

Chapter 4
Make or Take

In a coral reef, an animal (polyp) creates a hard shell around itself that protects many single-celled plants (zooxanthellae) living within its flesh that produce food and energy. Similarly, the state is needed to protect the makers of society's wealth from the takers. Without protection of property, people hoard their wealth instead of investing in the future. All countries have makers and takers of wealth, but the balance between them differs by place and time. Most rich nations today became wealthy because the state and social norms channeled the efforts of their citizens into making wealth.[1] Conversely, many poor nations stay that way because the state and social norms channel too much effort into taking wealth from others.

In striking the balance, much depends on law. The types of law needed to protect the makers of wealth include property, contracts, crimes, finance, corporations, regulation, antitrust, labor law, taxation, and torts. When law enables creative people who make wealth to keep much of it, the state channels their energies into enriching the nation by enriching themselves. Conversely, when laws allow the strong to take wealth from its makers, the state channels the energies of people into enriching themselves by impoverishing the nation.

What distinguishes making wealth from taking it? The distinction is easy when the contrast is stark. Artisans and merchants in Bukhara on the "Silk Road" enriched their city in the years before 1220, but then it opened its gates to an overpowering army sent by Genghis Khan. Instead of leniency, the invaders took Bukhara's wealth, enslaved the useful population, and reduced the city to a gravel pit. The people who take wealth from others in the modern economy do so more subtly than Genghis Khan. They include frauds, autocrats, commissars, cartels, stock manipulators, corrupt union officials, bribe-seeking politicians, gangsters, and monopolists of many kinds. We will distinguish three ways to take wealth from others: theft and bribes (criminal), subsidies and regulations (political), and cartels and monopolies (market power).

Theft and Bribes

Mineral resources are the most saleable assets in many poor countries. After communism collapsed in Russia in 1989, gangster-capitalists looted the state's mineral resources and sold them abroad. The richest three hundred people in the world in 2003, according to Forbes Magazine, included sixteen Russians, eleven of whom made their wealth in oil.[2] After oil was discovered in 1995 in Equatorial Guinea, its ruler, Teodoro Obiang, and his government deposited $700 million in private accounts in the Riggs Bank of Washington, DC. (These facts surfaced when regulators fined the bank for not reporting possible money laundering.) Forbes magazine makes an annual guess of the world's ten richest "kings, queens, and dictators." Most people on the list rule oil-rich countries.[3] Similarly, Mobutu Sese Seko, Congo's president from 1960 to 1997, ransacked billions of dollars from his country and deposited the money in Swiss bank accounts.

Instead of taking wealth from the state, some government officials take it from private citizens. Most constitutions require the state to compensate private owners for taking their property, but some politicians are above the constitution. When power overawes law, politicians expropriate the wealth of private citizens without compensation, especially their enemies. In 2000 Zimbabwean President Mugabe encouraged his political allies to expropriate the farms of white citizens—with disastrous economic effects for most people.[4]

Rather than stealing oil or land, many corrupt officials extort small sums of money from people who need something from them. The officials may demand a bribe for a license, performance of a duty, over-looking a regulatory violation or tax liability, obtaining a state document, granting a variance, or holding a hearing. The "corruption tax"—the cost that petty bribes impose on business—slows growth like a leak in a tire slows a car (see chapter 11 on crimes and corruption).

Subsidies and Regulations

We discussed illegal ways to take wealth from others, notably stealing and extracting bribes. Alternatively, instead of breaking the law, people can use law to take wealth from others. Politicians direct the state to sub-sidize various activities. One country or another subsidizes telephones, banking, railroads, electricity, steel manufacturing, farmers, airplane flights, windmills, coal mines, southern industries, northern industries, core industries, export industries, green industries, minority businesses, majority businesses, and so forth. The subsidies often go in opposite directions in different countries—thus farmers subsidized city workers in Peron's Argentina and Stalin's Russia, whereas city workers subsidize farmers in the United States, the European Union, and Japan.

Tax preferences resemble subsidies in their causes and effects. Lob-byists riddle tax codes with special provisions for influential groups of people. One country or another reduces taxes on income from cattle, oil, minority businesses, majority businesses, and small businesses, Internet sales, churches, solar panels, and owner-occupied houses. Critics call spe-cial tax provisions "loopholes," whereas admirers call them "incentives" for national goals like oil exploration, renewable energy, self-sufficiency in food, national security, small business development, sustainable farm-ing, and home ownership.[5]

Subsidies appear in budgets where taxpayers can easily see them. Tax preferences reduce the visibility of the transfer to favored groups. To reduce visibility further, politicians can use regulations to restrict compe-tition. To enrich yourself from restricted competition, obtain an exclusive license to operate cabs at an international airport, sell road signs to a city through closed bidding, own all of a country's electromagnetic spectrum for mobile phones, or build cars behind tariff walls in a country with two automobile plants. One country or another forbids selling aspirin without a pharmaceutical license, prohibits optometrists and lawyers from advertising their prices, requires banks to lend to political favorites at below-market rates, forbids dry cleaners from locating within a mile of each other, and requires farmers to sell coffee beans exclusively to a state exporter at prices below world market prices.

The shield against competition comes from licenses, charters, permits, restrictions, regulations, orders, variances, privileges, and government contracts. By such devices, administrators and politicians determine where a factory can locate, what goods it can produce, to whom it must sell, and whom it employs. These devices shield the friends of politicians from competition, and the friends repay the politicians with donations, bribes, and electoral support. Political power can restrict competition and create market power for politically favored factions of all kinds—entrepreneurs, unions, the upper class, the working class, the ethnic majority, the ethnic minority, men, women, optometrists, pharmacists, defense contractors, religious schools, state schools, to name a few. The beneficiaries of these state activities justify them in the name of fairness, employment, economic growth, national security, equal opportunity, social justice, public health, consumer protection, pollution abatement, and so on.

Are subsidies, tax preferences, and regulations mostly unjustified transfers of wealth or legitimate state activities? Your answer says a lot about your politics. Systematically evaluating subsidies, tax preferences, or regulations requires a general theory relating the state and the market. Conflicting ideologies grind against each other like ice in the Arctic Sea. Instead of taking sides, we will limit our analysis in subsequent chapters to the effects of subsidies, tax preferences, and regulations on innovation and growth.

Cartels and Monopolies

Whenever executives in competing firms talk to each other, consumers are in peril. Talk leads to restraint of trade—businessmen set prices and divide territory like Europeans divided Africa in the nineteenth century.

To combat this problem, most countries enacted statutes in the twentieth century that prohibit firms from collaborating to set prices or divide territory. If enforced impartially, these statutes can benefit the public, but administering them is often politicized. To limit politicization, the simplest and most reliable antitrust policy for many sectors of an economy is free trade. World markets are much harder to monopolize than national markets, because world markets are so much larger than national markets.

Although antitrust law forbids private businesses from organizing cartels, governments routinely do so. The firms in an industry sometimes capture its regulator, who operates a cartel on their behalf. To illustrate, a plane flight from Boston to Washington, which passes over several states, cost about twice as much in 1980 as a flight of similar distance from San Francisco to San Diego, which remains within the state of California. The fact that the federal government regulated air travel between states, and not within California, explains the price difference. On Boston-to-Washington flights that cross state lines, federal law allowed competing airlines to ask their regulator to increase the legal fares charged to passengers. On San-Francisco-to-San-Diego flights, however, the presidents of competing airlines who had such a conversation would violate antitrust laws and risk imprisonment.

We have discussed three ways that people take wealth from each other: illegally through theft and bribes, legally through state subsidies and regulations, and by monopolies and cartels that can be legal or illegal. Some examples of takings are transparent, and others are obscured by the complexity of a modern economy. The division of labor obscures exactly how much most people make in a complex economy. Do entrepreneurs, industrialists, farmers, laborers, shopkeepers, scientists, programmers, teachers, and laborers get more or less than they make? Sorting out their contributions is a fundamental task of economic theory. Some basic economic theories frame the question and suggest answers.

Are Workers Exploited?

A factory in Mumbai (formerly Bombay) makes cloth from Egyptian cotton and German dyes. It sells the cloth to a factory in Kolkata (formerly

Calcutta). A seamstress in the Kolkata factory uses the cloth, a pattern, a sewing machine, a building, and electricity to sew jackets. She sews ten jackets per week. The factory pays the seamstress 600 rupees at current exchange rates or roughly US$10. Six hundred rupees will buy enough in local Indian markets to survive, although US$10 will not buy enough in U.S. markets to survive.[6] Each week the Kolkata factory buys the cloth and electricity for the seamstress to use for US$300 and sells the ten jackets to an Italian wholesaler for US$400. The factory owner's net revenues thus equal $400 – $300 – $10, or $90.

Does the seamstress's wage of US$10 approximately equal the wealth that she makes, or does the factory owner pay her a fraction of her worth and retain the rest as profits? Two classical theories give opposite answers. The first is due to Karl Marx, who remains an icon in many universities in developing countries (although seldom in their economics departments). According to Marx's labor theory of value, workers make everything and capitalists keep much of it.[7] Thus the value of the seamstress's work is closer to $100 per week than to her wage of $10. The difference of US$90 measures the factory owner's profit and the seamstress's exploitation.

Turning from Marx to microeconomics, its classical theory of wages is "marginalism." The seamstress provides labor to the factory, which increases its production. The increase in the factory's production is the marginal product of the seamstress's labor. Competition in the labor market causes the seamstress to get paid her marginal product. To see why, consider that fact that the seamstress could quit her job at the original factory and go to work at an alternative factory. The alternative factory's production would increase from her additional labor. If this increase in production exceeds her wage in the original factory, then the alternative factory can make a profit by offering a higher wage to lure her away from the original factory. Thus the self-interest of the alternative factory causes it to offer a higher wage and the self-interest of the seamstress causes her to accept the offer. This competitive process bids up the wage of the seamstress until it equals her marginal product in the best use of her labor. If the labor market for seamstresses in Kolkata is competitive, the seamstress's wage of US$10 should roughly equal her marginal product.

The logic of marginalism also applies to the factory owner. He provides the seamstress with a sewing machine, electricity, and working space in the factory. The resulting increase in her production is the marginal product of his assets. Competition in the capital market causes the factory owner's profits to equal the marginal product of his assets. The factory owner could withdraw his capital from the jacket factory and invest it in an alternative factory owned by someone else. If the increase in production from the alternative use is higher than the profits in the original use, then the alternative user can pay more for the assets than the profits in the original use. Self-interest motivates the alternative user to make such an offer and self-interest makes the factory owner accept. This competitive process bids up the profits of the owner of capital until it equals the marginal product of his assets in their best use. If the capital market is competitive in Kolkata, the owner's profits of US$90 roughly equals the marginal product of his capital.

Marxism and marginalism disagree over whether or not the owner of capital exploits workers. Marxists attribute all of a product's value to the labor used to make it, so Marxists attribute none of a product's value to the capital used to make it. In Marxist theory, the worker's exploitation equals the difference between a product's sale price and the wages paid to make it. In contrast, marginalism holds that competition causes the price of each factor of production (capital, labor, land, and so on) to equal its marginal product. If a worker's wage equals her marginal product, then she is not exploited, and if the capitalist's marginal product equals his profits, then he is not an exploiter.

Which theory of wage determination is more nearly correct? Most modern economists think that the answer depends on the structure of labor markets. When employers must compete with each other to hire able workers, they lack the power to pay someone less than the market value of what she makes.[8] Competition roughly equates wages and marginal product. Later we review some data showing that in large cities or in countries where people can move and freely choose their working place, marginal productivity theory is approximately correct and the pay of most workers roughly equals the market value of what they produce.

In contrast, keeping wages below marginal productivity requires thwarting competition by cartels, serfdom, bonded labor, and the like.[9] Earlier we described cartels and monopolies as one of the three ways to take wealth from its makers. Without competition, employers can exploit workers. Thus millions of people in India, Pakistan, and Nepal are forced to work for an individual employer in order to repay the loans he has made to them—a practice called "bonded labor" that international conventions ban.[10] Bonded labor concentrates in villages where competition is weak, but it also exists in big cities ("slum dogs"), including among some textile workers. Bonded labor would disappear if effective laws allowed debtors to escape their creditors through bankruptcy.

As innovation increases the productivity of workers, Marxism predicts that wages will not increase because exploitation will increase. In contrast, as innovation increases the productivity of workers, marginalism predicts that wages will increase because the worker's marginal product will increase. In fact rising productivity has accompanied rising wages in countries around the world. Further, the countries with relatively high wages also have relatively high labor productivity. Thus the historical and comparative data fits marginalism better than Marxism. In the end, Marx's labor theory of value fails and marginalism succeeds in explaining the most central fact about wages and economic growth: innovation makes workers more productive and causes their wages to rise. Rising productivity and wages is the main mechanism that lifts workers out of poverty.

The reader, however, should draw inferences cautiously from this simple account of marginalism. Modern labor economics encompasses many departures from marginal productivity theory such as cartels, regulations, tariffs, unions, minimum wage legislation, and executive compensation in public companies. It also encompasses a hot political issue in many countries—discrimination that favors men over women, high caste over low caste, the dominant ethnicity or tribe or religion over the subordinate ones, and so forth.[11] Simplicity is the prelude to complex analysis, not its conclusion.

Oliver Cromwell, the seventeenth-century English revolutionary and dictator, was dug up and beheaded three years after he died. To some of our readers, revisiting the dispute between Marx and marginalism may seem like an exhumation, especially since Marxism is dead in the economics departments of most universities. Outside of economics departments, however, Marxism still engages deep political passions between left and right in many developing countries about the market and the state, and the owners and the workers.

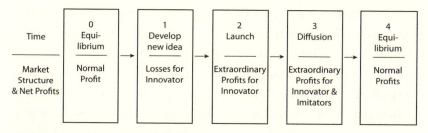

Figure 4.1. Life Cycle of an Innovation

Are Entrepreneurs Too Rich?

Marginalism provides a better answer than Marxism to the question, "How much does a worker make and how much does she keep?" Neither marginalism nor Marxism can answer the question, "How much does an innovator make and how much does she keep?"[12] To answer it, we divide the life cycle of an innovation into phases as depicted in figure 4.1. Before the innovation, the industry is in competitive equilibrium and its firms receive the normal rate of profit. In the first phase of innovation, one firm has a new idea and invests to develop it. In the development phase, money goes out and none comes in. Many innovators try and few succeed. Thus recent U.S. data suggests that 40 percent of new businesses survive and 60 percent disappear within four years.[13] If development succeeds, the innovator goes to the second phase and launches the innovation in the market. On launch, the innovator earns extraordinary profits because the product has no competitors. In the third phase, the new idea disseminates to imitators, whose competition causes a fall in the innovator's profits. In the fourth and final phase, the industry settles into equilibrium like a football team that eventually stops yelling after its star player scores a goal. The innovator's profits fall to the normal rate of return, as they were in the beginning.

Averaged over the life cycle, the successful innovator receives extraordinary profits, which exceed the normal profits earned by noninnovators. However, even the most successful innovator earns much less than the innovation's economic value to society. When the innovator sells the innovative product to buyers, they presumably value it more than they pay for it. Otherwise they would not buy it. The "surplus" is the difference between an innovation's value to a buyer and the price he pays for it.[14] In addition, as the innovation disseminates, some of its value goes to the imitators as extraordinary profits. Thus the innovation's social value is divided among innovators, imitators, and consumers.

Is the innovator's share too high or too low? Few people will object to small producers keeping much of the value of their innovations, like Indian farmers adapting "miracle rice" to local conditions, or Beijing shopkeepers discovering that their customers will buy coffee, or a Malaysian converting a craft shop into a textile factory.

What about rich people? A few stars in the Milky Way are brightest, and a few entrepreneurs are richest. The five richest people in the world in 2008 were, in order, Warren Buffett, Carlos Slim, Bill Gates, Lakshmi Mittal, and Mukesh Ambani. They averaged approximately $50 billion in wealth each.[15] If you invested that much money in no-risk bonds, you would have to spend approximately $3,800 per minute to keep your wealth from growing larger.[16]

Besides great wealth, these five people have something else in common: they did not inherit vast agricultural estates like Indian maharajas in colonial times, or own desert sands that float on oil like Saudi princes, or divert taxes into Swiss bank accounts like African dictators, or collect massive bailouts from taxpayers like American investment bankers. Rather, they created extraordinarily profitable businesses.[17] To become superrich, you should identify companies that will grow fastest and invest in them (Warren Buffett), supply mobile phone service to Mexicans (Carlos Slim), develop a computer operating system that becomes a world standard (Bill Gates), reorganize steel manufacturing in the world's rust belts (Lakshmi Mittal), or develop the Indian petrochemical industry (Mukesh Ambani).

For all five, a significant portion of their wealth apparently came from developing new ideas that caused wealth to grow unimaginably quickly. Presumably they also gained from unproductive advantages like natural monopoly, political patronage, and regulatory favoritism. We can only guess at the combination of creative and nonproductive sources of their wealth. In any case, their creativity benefitted consumers, producers, and themselves by billions of dollars. Such is the power of innovation and compound growth.

Conclusion

Clear thinking about the economy requires skepticism about people. For predictive accuracy, economic theorists since Adam Smith in the eighteenth century assume that most people want more wealth, and they will devote talent and energy to getting it. Oliver Wendell Holmes, the American legal theorist and Supreme Court justice, thought that law should aim at bad people who will disobey unless coerced, not good people who obey willingly. Combining Smith and Holmes, law and economics scholars usually assume that most people devote talent and energy to getting more wealth, and law's coercive force must channel and constrain their pursuit of it.

People can acquire wealth by making or taking it. If people mostly get wealth by taking it, then they will devote their energies to taking what others make and protecting what they possess. They will impoverish the nation by trying to enrich themselves. Thus legal and illegal practices that thwart competition enable employers to exploit workers. Conversely, given competition, the wages of workers will rise with their productivity.

Productivity especially increases through innovations made by entrepreneurs. If entrepreneurs mostly get wealth by innovating, then they will devote their energies to enriching the nation by enriching themselves. Securing their property through law will cause faster growth, like feeding a puppy. Conversely, if business people mostly get their wealth by bribes, theft, subsidies, tax preferences, or monopolistic practices, then they burden economic growth like parasites in a puppy's intestines.

Innovators retain a fraction of the wealth that they create for society, and law affects the fraction's size. Would taking less from entrepreneurs benefit the nation by causing wealth to grow, like catching fewer anchovies would cause the stock of fish to grow in the ocean off Peru?[18] Or would taking more from entrepreneurs benefit the nation by giving the money to people who need it more, like giving some of a fat puppy's food to a skinny puppy? For an answer, you'll have to read the next chapter.

Chapter 5
The Property Principle for Innovation

For an economy to grow, according to the preceding chapter, law and policy must channel peoples' pursuit of wealth into making it, not taking it from its makers. For entrepreneurs, innovation is risky and success is profitable. When innovators can keep much of the wealth that they make, greed overcomes fear, and entrepreneurs enrich the nation by enriching themselves. The *property principle for innovation* is the proposition that the makers of wealth should keep much of it.

Do entrepreneurs enjoy most of the gains from innovation, or do workers benefit through rising wages? In successful modern economies, growth compounds unimaginably fast and almost everyone benefits. In countries where productivity has grown, wages have increased over time, although not necessarily continuously or smoothly. Instead of trickling down from entrepreneurs to workers, historical and international comparisons suggest that growing income cascades down like the Blue Nile flowing from Lake Tana.

Does equality stimulate or retard innovation? Less equality sometimes causes faster growth, as when China relaxed egalitarian policies after 1980 and allowed entrepreneurs to keep more of what they make. Conversely, more equality sometimes causes faster growth. Thus high levels of education and health among workers in Denmark and Korea contribute to the robust economic performance of those countries, whereas poor education and health of workers partly explains the economic struggles of the Philippines. Facts about growth require rethinking the value of equality.

Are Innovators Too Rich?

How much of the value of an innovation should the innovator keep? The property principle for innovation provides a general answer: "much" of it. This answer is too vague for important policy problems like setting tax rates for rich entrepreneurs. More precision requires more detailed analysis of wealth and welfare. The hard cases occur when a law or policy that increases innovation also aggravates inequality. The aggravation of inequality decreases welfare because the poor need money more than the rich. However, faster growth eventually increases the welfare of everyone, including the poor. With compound growth, the poor quickly gain more than they immediately lost.

Assume that a change in policy allows entrepreneurs in an industry to keep 40 percent more of the social value of innovations than they kept in the past. While entrepreneurs get 40 percent more, others get 40 percent less, including workers and consumers. By making entrepreneurs richer, the change in policy aggravates inequality. Assume, however, that the additional payoff to innovators causes faster growth in the industry. Specifically, assume that the sustained growth rate increases from 2 percent to 10 percent. Recall that 2 percent growth compounded over a century increases approximately seven times, and 10 percent growth compounded over a century increases approximately fourteen thousand times. Most people would rather have a smaller proportion of an increase of fourteen thousand times than a larger proportion of an increase of seven times. Seeing these numbers, the gain in welfare from faster growth should overtake the loss in welfare from aggravated inequality.

Generalizing, the "welfare overtaking theorem" proved by Cooter and Edlin (2010) shows that when growth and equality trade off, the gains in welfare from increasing the rate of sustained growth overtake any loss from decreased equality, given reasonable preferences for equality.

This theorem implies that law and policy concerned with human welfare should aim to maximize sustainable growth.

The overtaking theorem applies to sustainable growth, not convulsive growth that soon collapses on itself like a sprinter attempting a marathon. Sustainable growth builds on itself, using yesterday's new ideas to find today's new ideas. Also, the growth that is relevant for human welfare encompasses nonmarket goods such as clean air, safe streets, handsome buildings, and rural land. The ideal is a comprehensive measure of consumption and wealth, as discussed in chapter 1. Narrow measures like GDP are proxies that we must use where data are scarce. Now we can use the welfare overtaking theorem to restate the property principle for innovation: "Innovators should keep the amount of wealth that maximizes the sustainable rate of growth in a comprehensive measure of consumption." This principle implies that law and policy should pursue equality to the extent that doing so increases growth, but not sacrifice growth to gain more equality.

A comparison between China in 1980 and today illustrates this principle. The Cultural Revolution, which ended approximately in 1975, impoverished an already poor country, and it also went far toward equalizing incomes. Beginning roughly in 1980, China began to allow innovators to make wealth and keep much of it. Consequently, China achieved double-digit economic growth, which dramatically increased wages. Growth also increased inequality, because unequal economic creativity causes unequal income.

Economists measure inequality of income in a nation by an index number (the Gini coefficient) that varies between 0 and 1. "0" indicates minimum inequality (or maximum equality) and "1" indicates maximum inequality. For comparison, table 5.1 gives the Gini coefficients for selected countries. We have no Gini coefficients for China in the 1960s and 1970s, but we presume that inequality was low so the Gini coefficient was low. As late as 1991, more than ten years after the start of market reforms, the Gini coefficient in China was 0.28. In 2000 the Gini coefficient for China had reached a value of 0.46, which indicates sharply greater inequality. In 1991, China's inequality resembled Scandinavia, and by 2000 it was higher than the United States (the most unequal Western country) and approaching Latin American levels.[1] However, most observers of China agree that

Table 5.1 Income Equality in Selected Countries

High equality	Index*	Medium equality	Index*	Low equality	Index*
Japan	0.25	India	0.33	Niger	0.51
Sweden	0.25	Canada	0.33	Nigeria	0.51
Belgium	0.25	France	0.33	Argentina	0.52
Denmark	0.25	Poland	0.34	Zambia	0.53
Norway	0.26	Indonesia	0.34	El Salvador	0.53
Finland	0.27	United Kingdom	0.36	Mexico	0.55
Hungary	0.27	Italy	0.36	Panama	0.56
Germany	0.28	Turkey	0.40	Chile	0.57
Ukraine	0.29	United States	0.41	Colombia	0.58
Ethiopia	0.30	Iran	0.43	Paraguay	0.58
Russia	0.31	China	0.45	South Africa	0.58
South Korea	0.32	Philippines	0.46	Zimbabwe	0.57
				Brazil	0.59
				Central African Rep.	0.61
				Namibia	0.71

*Gini coefficient

Source: World Bank, *World Development Indicators 2006* (Washington, DC: 2006).

the gains from growth overtook the undesirable consequences of more inequality. Only a few years absence are enough to strike returning visitors with the increases in wealth and welfare of ordinary people in China.

A similar analysis applies to communism's collapse in Central and Eastern Europe. Before 1989, the European communist countries had more income equality than any contemporary nation. Specifically, these countries had Gini coefficients around 0.2, which indicates significantly more equality than the countries shown in table 5.1, including prosperous capitalist countries. Communist countries achieved equality by central planning, and inequality returned when they restored markets and economic liberty. After the collapse of communism in roughly 1990, the Gini coefficients increased in Central and Eastern Europe to Western levels of around 0.3.[2]

What about growth? From the 1930s to the early 1960s, the Soviet Union and the Warsaw Pact countries achieved high growth rates. Mark Twain said that reports of his death were premature. Similarly, the proclamations of the Soviet Union's economic superiority were premature. Soviet growth came from squeezing more labor and savings out of people, such as sending women and peasants into the industrial work force whether they liked it or not, and diverting expenditures from consumption into building steel mills and sports stadiums. Creativity was as scarce as the western blue jeans that young people craved.[3] The growth spurt proved unsustainable because it came from mobilizing more capital and labor, not from innovation. Maximum growth requires creative entrepreneurs to control the flow of capital to industries, not politicians, civil servants, or bureaucrats. As data shows in chapter 2, growth improved remarkably after 1995 in those formerly communist countries that joined the European Union.

Equality and Growth

In general, the property principle for innovation requires law and policy to increase equality when doing so increases wealth, but not otherwise. Does faster growth generally increase or diminish equality? Does more equality generally increase or diminish growth? Most countries today are not like China in 1980, where more inequality increases growth. On average, equality and growth go together in nations, at least roughly. Table 5.1 sorts selected countries into low, medium, and high equality. Most low-equality countries are also low-income countries in southern Africa and Latin America. Conversely, most high-equality countries are high-income countries in Europe and East Asia. Table 5.1 thus shows that equality correlates roughly—but not perfectly—with income per capita in nations. Since income per capita is the result of past growth, equality in nations also correlates roughly with sustained growth in income per capita.[4] Econometric studies confirm the correlation found in table 5.1.[5]

Equality and sustained growth often go together, but does growth cause equality or does equality cause growth? Many causes in economic life respond to their effects, like a man courting a woman. The feedback between equality and growth is complicated. As explained above, central planning in communist countries stifled innovation by not rewarding it. Faster growth apparently required more economic freedom and less equality. Now consider the opposite—circumstances where equality promotes growth. An example is the education of workers. Better-educated workers are more productive and receive higher wages, which increases equality. Better-educated workers are also more innovative, which increases growth. So better schools for workers cause growth and equality.

Chinese agriculture provides another example where equality apparently caused growth. In the late 1950s, China's Communist Party forced farmers into communes and diverted much of their labor from agriculture into village industries. Farmers starved in the winters of 1959 and 1960. In the 1980s the Communist Party reversed itself, dissolved the communes and created family farms.[6] Agricultural production soared. When dissolving the communes, party officials divided the land roughly equally among families. Economic analysis of incentives suggests that an equal division of the land contributed to soaring productivity.[7]

Antitrust laws that disrupt cartels are another example of promoting growth and equality. Cartels suppress innovation in order to prolong monopoly profits, and monopoly profits aggravate inequality. For example, members of the New York Stock Exchange historically collected large fees for matching the buyers and sellers of stocks. Innovations allowed computers to make this match electronically. The controlling members of the NYSE, who are very rich, delayed adoption of electronic matching to prolong their monopoly profits. They enjoyed these profits at the expense of everyone who bought and sold stocks, including the pension funds of ordinary workers.

The most destructive cartels are oligarchies in which a few wealthy families hold all state power. When a few families control the state, they can use it to suppress economic competitors and secure monopoly profits.[8] Table 5.2 estimates the percentage of corporate assets owned by the fifteen richest families in selected Asian countries in 1996. The fifteen richest families owned more than half of the corporate assets in Indonesia, the Philippines, and Thailand. By contrast, the fifteen richest families owned roughly 3 percent of corporate assets in Japan and the United States.

Most people want effective state law to protect their property and enforce their contracts. When a few people control the state for years, however, they become the state. For them, wealth translates directly into power and power into wealth. Instead of needing the state to protect their property, they can make law and policy to restrict competition with their

Table 5.2 Ownership of Company Assets by the 15 Richest Families in Selected Asian Countries and USA in 1996

Country	Ownership	Country	Ownership
Indonesia	62%	Singapore	30%
Philippines	55%	Malaysia	28%
Thailand	53%	Taiwan	20%
Korea	38%	Hong Kong	34%
Japan	3%	USA	3%

Source: S. Claessens, S. Djankov, and L. Lang, "The Separation of Ownership and Control in East Asian Corporations," *Journal of Financial Economics* 58 (2000): 81–112.

businesses or take property from others by force. Laws that protect property and contracts mostly hinder these activities. These facts suggest that inequality undermines the rule of law, which partly explains the correlation between economic equality and the rule-of-law index.[9]

Russia in the 1990s provides an example. After the collapse of communism, Russia quickly privatized more than fourteen thousand medium- and large-size enterprises. Economic experts hoped that the new owners would secure their property by pressing politicians to create effective property law. This did not happen. Instead, a few tycoons called "the oligarchs" gained control over most of these firms. The oligarchs were so powerful that they did not need property rights to protect them, or so they thought until Vladimir Putin became president and used the state to stabilize the economy and dispossess the wealth of his enemies.[10]

Extreme economic and political inequality often causes the state to suppress innovation in order to protect existing wealth. To illustrate historically, eighty individuals owned approximately 50 percent of Iceland's agricultural land in 1700. To protect their power and keep wages low, they required all laborers and servants to reside and work on farms. Surrounded by rich fisheries, poor people starved when crops failed because law prevented them from leaving farms and taking up fishing.[11]

As another historical example, Caribbean plantation owners tied workers to their estates, originally by slavery and later by subtler means. Labor was cheap and workers were uneducated. Consequently, Caribbean economies were slow to adopt new technologies. Some authors apply a similar analysis to all of South America and assert that greater inequality caused slower historical growth rates in South America compared to North America.[12] Conversely, the good health and robust education of the workers in Denmark and Korea partly explains why these countries enjoyed high economic growth in recent history.

Three generalizations summarize the relationships between equality and growth:

1. Strict equality slows growth by weakening incentives to innovate.

2. Oligarchies, cartels, and uneducated workers cause extreme inequality and slow growth.

3. Market competition and educated workers cause moderate inequality and promote fast growth.

These relationships suggest that extreme inequality and strict equality slow growth, whereas moderate inequality maximizes growth, as depicted in figure 5.1. Furthermore, the welfare overtaking theorem implies that the growth maximizing level of equality also maximizes the welfare of the nation.

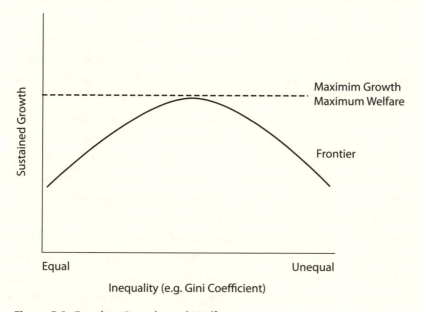

Figure 5.1. Equality, Growth, and Welfare

Do Wage Earners Benefit from Growth?

Does growth of national income correlate historically with growth in wages of working people? Historical evidence collected by Robert Allen indicates that economic growth in Europe raised everyone's wages. Allen collected data on money wages in various trades (masons, farm laborers, building laborers, etc.) in European countries since the Middle Ages. He also collected data on the prices of staples (bread, clothes, housing, etc.). He combined the data on wages and prices to measure real wages (the purchasing power of nominal wages).[13] Allen found that real wages in European cities were much the same in 1215 and 1800, despite some ups and downs. Real wages doubled and tripled after 1350 as a consequence of the Black Death, which killed up to one third of the European population. And they declined after 1650. But over the whole period there was no clear upward or downward trend. That changed after 1815, when real wages and production per worker began to increase in Europe. The rate of increase accelerated after 1850.[14]

To relate wages to poverty, Allen defined poverty as having just enough money to buy the staples needed for existence. He calculated that construction workers in three European cities—Amsterdam, London, and Paris—were living in poverty in 1820. Their real wages increased over the nineteenth century by more than 100 percent in London and Amsterdam, and by more than 50 percent in Paris. By World War I, wages had increased to two or three times above the poverty level.[15]

In developing countries with growing economies, today's trends in wages resemble Europe in the nineteenth century, with real wages and national income rising together. The second column in table 5.3 shows the average annual changes in GDP per employed person for selected countries and years. This number roughly measures changes in the average productivity of labor. The third column shows the annual changes in real wages. Changes in the productivity of labor in the second column correlate with changes in real wages in the third column. Thus real wages in China increased by 10 percent annually or 170 percent in a decade, and real wages in India increased by 2.5 percent annually or 30 percent in a decade. (Note, however, that real wages decreased in Brazil in these years

Table 5.3 Labor Productivity and Real Wage Increases by Country

Country (time period considered)	Average annual increase of labor productivity (GDP per person employed) in percent[a]	Average annual increase of monthly real wages in percent[b]
China (1995–2003)	9.15	10.36
Estonia (1995–2004)	4.99	4.66
Hungary (2000–2005)	4.55	3.19
India[c] (1994–2005)	4.78	2.68
Ireland (2000–2005)	3.97	2.47
Korea Rep. (1995–2005)	3.71	3.12
Egypt (1995–2003)	3.33	3.40
Poland (2000–2005)	3.11	1.92
Singapore (1995–2005)	2.83	3.01
UK (1995–2004)	2.45	1.85
USA (1995–2004)	2.42	0.05
Argentina (1995–2004)	0.95	− 2.20
Brazil (1995–2003)	0.94	− 1.96
Mexico (2000–2005)	0.06	0.98[d]
Zimbabwe (1995–2001)	−5.93	− 1.74

[a] Own calculations from *World Development Indicators 2008*.
[b] Own calculations from ILO, *Key Indicators of Labor Markets*, 5th ed. (Geneva: ILO, 2007), KILM 15, Manufacturing Wage Indices, KILM 16, Occupational Wage and Earning Indices, http://kilm.ilo.org/2007/register/.
[c] Data for India from C. P. Chandrachekar and J. Gosh, *Recent Employment Trends in India* (2008), real wages are wages of regular male workers at 1993–94 constant prices.
[d] Hourly wages.

at a time when productivity was increasing, which shows that average productivity is not the sole determinant of real wages.)[16]

Sustainability

For more than one hundred years, the United States and other Western capitalist countries have enjoyed sustained growth of 2 to 3 percent per year in per capita GDP.[17] Is growth sustainable, or must resource exhaustion stop it eventually?

Some physical resources are finite, but that does not mean that growth must stop. To see why, we contrast inexhaustible ideas and scarce resources. Many people can use products of the mind simultaneously, like theorems, principles, designs, inventions, expressions, and compositions. When one person uses an idea, just as much remains for someone else to use. Economists call this characteristic nonrivalry. Looking into the future, nonrivalry implies nondepletion: when the present generation uses an idea, just as much remains for future generations to use.

In contrast, scarce resources like capital, labor, land, and fuel have rival uses. When one person uses a scarce resource, it is unavailable for others to use. Some scarce resources renew like a forest, a river, or wheat. Use does not necessarily reduce their stock permanently, because the stock can be replenished. Other scarce resources deplete, like oil and iron. Use reduces their stock as long as we do not know how to replenish them. However, the stock can be depleted continually without ever exhausting it. Depletion is sustainable when its absolute rate always decreases, so exhaustion does not occur in finite time. Thus if the stock of oil falls by 50 percent in every period, the absolute fall diminishes in every period, and the stock never reaches zero, except in the mathematical limit when time goes to infinity. With sustainable depletion, the stock of exhaustible resources declines each year, but an infinite number of years must pass before it reaches zero. (This is a form of one of Xenophon's paradoxes—if you travel half of the remaining distance to your destination each day, you never arrive.)

Is increased consumption sustainable, or must we eventually freeze in the dark? If producing more consumer goods depletes resources at a constant or increasing rate, then increased consumption hastens resource exhaustion. If innovations enable the production of more consumer goods while depleting resources at a decreasing rate, then increased consumption may be sustainable. Innovation can probably sustain increased consumption indefinitely, although we cannot be certain because the path of innovation is uncertain.

Many scholars believe that the world is currently depleting resources at an unsustainable rate. Correcting this dangerous situation requires increasing innovation or reducing consumption. Innovation can conserve scarce resources as when new automobile engines economize on fuel or electronic communication substitutes for paper publishing. Innovations can also substitute renewable resources for exhaustible ones, as when hydropower replaces a coal-fueled electrical plant. Policies that decrease consumption face fierce political resistance, so policies that increase the pace of innovation may be our only long-term hope. Thus China is trying to slow resource depletion and improve the environment. To do so, China needs innovations that conserve resources and improve the environment, because Chinese consumers are unlikely to accept reductions in consumption.

Fairness and Justice

We have explained that maximizing sustainable growth requires innovators to keep much of what they make. Is this fair and just? Philosophers disagree. A famous book by Robert Nozick argues that fairness requires the people who make wealth to keep *all* of it.[18] People should keep all the wealth that they make, according to Nozick, because it is *theirs*. Taking their wealth away from them is unfair, including taxation for poverty relief or the supply of public goods.

In contrast, theories of social justice usually regard wealth as part of a comprehensive social system that should be fair as a whole. In a fair system, a person is not automatically entitled to keep what he makes. Instead, everyone gets a fair share of what the society makes.[19] A fair share of what society makes may take account of what a person needs, not just what he makes. A person with greater needs may fairly claim part of what others make.

Taking this approach, John Rawls developed the most influential theory of justice among Western philosophers in the second half of the twentieth century.[20] According to Rawls, a just society should maximize the "primary social goods" enjoyed by its worst off members. This is the *maximin principle*: maximize the minimum payoff. Applied to innovation, the maximin principle allows entrepreneurs to keep what they make to the extent that doing so benefits society's poorest members. In contrast, we discussed the property principle for innovation, which allows entrepreneurs to keep whey they make to the extent that doing so maximizes the sustainable growth rate of consumption as measured comprehensively.

To what extent do these principles conflict? Does maximizing the minimum well-being in society through law and policy come close to maximizing the rate of sustainable growth, or are they far apart? This is a question about the extent to which the wealth of the poorest citizens increases with the wealth of the nation. Wage earners broadly participate in the gains from rising national wealth. As workers become more productive, their wages rise and national poverty declines. China's Premier Deng Xiaoping devised a famous motto for the 1980s: "For everyone to get rich, some must get rich first."[21] People can accept others' moving ahead as long as they expect that their turn will come soon, rather like motorists waiting in line to enter a tunnel.[22] With sustained growth, most people get their turn for an increase in income.

But not everyone. Rising wages do not directly benefit people who do not work for money such as children, women-at-home, the elderly, subsistence farmers in remote regions, the disabled, the insane, vagabonds, criminals, people who sleep under railway bridges, people who pick through garbage at the dump, and homeless people who shuffle behind shopping carts piled with rags.[23] These people do not benefit directly from rising wages because they do not work for money. Some benefit indirectly from rising wages, such as the children of workers, and others benefit little or not at all, such as homeless beggars. "Residual poverty" refers to the people left behind as a nation gets rich. In low- and middle-income countries, approximately 22 percent of all people live in absolute poverty defined as less than one dollar a day.[24] They are the residual poor who still wait to get ahead.

Whereas rising productivity cures national poverty, the cure for residual poverty is efficient redistribution—sharing in families (relational redistribution), charitable gifts (private redistribution), and social expenditures by the state (public redistribution).[25] Governments reduce residual poverty by transferring income and services to people who cannot work or who can only do the lowest-paying jobs. In some countries, high social transfers increase personal incomes of the residual poor well above their market wages. Thus higher transfer rates in the Scandinavian countries cause lower poverty rates compared to other countries with similar national income and lower transfers, such as the United States and Ireland.[26]

Faster economic growth increases the tax base from which the state can collect and redistribute income to its poorest members.[27] Indeed, compound growth causes the income tax base to increase unimaginably quickly. This fact reduces the conflict between the property principle for innovation and principles of fairness that focus on residual poverty. To illustrate numerically, assume that the poorest 10 percent of the population receive transfers equal to 5 percent of the income taxes collected by the state. If national income grows at 2 percent for a century and transfers increase at the same rate, then transfers to the poorest 10 percent of the population would increase seven times. In contrast, if national income grows at 10 percent for a century and transfers increase at the same rate, then transfers to the poorest 10 percent of the population would increase over fourteen thousand times.

Growth benefits workers through rising wages, and growth benefits the very poor through transfers and social programs. The unimaginable power of sustained growth requires philosophers to rethink the application of theories of social justice to the economy. Any theory of social justice that precludes rapid growth should be modified or abandoned. Given background institutions that sustain transfers and social programs, fairness cannot rule out the property principle of innovation.

Conclusion

Economic growth increases the welfare of most people by causing wages to rise, and it increases the welfare of the residual poor by increasing tax revenues for transfer payments and social welfare programs. The welfare effects of sustained growth overtake redistribution, so law and policy should not sacrifice growth for the sake of equality. Rather, law and policy should implement the property principle for innovation: "Innovators should keep the amount of wealth that maximizes the sustainable rate of growth in a comprehensive measure of consumption." Redistribution often increases growth and it should be pursued, especially redistribution that increases the education and health of workers and poor people. Redistribution that slows growth should be abandoned. Much of the remainder of the book applies the property principle of innovation to particular bodies of law.

Chapter 6
Keeping What You Make—Property Law

A Brazilian landowner refuses to lease farmland for fear that the tenants will stay permanently without paying rent. A Chinese filmmaker foregoes making a movie for home viewing for fear that graduate students will circulate it freely on the Internet. Ecuadorian investors decline to buy stock issued by a profitable shrimp farm for fear that the managers will steal their money. What do these three examples have in common? In each case the fear that wealth will be taken stops someone from making it. Brazilian landowners need protection from deadbeat tenants in order to make land available for renting. Chinese filmmakers need protection from student-pirates in order to make films profitable. And Ecuadorian investors need protection from conniving managers in order to finance profitable businesses.

Effective law could assuage these fears—corporate law to protect investors, land law to protect lessors, and copyright law to protect filmmakers. These laws are necessary to satisfy the property principle for innovation: the makers of wealth should keep much of it. This chapter concerns how property law—specifically the law of real property (land and buildings), intellectual property (patents and copyright), and organizational property (corporations and partnerships)—helps people to keep what they make.

Land Reform, Squatters, and Dead Capital

The Peruvian economist, Hernando De Soto, recently estimated that Egypt's working poor own 92 percent of Egypt's asset base in the form of real estate. He calculated that relatively poor people own real estate in Cairo that is six times the value of all savings deposits in Egyptian banks, thirty times the value of the 746 companies registered at the Cairo Stock Exchange, and fifty-five times the value of foreign investments in Egypt until 1996.[1] While people can dispute these numbers, there is no disputing that many people own land and buildings that constitute a large fraction of any nation's wealth, especially in poor countries. The size and distribution of real estate gives vibrant real estate markets a special role in encouraging entrepreneurs in developing countries.

Land Reform

Anything called "reform" sounds good, but, in practice, land reform can be good or bad. The outcome usually depends on the mechanism to change owners. The worst historical example began in 1958 when China's communist government led by Mao Zedong forced peasants off small plots of land and into large communes. Abolishing private ownership gave the government unrestricted control over land. The government expected the communes, which were suited for heavy machinery and work groups, to increase agricultural production. The communes had to deliver high quotas of food to the state, even though the government shifted peasant labor from the countryside to cities for breakneck industrialization under the slogan "the Great Leap Forward." Instead of increasing, agricultural production fell disastrously. The government, however, did not acknowledge the problem, seek aid, or import food. As a result, millions of peasants starved, especially in the winters of 1959 and 1960. The best guesses of scholars put deaths at 20 to 30 million people, making it the deadliest famine in the history of the world.[2]

Zimbabwe provides another disastrous example of forced change in ownership. In Zimbabwe people of European descent owned prosperous farms that fed the country, employed workers, and earned foreign currency from tobacco exports. In 2000 President Mugabe asserted that whites had stolen the land from blacks early in the twentieth century, and he announced a program to take land from white farmers and redistribute it to blacks. Mugabe's loyalists seized land, most white farmers fled the country, agricultural production plummeted, food shortages developed, hyperinflation reduced trade to barter, and massive unemployment impoverished already poor people.[3]

Forced redistribution of land by politicians usually causes productivity to fall, sometimes disastrously as in the preceding examples and sometimes moderately. The history of Zimbabwe suggests two general reasons why productivity falls. The British originally conquered the region and distributed land to European settlers for farming.[4] Subsequently, many farms were bought and sold. The highest bidders tended to be the best farmers who could make the most money from farming. Markets continually redistribute land from less-productive to more-productive owners.[5] In contrast, President Mugabe took land from political opponents and gave it to loyal supporters. Loyalty correlates badly with productivity. Inferior farmers acquired the land. The first reason why production plummeted in Zimbabwe is that land was taken from buyers and given to loyalists.

Besides being worse farmers on average, the new owners in Zimbabwe were insecure. Fearing that someone else might take the land from them, they were reluctant to plant new crops, dig irrigation channels, or otherwise invest. Forced redistribution generally unsettles property rights, and uncertain ownership discouraged investment by increasing risk. The two reasons why production plummeted in Zimbabwe were putting worse farmers in control of the land and making them insecure.

Whereas land reform that destroys markets causes agricultural production to fall, land reform that creates markets usually causes agricultural production to rise. Again, the most dramatic example comes from China. After Mao Zedong's death in 1976, past policies were gradually reversed and China began to dissolve the communes in 1978. Land was redistributed from the collective to families who owned the agricultural products that they produced. Agricultural production consequently soared in the 1980s. The dissolution of the communes was relatively egalitarian, with each peasant family receiving a small plot of land, so the benefits from the surge in agricultural production were widely shared.[6]

Besides China, creating markets ("marketization") increased agricultural production in other times and places. Removing feudal restrictions on the sale and use of land caused a surge in agricultural production in eighteenth-century Silesia[7] and nineteenth-century Japan.[8] In the twentieth century, land reform in East Asia and Latin America had mixed success in dissolving feudal obligations and estates.[9]

In Poland, cooperative and state farms appropriated most agricultural land during the communist period that began in 1945 and ended in 1989. After 1989, the process reversed—privatization instead of socialization. By 1997–98, Poland had privatized 85 percent of its agricultural land.[10] While successful overall, privatization provoked competing legal challenges from people with past connections to the land.[11]

Private persons, not the state, must plant most of the nation's crops and build most of its barns, houses, apartments, shops, and factories. For private persons to make these investments, they must feel secure in owning the improvements that they make. A lease can provide this security, provided that the lease is long and easily renewed, even though the state retains ownership.[12] Countries where a communist tradition precludes privatizing land, strive to develop long-term leases as a substitute. China, Russia, and Vietnam have developed agricultural markets in recent decades based on use rights, without actually privatizing land. The land in these countries still belongs to "the people" (i.e., the state), but private persons own most of the buildings on top of it.

Other attempts to privatize land created chaos instead of markets. Most of the land in Papua New Guinea—the authorities say 97 percent—is in customary ownership by clans and tribes, who cannot sell it. Beginning under the Australian protectorate and continuing after full independence in 1975, the state tried to convert customary ownership, which does not allow land sales, to individual ownership under English common law, which allows land sales. Conversion had modest success in towns and failed in the countryside. Each clan and tribe claims the maximum land that it controlled in the past. Surveying boundaries and registering title requires resolving difficult disputes similar to deciding who owns Jerusalem.[13] In the 1980s the nation was awash with lawsuits and violence by customary owners seeking compensation or recovery of lost lands. The attempt of the state to create markets for land failed, although illegal markets flourished on the edge of towns.[14]

The desire to preserve a way of life lies behind restricting land sales in Papua New Guinea. Rural land traditionally passed from one generation to another according to fixed inheritance rules, with sales impossible. Allowing land sales raises the possibility that owners will sell the land, break the chain of inheritance, and disrupt the traditional social order. In societies where clans and kin groups still own land, creating lively real estate markets usually means clans die and agricultural production grows. With Papua New Guinea's clans as with Silesia's nobility in the eighteenth century, preserving the traditional social order seems to require retarding the sale of land.[15]

Kin groups sometimes obstruct land sales to preserve their way of life. In tribal areas in India, the law restricts sales of land to members of the same tribe.[16] Restricted land sales increase the likelihood that owners will continue using the land as in the past. Furthermore, many Indians—tribal or nontribal—can legally remove their property from the mortgage market by declaring that it belongs to the "undivided Hindu family."[17] This legal maneuver partly saves traditional families and saves on taxes.

Chapter 3 explained that kinship remains important in the most advanced economies because relational finance often funds the first stage of developing a business innovation. The Rothschilds in France, Agnellis in Italy, Onassises in Greece, and Birlas in India developed large, profitable family firms. Even in the best circumstances, however, family cooperation is too narrow to make a country rich. Firms must reach out beyond family for investors and managers. On balance, the historical trend of land ownership runs against clans and in favor of markets. In much of Africa, a more individualistic system of ownership is displacing a traditional system based on kin groups. A statistical analysis of Ghana established that more individual property rights cause more investment on improving the land. People apparently invest more to improve land when they share the benefits with fewer kin.[18] (Apparently, less sharing among kin also reduces savings.)[19]

In sum, agricultural land changes owners by market transactions and political fiat. Production usually falls when politicians redistribute land by force to their loyalists, and productivity usually surges in socialist, feudal, or tribal societies when legal reforms create active markets for land. Creating land markets requires quieting disputes over ownership so that people acquire land by buying it, not rousing disputes so that people acquire land by litigating or lobbying.

Squatters

King Charles II of England gave land encompassing the modern state of Pennsylvania to William Penn in 1681 in exchange for two beaver skins per year. Penn, however, had limited ability to survey and control the land, so squatters quickly occupied much of it. In the colonies that became the United States and later throughout much of the nineteenth century, poor people seized land illegally from large private owners and the state.[20] Seizures relied on intimidation, lapses in the owners' vigilance, and government officials who looked away.

Similarly, poor people in Latin America, Africa, and Asia squat on others' land and the law catches up later or never.[21] When the poor seize land from the rich, evocative slogans justify the seizures, such as "Land belongs to the people" or "Land belongs to those who farm it." In this spirit, the Brazilian constitution requires land to fulfill its "social function."[22] (Unlike the Brazilian constitution, ecologists deny that land left to nature has no social function.) Landless farmers can petition the state to expropriate "unproductive land" on their behalf. Or, instead of waiting for the state to act, landless Brazilian farmers can invade. When the signal is given, the invaders occupy part of a large ranch, quickly plant gardens, and erect dwellings. Afterward, the legal process gets complicated and unpredictable. Perhaps the court immediately issues an eviction order, or perhaps the eviction order comes after several years, or perhaps the state gives title to the invaders and promises to compensate the original owner.[23]

Given legal uncertainty in Brazil, owners who rent agricultural land to others take a big risk. After moving in, a tenant might stop paying rent and declare that the land was not fulfilling its social function. This possibility inhibits Brazil's rental market in rural land. A far smaller proportion of rural land is rented in Brazil than in other countries—less than 10 percent in Brazil compared to more than 40 percent in the United States, France, and Netherlands.[24]

Besides having difficulty renting land, poor Brazilian farmers face unnecessary difficulties when buying it. A constitutional right to housing causes some judges to refuse to evict a homeowner who has fallen behind in mortgage payments. Since courts sometimes shield homeowners from their creditors, banks reluctantly loan for the purchase of homes.[25] Compared to other countries, real estate credit operations in Brazil represent a much smaller percent of gross domestic product—only 1 percent.[26]

Land seizures in Brazil have a perverse logic. Thin rental and mortgage markets give many poor farmers few choices for acquiring land except to seize it.[27] Land seizures, however, are the main reason for thin real estate markets for poor farmers. By destroying markets, land invasions make themselves necessary. If courts promptly evicted people who seized rural land, and if courts made borrowers repay their debts, then renting and buying land would flourish. Markets easily dominate seizures as a mechanism to redistribute land and raise living standards.

Given political will, effective markets in land are immediately attainable in Brazil, but not in Papua New Guinea. The town of Madang expanded in recent decades where groups of people loosely called "clans" once planted crops, gathered food, and hunted. These clans still live there, encompassed by the town like islands in a lake, and the state still nominally recognizes them as owning much of the town's land in customary law. Customary owners cannot legally sell their land to anyone, and they cannot legally rent it to anyone without following prohibitively burdensome procedures. As Madang swells with immigrants from the countryside who need land for homes and gardens, the immigrants cannot legally buy or rent customary land. So the immigrants, who far outnumber the customary owners, seize the land, plant gardens, and build dwellings, as in Brazil. In the current legal situation, Madang's growth depends on seizures to increase the land's productivity and accommodate demographic change.[28]

The security of squatters decisively affects the quality of their dwellings. Squatters live in shanties of cardboard and tin when they feel too insecure to invest in them. An investment might draw the attention of the owners and increase the likelihood of losing everything. Fear of eviction creates some of the world's worst housing conditions. Conversely, when squatters feel secure, they invest time and money to improve their dwellings. To illustrate, the water authority in southeastern Sao Paulo, Brazil, owns land containing an underground aqueduct.[29] Squatters built houses illegally on the land over the aqueduct. The houses are mostly three-story brick or cinderblock buildings with plastered walls, bright paint, artistic cement balustrades, ornate ironwork balconies, satellite dishes on the roof, and often a garage with a car on the ground floor. Such investments increased the squatters' security, because the state is less likely to evict them from substantial dwellings than cardboard shacks. These squatters invest not only *because* they feel secure but to *make* themselves secure.[30]

Conversely, the presence of squatters significantly reduces the market value of land to its owner. A real estate agent in Mumbai (Bombay) told Hans-Bernd Schäfer that flats in high-rise buildings in the city center near Yuhu Beach sell for the remarkable price of US$1.7 million per 1,000 square feet (93 square meters), even though slums surround these tall buildings. To construct a high-rise building, the developer must first secure title and clear off the poor occupants, which is hard to do. Land rights are uncertain and fragmented between the poor occupants and formal owners. Modern apartments are so expensive because the difficulty of securing title constricts their supply.

Beside the poor seizing land from the rich, the rich often seize land from the poor. To illustrate, the state owns all land in China and small farmers have use rights. The state can terminate the use rights of small farmers and transfer them to large developers for factories, offices, and apartments. The ideology of progress and growth disguises this theft, although international news media sometimes publicize the protests and violence. The worst way to subsidize growth is to allow large developers to seize land from the poor.

Live and Dead Capital

Chapter 3 explained that innovators borrow money to develop new ideas. When a borrower seeks a loan, the lender usually demands that the borrower offer something valuable as security. If the borrower defaults, the lender will seize the security and sell it to recoup the loan. Lenders prefer "liquid" security, which means a good that is easy to sell in an active market with many buyers. When the borrower can offer a liquid asset as security, the lender will loan on good terms. Loans often pay for business investments. Consequently, liquid assets are "living capital" that finances growth, whereas illiquid assets are "dead capital" that cannot finance growth.

Real estate is the most valuable asset that many people own, especially the lower and middle classes. Furthermore, creditors in poor countries prefer real estate as collateral because land and dwellings are harder to hide than silver bracelets, bonds, or barrels of beer. To obtain a mortgage, which is a loan secured by real estate, the creditor must be able to seize it from a defaulting debtor and sell it to satisfy the debt.[31] Thus the ability to secure loans by real estate significantly affects the finance of innovation and growth.

When repossession and sale is easy, mortgage markets are liquid and real estate is living capital. However, bad laws and policy make much of the world's real estate illiquid. Throughout the world, cities like Cairo pulse with industry and enterprise from countless small businesses. Many families own small businesses, but they cannot use their real estate to secure a loan and grow into a big business. This problem is endemic in poor countries.[32]

Three obstacles to real estate transactions plague countries with weak property law. First, the buyer in a real estate transaction must ascertain that the seller truly owns the property. Defects in registries increase the risk of mistake or fraud in buying real estate.[33] In Vietnam, the state has not developed a registry of titles for apartments and houses. Some owners have a written document from a local authority acknowledging ownership, and others have no official documents. A statistical analysis of offers to sell real estate in two Vietnamese cities found that owners who claim to have a written document charge more for similar properties. The price increase approximately equals the value of having a telephone, which is less than the value of having a toilet.[34] An efficient registry of title would increase real estate sales in Vietnam.

After a defective registry, the second way that ineffective laws lower the sale value of real estate concerns its use. Besides ascertaining the seller's identity, the buyer must ascertain what he can do with the property. Obtaining a construction permit is so bureaucratic, slow, and costly in many countries that owners bribe officials to turn a blind eye to illegal construction. Height limits on buildings in many Cairo neighborhoods are unrealistic, so owners accommodate growing families by violating regulations and adding additional stories to their buildings. Since almost every owner in Cairo is a violator of one regulation or another, officials can extract bribes from anyone by threatening to enforce the regulations. Buyers face the uncertainty of not knowing exactly how much they will have to pay in bribes to use their new property.

Third, the creditor bears the burden of filing a complaint against a defaulting debtor and going forward with legal action. In some countries, the legal process of debt collection costs too much or consumes too much time, so legal debt collection is impractical.[35] In these circumstances, mortgages are unavailable, or only available on unfavorable terms. Conversely, the availability of mortgages increases dramatically when the creditor can obtain immediate control over property from a defaulting debtor without a trial.[36] Even in countries where evicting a family is practically impossible, evicting a corporation can be relatively easy. Consequently, creditors are willing to lend to a corporation on favorable terms when corporate real estate secures the loan. Thus a recent study of secured loans in sixty developing countries found that corporations secure 70 percent with mortgages and only 30 percent with movable capital.[37]

Creativity and Property

Illiquid real estate constitutes a large proportion of capital in poor countries, which inhibits credit and investment in growing businesses. A different problem with property concerns rampant theft of new creations. Humanity almost lost its greatest theatrical legacy because Shakespeare made only a few copies of each play that he wrote.[38] He did not want them published because he did not want others to perform his plays. With ineffective copyright laws, he profited from selling tickets to performances of his plays, not from publications. In contrast, J. K. Rowling sold 8.3 million copies of *Harry Potter and the Deathly Hallows* on the first day of its publication.[39] A modern author like Rowling uses copyright law to secure ownership of an original expression. With effective copyright, secrecy is unnecessary.

Like an author uses copyright, a modern scientist uses patent law to secure ownership of an original invention. Copyright and patents are "intellectual property"—intangible products of the mind that are owned like land and other tangible goods. No one can use another's patio, pants, or patent without the owner's permission. Permission to use a patent comes at a price—the fee for a permit, license, lease, or sale.

Intellectual property law, however, does not extend to important classes of business innovations. An entrepreneur cannot copyright or patent the discovery of a foreign buyer, reorganization of its sales force, or its training methods for quality control. The discoverer of a better way to organize a business or a new market for goods cannot own the innovation. When innovations are unowned, their creators must protect them the same way that Shakespeare protected his plays—by secrecy.[40] Chapter 8 on corporate law analyzes the firm as a way to keep secrets. For now, instead of discussing business secrets, we consider an intense conflict between rich and poor countries over intellectual property.

When two students share a cheese sandwich, each one gets a fraction of it. In contrast, when two students share a digital recording of music, each one gets the whole thing. Economists say that consumers of a sandwich are *rivals*, and listeners to recorded music are *not rivals*. The absence of rivalry is a reason to allow free use of a good.

However, free use has a big disadvantage. Explicit information is easily stored and retrieved, like the chemical formula for aspirin, the lyrics of the Beatles song "Imagine," and Microsoft's PowerPoint program. By not paying royalties to creators, competition among resellers drives the price of explicit information down to its copying cost. Shops in Hong Kong and Brasilia, consequently, sell American software at little more than the cost of a diskette, much to the consternation of U.S. businessmen and politicians. When people can copy freely, smart businessmen wait for others to create and then imitate the creators. Imitators gain a competitive advantage by escaping the costs of creating, including research and development costs, so creativity plummets. Should officials in China and Brazil try to stop piracy of intellectual property or look the other way? Free copying of creations expands use and slows creativity. Conversely, patents and copyright expand creativity (up to a point) and narrow use.[41]

Different countries prefer to balance incentives for use and creativity differently. Creators of intellectual property are disproportionately in countries with more educated people, well-equipped laboratories, and superior universities. These countries tend to favor restrictions on copying. In contrast, countries with many users relative to creators tend to favor free copying and using. Thus Brazilian and Chinese officials tend to look the other way when intellectual property rights get violated.

Pharmaceutical drugs are a poignant example. Europeans and Americans invent most drugs. India and Latin America historically refused to recognize pharmaceutical patents, so their consumers enjoyed cheap medical drugs that were invented abroad and manufactured locally.

In Brazil, the law compelled the owners of AIDS patents to license Brazilian manufacturers. Compulsory licensing lowered the price that Brazilian consumers pay for AIDS drugs, and the law also reduced the potential profits of Brazilian innovators in pharmaceutical. However, a recent study concluded that *all* of the potential pharmaceutical innovators are foreigners, not Brazilians.[42]

When users and creators are from different countries, national tensions rise over intellectual property.[43] Thus American businessmen, politicians, and diplomats scold China, India, and Brazil over lax enforcement of patents and copyrights. Conversely, these countries have fewer creators and more users, so, instead of creating for themselves, they hope to do better by copying American software, Japanese hardware, German pharmaceuticals, and Italian designs.[44]

An implicit bargain between relatively rich creators and relatively poor users ameliorates this tension between them. Poor countries with low labor costs want to export manufactured goods to rich countries with high labor costs. Rich countries with high technical abilities want poor countries to recognize and enforce intellectual property rights. So the two groups make a political bargain. By supporting the applications of poor countries to join the World Trade Organization (WTO), rich countries agree to accept imports from poor countries. In rich countries, these imports benefit consumers and harm workers in impacted industries. In return, the countries that seek admission to the WTO must join the World Intellectual Property Organization (WIPO) and agree to recognize and protect intellectual property rights. When poor countries fail to protect intellectual property, WTO rules allow rich countries to initiate legal proceedings and possibly to retaliate by curtailing imports. Thus, after fifteen years of negotiation, the WTO admitted China in 2001 with the support of the United States. China has historically tolerated piracy of intellectual property belonging to foreign companies, but accession to the WTO raises the risk of continuing this practice.

Diplomacy aside, development causes an economy to shift in a direction that naturally favors better legal protection of creativity. Newly industrializing countries focus on mass production of standardized goods. This kind of production gives a comparative advantage to a country with many uneducated workers who earn low wages. As education and wages increase, the mix of production shifts toward higher-quality goods. Finally, with better education of workers and higher wages, the mix shifts towards innovative products, as depicted below:

quantity → quality → creativity.

As a country's mix of production shifts to the right, it produces more creative goods. When creativity increases in importance, the benefits to a nation from effective intellectual property protection also increase. Thus ineffective copyright laws distort and retard the domestic software industry in China and India. Similarly, "Bollywood" in India makes more movies annually than Hollywood in California, and China also has a significant movie industry. Indian and Chinese production of movies would expand if the makers could reduce unauthorized use. Perhaps this fact partly explains the recent newspaper headline: "42 Million Pirated Discs Destroyed in Latest Chinese Anti-Counterfeiting Effort."[45] Unfortunately, theft is much harder to prevent for intellectual property than automobiles or real estate. Even with relatively effective intellectual property laws, Americans and Europeans steal much more software and recorded music than cars or land. For intellectual property, fixing law-on-the-books is easy and fixing law-in-practice is hard.

Filings for patents indicate the rate of technical innovation. In the world as a whole, patent filings are increasing, which apparently indicates that technical progress is accelerating. Residents in rich countries file the most patents by far, but filings from middle- and low-income countries are increasing. Chinese and Indian patent filing in the United States have increased dramatically.[46] Creative industries apparently thrive in some countries and languish in others. During the twenty-year period between 1980 and 1999, South Korea registered 16,328 patents for inventions in the United States, whereas the nine leading Arab economies registered 370 patents in the United States for the same period.[47]

If economic development shrinks the advantage to poor countries of pirating intellectual property, a common interest will emerge for developed and developing countries to find effective ways to enforce intellectual property rights. With more effective intellectual property law, developing countries will participate more fully in the explosion of creativity throughout the world.[48] Because ideas come from ideas, more innovation by developing countries would increase its rate everywhere, including in developing countries.

Everyone can gain more from the expansion of creative industries in developing countries. Chapter 5 explained that when less equality causes more growth, the increase in human welfare from faster growth quickly overtakes the decrease in welfare from less equality. Intellectual property law in developing countries is a case in point. By enforcing intellectual property rights in developing countries, faster innovation will overtake the transfer of income to developed countries. Many developing countries and all developed countries would gain more from the expansion of creative industry in developing countries than those countries gain from lax intellectual property rights.

Trademark is another type of intellectual property, but its usefulness is fundamentally different from patents or copyright. People like to gossip about the quality of products almost as much as the morality of people. In marketing and socializing, reputation matters. Trademark law gives the owner of a brand name the power to build its reputation, which can protect consumers from inferior products. Thus Coke commands a price premium in India over domestic competitors such as Campa Cola and Thumbs Up, partly because "Coke" signals uncontaminated bottles to consumers.[49] Conversely, without branding, consumers confuse goods from different manufacturers, and confusion creates an incentive to save costs by debasing quality. Before the fall of communism in 1988, Moscow stores sold many goods with generic labels such as "milk," "ink pen," and "pants," so Moscow consumers sometimes bought adulterated milk, leaky pens, and holey pants.

We discussed examples where effective trademark laws prevent consumers from buying fake goods unknowingly. Conversely, people *knowingly* buy fake Gucci bags, Nike shoes, and Rolex watches, especially in Korea and China. Where a savvy consumer can perceive quality by careful inspection, a good counterfeit provides similar quality and prestige at less cost. Rich countries pressure poor countries to stop producing the counterfeits that consumers love.

Do consumers gain more from buying counterfeits knowingly than the manufacturers of the authentic item lose? Some people delight in prestige brands, and for others Gucci represents "manipulative fashions," Nike represents "American imperialism," Rolex represents "conspicuous consumption," and all of them represent snobbery. Many people who sneer at prestige brands would welcome their death. Like most economics, this book does not take sides on what people ought to want.[50] Note, however, fake gods are like a parasite that dies without a host. If trademark violations destroy the prestige of the Guicci brand, Guicci counterfeits will lose their appeal to fashionistas.

Organization as Property

Organizations are a different type of property from real property or intellectual property. An organization includes offices such as chairman, chief financial officer, and vice president. Besides offices, organizations divide labor through roles such as bookkeeper, mechanic, or purchasing agent. Through offices and roles, an organization coordinates its members and pursues goals. With sufficient coordination, the organization acts coherently like a rational person.[51]

An organization's goals depend partly on whether or not it is *owned*. Owned organizations such as partnerships and corporations can be sold. The acquirer has rights to the firm's profits and the power to restructure its offices and roles. Since the owner can do what he or she wants with a firm, ownership allows for quick decisions at low cost.

In contrast, no one can buy or sell a club, church, cooperative, trust, charity, or the state. These organizations are unowned. They can sell their property—land, buildings, machinery, etc.,—but not themselves. Unowned organizations often make decisions collectively, following rules of governance that involve politics. Thus some clubs, churches, cooperatives, and governments proceed by majority rule. Compared to ownership, nonownership often leads to slow decisions and high transaction costs.

Ownership affects an organization's goals. When an owned firm underperforms financially, a buyer can purchase it and increase its profits by restructuring it. Expecting higher profits, the buyer should be willing to pay more for the firm than its current owners can earn. Markets for organizations thus pressure the owners to maximize profits or sell the firm to someone else.[52] No wonder that owned organizations stay more focused on making money.[53] This focus is good for price, quality, and innovation in market goods. Privately owned firms play the central role in the production of market goods in all of the world's rich countries.

In contrast, since no one can sell an unowned organization, the people who control it escape the pressure to maximize profits. They can pursue other goals—saving the rhinoceros, helping the poor, praising the Lord, organizing bridge tournaments, curing cancer, training graduate students, and so on. Unowned organizations play the central role in government, religion, education, and social life, where profits are not the organization's main goal.

Owned organizations tend to focus on making money, whereas unowned organizations pursue more diffuse goals. The difference shows when nationalizing or privatizing firms. Nationalizing a firm eliminates private ownership and usually increases the influence of politicians and other state officials, who broaden its goals. Conversely, privatizing a state enterprise usually refocuses it on profitability.[54] This happened in the 1990s in the formerly communist countries of Europe that joined the European Union. Privatization in these countries refocused firms on profitability and their economies prospered.

For privatization to refocus a firm on profitability, however, laws and policies must provide the foundation for markets. Otherwise privatization can degenerate into looting the state, which is what happened all too often in the 1990s in the formerly communist countries of Europe that did not join the European Union. To illustrate the difference concretely, Ukraine's government agreed to sell the country's largest steel mill in 2004 for $800 million to a consortium that included the son of the country's president, Leonid Kuchma. In 2005, the new president of Ukraine, Viktor Yushchenko, succeeded in undoing the sale and auctioning the steel mill for $4.8 billion. The price difference between an insider deal and a relatively competitive auction was 600 percent. The insider deal would have looted approximately $4 billion from Ukraine's treasury.[55]

A market for firms keeps owned organizations focused on profitability, which contributes to prosperity, innovation, and growth. Subsequent chapters discuss how the laws of finance, corporations, and bankruptcy make these markets work by keeping firms productive and preventing powerful insiders from looting them.

Conclusion

Squatters improve real estate when they secure title of it, managers improve firms when they own them, and creators innovate when they can patent their inventions. In general, effective rights give owners the security to invest and develop their property. To invest, the owners of land, organizations, and intellectual property often need to borrow money. Owners can borrow money when a lender can acquire the collateral of a defaulting debtor. Using loans, a superior farmer can buy land, a superior entrepreneur can buy firms, and a more creative person can buy patents. A market for farms reallocates land to better farmers, a market for corporations reallocates firms to superior entrepreneurs, and a market for innovations reallocates them to more creative people. For real estate, organizations, and inventions, property law provides the basis for investing, borrowing, and selling. These laws are necessary to satisfy the property principle for innovation: the makers of wealth should keep much of it.

Besides needing effective property rights, innovation requires coordinating the efforts of different individuals. People coordinate by saying what they will do and doing what they say. Contract law, which enables people to commit to doing what they say, is the subject of the next chapter.

Chapter 7
Doing What You Say—Contracts

The Soviet commissar needed to cooperate with the director of the State Steel Combine in Russia in the 1960s. They were also rivals, so the commissar kept an eye on the director's movements. One day they met in the Moscow railway station. The commissar asked the director, "Where are you going?" The director replied, "To Leningrad." The commissar thought to himself, "He says that he is going to Leningrad because he wants me to think that he is going to Minsk, but I know that he really is going to Leningrad." So the commissar said to the director, "You're lying!"

This joke depicts the problem of credible communication. To coordinate their behavior, people must say what they will do and do what they say. How do we know when to believe them? Businessmen relentlessly scrutinize the demeanor of others for clues about what they are really thinking. In Warm Springs, Oregon, a painting on the courthouse wall in an Indian reservation shows a witness testifying while holding his fingers in a bowl of water. If his hand trembled and made ripples, then he was presumably lying. The polygraph, or "lie detector," used by police works on similar physiological principles. An accomplished deceiver, however, can fool a water bowl or a polygraph. Fortunately, the law invented a superior mechanism to make people tell the truth in business transactions: the contract.

To understand how contracts work, consider what the Chinese philosopher Sun Tzu wrote in the sixth century BCE: "When your army has crossed the border [into hostile territory], you should burn your boats and bridges, in order to make it clear to everybody that you have no hankering after home."[1] Burning the bridges commits the army to attack by foreclosing the opportunity to retreat.

In business as in war, an actor commits to performing an act by raising the cost of not performing it. We use the term *contract* to refer to a promise with sanctions for breaking it, especially legal sanctions. Like burning bridges, an effective contract commits a person to doing what he says he will do by raising the cost of not doing it. The cost is raised by the sanction for breaking the promise. When businessmen bargain, they begin with "cheap talk" involving words without commitments or sanctions, and they end with contracts involving enforceable obligations. According to the *contract principle for coordination, the law should enable people to commit to doing what they say.* When this principle is implemented, people can trust each other enough to work together, even though money is at stake.[2]

Chapter 3 describes three types of finance: relational, private, and public. As a start-up firm passes from one stage to another, finance relies increasingly on state law, without abandoning the earlier forms of relational finance. The same three-way distinction for finance applies to contracts in general, as depicted in figure 7.1.

"Relational contracts" refer to promises among friends and relatives who are embedded in enduring relationships, such as the promise that an uncle makes when hiring his nephew. To enforce relational contracts, the parties rely on social sanctions. We use "private contracts" to refer to promises individually negotiated among nonrelatives, such as bank loans. To enforce private contracts, the parties use civil sanctions as well as social sanctions. And "public market contracts," or "public contracts" for short, refer to promises with standardized terms and prices, such as stocks sold in an exchange.[3] (These terms also have other meanings.)[4] In these contracts, the standardized terms and prices are known, or knowable, by many people. To enforce public contracts, the parties rely on

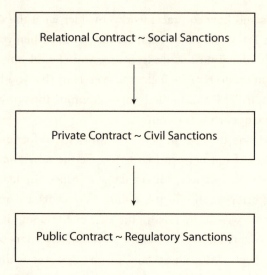

Figure 7.1. Three Types of Contracts and Sanctions

regulatory sanctions as well as civil and social sanctions. As a legal system becomes more reliable in a developing country, business shifts toward more law-intensive forms of contracting as indicated by the arrows in figure 7.1, without abandoning the less law-intensive forms.

Relational Contracts and Social Sanctions

This chapter explains each of the three types of contracts in turn, with emphasis on the distinctiveness of developing countries.[5] Human beings originally lived in small groups of kinsmen and friends who relied on each other. Although tribal life has faded, relatives and friends remain important for economic life, even in big firms and large cities. In northern Italy and Hong Kong, kinship glues together many firms, some of which have grown into business empires like the manufacturer Fiat and the fashion house Prada. In Switzerland and Israel, friendships formed in the army shape industries. And in the nineteenth century, men who fought beside each other in the United States' civil war subsequently created corporate America.

Where states do not enforce contracts effectively, businesses rely on relationships.[6] In the eleventh century, the states around the Mediterranean Sea were fragmented, without effective international laws. Yet Jews based in Egypt traded extensively in the region by contracts among relatives and friends.[7] Much the same is true today among Indian traders in Africa, Chinese merchants in Papua New Guinea, and Vietnamese businessmen.[8]

The scale of modern business necessarily involves interactions with people who are not relatives or friends. In these circumstances, businessmen often rely on a substitute for kinship and friendship: they deal with the same people over and over again. In Japan workers in large companies traditionally enjoyed lifetime employment, manufacturers traditionally preferred to deal with one or two suppliers for each input, and companies traditionally financed themselves through one main bank. Outside Japan, repeat transactions dominate some economic sectors in most countries. Thus civil servants worldwide seldom change jobs, many Apple computer users are fiercely loyal, depositors seldom change banks, retailers buy repeatedly from the same wholesaler, and franchisors and franchisees seldom separate their businesses.

How do people use relationships to enforce promises? When chimpanzees groom each other, they apply the principle, "Clean my fur today and I'll clean yours tomorrow." Like a chimpanzee troop, kinship and friendship provide a framework for reciprocity that remains fundamental to social life. In business the principle of reciprocity is, "Create a benefit for me now and I'll create a benefit of similar value for you in the near future." The principle has two elements: the implicit promise to give a future benefit and the commensurability of benefits given and received, which is a matter of fairness. A businessman who breaks his promises to return a favor will be called dishonest, and a businessman who gives a small favor in return for a large one will be called unfair. Whether in markets or organizations, people in repeat transactions reciprocate like grooming chimpanzees. Similarly, laboratory experiments confirm business experience: in repeated games, the form of reciprocity called "tit-for-tat" is the most popular strategy, and often the most profitable.[9]

With reciprocity each person punishes someone who wrongs him, and with "generalized reciprocity" people punish someone who wrongs someone else. For social sanctions, generalized reciprocity especially relies on gossip and ostracism. Families, small towns, firms, and networks hum with gossip that provides information (and misinformation) about who wronged whom. A bad reputation can trigger ostracism in the form of refusing to deal with someone else. Gossip provides the information and ostracism provides the sanction. A good reputation is valuable for its own sake and to overcome gossip that might trigger ostracism.

Earlier we characterized a contract as a promise with material sanctions for breaking it. "Relational contract" refers to a promise made by people in a relationship who can enforce it through sanctions that come from society, not the state.[10] People in relationships can commit to doing what they say by submitting to the threat of social sanctions. If you break your promise to come to family dinner on Sunday evening, your mother can punish you in a thousand small ways. The same is true in repeated business transactions. The most common problems of contracting are nonpayment of bills, late delivery, and poor performance. For nonpayment, a typical reciprocation is suspension of supply; for late delivery, it is delayed payment; and for poor performance, it is partial payment.

With relationships, the parties often make vague promises and adapt their behavior to circumstances as they arise. For example, when you promise your mother to be home in time for dinner, you do not list acceptable excuses for arriving late. Similarly, the parties in repeated business transactions rely heavily on implicit understandings that adapt to changing circumstances. Thus a wholesaler and retailer in a good relationship are flexible about what counts as late delivery of goods and the remedy for it. Flexibility can stop quickly if the relationship deteriorates or ends.[11]

Organizations can enforce reciprocity by formalizing sanctions for wrongdoing. Thus London merchants in the eighteenth century signed notes promising to repay the named party on presentation of the note. As these notes circulated, other people endorsed them and guaranteed repayment of the debt. Quakers, a small Protestant religious sect, expelled anyone who endorsed a note and failed to repay. As a result, merchants were especially willing to take notes from Quakers as payment.[12]

As another example, medieval European towns and guilds held their merchants collectively responsible for contracts with outsiders. If merchant α in town A failed to pay debts to merchant β in town B, then the merchants in town B could seize and hold any merchant from town A until the debt to merchant β was repaid. Foreseeing this fact, the merchants in town A pressured their members repay their debts. Collective responsibility facilitated trade over long distances. As we will explain in the next chapter, collective responsibility remains important today for lending to the poor.[13]

With reciprocity each person punishes someone who wrongs him, and with "generalized reciprocity" people punish someone who wrongs someone else. The main social sanctions are reciprocity, reputation, and ostracism. In business, ostracism usually takes the form of refusing to deal with someone. Families, small towns, firms, and networks hum with gossip and ostracism. Gossip provides information (and misinformation) about who wronged whom, and ostracism provides the sanction.

We mentioned that business relies on relational sanctions to enforce contracts when state law is ineffective. Even where states enforce contract law effectively, however, businesses prefer to avoid state enforcement. Relational enforcement is so much cheaper and quicker, if it works. To avoid relying on state law to enforce contracts, people cultivate "relationships" or "connections," which Chinese call "guanxi." Besides cultivating relationships, businesses avoid state enforcement by writing good contracts. The art of writing good contracts includes reducing a large exchange into a series of small, reciprocal exchanges. Social sanctions may be enough to enforce each of the small exchanges, but not enough to deter cheating in one large exchange.

To illustrate, when I buy a sausage at a street fair, I pay and I get the sausage simultaneously. Simultaneous exchange does not require promises. In contrast, when I pay you now for the promise of future delivery of a good, a gap in time allows promise breaking to slip in. A good contract divides the large exchange into a series of small exchanges. Thus a contract to construct an office building that takes a year to complete usually provides for small, periodic payments for completing each stage in the project. The ultimate goal is a "self-enforcing contract" in which each party expects to gain more at each stage by keeping his promises than breaking them. Good contracts are drafted to come as close to self-enforcement as possible, but perfect self-enforcement is often impossible without the threat of state enforcement.[14]

Innovative businesses need talented lawyers who can write contracts that accurately express the parties' commitments in language that judges can easily interpret and apply. With good contracts, judges and other officials help the parties to achieve their business purposes by interpreting the contracts as written. However, contracts often fail to address precisely the circumstances that give rise to a legal dispute. When courts must enforce terms in a relational contract, judges disagree about the extent to which they should enforce the terms as written, or impose the remedy most likely to repair the relationship.[15]

Besides these strengths, relational contracts have characteristic weakness. To sustain a business relationship, a person must deal with someone for reasons of history and sentiment, instead of dealing with the cheapest seller, richest buyer, hardest worker, or superior creator. In brief, relational contracting increases trust by reducing competition. For example, a cooperative factory in the city of Palampur, India, burns coal to roast tea. The cooperative buys coal at the beginning of the tea harvest and stores enough on its grounds to burn over several months. Keeping a large inventory of coal ties up scarce capital. Instead of storing coal, the cooperative could develop a relationship with one reliable seller to deliver coal as needed. A relationship with one seller, however, would preclude buying from a cheaper seller. Buying from the cheapest seller apparently saves enough money to pay for storing coal.[16]

If the state enforced contracts more effectively in Palampur, the tea cooperative could seek bids for future delivery of coal. A future contract allows competitive pricing without the need for inventories. In general, statistical research shows that companies in poor countries with ineffective contract law keep larger inventories than equivalent businesses in rich countries with effective contract law. Comparable enterprises like cement factories or breweries keep 30 percent to 50 percent higher inventories in countries with ineffective contract law.[17]

Ineffective state law channels transactions into long-run relationships and away from the best deals. Thus a survey asked businessmen in Peru how much the price of an input would have to fall to induce them to switch from their current supplier to a new supplier. The average answer was 30 percent. They explained their reluctance to change by ineffective contract enforcement. In Peru, the security provided by a long-run relationship with a supplier is apparently worth 30 percent of the cost of the supplies on average.[18]

We have explained that relational contracting has the disadvantage of reducing competition. Besides this economic cost, relational contracting facilitates discrimination and distrust among groups of people. Insiders often give lower prices, higher wages, and fairer terms to each other than to outsiders, who often exaggerate their mistreatment. These abuses can aggravate the natural vulnerability of a wealthy, inward-looking minority to racism and scapegoating. Thus in the 1960s many African countries drove out merchants of Indian descent, and Indonesian politicians episodically unleashed mobs on Chinese shopkeepers.

Besides the economic and social disadvantages of reduced competition, relational contracting has another problem: sometimes it is impractical or impossible. Most people do not buy enough cars, houses, or corporations to deal repeatedly with the same seller. One-time transactions yield an immediate payoff to unscrupulous behavior, without significant future costs such as damaged reputation. Only a naïve buyer would rely on the representations of a car salesman, real estate agent, or financier in most countries.

Our final example of the limits of relational contracts concerns proximity.[19] Nearness strengthens relationships. Thus a clothes wholesaler in Dar es Salaam, Tanzania, has strong relationships with retailers in shops around the city and delivers goods to them on credit. The wholesaler in Dar es Salaam would like to supply retailers in Mwanza in northern Tanzania, but her relationship with them is too thin to rely on credit. Local business can flourish in spite of ineffective state enforcement of contracts, but distance attenuates relationships. Ironically, the merchant in Dar es Salaam may be able to deal on credit with London by using letters of credit enforceable in English courts. In some countries, transactions are easy locally due to relational contracts, difficult nationally due to ineffective domestic law, and easy internationally due to effective foreign law.[20]

Relational contracting at a distance creates profitable opportunities for "middlemen" to complete the sales chain.[21] Thus the merchant in Dar es Salaam in the preceding example may find a relative in Mwanza to serve as middleman for local retailers. By establishing enduring relationships with buyers and sellers, middlemen can trade over distances without enforceable contracts, as shown by studies of Ghana,[22] Southeast Asia,[23] and overseas Chinese.[24]

Middlemen perform a valuable service by moving goods from people who value them less to people who value them more.[25] However the public, which does not appreciate this fact, asks "How can they get wealthy without making anything? They must be up to something crooked!" In weak legal systems, middlemen often belong to relatively small, ethnic minorities, like Indians in black Africa, Arabs in Mexico, and Chinese in Papua New Guinea. As middlemen, such a group builds trust among its members and provokes distrust among outsiders.

Private Contracts and Civil Sanctions

No one has enough relatives, friends, or repeat customers to achieve the scale of economic activity required for affluence. Relational contracting narrows the scale of cooperation, reduces competition, and fails altogether in one-time transactions or high-value transactions. Rather than just relying on social sanctions, people need the state's help to commit to keeping their promises. Economic development must extend the sphere of cooperation beyond relationships to encompass strangers.[26] When dealing with strangers, social sanctions are not enough protection from unreliable, careless, unlucky, mistaken, confused, or misleading promises, as well as from dissemblers, liars, rationalizers, frauds, and cheats.

We use "private contract" to refer to those promises where the victim of breach can obtain a remedy from the promise-breaker in a state court or similar body.[27] Unlike relational contracts, the remedy for breach of a private contract is a state sanction, not just a social sanction. Effective private contracts enable strangers to commit to doing what they say, so strangers can cooperate even when significant money is at stake.

Conversely, private contracts are ineffective when the threat of a state sanction does not give most self-interested people sufficient incentive to perform as promised.

Defects in the law of private contracts especially afflict poor countries and inhibit cooperation in business. Written contract law in developing countries mostly resembles written contract law in developed countries. For contract law-on-the-books, Mexico and Columbia resemble Spain and France, India and Nigeria resemble England, and Taiwan, China, and Korea resemble Germany. The writing is more similar than its application. Application of law causes the most important differences in the effectiveness of contract law in different countries.

Before becoming Germany's greatest poet, Johann Wolfgang von Goethe worked as a lawyer at the Imperial Court in 1771 where he saw "a monstrous chaos of papers lay swelled up and increased every year." Some legal cases remained on the docket for more than a hundred years, and one case filed in 1459 was still awaiting a decision in 1734.[28] When someone breaks a contract and the victim seeks a state remedy, delays can occur at each stage in the legal process—filing a legal complaint, discovering the facts, settling or litigating, appealing a decision, and enforcing a judgment against the defendant. Slow, uncertain legal processes cause a rational person to discount the court's remedy, like a ten-year junk bond.

For example, assume that a Mexican borrows 10,000 pesos from a bank and promises to repay 1,000 pesos each month for twelve months. Having received the loan, the borrower makes eight monthly payments and then stops paying when he still owes 4,000 pesos. The bank must go through legal proceedings to collect it. If the legal process is too slow and uncertain, the bank may give up without trying. Foreseeing the outcome, banks stop making such loans.[29] With deep discounting of remedies, state law cannot empower people to commit to keeping their promises.

Is this hypothetical example typical? Using survey data collected by the World Bank, table 7.1 ranks countries according to the number of days required to enforce a contract by means of a lawsuit. Interpreting this data requires caution.[30] The data apparently show large differences

Table 7.1 Time in Days to Enforce a Contract by Means of a Suit

Short delays		Medium delays		Long delays	
Country	Days	Country	Days	Country	Days
Singapore	150	Turkey	420	Bolivia	591
New Zealand	216	Peru	428	South Africa	600
Belarus	225	Nigeria	457	Czech Rep	611
Korea	230	Kenya	465	Morocco	615
Hong Kong	280	Chile	480	Brazil	616
Russia	281	Belgium	505	Ethiopia	620
Vietnam	295	Sweden	508	Algeria	630
USA	300	Venezuela	510	Botswana	687
France	331	Taiwan	510	Uruguay	720
Ukraine	345	Romania	512	Greece	819
Japan	360	Netherlands	514	Poland	830
Finland	375	Ireland	515	Philippines	842
Denmark	380	Spain	515	Israel	890
Germany	394	Iran	520	Pakistan	976
Australia	395	Portugal	547	Egypt	1010
Hungary	395	Rep. Congo	560	Italy	1210
Austria	397	Bulgaria	564	Colombia	1346
UK	399	Canada	570	India	1420
China	406	Indonesia	570	Bangladesh	1442
Switzerland	410	Malaysia	585		
Mexico	415	Argentina	590		

Source: World Bank, *Doing Business* (Washington, DC: World Bank, 2010).

around the world that correlate roughly with per capita income. The countries in the first column with enforcement delays of less than 415 days are disproportionately high-income countries (except for some misleading cases).[31] Conversely, the countries in the third column with long delays exceeding 590 days are disproportionately low-income countries.

Besides delays, another defect is vague laws with unpredictable consequences. Article 7 of the Chinese Civil Code stipulates that

> In concluding or performing a contract, the parties shall abide by the relevant laws and administrative regulations, as well as observe social ethics, and may not disrupt social and economic order or harm the public interests.

Is there any private activity that some official would not construe as violating article 7? If you are the victim of breach of contract, instead of suing, you might prefer to keep your head down and hope the authorities do not scrutinize your business to see whether your activities harm ethics, social order, or the public interest. Indian law does better. Section 23 of the Indian Contract Act regards any contract as void if it "would defeat any provision of law . . . or the Court regards it as . . . . opposed to public policy."[32] Although open ended, at least this proposition refers to laws and policies, rather than ethics, social order, or public interest.

The problem of legal vagueness has no simple cure. Like most bodies of law, the law of contracts navigates between precise rules that have the advantage of predictability, and imprecise principles that have the advantage of flexibility. Thus an imprecise contract principle in civil law is "good faith" (bona fides) and its opposite "bad faith" (exceptio doli generalis). Acceptance of the good faith rule has spread across civil law countries in recent decades.[33] Using "good faith," German judges can alter almost any aspect of a contract that they regard as dishonest, unfair, unreasonable, or bad for business. They can impose an obligation not stipulated in the contract, set damages to undercompensate the victim, set damages to overcompensate the victim, fix specific levels of due care, create a duty to disclose information, or render a contract void. (In some other countries, the judges use the principle of good faith more cautiously.)[34]

At the polar opposite from Germany, English judges follow the common law tradition and reject the principle of good faith.[35] They defer more strictly to the explicit terms written into the contract.[36] This fact marks a difference between contract litigation in Frankfurt and London.

Recent papers in development economics get the difference backward.[37] These influential papers characterize civil law as formalistic and common law as flexible. This characterization will surprise German judges in Frankfurt who apply the civil law principle of good faith so flexibly, and it will surprise English judges in London who reject the principle of good faith and interpret contracts literally. As the principle of good faith diffuses to developing countries, we cannot detect a difference in its acceptance that depends on the country's civil or common-law origins.[38] We believe that formality and flexibility depend on the way a nation has developed its legal heritage, not whether it began with civil or common law.

Vague, flexible principles like "good faith" can be compared to a Lamborghini automobile—the fastest car demands the best driver, or else expect a crash. High-quality judges have good educations, understand business, refuse bribes, and resist political influence. They can make good use of discretion by interpreting contracts flexibly. Conversely, when judges fall short on quality and independence, formalistic rules will work better than flexible rules. Indian law apparently recognizes this fact. The judges in India's Supreme Court and the High Court, who are well educated and independent, have authority to use the principle of good faith to develop law. In contrast, the lower courts judges, who are poorly educated and too often corrupt, are not allowed to use the principle of good faith to develop law.[39] Formality insulates Indian litigants against the quirks of lower court judges. Formality can also insulate judges against political pressure. Making the courts follow formal laws has an advantage in states like Russia where politicians interfere with judges in private disputes.

Next consider a special problem in developing countries concerning remedies for breach of private contracts. The usual court remedy for breaking a contract is money damages.[40] Collecting money damages from poor people is often impractical because they cannot pay, or they have no bank account to garnish wages, or their wages are unrecorded and unprovable, or their wealth is hidden, or their property is inseparable from their relatives' property. According to a recent estimate, roughly 11 percent of the population is in this situation in rich countries, and the proportion is much higher in poor countries.[41] The inability to collect money damages from poor people stops them from making legally effective contracts, which erodes their ability to cooperate with strangers.

In some countries, courts aggravate the problem by deciding contract disputes in favor of the poorer party, regardless of the case's merits. Thus Brazilian courts sometimes use the constitutional doctrine of the "social function of contract law" to refuse enforcement of contractual obligations of poor people.[42] This practice inhibits people from contracting with those who are poorer than themselves. Poor people have difficulty legally committing to keeping their word. Like a gift of contaminated cream, this doctrine is a sharp punishment disguised as a reward.

Money damages also require pricing broken promises, which can be difficult or impossible. To illustrate, assume that someone pays her neighbor for a used refrigerator and the seller fails to deliver it. To award money damages, the court will have to determine the used refrigerator's market value. The quality of used refrigerators varies and the court cannot inspect it. Or, even worse, perhaps price controls, import licenses, multiple exchange rates, and buying privileges cause people to queue for refrigerators. When meaningful prices are not public, courts have difficulty getting the information needed to assess money damages. (Money damages have other problems as well.[43])

These difficulties with money damages suggest that courts in poor countries should look for an alternative remedy for breach of contract. What other remedies are there? The other leading remedy is a court order requiring the defendant to perform as promised ("specific performance").[44] Defendants usually comply with court orders because defying them can ripen into the crime of contempt of court. In some circumstances, however, performance is infeasible. Thus a contractor cannot meet a deadline that has already passed, and a seller cannot deliver a refrigerator that it already shipped to someone else. When performance is impossible as in these examples, a court order to perform is pointless.

However, cases often arise in which specific performance has fewer problems than the damage remedy. If the court orders the defendant to perform as promised, the court obviously does not have to collect money from the defendant or determine the market value of performance. In the refrigerator case, the court can order the seller to give the refrigerator to the buyer as promised. To execute this order, a policeman may need to find the refrigerator, which is probably easier than finding the money paid for it.

We have explained that poor defendants and thin markets tilt the preferred remedy for breach of contract toward specific performance when it is possible, and away from money damages. Thus legal scholars in communist countries where markets were thin associated "socialist contract law" with specific performance, whereas money compensation belonged to "capitalist contract law."[45] Conversely, as an economy becomes more commercialized and monetized, thicker markets and liberalized prices tilt the preferred remedy for breach of contract toward money damages. Thus European countries that replaced communism with capitalism after 1989 moved toward money damages and away from specific performance, and China has apparently done the same.[46]

Public Contracts and Regulatory Sanctions

Private contracts enable strangers to cooperate by making commitments to do what they say. Private contracts widen the scale of cooperation compared to relational contracting. Sometimes, however, people widen the scale further by exchanging in public markets. The difference between the Old Delhi bazaar and the supermarket illustrates the contrast between private and public contracts. Grocers in Old Delhi bazaars compete vigorously to sell rice, wheat, peas, nuts, spices, fruits, cookies, bottled drinks, and other foods. Traditional Indians do not trust the quality of prepackaged food. A bag of rice might contain stones to increase its weight, a bag of peas might contain rat feces, or fruit might be old. Food is sold in open bags or piled on counters so buyers see and taste it.

Instead of seeing and tasting the food, repeat dealings with the same sellers could protect buyers against hidden defects. To build loyalty, sellers would not sell impure, unclean, or spoiled food to their repeat customers. Instead of repeat dealings, however, most consumers in Old Delhi apparently prefer to buy from the seller who offers the best price that day.

Unlike Old Delhi market vendors, supermarkets sell prepackaged and preweighed foods. Regulators punish sales of impure, unsafe, unhealthy, falsely labeled, or underweighed food. To avoid complaints to regulators, many sellers give disgruntled consumers a replacement or their money back. When regulations sustain the purity, safety, health, truthfulness, and accuracy of weights and measures, buyers can focus more on getting the best price, not on who is making the offer.

Failed regulations for food can have tragic consequences as Chinese consumers recently experienced. At least thirteen thousand Chinese children were hospitalized and four died in 2008 because Chinese regulators closed their eyes to adulterated baby food, milk, and yoghurt. Consumers of imported food in Taiwan, Japan, and Singapore were also affected.[47] After such an experience, how long will parents wait before they trust these sellers enough to buy from them again?

We have discussed foods where sellers know more about quality than buyers. The gap in information between sellers and buyers is wider and harder to close for complicated contracts like insurance, loans, mortgages, and employment. People who buy health insurance must trust that their insurer will reimburse reasonable claims, lenders must trust that borrowers will repay their loans, stockholders must trust that firms have honest audits, and employees must trust managers of their pension plan. (Note that important advances in economic theory in recent decades explain how differences in the information of buyers and sellers affect markets.)[48]

Regulators can increase competition in these markets by enforcing standardized terms. When law standardizes terms, one seller cannot mean something different from another who says that a basket contains two kilograms of rice, and one company cannot mean something different from another who tells an investor that the company's books have been audited. With standardization, buyers can easily compare offers from many sellers. Thus buyers purchase stocks from the cheapest seller on the Singapore stock exchange. Without standardization, buyers and sellers need to negotiate, as often happens when a Singapore business borrows from a local bank.

In sum, standardized contract terms and regulations can increase competition by reducing the information gap between buyers and sellers. More trust by buyers enables them to focus on getting the best price, not on who is making the offer as in relational contracting, and not on differences in nonprice terms as in private contracts. When the legal system strengthens, people buy more packaged food, health insurance, stocks, refrigerators on credit, and so forth.[49]

Markets approximate the model of "perfect competition" when buyers and sellers compete over price. To focus on price competition, the quality of the goods must be uniform in the market. Thus firms can compete over the price of coal more easily when buyers correctly believe that all coal sold as "grade A" has the same quality. Most goods, however, differ in quality. They are naturally heterogeneous. Inducing a high level of price competition requires standardizing the nonprice characteristics of exchange, such as weight, color, freshness, promptness, guarantees, warranties, risks, insurance, liabilities, services, and so forth.

When nonprice terms are standardized, buyers and sellers can focus on competing over price. Conversely, unique nonprice terms blunt price competition. Markets for unique goods are "illiquid" because they are not readily sold. To illustrate concretely, financial institutions in New York created idiosyncratic bundles of mortgages called "derivatives" with individually negotiated prices. When the U.S. financial system collapsed in the fall of 2008, banks that suddenly needed cash to pay their debts could not readily sell their derivatives. The illiquidity of derivatives tightened the credit squeeze on financial institutions that needed to raise cash quickly. Without public prices, the banks did not even know how much value their derivatives had lost.

The phrase *public market* usually refers to markets where many people freely buy and sell goods at known prices. Price competition and liquidity characterize public markets. Our concern is with the legal prerequisites for price competition and liquidity. The legal prerequisites include standardized nonprice terms in contracts. Sustaining standardization requires legal support, including mandatory legal rules and some regulations policed by judges and administrators.

Gray Contracts

The regulations discussed above contribute to the legal foundation of competitive markets. In contrast, many choice-choking regulations retard contracting. In Great Britain in the 1960s, running the trains required disobeying many regulations. The railroad unions, consequently, could shut down the rail system for a few days by following all of its rules. "Work-to-rule," as it was called, was a ministrike that paralyzed the railroad system. Similarly, businessmen and workers must violate many regulations in order to get things done, especially in poor countries. Thus a builder in Cairo violates building restrictions, a worker and employer in Brazil evade employment taxes, and a manufacturer in Russia runs a factory without a permit to do business.

Throughout the world, much of the economy operates in the "grey market" between the "white market" of legality and the "black market" of criminality, especially in developing countries. A survey of 145 countries estimated that gray markets activities produce between 30 percent and 40 percent of GDP (gross domestic product).[50] The gray market's share of total employment is even higher than its share of GDP.[51]

The gray market would be even larger if legal uncertainty were reduced for gray contracts. Judges in some developing countries believe that legal doctrines require them to refuse to enforce gray contracts.[52] Even when judges will enforce gray contracts, the parties may be unwilling to sue in public courts. When a gray market business goes to court, officials may notice that some of its operations violate regulations. The plaintiff often loses more by bringing himself to the attention of government regulators than he can win in a civil suit. Gray market businesses shun civil courts because their contract might be void, and the state may prosecute them for regulatory violations.[53]

Unlike many developing countries, German legal doctrine and practice avoid this result. German regulatory violations seldom void contracts, and German prosecutors seldom act on regulatory violations revealed in a civil trial. Thus a gardener in the German gray market who does not pay taxes can sue an employer for unpaid wages without fear of triggering an investigation by tax collectors. And a customer who buys a restaurant meal at an hour when law requires the closing of restaurants still has to pay his credit card bill. The same applies to a construction contract that violates zoning regulations, or a credit contract that violates banking regulations. Although seldom discussed in constitutional law, separating the civil courts from the regulators and police is an important part of the separation of powers, especially in countries with a large gray market.

Conclusion

The preceding chapter formulated the property principle for innovation: people who create wealth can keep most of it. Successful implementation of the property principle gives people motivation to make wealth, not to take it. Besides needing motivation, people who make wealth need to coordinate the efforts of different people. This chapter concerns the contract principle for economic cooperation: the law should enable people to commit to doing what they say. When this principle is implemented, people can trust each other enough to work together, even when money is at stake.

Taken together, the property principle and the contract principle provide motivation and coordination for innovation and growth. Developing a new idea requires innovator and investor to overcome their distrust, which we called the double trust dilemma. In the first stage of finance in Silicon Valley, immeasurable risk[54] and unobservable activity are so great that explicit contracts are infeasible, so relational contracting dominates. As development of the innovation proceeds in the second stage, risk falls, cooperation extends to more strangers, and the parties rely more on private contracts with explicitly negotiated terms. Finally, when the innovation diffuses in the third stage, finance encompasses a broader public, which requires more standardization and regulation of contracts as with stocks and bonds.

The three stages in a start-up firm resemble stages in a nation's development of effective contract law. More effective laws shift the proportion of activities from relational contracts to private bargains, and from private bargains to public markets. The shift toward more law-intensive forms of exchange widens the sphere of cooperation, which quickens the pace of creating and assimilating innovations.

Chapter 8
Giving Credit to Credit—Finance and Banking

In Afghanistan the wives of Pashtu herdsmen traditionally wear heavy silver bracelets to show off their beauty and to store the family's savings. Robbing a woman provokes clan revenge feared by thieves, so women are good protectors of wealth. In India poor people developed another way to save—the "chit fund." A small group of friends, say twelve of them, agree to meet each month for a year. At the first meeting in January, each one contributes $10 into a pot, receives a chit, one chit is drawn at random, and the winner gets the pot of $120. In February the twelve people repeat this process, except January's winner is ineligible to win. The process repeats itself each month until December, so everyone wins $120 exactly once. The monthly winner uses the money for a relatively large purchase—a bicycle, seed corn, a refrigerator, a television, or a wedding.

How do silver bracelets and chit funds differ? Like gold buried under the floor, the silver bracelets do not produce anything. In contrast the chit fund produces something. To see why, suppose each of the twelve individuals buried $10 under the floor each month. At the year's end, all twelve of them would have $120. In contrast, by forming a chit fund, eleven people get $120 before the end of the year and one person gets $120 at the year's end. So the chit fund makes eleven people better off and one person no worse off than burying the money.[1] The chit fund creates credit, which enables its members to spend sooner rather than later.

Some of the money that they spend goes to investment. Perhaps someone in the chit fund buys "miracle rice" for a better harvest, or a refrigerator to sell kebabs on the street, or a bicycle for a messenger service. So credit can create more rice, kebab, and messages. The chit fund's capital is economically alive, whereas capital in bracelets is economically dead.

Given the profitability of lending, why would anyone bury wealth instead of loaning it? Loans risk nonpayment. Thus the person who wins the chit fund's pot of $120 in January may refuse to contribute the $10 that he owes in February. Members of the chit fund trust each other enough to take this risk. Perhaps the Pashtu herdsman has no such group of people who trust each other enough to form a chit fund. In any case, financial organizations from a village chit fund to the Deutsche Bank finance investment by collecting savings, creating credit, and loaning or investing the money. These are core activities of banks. How important are they to economic growth? A famous economist named Joan Robinson said, "Where investment leads, finance follows." This phrase suggests that financiers will find their way to innovators like ants find a picnic. Influenced by this thought, most textbooks on development economics neglect finance and financial law,[2] which does not give credit to credit. In fact, investors come to innovative ideas like a man and a woman come to marriage—with caution and fear. Risk is great because the stakes are high: the investor fears losing his money and the innovator fears losing her idea. This is the "double trust dilemma" as explained in chapter 3.

The tectonic plates of the world economy shifted twice in the last fifty years: once when central planning collapsed after 1990 in the former Soviet Union, and once in 2008 with the near-collapse of the world's financial system. The aftershocks of the financial crisis continue, notably in the Euro crisis that began in 2010. Banks do not just make a few people rich by moving paper money around in obscure ways. When the financial system works, economies grow, and when the financial system fails, economies decline. With competition and a good regulatory framework, banks search relentlessly for the most profitable investments. With little competition or a bad regulatory framework, banks fail to finance profitable innovations, or, even worse, banks destabilize the economy. The efficiency and creativity of the banks in a developing country significantly affect its rate of economic growth.[3]

Relational Banking

Chit funds, cooperative banks, and similar organizations played an important historical role in rich countries, and they continue to play that role in poor countries. More than 20 percent of the people in poor countries live from less than a one dollar per day and more than 50 percent live on less than two dollars per day.[4] If these people had the ability to borrow money, some of them would invest in agriculture, small business, or education, where the rate of return is high.[5] The poorest people, however, cannot borrow from a bank because they have no regular income and they own nothing to pledge as security.[6] They live outside the formal banking system. According to a recent estimate, between 50 percent and 85 percent of Latin Americans live outside the banking system and lack access to bank credit.[7]

For credit, the poorest people must rely on informal organizations like the chit fund.[8] Chit funds originally developed spontaneously among friends and relatives without state approval, encouragement, or subsidies. Social norms originally controlled them, not state law. These organizations use personal relationships and group responsibility to collect debts. Unregistered chit funds that serve the poorest people remain uncounted and unregulated by Indian state law. Chit funds at this early stage resemble relational finance in Silicon Valley as described in chapter 2.

To create more credit, chit funds in India evolved and stretched beyond friends to encompass acquaintances, which increases the risk of nonpayment. To contain risk, members form a club and screen applicants for trustworthiness before allowing them to join. The club may hire a professional to organize and operate the chit fund in exchange for a commission. Dealings with a professional manager require contracts. The expansion of chit funds from friends to clubs resembles the movement in Silicon Valley from relational to private finance described in chapter 2.

The evolution of chit funds, however, did not stop with clubs. Indian companies that organize chit funds have become so large that they resemble commercial banks. They offer different chit funds with different terms, evaluate the creditworthiness of applicants, charge commissions, and assume responsibility for nonpaying members.[9] After chit funds evolved to include strangers, laws were enacted to regulate them. Large chit funds must register and comply with state regulations. The movement among chit funds from clubs to regulated markets resembles the movement in Silicon Valley from private to public finance described in chapter 2. Regulations ideally improve chit funds by suppressing fraud and increasing the trust that consumers have in them. In 2005, nonbanking financial institutions in India accounted for 6.5 percent of total assets in the financial sector, and registered chit funds are prominent among them.[10]

Much like chit funds, small cooperative banks developed in nineteenth-century Europe to pool funds, finance development, and share responsibility. One of the most successful cooperatives was the Raiffeisen bank in Germany in the late nineteenth century and early twentieth century. Friedrich Raiffeisen was a conservative Catholic who became the mayor of several villages in Prussia. During the winter of 1846–47 famine struck the region, including his village of Weyerbusch. In response, Raiffeisen founded a bread cooperative with money from a charity. Later he transformed this organization into a cooperative bank, which became a runaway success. Starting from several hundred in 1885, they grew into a network of 14,500 affiliated banks in rural Germany in 1910. Many of them still exist today.

Each Raiffeisen bank was organized as a cooperative in which old members picked new members. The members bought shares in the bank, made a deposit, and then they were entitled to borrow. Individual members were liable for all of the bank's debt if it failed. Group responsibility for debts and shared profits made each member screen applications for membership and monitor loan making and debt collection.[11] The central Raiffeisen bank pooled funds of the member banks, served as lender of last resort, and supplied an outside professional to supervise and audit the member banks.

To grow into a large network, the Raiffeisen banks needed two legal innovations. The first innovation allowed charities to accept deposits and lend money against interest to poor people. This innovation shifted activity away from poor relief and toward commercial lending. The second innovation concerned liability. Originally each of the members was liable for the debts of the group ("unlimited joint and several liability"). The second innovation replaced group liability for everything with individual liability for part of the whole.[12]

Cooperation banking depends on group responsibility, as do chit funds and most forms of relational lending. Raiffeisen banks succeeded in German villages and rural areas where enduring relationships made group responsibility feasible, and they mostly failed in German towns where people have more anonymity and mobility. Raiffeisen banks were transplanted to Holland, the Austrian-Hungarian Empire, Switzerland, and Italy, but they failed in Ireland and India in the early 1900s.[13] In the 1960s and 1970s development agencies tried to transplant cooperative banking to developing countries, but they mostly failed due to corruption, especially loans to politicians and the families of managers.

Many development experts regard cooperative banking as an outdated model.[14] As an alternative, many developing countries set up rural development banks run by the state. For example, Indian commercial banks are legally obliged to channel some of their liquid assets into rural development banks that give credits to small farmers. However, the borrowers often regard the loans as gifts for political loyalty that they need not repay.[15] Rural development banks in most of the world are not commercially viable and their lending is political, unlike chit funds or Raiffeisen banks. Chit funds never received subsidies, so they were commercially viable from the beginning. The Raiffeisen banks began as charities and became commercially viable within twenty-five years of their founding.

Next we turn to another form of group responsibility called microlending, which has multiplied faster than the rabbit in Australia. In 1976 Muhammad Yunus, an economics professor in Bangladesh, left his university office and began a project to help the poor, which grew into the Grameen Bank of Bangladesh ("gram" as in very light + the word for "village"). It reported in 2006 that it has 6.23 million borrowers in 2121 branches serving 67,670 villages covering 99.51 percent of the total villages in Bangladesh.[16] His efforts won him the Nobel Peace Prize in 2006.

The Grameen Bank continues to expand both geographically (e.g., projects in Bosnia-Herzegovina) and functionally (e.g., new program of loans to beggars). Similar microcredit organizations include the Banco Sol in Bolivia and Bank Rakyat in Indonesia.

The Grameen Bank works roughly as follows. A bank employee, who believes in the bank's philosophy, attracts members from poor people, each of whom buys a share for approximately $2 and receives a loan. A typical loan might equal $75 and extend for one year at 20 percent interest, with repayment in weekly installments. The loan might be utilized for fertilizer on a farm or handicraft materials for a small business. Early in its history, the Grameen Bank found that women repay debts more reliably than men, so it mostly recruits women as members. In 2006 the Grameen Bank proclaimed that 97 percent of its borrowers were women.

The members are organized into groups of five. The bank employee works intensively with the group to assure prudent use of loans and timely repayment. Each borrower is individually liable to repay her debt. Individuals, however, are not liable to repay the debts of others. If someone in the group fails to repay, however, the bank will not loan to anyone in the group in the future. Thus the Grameen Bank principle is based on individual liability and group responsibility.

Is the Grameen Bank commercially viable, like chit funds and Raiffeisen banks? A study commissioned by the Grameen Bank in the late 1980s calculated that its subsidy on operations was between 39 percent and 51 percent.[17] A more recent study calculated that, for the period 1983–97, loans are subsidized at 22 percent. In recent years its annual reports claim a modest profit (although not in 1996 when it went bankrupt), but this claim is misleading because it is heavily financed through development aid.[18] Organizations like the International Fund for Agricultural Development give it credits at below market rates. Apparently, Grameen Bank loans are partly commercial and partly charitable.

Politicians often pressure state banks and private banks to make charitable loans. This pressure contributed to the wave of bank failures in the United States in 2008.[19] Instead of pressuring banks to make charitable lending through organizations like the Grameen Bank is probably a better way to extend credit to the poor.[20] The Grameen

Bank, however, is an improbable way to eliminate poverty. Microfinance supposedly makes the poor into microcapitalists. The philosophy of microcapitalism is: "Give them credit and they will invest their way out of poverty." If this picture were true, then developing countries like Bangladesh would follow a completely different path out of poverty than the one taken by countries as different as Sweden, Brazil, and Taiwan. In these countries, workers moved out of agriculture and handicrafts into factory and service jobs, which also reduced self-employment.[21] They did not become microcapitalists. Instead, rising wages lifted them out of poverty. A recent study found that the twenty richest countries have a self-employment rate of 14 percent and the 20 poorest countries a rate of 43 percent.[22] In the future, developing countries will presumably lift themselves out of poverty by the same path as taken by successful countries in the past.

Statistical studies have yet to show that providing credit to the very poor reduces poverty.[23] Specifically, the Grameen Bank's effect on reducing national poverty is unproved statistically. During the rise of the Grameen Bank, absolute poverty in Bangladesh increased substantially according to some statistics and decreased moderately according to others.[24] Without the Grameen Bank or anything like it, China reduced absolute poverty from almost 60 percent in 1980 to less than 20 percent in 2005.[25] Viewed statistically, poverty reduction goes with rising productivity and wages, and less self-employment.

Instead of converting poor people into microcapitalists, another philosophy seeks out the small fraction of poor people who can grow tiny businesses into larger ones. Lending money to the entrepreneurial poor may grow new businesses that will employ other poor people and raise their productivity and wages. Instead of creating a not-for-profit organization like the Grameen Bank or Pro Mujer in Bolivia, the alternative approach creates for-profit organizations that loan to poor entrepreneurs. Acción International, the Omidyar Network, Citigroup, Kiva, and some high-tech billionaires from Google have implemented this approach in developing countries.[26] Whereas the Grameen Bank prides itself on a high rate of loan repayment, a bank loaning to poor entrepreneurs must expect mostly failures and a few spectacular successes, as with all innovations. A recent magazine article contrasted the two approaches as "not-for-profit-do-gooders" and "for-profit-do-gooders." The world needs more contests in which the winner is the one who does the most to reduce poverty.

Microfinance is the newest fashion, whereas money lending is the world's second oldest profession. In rural villages or poor urban districts around the world, lenders live among their borrowers, so they know who is thrifty and who is profligate, who works regularly and who works episodically, who keeps his word and who breaks his promises. With this information they can make loans to people who lack collateral or steady income. They can also extend loans in response to misfortune, thus acting as insurers as well as lenders. Moneylenders generally provide loans and insurance based on local knowledge.

Moneylenders profit most when reliable people stay in debt. Instead of helping customers to pay off their loans, they prefer for people to pay only the interest on their loans, and to pay it forever. Some borrowers fall farther and farther into debt.[27] As long as they continue paying interest, lenders profit from their distress. Moneylenders behave like modern credit card companies that push loans at poor people.[28] Whether in Bangladesh or Baltimore, lending to the poor and collecting their debts is a heartless business. Modern social critics describe moneylenders in scathing terms, like Christians described Jewish bankers in medieval Europe. For each defaulting debtor in India whom a moneylender throws into the street, however, how many people avoid being thrown into the street by such a loan? For every debtor whose interest payments grow and grow, how many successful businesses began by borrowing from a moneylender? The scathing critics whose rhetoric is one-sided have no information on these points, and neither do we.

Development economists increasingly believe that modern finance should encompass moneylenders who extend credit to poor people whom banks cannot reach.[29] Compared to banks, moneylenders have superior information on their debtors; more flexible terms of repayment; and they use social networks to enforce debt collection. Instead of suppressing money lending, the state should make moneylenders obey the law. Thus the state should suppress strong-arm debt collection, allow consumers to escape their creditors through bankruptcy, and protect consumers from fraud. Most important, the state should facilitate competition with moneylenders through chit funds, cooperative banks, and microlending.

Expanding the Circle

Unlike relational lending, formal banking activities differ according to the sources and uses of funds. Commercial bankers take deposits and make loans secured by collateral. Investment bankers use money from the sale of the bank's stocks and bonds to invest in other companies. Finally, brokers receive and execute orders to buy and sell stocks and bonds on commission (see table 8.1 for a sketch of these organizations).[30] Bear in mind that a single bank can perform all of these activities as in Germany's "universal banks," or the law can confine different activities to different kinds of banks such as separating commercial and investment banks.[31] Each of these banking activities has a different legal foundation.

Commercial Banking

With effective state law, finance can expand beyond relationships to encompass strangers. Instead of social sanctions, private banking relies heavily on state law to make debtors repay. A particular form of private banking called "commercial banking" serves most households and businesses. People deposit money in commercial banks in order to store wealth and transact conveniently. Commercial banks use deposits to make low-risk loans. To reduce risk, commercial banks mostly require collateral from the borrower, such as land and buildings, machines, inventories, or financial

Table 8.1 Banking Activities

	Source of funds	Use of funds
Commercial banking	Deposits	Secured loans
Investment banking	Bank's stocks and bonds	Risky investments
Brokering	Client's orders	Execute orders

claims. If the borrower defaults, the lender seizes the collateral and sells it to satisfy the debt. Commercial banks also make personal loans without security to borrowers with a steady income like a government job.

Commercial banks mostly secure their business loans with the specific assets of the borrower, especially capital goods that the borrower buys with the loan such as machines or buildings. The bank is confident of being repaid as long as the collateral retains its value.[32] Chapter 1 explained that innovation creates a double trust dilemma: the innovator is afraid that the investor will steal his idea, and the investor is afraid that the innovator will steal his capital. Collateral thus halves the double trust dilemma—the bank monitors collateral to assure that the borrower does not steal the money, but the bank does not need to know the borrower's trade secrets or business plan.

A legal problem plagues commercial banking in developing countries, as captured by this historical example. In early nineteenth-century France, the Emperor Napoleon possessed almost absolute power. Since he could cancel his own debts, he could not commit to repaying others, so his subjects would not buy his bonds. The British king, in contrast, had less power—he shared it with Parliament—and he had to repay his debts. His subjects would buy his bonds, and he sold them in London to finance his wars. The British king thus outspent Napoleon, England won the war with France, and Britain's debt grew to more than two times the British national income.[33]

Like Napoleon, some people in developing countries do not have to repay their debts. The World Bank identified forty countries where legal devices allow debtors to drag out the process of seizing collateral.[34] In Brazil the law forbids a creditor from seizing the debtor's collateral without first obtaining a valid court order, which makes debt collection costly. In contrast, a creditor in Germany can repossess the debtor's collateral within weeks of default without a court proceeding. Peru has more than twenty different registries for different types of collateral (one registry for collateral of farmers, another registry for collateral of industrialists, etc.), and the registries in one part of the country are unconnected to those in another part of the country.[35] Besides obstacles to seizing collateral, laws sometimes create obstacles to pledging it. Thus civil law doctrines sometimes prevent pledging a herd of cattle or the stock in a warehouse as security.[36] People who do not have to repay their debts cannot borrow money, or they can only borrow on unfavorable terms. Obstacles to debt collection shrink the pool of commercial loans in developing countries.

When laws and institutions pose obstacles to debt collection, the rewards are great for overcoming them. One of Mexico's richest businessmen, Ricardo Salinas, first built his fortune by finding an economical way to collect consumer debts. His Elektra stores, which now number more than six hundred, sell televisions, refrigerators, washers, and other household appliances. Many of the buyers are poor people who purchase on credit. When deciding whether or not to make a loan, the account manager in the store obtains the names of the borrower's relatives. If the borrower subsequently falls behind in his monthly payments, the account manager will enlist the help of relatives to collect the debt. This approach to debt collection relies on reputation and group responsibility, similar to a Raiffeisen bank or Grameen Bank.[37] Similarly, banks in Ghana are more willing to make business loans when family members of the debtor own houses, which increase the bank's power to identify and harass them.[38]

Data shows that obstacles to making loans and collecting debts raise the cost of borrowing money. The "spread" is the difference between the interest rate that the bank charges to borrowers and the interest rate that it pays to depositors. (Commercial banks make much of their profits from the spread.) Inefficient debt collection raises the bank's cost of loaning money, which increases the spread. Figure 8.1 summarizes the facts about the interest rate spread in groups of countries. The difference between borrowing and lending rates by banks is roughly three times higher in developing countries than developed countries, which suggest a big difference in the efficiency of bank collections. (Other causes also matter.)[39]

Improving debt collection is easy legally and hard politically. The public naturally sympathizes with the poor debtor, not rich lenders. The public also sympathizes more with a particular debtor who defaults than with unidentified future loan applicants. So the public wants a poor debtor

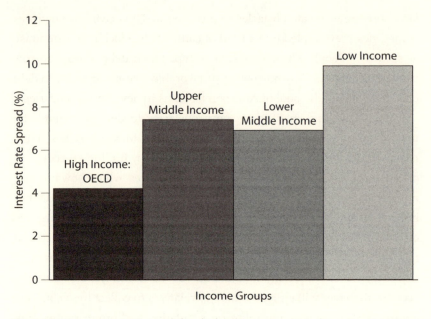

Figure 8.1 Interest Rate Spread (banks lending rate minus deposit rate, average from 1980 to 2008)

excused from repaying his debt, without thinking about the resulting loan denials to poor people in the future. In a highly disputed legal case that the media characterized as "Mexico versus the bankers," Mexican banks charged interest on the total debt owed to them by consumers, including interest on unpaid interest. When this fact was publicized, 9 million debtors refused to pay, and it took years until the Supreme Court decided in favor of the banks.[40]

Religion poses another obstacle to commercial banking in some countries. Both Christianity and Islam traditionally objected to their members charging interest on a loan. Among Christians the ban against interest disintegrated over centuries, although its language persists in "usury" laws that impose legal caps on interest rates.[41] In Muslim countries, the ban on interest mostly remains in form but not substance. To preserve form and not substance, some Arab banks recharacterize interest as profits.[42] This makes modern banking legally possible, while enraging some devout Muslims.

Investment Banking

From commercial banking, we turn to investment banking. Financial organizations that engage in investment banking activities may be called "banks" or something else such as venture capitalists, hedge funds, wealth managers, or private equity.[43] Instead of names, we focus on activities. Whereas commercial banks take deposits that are easily withdrawn, investment banks mostly obtain funds by selling their own bonds and stock. Investment bankers use their funds to invest in risky ventures by giving credits, making loans, buying bonds, or purchasing stock. The parties bargain to decide the terms of the bank's participation in the firm, such as holding a seat on its board of directors.

Investment banks share the borrower's risk of failure in exchange for a share of its gains from success. To assess the risk, the investment bank needs to know the borrower's secrets. The entrepreneur must disclose his secrets to get the investment banker's money. The investment bank must trust the borrower with the money, and the borrower must trust the investment bank with its secrets. In investment banking, the trust problem is often double sided. (In contrast, commercial banks secure their business loans with collateral, which makes the trust problem single sided.)[44]

As explained in chapter 2, investment banking solves the double trust dilemma primarily by aligning the interests of banker and entrepreneur. In Silicon Valley the founders of a start-up company expect to gain much more from its success than they could gain by stealing the money that others invested in it. Complicated contracts create these expectations by using preferred stock, options to buy, options to sell, and other financial instruments. In general, a successful firm is more valuable than its assets,[45] so a person who steals the assets of a successful firm gains less than the firm's value. This fact provides a way to deter managers from stealing a firm's assets. If the managers stand to gain a significant share of the value of a successful firm, then they may gain more by making it succeed than by looting it.

If managers gain most by making a firm succeed, then investors may be able to trust managers enough to loan them money. Contracts and business law induce the alignment of interests between investors and managers. Thus an obvious way to protect investors is to turn them into insiders so they participate in management by holding board seats, designating officers, or controlling the compensation committee. As insiders, bankers can detect slights of hand and protect their interests much better than outsiders.

Conversely, ineffective contract and business law plagues investment banking and slows growth. In a Las Vegas magic show, slight of hand makes a beautiful woman disappear before your eyes. With ineffective law, the same thing happens to business profits. After 1989 gangster capitalists in Russia made profits disappear from the books of state companies and reappear in their own pockets. They used tactics such as the following: seize control of a state company with mineral assets, sell the minerals to your privately owned corporation at low prices, and then resell the minerals on the world market at high prices. When corporations can make their profits magically disappear and reappear, investors face massive risks.

Chapter 3 described three general ways to create trust between investors and the insiders who manage an enterprise: relationships, private contracts, and public markets. Most countries finance growth by combining relational finance and private agreements. Thus in India stocks are often sold through informal networks to people with long-run relationships.[46] In Japan and Germany each manufacturer traditionally has a "main bank," or "house bank," that provides most of its finance. The main bank might arrange for a manufacturer and one of its suppliers—say, a car manufacturer and a supplier of specialty steel—to deal exclusively with each other instead of trading on the open market. To seal the agreement, the bank arranges for them to exchange their stock. "In Japan the companies choose who will buy their stock," observers say, "and in Britain the buyers choose which stock they will buy."

Foreign investors without political protectors face especially severe risks in many countries. Worshippers at shrines in East Asia give the gods play money and ask them to repay in real money. Similarly, in joint ventures with foreigners, Chinese entrepreneurs sometimes give paper rights to foreign investors who pay with real money. The assets of the project disappear through connivance between local partners and state officials.[47] In general, outsiders are reluctant to buy stocks in a company unless corporate insiders can give a credible guarantee that they will not divert the company's assets into their own pockets. Statistical analysis shows that when ineffective laws make outside investors insecure, they will not invest, so a greater proportion of companies must finance themselves internally.[48]

Effective legal reforms to protect minority shareholders can significantly increase the value of companies. To conform to requirements for joining the European Union, Bulgaria introduced dramatic reforms in 2002 to protect minority shareholders against dilution (distributing shares to insiders at prices below market value) and freeze-out (involuntary purchase of minority shares or delisting of the company). A statistical analysis showed that these reforms caused an equally dramatic increase in various financial measures of the value of companies to minority shareholders, such as the price-earnings ratio.[49]

Another kind of financial problem concerns politics and banking. The state can direct bank loans toward large conglomerates as in South Korea, channel credits into sick industries as in India, create a military-industrial complex as in Germany and Japan prior to World War II, or extract wealth to benefit the ruling family as in Suharto's Indonesia. Political intrusion mostly worsens the economic performance of banks. In business, sports, and war, leaders who fail lose their power. Business has a formal legal procedure to dispossess a failed leader: bankruptcy. Bankruptcy quickly transfers resources from failed managers to new managers. Political intrusion protects failed business leaders by preventing rescuing their firms from bankruptcy.

When a small or medium firm runs out of money, it often disappears because its budget constraint is hard. When a very large firm runs out of money, it often negotiates for government subsidies. Thus the United States secretary of the treasury loaned billions of dollars of the government's money to his banker friends in the financial crisis that began in 2008.

Very large firms in China also enjoy soft budget constraints. The dinosaurs in China's old industrial core—heavy industries like steel—were reorganized after the demise of central planning as companies that issue stocks. The government owns enough shares to retain control over these enterprises.[50] When these enterprises lose money, as they inevitably do, the government makes state-controlled banks provide fresh loans to cover the losses. In a summit meeting for China's top economic officials in 2005, several speakers identified the soft budget constraints on state enterprises as China's biggest economic problem.[51]

China's startling economic growth has occurred in export industries outside of its old industrial core. Many of these new enterprises are privately owned, and others involve a partnership between private businessmen and local government officials, especially in China's many "village enterprises." In dealing with village enterprises, the Chinese government shows remarkable toughness: succeed or fail, they cannot expect subsidies from the central government. The old industrial core, however, receives subsidized loans. Ironically, China's failing enterprises in the old industrial core pay a lower price for capital than China's innovative new enterprises.

Similarly, India nationalized its banks in the 1970s, and now they suffer from bureaucratic sclerosis and political intrusion. Many other developing countries nationalized banks with the same results. As in China, state banks soften the budget constraint for state-owned enterprises and other politically preferred borrowers. Instead of losing power, managers in failed enterprises go to state banks for more loans.

When factories close, employees lose their jobs, which is painful.[52] The large firms in China's industrial core are not just factories that supply jobs. They are also social centers that supply housing, schooling, recreation, and medical care to their workers. Closing these enterprises endangers a system of social support, not just jobs. Even so, other citizens may eventually tire of subsidizing old industries.[53]

In much of the world, the budget constraints on commercial banks are soft. Banks make risky investments in which they win or else the taxpayer loses. In the 1980s U.S. regulators in the Reagan administration allowed government-insured banks called "savings and loans" to try to gamble their way out of bankruptcy. If their highly risky investments succeeded, the bankers would win, and if they failed, the taxpayers would lose. This gamble delayed the collapse of these banks until after

President Reagan left office, when massive failures in these banks triggered the government's liability as insurer of the depositors. The federal government apparently lost more money in reorganizing these banks than in any other bailout or financial scandal in U.S. history, until 2008 when the U.S. government began lending vastly more billions of dollars on failed banks than ever before.

Brokers

From investment bankers, we turn to financial brokers. Customers pay commissions for brokers to act as intermediaries in buying and selling securities. Brokers also purchase securities for their clients on credit and hold the securities as collateral. To flourish, brokers need public securities markets with high volumes of sales. Brokers contribute to innovation and growth by helping to create these markets.

In Silicon Valley, after an innovation has proved its profitability, the founders often sell securities to the public directly in an initial public offering of stock or indirectly through acquisition by a public company. Public markets thus enable the founders of a company to diversify their portfolio and exit from the business that they started. The possibility of eventual exit through public sales provides incentives for entrepreneurs to create start-up firms and for venture capitalists to finance development of new ideas. Conversely, small or illiquid public stock markets inhibit venture capitalism.

Public markets require protecting a broad group of outside investors, who play a passive role in managing a company, against the firm's insiders. The owners of only a few shares in a company are the most vulnerable outside investors. After 1989 Russia and the Czech Republic privatized state companies by equally distributing shares among the public, but the insiders quickly appropriated the public shareholders. Instead of equality, the result was cynicism. In a popular joke, the wife says to her husband, "Play cards if you must, dear. At least you win sometimes. But don't buy any more stocks."

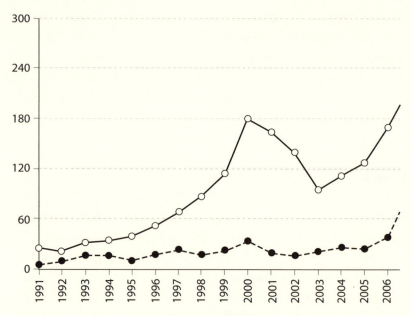

Figure 8.2. Stocks Traded, Percentage of GDP (line with white circles depicts rich countries, line with black circles depicts low- and middle-income countries)

Since private finance requires less effective law than public finance, weak law tilts finance toward private deals by banks and away from public markets.[54] Conversely, public stock markets play a more decisive role when the legal system strengthens. Econometric analysis concludes that better banking law leads to more activity on bond and stock markets.[55] Figure 8.2 shows decisively that stocks are traded far more in rich countries than in low- or middle-income countries.

Protecting diffuse stockholders against insiders is so difficult that few countries succeed. Recent empirical research shows that firms with dispersed ownership play almost no role in developing countries, and even in rich countries they dominate only in the United States and the United Kingdom.[56] Instead of being widely held, most corporations in the world are closely held by a few people with a controlling share of stock. Although closely held, these companies often sell some stock to outsiders, especially as law strengthens. Statistical evidence indicates

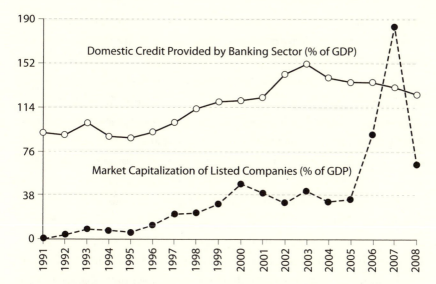

Figure 8.3. Market Capitalization and Banking Credits in China, Percentage of GDP
Source: World Bank *World Development Indicators 2009*

that bank finance has a relative advantage over capital markets in poor countries, and that securities markets surpass the importance of banks when the economy gets rich.[57]

When a country goes through a period of rapid industrialization, the law of contracts, corporations, and finance is usually weak, so bank finance should predominate. Thus bank credits played the pivotal role during industrialization in Germany.[58] Until recently the stock market played an insignificant role in financing China's explosive growth. Thus figure 8.3 compares total bank credits to the total market value of the stock of all Chinese companies ("market capitalization"). The total market value of the stock of all companies depends on the number of public firms and the price of their stock.[59] Until 2005, the ratio was large, which shows that bank loans were much more important than the sale of stock in financing China's economic growth. In 2005 the situation changed as stock prices rose and then fell.

A tilt in finance toward bank credits and away from stocks, which is a natural result of ineffective law, imposes a heavy economic cost: it dampens risk taking and slows innovation. To see why, assume that an entrepreneur uses his own money to start a company and then obtains additional funds from bank credits. If revenues do not flow into the business fast enough to redeem the credits, the business will go bankrupt and the entrepreneur will lose his entire investment. In contrast, if he were able to obtain funds by selling stock, he would not need to make fixed payments, so a downturn would not jeopardize his business. With stock financing, the entrepreneur could grow the company faster with less personal risk.

In exceptional cases where laws are strong, public finance predominates. Thus stock markets in the United States and Great Britain financed industrialization in the nineteenth century more than banks. In Japan, the pattern was more complicated. Finance was not bank based when industrialization exploded in the early twentieth century; bank finance became predominant in the 1930s when regulation favored it; and in recent years, large Japanese firms have increasingly sold shares on public markets.[60]

Conclusion

When property protection is uncertain and promises are not enforced, savings flow to the best protector, but when property protection is certain and promises are enforced, savings flow to investors who use money creatively. To go from savers to investors, money mostly passes through financial intermediaries. Financial intermediaries do not merely move paper money around in obscure ways that baffle ordinary people and enrich bankers. Rather, banks collects savings, magnify them by credit, and invest. Creative investments drive innovation and growth.

To produce innovations, money and ideas must come together like the rings in Solomon's knot. Different financial organizations solve the double trust dilemma of innovation in different ways. From chit funds to hedge funds, the borrower who gives a promise to the lender in exchange for money must be able to commit to doing what he says. In relational lending, social sanctions and group responsibility constrain the borrower to keep his promises. In commercial banking, the lender must be able to seize the defaulting borrower's collateral at low cost, whether it is a car, a building, a paycheck, or a company. In investment banking, if the borrower promises a future share of profits, the lender must be able to force the borrower to perform. Similarly, in brokerage, outsiders who hold bonds or stocks in a firm must be able to get their share of the money away from the firm's insiders. As financial law strengthens, group responsibility is supplemented by individual responsibility, relational lending is supplemented by private lending, bonds are supplemented by stocks, and private banks are supplemented by public markets.

Any discussion of finance must mention financial crises, including the collapse that began in 2008 in the United States. A reporter asked a prolific American bank robber named Willie Sutton why he robbed banks, and he allegedly replied, "because that's where the money is." Ingenious people dedicated to getting rich will always be drawn to banks because that's where the money is. Their creativity can make an economy hum or bring it crashing down. Much of the modern economy runs on banks. Commercial banks make deposits and loans to each other, so the bankruptcy of one threatens the solvency of others. With a string of bank failures, an economy can slow down like traffic when an interstate highway closes.

What is to be done? Almost every country regulates banking to guarantee solvency, as well as to control fraud, manipulation, and recklessness. Bank regulators especially focus on the ratio of bonds to stock issued by a bank.[61] Issuing bonds is risky to the bank, because the bank must repay the creditors as the bonds mature. If profits fail to materialize, the bank may be unable to redeem its maturing bonds. Alternatively, issuing stocks is not risky to the bank because it gets money without a fixed obligation to repay. Thus the ratio of bonds to stocks ("leverage") simply measures an investment bank's risk.

In the prelude to 2008, American investment banks vastly increased their leverage. To redeem their maturing bonds, investment banks needed to issue new bonds. When real estate prices turned down and the economic outlook darkened, investment banks had difficulty issuing new bonds to meet their obligations on maturing bonds. Other factors aggravated the problem—derivatives,[62] risky investments,[63] panicky depositors,[64] and lax regulators,[65] to name a few. Ideally, investors would have prevented the crisis by selling bank stocks and bonds much earlier, thus forcing banks to invest more conservatively. The market failed. Regulators could have prevented the crisis by limiting leveraging and constraining risk taking. The regulators failed. So banks failed, the taxpayers paid many of their bills, and the economic downturn threw people out of work.

In developing countries as in the United States, banking crises undermine economic growth.[66] The best way to avoid them is unclear. Banking regulation differs from one country to another. No country, it seems, has created a superior regulatory structure that easily transfers to other nations. International agreements to regulate banking induce participation by some countries, with mixed results,[67] but the topic of bank stability is too large and too far from innovation for us to say more about it.

Chapter 9
Financing Secrets—Corporations

How did the corporation become the dominant form of business organization? To answer this question, recall chapter 1's example of the spice trade between Europe and Asia in the seventeenth century: in a port such as London, a bold ship's captain would propose that investors finance a voyage to Asia to obtain spices. The investors had to provide capital for a voyage lasting at least two years, and the ship's captain had to share secrets about how to get to Asia and where to go when he arrived. When the voyage succeeded or failed decisively, the captain and investors usually ended this collaboration. Exit after success occurred through a general court at the dock. Similarly, in twentieth-century Silicon Valley, a bold innovator would propose that venture capitalists finance a new technology. The investors had to provide capital for development lasting at least two years, in exchange for which the innovator had to share many secrets about the new technology and his business plan. When the venture succeeded or failed decisively, the innovator and investors usually ended their collaboration. Exit after success occurred through the sale of the start-up firm to an established company or an initial public offering of its stock.

In the seventeenth-century spice trade and twentieth-first-century Silicon Valley, capital and secrets combine in a risky venture. The investors fear losing their wealth and the innovators fear losing their secrets—the "double trust dilemma." To solve it, seventeenth-century firms in the spice trade developed the modern corporation, which they called the "joint stock company." Three hundred years later, firms in Silicon Valley still use this form of organization. Business ventures generally face a dilemma in joining capital and ideas, and with the right background conditions, the joint stock company is the best solution anyone has devised. A corporation that issues stock can reliably guarantee its owners a share of the firm's profits. Profit sharing gives the innovators an incentive to use the investors' money for the venture, and profit sharing provides the investors with an incentive to preserve the innovator's secrets. Being marketable, shares enable both parties to exit from the deal as soon as it succeeds or fails decisively. The secret of growth is financing secrets, and the corporation provides the best organizational form for doing this. This is the corporation's decisive advantage, as explained in this chapter.

Organizations and Markets

Business organizations differ from the markets that surround them. Organizations generally have a structure of offices created by contract and law, such as chairman, treasurer, or ombudsman. While some members of organizations have offices, all members have roles to play. Standardization in the division of labor creates roles like bookkeeper, mechanic, or purchasing agent. By supplying a structure of offices and roles, organizations coordinate the behavior of its members.

When the behavior of different people is tightly coordinated, observers speak as if the group has goals, purposes, intentions, strategies, interests, wishes, and acts. These are the mental attributes of a person. An organization can be described as a *personified* group of individuals. The structure of offices and roles in an organization makes its individual members capable of corporate action. Its members coordinate their behavior to pursue common goals, as with a football team, symphony orchestra, church, army, partnership, or corporation. In the case of a corporation, the organization is personified in law: it is a legal person who can own assets, make contracts, sue, and be sued.

As coordination and discipline tighten in a group of people, they become an organization. Conversely, as coordination and discipline loosen in a group of individuals, an organization dissolves into a collection of individuals, like voters in an election or competitors in piano recital. Markets are organized, but they are not organizations. Markets have causes and effects, but they do not have goals, purposes, intentions, interests, wishes, or actions, except metaphorically. Participants in markets often have legal contracts with each other, but the market is not a legal person. A nexus of contracts often sustains an organization, but an organization is not just a nexus of contracts.[1] Organizations buy their inputs and sell their outputs in markets that surround them, but organizations are not markets.

What kind of organization is a corporation? Let's converge toward an answer. Many organizations own property. A club, church, cooperative, trust, charity, or the state can buy and sell property such as land, buildings, and machinery. However, no one can buy or sell these organizations because they are unowned. In contrast, some organizations such as corporations and partnerships *are* property —they can be bought and sold. Chapter 6 explained that a market for organizations keeps them focused on making money, so owned organizations play the central role in economic life. In contrast, unowned organizations that focus on goals other than making money play the central role in government, religion, and social life.

What distinguishes the corporation from other owned organizations? As the state's creation, a corporation has whatever legal powers the state gives it.[2] Different legal traditions give different legal powers to different kinds of corporations, such as the joint stock company, the public limited liability company (Aktiengesellschaft), the private limited liability company (Gesellschaft mit begrenzter Haftung), the nonprofit corporation, the S corporation, the banking corporation, the codetermined corporation, and the cooperative corporation. When people speak of "the corporation," they usually have in mind a joint stock, limited liability corporation, which is our focus. Figure 9.1 puts this kind of corporation in the perspective of markets and organizations.

In the traditional form of the joint stock, limited liability corporation, investors own stock that entitles them to a share of the profits and

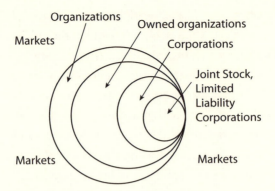

Figure 9.1. Perspective on Corporations

a voice in governance. In company elections, shareholders have votes in proportion to their investments (one stock, one vote), so they control the organization jointly and unequally. In most companies, a small block of shareholders—the "control block"—owns enough shares with voting rights to control the company. Each investor can sell his shares to another person without obtaining the consent of other shareholders. The corporation, not its shareholders, is liable for its debts. The corporation's creditors cannot reach into the wealth of its owners. The corporation pays taxes on the profits that it earns. When it distributes profits to its investors, the investors also pay personal income taxes on these dividends.

The joint stock, limited liability corporation contrasts with a personal organization ("sole proprietorship"). A personal organization is the owner's property like his clothes and furniture, not a distinct legal person like a corporation. It cannot own property, contract, sue, or be sued. Its income is his income and its liabilities are his liabilities. The owner has complete power to sell the organization or reorganize it. Unlike a corporation, its creditors can reach into the owner's personal property to recover their debt, and its profits are taxed as part of the owner's personal income.

A corporation also contrasts with a partnership ("general partnership"). Like a corporation, a legal partnership is a person in law, distinct from the partners in it. It can own property, contract, and sue or be sued. Power among partners is negotiated when they form a legal organization

Table 9.1 Characteristics of Three Types of Firms

	Corporation	*Personal*	*Partnership*
Legal person	Yes	No	Yes
Power	Controlling shareholders	Individual owner	Partners negotiate
Liability	Limited	Unlimited	Unlimited
Tax basis	Corporation and stockholders	Individual owner	Partners

by drafting a partnership agreement, which specifies its governance. In the simplest form of governance, the partners vote equally on fundamental matters affecting the partnership. Unlike a corporation, partners traditionally have unlimited liability for the partnership's debts, although this law is evolving. The partners usually want control over who can join them. Consequently, the partnership agreement usually restricts the ability of a partner to sell his membership to another person, which makes exit from a partnership more difficult than from a corporation. Unlike a corporation, the partnership traditionally does not pay taxes directly. Instead, its profits are attributed to the partners, who pay personal taxes on their income from the partnership.

Table 9.1 summarizes these broad generalizations about the traits of three fundamental types of firms: a (joint stock, limited liability) corporation, personal organization (sole proprietorship), and a partnership.

Markets and different types of organizations have a place in modern economies. Among organizations, however, corporations dominate. According to the theory of this book, innovative ventures confront the double trust dilemma. Solving it requires organizations with tight coordination and discipline. The corporation dominates other forms of economic organization because it solves the double trust dilemma the best. We sketched how it does so in comparing ventures in Silicon Valley and the seventeenth-century spice trade. The corporation is a decisive improvement in financing innovation because investors receive a *marketable share of future profits*. In contrast, a personal organization provides no mechanism to guarantee investors a fraction of its future profits, and a partner's rights in a firm are not freely marketable.

How Big?

The distinctive advantage of corporations enables them to grow faster than other firms, but all firms eventually stop growing. What determines a particular firm's size? To appreciate the problem, contrast two Indian examples of large and small firms. Shopper's Stop is a department store in Mumbai that sells much the same goods as the Connaught Place market in New Delhi, but in a very different way. Shopper's Stop is a one massive store with hundreds of employees selling goods in different departments. In contrast, hundreds of small, independent shops rent space in an underground structure at Connaught Place. Why doesn't Shopper's Stop dismiss its employees, divest its departments, and rent space to many small sellers as in Connaught Place? Conversely, why don't the small firms in Connaught Place merge to form one large firm like Shopper's Stop?[3]

In general, two firms can merge to make one, or one firm can divest to make two. This is the "merge-or-divest" question. Similarly, consider a choice faced by Kia, a Korean car manufacturer. It needs tires for the cars that it makes. If it makes tires in a subsidiary, then Kia becomes that much bigger. If it buys tires from another firm, then Kia remains that much smaller. This is the "make-or-buy" decision. These two decisions—merge-or-divest and make-or-buy—are examples of choices by which firms grow or shrink. To understand what determines the size of a particular firm, we need to know how they make such decisions.

Competition drives a firm toward its most profitable size. If a smaller firm is more profitable, then the firm will divest and buy inputs. If a larger firm is more profitable, then the firm will merge and make inputs. In "The Nature of the Firm" (1936), the Nobel Prize winner Ronald Coase argued that the more profitable choice depends on *transaction costs*. Manufacturing tires requires KIA to contract with employees and supervise them. These are transaction costs of *making* a product. Buying tires requires KIA to contract with sellers and monitor the quality of the tires. These are transaction costs of *buying* a product. Similarly, merging two companies requires supervising both of them, and divesting a line of production ends the firm's supervision of it. Competitive pressure should cause firms to choose the cheaper alternative between buying and making inputs, or merging firms and divesting activities.[4]

Coase's theory implies that competition should cause firms to adjust their size (large or small) and form (sole proprietorships, partnerships, corporation) to minimize transaction costs. When combining capital and private information in a firm, the investor risks losing his capital and the innovator risks losing her ideas—the double trust dilemma. To reduce these risks, the investor and innovator form a firm. The cost of organizing the firm can be regarded as the transaction costs of preventing the diffusion of information and appropriation of capital. Following Coase, we say, "The corporation achieved its dominant position by reducing the cost of preventing the diffusion of innovative ideas and the appropriation of investors' money."

Innovation and growth determine the size of firms in a market economy, but not in a nonmarket economy. Socialism replaces capital markets with politics. Under central planning, firms throughout the communist world, such as the Nowa Huta steel plant in Poland, grew vastly larger than under capitalism. Transaction costs theory suggests why this happened. Political influence determined the central plan, which allocated capital for firms to grow. In many institutional settings, one large firm has more political influence than two smaller firms. When political influence increases more than proportionately with a firm's size (increasing returns to scale of lobbying), large firms beat out small firms. Thus a politicized economy under socialism helped large firms to grow larger.[5] This explanation of gigantic firms under socialism also explains the large size of firms that sell mostly to the central government in a mixed economy, such as military suppliers.

Keeping Secrets

In the 1950s, socialist countries around the world built gigantic steel plants like Nowa Huta in Poland. By the 1980s they were losing vast amounts of money, and they seemed destined to die a slow death by rust. Lakshmi Mittal, who led the international operation of an Indian steel business built by his father, believed that these industrial dinosaurs could flourish in the age of nimble business "mammals." In the late 1980s he used family money to buy ailing steel companies in Indonesia, Mexico, and Kazakhstan. More acquisitions followed, including Nowa Huta in 2003. He had novel ideas about making them profitable by shrinking and reorganizing them, and he thought that the Asian construction boom would lift world steel prices. He proved right on both counts. In 2005, Forbes rated him as the third richest person in the world.

What do entrepreneurs such as Mittal know that others don't know? First, they know how to organize a business. Reorganizing gigantic steel mills to make them smaller and more profitable requires massive changes in offices, roles, and the people who fill them. Second, entrepreneurs such as Mittal know better than others what prices the future will bring, so they know which lines of business to expand and which to contract. Knowledge of organization and future prices convey a decisive advantage over competitors.

Since Mittal knew things about organization and future prices that his competitors did not know, economists say that he had "private information." The discovery of private information begins the life cycle of innovation described in chapter 3. At the start, the innovator and investor need to combine the new idea with capital, thus solving the double trust dilemma. Solving it requires an organization, and the corporation is usually the best organization to solve it. Given effective law, the parties can structure the corporation so that investors make more money by keeping the firm's secrets than by sharing them with others, and entrepreneurs make more by developing the business than by appropriating the investors' money. After developing an innovation and bringing it to the market, the innovation conveys a competitive advantage and yields extraordinary profits. When the entrepreneur succeeds, however, competitors smell money and try to imitate the innovator. The innovator tries to prolong extraordinary profits as long as possible by withholding the information needed by the imitators.

The longer an innovative firm can delay competitors from understanding or improving on what it knows, the more it profits and the larger it grows. Once the firm's private information stops being innovative, it loses its competitive advantage and stops growing. A firm should conserve the value of its private information, which often requires keeping its secret. The firm protects its secrets partly by using legal devices such as nondisclosure agreements, noncompetition clauses, and trade secrets laws. These devices have little value in countries with strong state law, and no value elsewhere. Thus when technology firms negotiate in Silicon Valley they usually sign nondisclosure agreements, which might be enforceable. In contrast, when technology firms negotiate in India, they seldom sign nondisclosure agreements, which are certainly unenforceable.[6] Much the same contrast between Silicon Valley and India applies to suing employees or trading partners who disclose trade secrets.

The main way to protect business secrets is through organization. Compared to other forms of organization, a corporation provides a superior incentive structure for keeping secrets from imitators. Since the corporation usually provides the best solution to the double trust dilemma, corporations have grown faster than other forms of economic organization, and they dominate the modern economy. These considerations suggest a general principle: "Secrets are easier to preserve when interactions that require sharing them occur inside a firm rather than outside of it."[7] Consequently, a firm should internalize production that utilizes its secrets.

Applied to the merge-or-divest decision, this principle implies that firms which need to share secrets can keep them better by merging. Applied to the make-or-buy decision, this principle implies that firms can keep secrets about an input better by making it than buying it. The same logic extends to many other decisions. Consider whether to hire an employee or buy a service. If performing a task requires understanding a firm's secrets, the firm should hire an employee to perform the task. Conversely, if performing the task does not require understanding a firm's secrets, the firm can buy the service from an outside contractor.[8] Or consider whether to sell a service or the product that produces it. A firm invents a computer program to perform an accounting task. If a firm owns an effective patent, it can sell the program to others to use. Conversely, if it does not own an effective patent, it should sell the accounting service to others and keep the program secret. Or consider

Table 9.2 Organizational Decisions and Informational Criteria

Decision	Criterion
Merge or divest?	Does the activity require sharing secrets?
Make or buy an input?	Does the firm have secrets about the input?
Hire an employee or buy a service?	Does the worker need to know firm's secrets?
Sell a product or sell a service?	Can a product's user appropriate its secrets?
Buy a firm or its product?	Do you want the target's imbedded information?

whether to buy a product or buy the firm that makes it. Special know-how imbedded in a successful firm's routines, organization, and culture gives it a competitive advantage, sometimes called its "core competence." If one firm wants the information imbedded in another firm, it should buy the other firm. Conversely, if a firm does *not* want information imbedded in another firm, it can buy the other firm's assets, products, services, patents, and so forth.

Table 9.2 summarizes these decisions and the criteria for making them.

Chapter 7 explained the difference between relational and private contracting. When state law is ineffective, businesses organize on the basis of relationships. The firm provides a framework for relational contracting. Concentrated ownership tightens relationships among the most powerful people in a firm. Conversely, when state law is effective, firms organize more impersonally. The law provides a framework for formal contracting. Ownership disperses.

Empirical evidence in table 9.3 suggests that loose state law for business concentrates ownership, and tight state law disperses ownership. The figure divides large firms with publicly traded stock into three types: (i) closely held—controlled directly or indirectly by one person, a family, or a small group; (ii) widely held—controlled by professional managers; or (iii) state owned. Countries are arranged in descending order by the proportion of closely held companies. Thus the first row indicates that all Mexican companies in the sample were closely held, and none were publicly held or controlled by the state. At the other extreme, all large

Table 9.3 Control of Large Publicly Traded Corporations in Selected Countries (in percent), 1995[a]

	Closely held	Widely held	State
Mexico	100	0	0
Hong Kong	70	10	5
Argentina	65	0	15
Singapore	30	15	45
South Korea	20	55	15
France	20	60	15
USA	20	80	0
Italy	15	20	40
Germany	10	50	25
UK	0	100	0

Source: R. La Porta, F. Lopes-de Silanes, A. Shleifer, and R. Vishny, "Corporate Ownership around the World," *Journal of Finance* 54.2 (1999): table 2.
[a] We thank Florencio Lopez-de-Silanes for help interpreting this table.

UK companies in the sample in table 9.3 were publicly held. According to table 9.3, the widely held corporation represents less than half of large publicly traded firms in Mexico, Hong Kong, Argentina, Singapore, and Italy, and more than half of large publicly traded corporations in South Korea, France, the United States, Germany, and the United Kingdom.[9] Our hypothesis is that an ascending order of state law explains the descending order by closely held companies.

Financing Inside and Out

Having discussed how firms protect secrets, we next discuss how firms protect the investors' money. Outsiders demand legal protection to invest in companies controlled by insiders, whereas insiders who control the firm can protect themselves. To illustrate, after the collapse of communism in 1989, Czechoslovakia privatized state firms. To implement wide ownership, the state gave the stock in newly privatized firms to large mutual funds, and the state distributed vouchers to citizens entitling them to obtain shares in the mutual funds at little or no cost. However, weak law could not stop insiders from grabbing profits from the privatized firms. Without effective legal protection, individual citizens correctly placed little value on the vouchers, so public prices plummeted, insiders snatched up shares at bargain prices, and widely held firms collapsed into closely held firms. The Czechoslovakian state tried and failed to achieve broad ownership of privatized firms. Voucher privatization, which Western economists recommended, also failed miserably in Russia during the transition from communism to capitalism after 1991.[10]

Weak investor protection has an observable effect on stock prices. A stock yields a stream of future dividends to its owner.[11] Without effective investor protection, insiders grab a disproportionate share of a firm's earnings and little is left to pay dividends. A few shares in such a company have little value, but a controlling block of shares has much value. The price per share that people will pay for a controlling block of shares is larger than the price per share that they will pay for a small number of shares. The difference in price per share for the control block and individual shares is called the *control premium*. To illustrate, if insiders are willing to sell the controlling block for $1.50 per share, whereas outsiders are willing to pay $1 per share for individual shares, then the control premium is $0.50 per share.

The control premium is especially large when insiders can divert profits to themselves rather than sharing them with outside investors. Conversely, the control premium is small when effective law gives outsiders their fair share of profits. Nenova calculated the control premium in different countries. In the Czech Republic, a controlling block of shares commands a premium of 58 percent relative to the stock market price. In the Republic of Korea the premium is 47 percent. In France and Italy—countries with a strong legal system but weak minority shareholder protection—it is 28 percent. In Brazil and Chile it is 23 percent. In Germany and the United Kingdom, it is 10 percent. In the Scandinavian countries, the United States, and Canada it is less than 5 percent. According to a statistical study, the control premium falls when the rule of law strengthens as measured by the "rule-of-law index."[12]

Better investor protection should cause an increase in the stock market value of firms, or their "market capitalization."[13] To test this proposition, economists compare the market capitalization of firms in different countries. Firms are the main source of national income in most countries. Consequently, better investor protection should cause an increase in the ratio of market capitalization to gross domestic product for a country. Empirical research confirms this prediction. The ratio of total market capitalization to GDP is roughly twice as large in high-income countries compared to low-income countries. Furthermore, the ratio of total market capitalization to GDP increases with improved investor protection, as measured by an index of shareholder rights or an index of public disclosure.[14]

Reform

How can better law increase the pace of economic growth? The preceding analysis suggests an answer: improve the laws for joint stock, limited liability corporations. Legal reforms that facilitated this form of organization in Europe and the United States suggest how developing countries should proceed today.

Cheap Freedom

To become the dominant form of economic organization, the joint stock company had to extend from the spice trade to manufacturing. This extension required dismantling restrictive rules by which the state controlled the economy. In the seventeenth and eighteenth centuries, British monarchs created monopolies for privileged subjects in exchange for loyalty and money. A patent or license gave the holder an exclusive right to engage in a certain line of business. Thus local patents were given for many small businesses such as brewing beer. At the opposite extreme, the Hudson's Bay Company was incorporated in 1670 with a charter from King Charles II granting a monopoly over trading with Indian tribes in much of northern Canada. Adam Smith's famous critique of mercantilism claimed that these monopolies enriched the king and his friends and impoverished the nation.

In the eighteenth and nineteenth centuries, British law changed under the influence of thinkers like Adam Smith. Important changes included routine incorporation (incorporation by anyone using simple laws, not by a grant of executive privilege to a political favorite) and broadening the range of businesses that a corporation could enter (general incorporation instead of incorporation for a single line of business). Entrepreneurs gradually acquired the right to form a corporation for almost any business purpose without a special license, patent, or grant of royal privilege. In the modern world, some contemporary countries still require a separate license for pharmaceuticals, securities, cable television, exports, restaurants, real estate, hotels, haircuts, opticians, and so forth. Some of these restrictions provide justifiable protection of consumer against incompetence and fraud. However, many of these restrictions reserve some lines of business for politically privileged groups. In every country, restrictive licensing shields privileged firms from competition, and they reciprocate with bribes, contributions, and other forms of support for politicians.

Similar to nineteenth-century Britain, most developing countries today have a general corporate form for entering many lines of business. This development increases liberty by allowing people to organize and exchange without special permission from the state. The law should provide entrepreneurs with a menu of legal forms for organizing the firm's governance. By removing prohibitions and allowing choice over organizational forms, economic liberty releases the energies of entrepreneurs and sends innovation on its creative, unpredictable path. According to the *principle of organizational liberty, people should be free to organize firms to pursue business opportunities as they see fit and to select a form of governance from a menu of legal alternatives.*

The law imposes a price for exercising economic freedom, which varies from country to country. The price includes fees for licenses and registration, bribes paid to expedite processing or relax rules, minimum capital requirements for establishing a company, business taxes, and many restrictions involving employees. The World Bank survey reported in table 9.4 gives the number of days and procedures needed to establish a new business in various countries. According to table 9.4, the regulatory

Table 9.4 Legal Barriers to Establishing a New Business

	Time (days)	Number of procedures
Venezuela	141	16
Brazil	120	16
Indonesia	60	9
Vietnam	50	11
China	37	14
Kenya	34	12
Poland	32	6
Nigeria	31	8
India	30	13
Russian Federation	30	9
Argentina	27	15
Chile	27	9
Pakistan	20	10
Czech Republic	15	8
Mexico	13	8
Malaysia	11	9
Iran	9	7
Egypt	7	6
Turkey	6	6
USA	6	6
Canada	5	1

Source: World Bank, *Doing Business* (Washington, DC: World Bank, 2010).

burden on new businesses varies from one country to another, and the burden is especially heavy in developing countries.[15] (The general pattern in table 9.4 is convincing, but the numbers contain measurement errors, so comparisons between any two countries must be treated with caution.) Innovation would increase if business freedom were cheaper to exercise.

Partitioning Assets

Besides dismantling restrictive rules, innovations in law and institutions have broadened the basis of corporate finance. Broad finance requires a firm to attract investors from outside the inner circle of people who control it. The outsiders must trust the representations of the insiders. Special features of the seventeenth-century voyages from Europe to Asia made stockholders relatively easy to protect. For the ship's crew to get home, the ship usually needed to return to the port of embarkation, where investors could see the cargo and divide it. In contrast, a factory yields a stream of production over time, so insiders can disguise profits and divert them relatively easily. The preceding chapter explained that investors in innovative ventures need a share of profits to compensate for risk. The legal power to guarantee outside investors their share of profits was necessary for the corporation to dominate manufacturing.

The problem was solved through many small improvements in law and institutions in the United States and Europe in the eighteenth and nineteenth centuries. Improvements that helped to extend stock financing to manufacturing include better accounting techniques, limited liability, reporting requirements, and banking regulations. These improvements mostly have a single purpose: to separate the company's assets and liabilities from those belonging to other legal persons. Separation prevents insiders from converting the company's assets into their personal wealth, and separation prevents the company's creditors from converting its debts into the personal debts of its investors.[16]

Improvements in partitioning assets enabled the corporation to spread in the nineteenth century. The corporations that first attracted outside investors especially concentrated on infrastructure and utilities—roads, canals, railroads, water, and so forth. These firms reassured outside investors by securing state participation and supervision. Gradually the stock market in the United States spread from infrastructure and utilities into manufacturing. Legal and nonlegal improvements in partitioning assets probably contributed as much to the industrial revolution as factors usually cited like scientific progress, capital accumulation, and labor mobilization.[17]

Econometric evidence shows that improvements in corporate law can increase the value of firms today. Before 1947, India was a British colony, so its rules of corporate governance were British. From independence in 1947 until roughly 1999, socialist policies made firms increasingly dependent on state finance. Nationalized banks crowded out private financing of large firms. In the 1990s, however, socialist policies were reversed and private investing recovered. In 1999, India adopted major reforms in the law of corporate governance, known as Clause 49, which protect outside investors against wrongdoing by corporate insiders. Provisions include mandatory disclosure, stricter accounting, and managerial responsibility for reporting. Clause 49 reforms applied immediately to large firms and gradually to smaller firms. The difference in timing permitted Black and Khanna to estimate the effect of these laws on stock values. Regression analysis concluded that the laws caused the stock prices of affected firms to increase by 4 to 5 percent.[18]

Another econometric test of the effect of corporate legal reform on stock prices comes from Korea. In 1999 Korea enacted new laws on corporate governance that became effective in 2000. Under the new law, large firms were required to appoint independent directors, create an audit committee, and form a nomination committee. The result as shown by Black and Kim was a measurable increase in the stock value of affected firms.[19] Apparently these legal reforms made outsiders more secure about investing in Korean firms, all of which are closely held by insiders.

Even with ineffective state laws, a firm can take steps to make outside investors more secure. The firm can voluntarily introduce transparent reporting, hire reputable accountants, and offer seats on the board of directors to minority shareholders. Empirical studies from East Asian countries suggest that such measures taken by firms protected outsiders to some extent during the financial crisis of 1997, but better protection would improve the region's economies.

Summarizing a decade of econometric research on economic development, Lopez de Silanes concludes, "Investor protection explains the development of financial markets." He favors laws requiring full disclose to outside shareholders of self-dealing by insiders, with effective private enforcement of this right. He stresses that private enforcement of investors' rights is more effective than public enforcement.[20]

This chapter described the firm as a repository of private information, whose dissemination reduces its profits and increases the productivity of others. Direct foreign investment is the quickest way to diffuse innovations in markets and organizations from developed to developing countries. A foreign firm that operates in a developing country transfers capital and innovative ideas to the host country, which increases productivity and wages. Obstructing foreign investment deprives a country of valuable ideas, especially unpatentable ideas about organizations and markets.

Rent a Regulator

Outsiders need the legal system to protect them against insiders. However, improving a country's courts can take years. In the meantime, a firm can reassure outside investors by bringing itself under the jurisdiction of foreign courts. Cross-listing companies on more than one stock exchange makes the firm comply with foreign regulations policed by foreign regulators, which can signal that the firm wants its shareholders protected better than its own legal system provides. In effect, firms gain access to outside investors by renting a regulator.[21]

To illustrate, the Russian gas company Gazprom resembled Exxon in its size and scope of operations, but the market value of Gazprom's stock ("market capitalization") in 2001 was 10 percent of Exxon's. This difference in value mainly reflected the difference in the protection of minority shareholders in Russia and the United States. In 2005 Russia removed restrictions against foreign investors in Gazprom, its biggest state-owned company. Gazprom promptly applied to list its stock on the New York Stock Exchange, as well as in London. To list on the New York Stock Exchange, Gazprom must comply with its rules and also the rules of the U.S. Securities and Exchange Commission.[22] In general, empirical evidence from various countries shows that cross-listing a stock increases its price.[23]

Beyond cross-listing, a firm can try to relocate its corporate charter in another jurisdiction. The United States allows its firms to incorporate under the laws of any one of the fifty states, without regard to the location of their operations. Thus a company whose business operates entirely in Nebraska can incorporate in Delaware, so Delaware law would control most corporate disputes involving the company. Empirical evidence from the United States suggests that competition for corporate charters among states probably improved the quality of corporate law.[24] Similarly, the European Court of Justice allowed firms to incorporate in any EU country, regardless of where they operate. Thus Germans established many firms under English law which will operate mostly in Germany. This example shows that courts can facilitate or impede cross-listing and foreign chartering.[25]

Conclusion

The (joint stock, limited liability) corporation is the best organization to combine capital and innovative ideas. In the right circumstances, the corporation can contain business secrets and use investors' money to develop innovations. After development, a successful innovation yields extraordinary profits temporarily. These venture profits drive economic growth by rewarding innovators. Thus the corporation's social justification is much the same as the justification of patent: consumers pay more to give entrepreneurs the extraordinary profits that drive growth.

Like the fairest youth, the most vigorous corporation eventually dies. When a person dies, an effective will disposes of his assets. The next chapter explains that when a corporation dies, effective bankruptcy law redeploys its assets.

Chapter 10
Hold or Fold—Financial Distress

In Silicon Valley start-ups, the World Cup, and the elk rut, some win and many lose. Success and failure are two sides of risk taking in sports, business, and biology. The previous chapters concerned how law unites capital and ideas to create winning firms. This chapter concerns how law resolves financial distress in failing firms. Firms owe money to commercial banks that make loans, investment banks that buy bonds or preferred shares, suppliers who deliver goods on credit, consumers who pay for goods before their delivery, employees with unpaid wages, accident victims awarded compensation, among others. When a firm loses money for long enough, it cannot service its debts. If losses are temporary, the firm can eventually repay its creditors when it returns to profitability. Such a firm needs temporary financial relief. Refinancing temporary failures preserves firms with good ideas and management. However, if the losses are permanent and the firm can never return to profitability, it needs liquidation. Quickly liquidating permanent failures redeploys capital to better ideas and management. The first problem of bankruptcy law is distinguishing between temporary distress and permanent failure. When gambling with cards, according to a popular song, "You got to know when to hold 'em, know when to fold 'em."[1]

The firm's main stakeholders are its managers, employees, stockholders, and creditors; other stakeholders include consumers, politicians, and communities. The resolution of financial distress alters the status and wealth of its stakeholders. In a distressed firm, these groups have different aims: managers and employees want to keep their jobs, shareholders want a high stock price, and creditors want full repayment of debts. Different stakeholders have different powers, and they often bargain with each other in an attempt to agree on how to resolve the firm's distress.

Their bargaining power partly depends on the terms of a resolution that judges or other state officials will impose if the stakeholders cannot agree. The laws affecting a state-imposed resolution include bankruptcy, contracts, finance, corporations, employment, and consumer protection. The formal law, however, is less effective in many poor countries than in rich countries. In some developing countries, bankruptcy law is so ineffective and costly that firms never use it to resolve their distress. Furthermore, politics pervades the resolution of financial distress in some countries. The problems of distressed firms, consequently, differ significantly in developed and developing countries. General principles about distressed firms require modification in light of the special problems of developing countries.

Causes and Cures of Financial Distress

A firm combines capital and ideas under managers. Failure in capital, ideas, or managers can cause financial distress. First, consider distress caused by inadequate capital in a firm with good ideas and managers. Even good managers often miscalculate the timing of the firm's revenues and costs. Thus start-ups in Silicon Valley often underestimate how long they will lose money before turning profitable. Similarly, a downturn in the business cycle sometimes causes a temporary cash crisis in a successful firm. Or a successful firm may experience an unanticipated shock that demands immediate cash, as when OPEC increases oil prices. If capital runs short in a firm with good ideas and good managers, the firm should refinance by seeking additional funds or restructuring its debt to slow repayment.

Second, consider distress caused by bad management of a firm with adequate capital and good ideas. If management falters, even a firm with

Table 10.1 Causes and Cures of Financial Distress

Cause	Cure
Insufficient capital	Refinance
Bad management	Reorganize
Unprofitable core idea	Liquidate

adequate capital and good ideas can turn unprofitable and experience financial distress. In these circumstances, the owners should replace the managers and reorganize the firm. To illustrate, the creative people who found firms in Silicon Valley often manage them badly, so venture capitalists must replace the founders with new executives. The board of directors may replace the managers and hire new ones, or the board may sell the firm and let the buyer replace the managers.

Third, consider distress caused by bad ideas in a firm with good managers and adequate capital. Many firms build around a few activities that they do best, sometimes called the firm's "core competence." In a mature company, the core activity may become obsolete and lose its value. In a start-up, development of the firm's core idea often exposes fatal weaknesses in it. In either case, if a firm's core idea is unprofitable and managers cannot reinvent the firm, the owners should liquidate it. Liquidating a firm involves selling its assets, paying its creditors, and dissolving the firm. The general principle for liquidating a firm has the same basis as the decision to start a firm: "Start firms with positive expected profits, and liquidate firms with negative expected profits."

Table 10.1 summarizes these general causes and cures of financial distress in firms.

Bargains and Quarrels

In a successful firm, the hope of mutual gain encourages cooperation among stakeholders, as explained in earlier chapters. Similarly, in an unsuccessful firm, the fear of mutual losses encourages cooperation among stakeholders. When the same spirit of cooperation persists in a distressed firm as in a successful firm, the stakeholders converge on the best solution among bad alternatives, which imposes the least costs on them. Costs include reduced salaries of managers, lost wages of employees, lower prices of stock, and incomplete or delayed repayment of debts. For example, refinancing a good firm in temporary distress creates more wealth than liquidating it, and quickly liquidating a bad firm in permanent failure creates more wealth than refinancing it.

Cooperation among stakeholders comes from give and take. For example, creditors might offer to refinance the firm in exchange for preferred shares and an agreement by the workers to accept lower wages. After identifying the cost-minimizing solution, the best resolution distributes the costs so that all of the stakeholders benefit relative to the alternatives.[2] The extent of the benefit to each one depends on the terms of the bargain that they reach. In economic theory, a bargaining situation exists when parties can create a surplus by agreeing on its distribution. This is true when selling a used car, settling a liability claim out of court, or resolving a firm's financial distress.

In practice, however, the spirit of cooperation often breaks down in a distressed firm and the stakeholders quarrel. The quarrels usually follow predictable lines as depicted in table 10.2. The managers and employees, who want to keep their jobs, prefer to refinance the firm and retain its current organization. The shareholders, who want a high stock price, prefer to reorganize the firm, or else to sell it and let the acquirer reorganize it. The creditors, who want repayment of debts as fully as possible, prefer to sell the firm or liquidate its assets.

Earlier chapters explained that bargaining is more likely to overcome disagreement when the parties have clear legal rights. The rights are clear when everyone can predict what will happen if they fail to agree. Absent agreement, the state often imposes a resolution by judges or other officials. The relevant laws concern **bankruptcy**, contracts, finance,

Table 10.2 Typical Alignment of Stakeholders in Distressed Firm

Stakeholder	Preferred remedy
Managers & employees	Refinance
Shareholders	Reorganize
Creditors	Sell or liquidate

corporations, employment, and consumer protection. Clear rights come from predictability in the application of the underlying contracts and legal rules.

Contracts and laws favor some stakeholders more than others. Where law unduly favors managers, failed executives retain control of a distressed firm for too long and deplete its assets. The executives keep the firm going to retain their jobs, while the depletion of assets reduces the creditors' chances of repayment. Similarly, where law unduly favors stockholders, a firm with bad core ideas goes on for too long and depletes its assets. The stockholders keep hoping that fortuitous events will raise the stock's price, while the depletion of assets reduces the creditors' chances of repayment. The problem of failed firms going on too long allegedly afflicts bankruptcy law in the United States, or it used to.[3]

Conversely, where law unduly favors creditors, the opposite occurs: able executives with good ideas lose control of distressed firms too quickly. They lose control because the creditors sell or liquidate the firm in order to avoid any risk of depleting its assets, even though there may be a small risk of loss and a high probability that losses will end soon and turn to profits. This problem allegedly afflicts bankruptcy law in Germany.[4] (Some observers believe that the Swedish bankruptcy code solves these problems better than the United States or Germany by making better use of market prices for valuing the failed firm and its assets.)[5]

Some Creditors Are More Equal than Others

We have been discussing creditors as if they were alike. In fact, they differ in two ways that matter to bankruptcy law. First, the law distinguishes between secured and unsecured creditors. To illustrate, a firm's assets may consist of cash and a cement truck. The firm offers the cement truck as security for a loan. If the firm subsequently goes bankrupt, the secured creditor can sell the cement truck to repay himself. In contrast, the unsecured creditors must divide the cash in the same proportion as the firm's debt to them.[6] When a firm fails, its assets are worth less than its outstanding debts. Like ten vultures on one dead rabbit, there is not enough to satisfy the unsecured creditors.

Securing a debt by a cement truck or something similar obviously reduces the creditor's risk. Besides reducing risk, security also simplifies the creditor's monitoring of the debtor. In the preceding example, the secured creditor must monitor the cement truck, which is relatively easy. With low risk and low monitoring costs, secured creditors can make loans at low interest rates. In contrast, the unsecured creditors must monitor the firm's cash, which is relatively difficult.

In recent decades, the creation of new securities revolutionized finance in the United States. Instead of securing a loan by something tangible such as cement truck, loans were secured by intangibles like accounts receivable (uncollected bills owed to the firm), a farmer's unplanted crop, and the interest owed on home mortgages. In the last decade, new securities helped to finance an explosion in corporate debt in the United States. High levels of debt are inherently risky, especially when the underlying securities are unsound, as were mortgage-backed securities in the United States. (The worst case materialized in the financial crisis that began in 2008, but that is another story.)

Besides security, the second difference among creditors that matters to bankruptcy law is priority. The debtor must repay fully the creditors with higher priority before repaying anything to creditors with lower priority. Thus a firm might borrow money to buy a building using a loan secured by the building—a "first mortgage." Later the firm might borrow more money secured by another loan on the building with lower priority—a "second mortgage." If the firm goes bankrupt, the first mortgage gets repaid in full before any repayment of the second mortgage.[7]

Financial contracts between the firm and its creditors give some of them security and priority. Thus a financial contract might stipulate that a particular borrower has the exclusive right to sell the firm's cement truck to satisfy its unpaid loan. Or the contract might specify that a preferred shareholder must get repaid in full before any dividends are paid to other shareholders. In general, financial contracts that include priority or security for one party preclude it for others. Consequently, contracts giving security or priority must hurdle an information obstacle. How does the new lender know whether or not the firm has already given security or priority to someone else? To illustrate, assume that a distressed firm seeks a new loan and the lender demands that the firm pledge its cement truck as security. The firm has legal power to make this pledge only if it has not previously pledged the cement truck to a prior lender. The new lender needs information on the borrower's prior loans.

Some states hurdle this information obstacle by maintaining a registry to record security and priority. By checking the registry, the new lender can find out whether or not the firm already pledged its cement truck to someone else, just like a purchaser of land in most countries can check the real estate registry for "liens" on the deed.[8] Most European states have registers for real estate, ships, and airplanes, but not for trucks. Without state registries or similar mechanisms, lenders must rely on the representations of the borrower about security and priority, backed by criminal prohibitions against fraud.

Security and priority make creditors unequal. Should the law permit inequality or compel equality? Chapter 5 explained that state enforcement of contracts generally increases prosperity and growth. This principle applies to financial contracts that grant unequal security and priority to lenders, which increase the volume of loans to finance economic growth. Some numbers show why. Assume that a start-up firm needs 100,000 euros, yen, pesos, or whatever other currency is used in the start-up country to develop its new business. Family and friends loan the founders 40,000, and they need to borrow 60,000 from outsiders. An outside lender may reasonably insist on priority of his loan over loans from family and friends, who have more information and influence over the borrower. If the law were to deny priority and insist on equality among creditors, then the firm could not borrow the 60,000 it needs from outsiders. In these circumstances, everyone—founders, family and friends, and outsiders—wants the law to enforce the contract's terms giving outside creditors priority over insiders.

To promote economic growth, the state should enforce contracts giving security or priority, and the state should facilitate access to information about them.

Instead of enforcing contracts giving security and priority, however, the law sometimes treats all classes of creditors equally. The principle of equality among creditors is prescribed in Roman law,[9] whose remnants survive today in some countries. Thus, Italians cannot buy a house by using a first mortgage and also a second mortgage.[10] Short of strict equality, the law sometimes limits inequality. Thus developing countries whose bankruptcy law follows the French tradition may guarantee unsecured creditors a minimum percentage of the firm's liquidation value.[11] Mandatory equality among creditors has some advantages,[12] but it usually reduces the supply of loans that fuel economic growth,[13] because creditors lend less money on worse terms when denied security or priority.[14]

Three Ways to Implement a Cure

The cures for financial distress depicted in table 10.1 can be implemented in three ways: relational, private, and public. Reorganization, refinance, or liquidation of businesses owned by families often occurs internally, with little regard to state law. Thus creditors of distressed family-based firms in Asia prefer private workouts rather than in-court procedures.[15] Similarly, contractual workouts are common in Central and Eastern Europe.[16] Defaulting debtors who belong to merchants' associations often try to resolve financial distress without loss of reputation.[17] "Relational bankruptcy," to coin a term, minimizes the needs for participation by state officials, including judges.

In contrast, private resolution of financial distress relies on contracts to refinance, reorganize, or liquidate a firm. Ideally, private markets resolve financial distress before it deepens, as when a successful firm acquires a distressed firm in a friendly or hostile takeover.[18] Financial contracts between the firm and its investors often prescribe how to resolve financial distress, or who has the power to resolve it. Thus the financing arrangements for start-up firms in Silicon Valley often allow preferred shareholders to seize control of a failing firm, replace executives, redirect activities, or liquidate it. When Silicon Valley start-ups fail, as they often do, these financial agreements substitute for formal proceedings prescribed in bankruptcy law that firms seldom use.

In England, private contracts to resolve financial distress coalesced into something called the "London Approach"—a set of standardized private bankruptcy contracts used by banks and firms. The London Approach includes a "standstill" of all creditors (no debt collection for a prescribed period of time), refinancing with "super priority" for the new lenders (they get paid ahead of all other creditors), a sharing rule for future gains or losses, creation of a creditors' committee to make decisions, and a requirement of unanimity among creditors to change the standard terms in their contracts.[19]

Having discussed relational and private bankruptcy, consider public bankruptcy. In public bankruptcy, the court applies bankruptcy law that is not necessarily prescribed in financial contracts. Public resolution of financial distress requires courts, or state organizations like courts, to supervise refinancing, reorganizing, or liquidating the firm. The bankruptcy procedure usually suspends collection of debts for a period of time, which stops creditors from breaking up the firm immediately and allows it to reorganize.

A firm that suffers financial distress often refinances on terms that give the new investors complete control in the event that the firm fails to return to profitability. Chapter 11 of the U.S. bankruptcy code thus allows a firm to suspend repaying its debts while it develops a plan to resolve its distress. It presents the plan to a court-appointed trustee, who supervises the firm during the resolution of its distress.[20] The plan may propose the acquisition of fresh capital by giving a new investor a seat on the board of directors and priority over old investors in collecting its debt. Alternatively, instead of refinancing and reorganizing under chapter 11, the firm may liquidate as prescribed under chapter 7 of the bankruptcy code. In liquidation, a court-appointed trustee auctions the firm's assets.

In sum, relational procedures for resolving financial distress require little from the state; private resolution requires the state to enforce the terms of contracts to refinance, reorganize, or liquidate the firm; and public resolution requires courts to approve a plan of action by the creditors or develop a state plan. Figure 10.1 depicts the increasing involvement of the state in movement from relational to private to public bankruptcy.

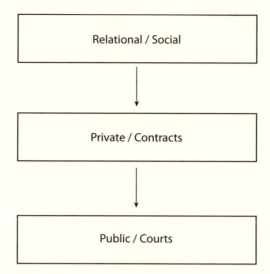

Figure 10.1. Processes to Resolve Financial Distress
Source: *World Development Indicator 2009*

Bankruptcy in Developing Countries

Earlier chapters distinguished between private finance through bank loans and public finance through markets for stocks and bonds. Empirical research shows that developing countries that rely on bank financing also rely on private resolution of financial distress.[21] This makes sense since banks have so much knowledge and control over firms. When distress hits the firm, the banks can help themselves by private workouts and contracting, without relying on the state. Conversely, ownership of stock and bonds by a broad group of outsiders increases the transaction costs of negotiating agreements among the firm's creditors. Public finance thus leads to more reliance on public bankruptcy procedures.

The law ideally promotes economic growth by helping stakeholders to resolve the financial distress of firms. In practice, however, the law often fails in this task in several predictable ways. Distress demands quick resolution before the firm's assets disappear. With distressed firms, justice delayed is justice denied.[22] If the public bankruptcy procedure is too slow, creditors will not use it. The bankruptcy procedure varies in duration by country, such as several months in Singapore and Finland, 1.9 years in Taiwan, 4 years in Brazil, and 7 years in India.[23]

In addition to delays, insolvency proceedings are expensive, which discourages their use. As insolvency proceedings become more costly, firms use. The World Bank collected data on the average cost of insolvency proceedings as a percentage of the value of the bankrupt's assets. Countries were arranged into three groups as shown in table 10.3. The number in parenthesis indicates the average cost of bankruptcy proceedings as a percentage of the estate in bankruptcy.

Why are insolvency proceedings more costly in some countries than others? Many economists believe that prodebtor laws are the cause. Chapter 6 provided the example of Brazil's legal obstacles to repossessing land and dwellings from defaulting homeowners, which sharply reduces the

Table 10.3 Average Cost of Insolvency Proceedings as a Percentage of the Estate

Low cost	Medium cost	High cost
Norway (1)	Argentina (12)	China (22)
Singapore (1)	Brazil (12)	Egypt (22)
Canada (4)	Bolivia (15)	Ghana (22)
Japan (4)	Chile (15)	Italy (22)
Netherlands (4)	Hungary (15)	Kenya (22)
South Korea (4)	Spain (15)	Nigeria (22)
Taiwan, China (4)	Turkey (15)	Tanzania (22)
United Kingdom (6)	Vietnam (15)	Thailand (36)
Algeria (7)	Indonesia (18)	Philippines (38)
United States (7)	Mexico (18)	Venezuela (38)
Uruguay (7)	South Africa (18)	Ukraine (42)
Australia (8)	Poland (20)	
Germany (8)		
France (9)		
India (9)		
Russia (9)		
Sweden (9)		

Source: World Bank, Doing Business (Washington, DC: World Bank, 2010), stat. appendix (cost as % of estate in parentheses).

supply of mortgages. In general, overly generous legal treatment of current debtors reduces credit for future borrowers, which reduces investment and stifles growth.

Some economists try to trace prodebtor laws back to the origins of private law. A study ranked bankruptcy laws in different countries, compared them according to their legal origins, and concluded that countries with a French civil law tradition are relatively prodebtor, whereas countries with a British common law tradition are relatively procreditor.[24] If this explanation is correct, then developing countries with bankruptcy laws modeled on Britain have a distinct advantage over those modeled on France.

Another study finds that powerful judges raise the cost of insolvency proceedings. In some countries, the law assigns all power to the judge—the court appoints and replaces the bankruptcy administrator without restrictions, the trustee reports exclusively to the court and not to the creditors, and the court alone can decide on a plan for restructuring the company. In other countries, the stakeholders have more say. Data suggests that the average cost of insolvency proceedings correlates positively with the power of courts over the bankruptcy process. Conversely, the average cost of insolvency proceedings correlates negatively with the power of stakeholders over the bankruptcy process. The facts suggest (but do not prove) that judges with much power over the bankruptcy process increase its costs.[25]

Politics of Bankruptcy

Politics intrudes into bankruptcy proceedings of private firms in two distinct ways. First, politicians sometimes use bankruptcy procedures to expropriate firms. The most notorious example involved Russia's largest private oil company, Yukos. Like many natural resource exporters in Russia during the 1990s, Yukos engaged in various practices of doubtful legality. The state eventually charged Yukos with tax evasion, which reduced the company to near bankruptcy and depressed the price of it stock, and then the state bought it. The state also charged its biggest shareholder and chief executive, Michail Khodorkhovsky, with fraud and corruption. He was convicted and sentenced to eight years in prison. Khodorkhovsky was an outspoken opponent of Russian President Putin. Was the state's deepest motive to get a criminal out of business or to punish the president's political opponents and to transfer their wealth to his friends? Experts disagree.

Yukos exemplifies a general practice of the Russian state after 2000 to reestablish state ownership of firms that were privatized in the 1990s. Here is how it worked. Under communism, firms systematically overstated their production in order to meet the quotas assigned to them by central planners. By 1990 the situation reversed with communism's collapse: firms systematically understated their revenues to avoid paying taxes, which were often set at unrealistically high rates. For many Russian firms, the crime of evading taxes was a business necessity. In Western Europe private creditors initiate most bankruptcy proceedings, not tax authorities. In Russia and other Eastern European countries, however, the tax authorities initiated most bankruptcy proceedings during the transition from communism to capitalism.[26] By threatening an investigation for tax evasion, the authorities raised the possibility of bankrupting the firm and imprisoning its management. Under this threat, firms readily agreed to reorganize and change their management as demanded by the state, or sell their stock to the government at bargain prices. With so many firms owing taxes, the tax authorities could pick and choose whom to threaten. As with Yukos, who can say how they chose?

Sometimes politicians use bankruptcy to expropriate firms, and sometimes politicians use bankruptcy to subsidize firms. When a politically powerful organization runs out of money, it lobbies politicians to get more. With a soft budget constraint, efficiency-oriented bankruptcy becomes unworkable. Thus India's "Sick Industry Act" of 1985 aims to resurrect failing firms by giving low-priced credits to existing management. Some countries constrain the influence of politics on financial distress to very large firms, such as big banks whose failure can destabilize the national economy. Very large firms are sometimes "too big to fail"—their political clout forces the state to rescue them from financial distress.[27] Debtors lobby politicians to ease the terms of repayment, as in mortgage crisis of 2008 in the United States.[28]

In other countries, however, politics pervades the resolution of financial distress in routine cases, whether or not their bankruptcy would endanger the economy.

National identity can affect the politics of bankruptcy. In developing countries, domestic firms often borrow from foreign lenders. In bankruptcy, foreigners are creditors and nationals are debtors. Politicians often favor their domestic supporters and disfavor foreign investors.[29] Foreseeing this fact, foreigners are reluctant to invest in domestic firms.[30] To overcome this reluctance, governments in developing countries sometimes guarantee foreign lenders against default by domestic borrowers.

Thus, when a German bank loans to a Tanzanian developer, the Tanzanian government may guarantee the loan's repayment. A government guarantee enables the domestic developer to borrow from foreigners at a lower interest rate. The German bank's interest rate reflects the risk of the *government's default*, not the *debtor's default*. The lender, the borrower, and the politicians benefit from the guarantee. The loser is the taxpayer, who must repay the loan if the debtor defaults.

Government guarantees for loans are insidious because ordinary citizens know nothing about them, unless a crisis forces citizens to confront their potential tax liabilities as with the mortgage meltdown of 2008 in the United States.[31] In fact, new research has shown that interest payments on international loans by overindebted developing countries crowd out social spending and investment, which impacts economic growth and poverty.[32]

Bankrupt States and Odious Debt

Like a firm, a state can become financially distressed. "Sovereign bankruptcy" occurs when a state declares itself unable to repay its debts. Unlike a firm, however, the state cannot resolve its financial distress by selling or liquidating itself. Instead, a bankrupt state must reorganize its debts or renounce them. States reorganize their debt by one of three procedures. First, the distressed state may negotiate an ad hoc agreement with other states, like negotiating an international treaty.[33] Second, the distressed state may negotiate with other states by following preestablished procedures, such as the procedures of the "Paris Club."[34] Third, the distressed state may ask for relief from the International Monetary Fund. The IMF, which includes almost all of the world's nations, loans money to financially distressed member-states.

The IMF is a financial fire department: it hoses down the flames of financial distress in states. Fire departments are necessary, although they increase the incentive to play with matches. Government loans to financially distressed firms create a "soft budget constraint," which makes the firms inefficient and reckless. The same is true of IMF loans to financially distressed nations. To counteract this effect, IMF loans often impose conditions to stabilize the currency, increase exports, reduce imports, and constrain government spending. The IMF's stated goal is macroeconomic stabilization, but empirical research finds little stabilizing effects from its loans and much protection of large private lenders, notably American and European banks.[35] For example, the IMF applied this policy during the financial crisis in Greece, which led to a bailout package of 135 billion euros in May 2010. The bailout transferred all risks and costs of adjustment exclusively to the IMF, the European taxpayer, and the Greek people. The beneficiaries were holders of Greek government bonds, especially large banks that obtained high interest rates for buying risky assets and then the bailout reduced their risk.[36]

The IMF should not stop lending to poor countries altogether,[37] but it should reform its practices.[38] Banks extend loans recklessly when they can rely on the IMF to bail out the debtor. To improve incentives, the IMF should make loans to a state contingent on rescheduling its debts to private creditors, thus obliging banks and bondholders to take more responsibility in large rescue operations. Under this proposal, private banks would help the IMF to save distressed states, instead of the IMF helping the distressed states to save private banks.

Government debt can take a morally troubling form called "odious debt."[39] Under international law, a dictator can borrow for his country without the citizens' consent and spend the money without benefitting the nation, yet international law does not allow a subsequent government to renounce national debts of a dictator, no matter how odious.

Thus, the unelected dictator of Iraq, Saddam Hussein, borrowed money internationally in the 1990s, especially from Russia and France. After the United States invaded and overthrew him in 2003, the Iraqi nation remained liable under international law for the national debts contracted by Saddam Hussein, even though he terrorized the citizens and plundered the nation.[40]

Reformers want to change international law by recognizing the principle that an odious government cannot create national debt owed by its citizens.[41] Implementing this principle requires defining "odious debt." Some precedent exists in international practice and law for defining this term.[42] The hardest question, however, is not the definition but who will apply it and decide whether a debt is odious.[43] Most proposals want an international body, such as an international court set up by the United Nations, the IMF, or the WTO, to decide. Alas, these organizations have the usual frailties and susceptibilities of political bodies.[44] A more realistic view concludes that odious debt is inevitably a political concept that acknowledges the power of different nations, not a purely legal concept. The odiousness of a debt and its forgiveness should be decided through political bargaining among creditors. The aim is to save us from hell, not to get us to heaven.[45]

Conclusion: Recycling Capital

"To win a war, promote officers who win battles and demote officers who lose battles," according to a prescription attributed to Winston Churchill.[46] How else can the head of state tell good officers from bad ones except by their victories and defeats? Similarly, an economy must put resources under the control of the best entrepreneurs, and the best way to identify them is by how much money they make. Profitability reveals itself over time, albeit with random errors. In innovative economies, some firms succeed spectacularly and many fail. To speed innovation, capital must recycle quickly from failures to successes.

Formal law is less effective in many poor countries than in rich countries. In some developing countries, bankruptcy law is so ineffective and costly that firms never use it to resolve their distress. Instead they work out a firm's distress through relationships among the parties. As law becomes more effective and cheaper to use, relational bankruptcy is supplemented by private bankruptcy. The best laws for financial distress in firms enforce the private agreements among stakeholders so that entrepreneurs quickly recycle capital.

Unlike recycling metal scraps, recycling capital alters the status and wealth of stakeholders in firms. People do not lose status and wealth passively. The firm's stakeholders systematically disagree about how to resolve financial distress according to their roles as managers, employees, stockholders, general creditors, secured creditors, or politicians. When stakeholders cannot agree on a private plan to resolve a firm's financial distress, they fall back on the prescriptions of public law. State bankruptcy law should resolve financial distress quickly, and it should apply transparent rules that assign clear rights to each group of stakeholders. Ideally, the assignment of rights should minimize the loss from the stakeholders' inability to cooperate.[47] Unfortunately, politics pervades the resolution of financial distress in some countries. Favoring debtors over creditors dries up business loans; favoring unsecured over secured creditors reduces high-risk loans; favoring insiders over outsiders discourages outside investors; and favoring managers and employers over taxpayers perpetuates business failures.

Chapter 11
Termites in the Foundation—Corruption

In the Georgian Soviet Socialist Republic of the 1970s, patients bribed medical doctors for better treatment in state hospitals, high school students bribed teachers for higher grades, farmers bribed policemen to sell in town markets, and builders bribed inspectors to overlook inferior construction. Citizens generally expected to bribe state officials for permits, licenses, services, exemptions, and favorable decisions. Many corrupt results were sinister: low-quality goods, high prices, uneven public services, unsafe buildings, environmental degradation, and slow growth. Some corrupt results were comic, as when officials permitted construction of a synagogue provided its sign read, "A meeting hall where prayer is forbidden."[1]

"Corruption" often refers to improper influence of state officials. Improper influence is sometimes illegal such as bribing a procurement officer, and improper influence is sometimes legal such as contributing to the political party controlling the procurement office. This chapter focuses on illegal corruption, especially bribery. Some officials in every country, and most officials in some countries, take bribes. We described Georgia in the 1970s because, having passed into history, its corruption is documented. Many contemporary countries resemble it, but documentation is difficult because corruption hides from view. Politicians who fear prosecution suppress the facts. Thus the World Bank originally did not discuss the bribery that afflicts many of its biggest aid projects. Such a discussion was thought to violate the bank's prohibition against interfering in the politics of recipient countries.

Susan Rose-Ackerman estimated that the world's bribe payments per year approximately equal 3 percent of global GDP, or roughly $1 trillion.[2] This is too big to hide. In 1996, the World Bank's president, James Wolfensohn, violated the organization's taboo by referring to the "cancer of corruption" in developing countries. Two years later, the bank published an influential paper, "Assessing Aid," which argued that aid is ineffective unless given to countries with honest government.[3] As this story suggests, the world's toleration of corruption has diminished with increased appreciation of its costs to society.[4]

Although hidden, pervasive corruption weakens the legal, physical, and social foundation of economic development like termites weaken the foundation of a house. A rich economics literature explains how corruption slows economic growth and suggests strategies for dealing with it.[5]

Facts

To estimate hidden corruption an organization called Transparency International surveys the opinions of experienced people. Using these surveys, it publishes an index of the extent of corruption that observers perceive in their country's public sector. In 2009 the index ranked 180 countries by perceived public sector corruption. The following table gives a sample of countries ranked from low to high. According to the figure, New Zealand is perceived as the least corrupt country in the survey (ranked 1), and Somalia is perceived as the most corrupt country (ranked 180).

On average, observers tend to perceive low corruption in high-income countries, medium corruption in middle-income countries, and high corruption in low-income countries. By our calculation, the simple correlation between a country's ranking on the corruption perception index and its ranking on income per capita in 2009 is 0.75.[6] This correlation

Table 11.1 Corruption Perception Index, Transparency International, 2009

Ranking from least to most corrupt for selected countries					
1	New Zealand	55	Namibia	106	Argentina
2	Denmark	63	Italy	111	Indonesia
3	Singapore	69	Ghana	146	Russia
14	Germany	75	Brazil	158	Cambodia
17	Japan	79	China	162	Venezuela
19	U.S.A.	8	India	168	Iran
25	Chile	89	Mexico	180	Somalia

is imperfect, with some wealthy countries like Italy being perceived as more corrupt than some poor countries like Namibia.

Also, in states where perceived corruption is high overall, important sectors are uncorrupt. Thus observers agree that Indian elections are as clean as in Western countries; the Indian Supreme Court (APEX) enjoys a reputation for honest judges; and India's space agency (OSRA) launches rockets and satellites that require honest administration. However, experts estimate that up to two-thirds of the Indian government's expenditure on cheap food for the poor gets diverted through corruption.[7] Also some countries that harshly punish domestic corruption tolerate its firms paying bribes in foreign countries.[8]

Unlike *perceived* corruption, little meaningful international data exists on *actual* corruption. Various inferences attempt to solve the problem indirectly.[9] The United Nations and other international organizations collect data on reported crimes, which they receive from national justice departments. Most reported crime data is useless for international comparisons. Thus combining all reported crimes from shoplifting to murder, Germany and New Zealand are the countries with the highest crime rates per 100,000 people, whereas Russia and India are among the lowest. Would anyone actually feel safer walking down a street in Moscow or Kolkata rather than Frankfurt or Auckland?[10] This data reflects differences in crime reporting, not crime committing.[11]

In contrast, statistics on homicide are somewhat reliable,[12] so we use them to gain a perspective on illegal activities. The following figure shows reported homicide rates for selected countries, where some patterns are

Table 11.2 Reported Homicides per 100,000 Inhabitants in Selected
Countries, 2008

Country	2008	Country	2008	Country	2008
Venezuela	39.5	Iran	2.93	Australia	1.45
South Africa	38.6	India	2.82	Poland	1.28
Colombia (1996)	33	Bangladesh	2.64	Niger	1.28
Brazil	25.7	China	2.36	Syria	1.14
Russia	16.5	Malaysia	2.31	Vietnam	1.08
Mexico	10	South Korea	2.18	Italy	1.06
Pakistan	6.86	United Kingdom	2.03	Indonesia	1.05
Turkey	6.23	Chile	1.9	Saudi Arabia	0.92
United States	6.8	Israel	1.87	Germany	0.88
Kenya	5.72	Canada	1.80	Algeria	0.64
Ethiopia	5.48	Jordan	1.75	Japan	0.44
Argentina	5.27	France	1.59	Singapore	0.39

discernable. Many middle-income countries in Central and South America have high homicide rates. The homicide rate in the United States is much higher than in Europe, but lower than in Central or South America. In Asia we find poor and middle-income countries with low homicide rates similar to rich countries in Europe. In general, homicide does not concentrate in poor countries, nor does more wealth correlate closely with lower homicide rates. The correlation between poverty and murder across nations is 0.43,[13] which is weaker than the correlation with perceived corruption.

Some crimes such as drug dealing, prostitution, and extortion usually involve cooperation by several criminals, which requires organization. In a comprehensive cross-country study, Jan van Dijk constructed an index of organized crime based on data from 2005. Countries are rated from 0 to 100, with a higher number indicating less organized crime. The numbers in the following table indicate that organized crime tends to be lower in richer countries, with notable exceptions. Thus Italy has high organized crime for a rich country, and Gambia has low organized crime for a poor country. The correlation is –0.7 between the organized crime index in the figure and income per capita.[14]

Table 11.3 Organized Crime Index (2005) by Jan van Dijk[a]

Iceland	100.0	United States	76.4	Vietnam	36.3
Sweden	98.1	Taiwan	72.6	Algeria	31.8
Malta	96.2	South Korea	70.7	Brazil	31.2
Australia	94.9	Korea, Rep.	68.2	Mexico	30.6
Switzerland	94.3	Japan	65.0	Paraguay	24.2
Norway	93.6	Israel	64.3	South Africa	18.5
Germany	90.4	Ghana	62.4	Indonesia	17.4
United Kingdom	89.2	Tanzania	61.1	Philippines	16.6
Gambia	88.5	Morocco	54.1	Bangladesh	14.6
Belgium	87.3	Italy	51.6	Kenya	12.7
Netherlands	86.6	India	51.0	Nigeria	10.8
Canada	86.0	Turkey	47.1	Russia	9.6
Tunisia	85.4	Poland	43.9	Venezuela, RB	8.9
Chile	82.2	China	38.9	Ukraine	7.6
France	77.1	Argentina	38.2	Haiti	3.8

[a]van Dijk, *The World of Crime* (2007), see chap 11, n3.

Using international data, we found a rough negative correlation between national wealth and perceived corruption, reported homicide, and organized crime. Does corruption cause poverty or does poverty cause corruption? Previous chapters explained that effective laws for property, contract, and business cause economic growth. Corruption makes these laws less effective, which contributes to national poverty. By this means, corruption causes national poverty. However, a simple economic theory suggests that causation also runs in the opposite direction: as people get wealthier, they spend more to clean up corruption, just as they spend more to clean up the air. Rising incomes generally increase the demand for public goods, including honest administration.[15]

Corruption with Strong and Weak Governments

Corruption and national poverty feed back on each other, and this vicious circle may sustain the rough correlation between them. However, the data also show that some countries in every region defy this correlation, and so do some sectors in every country. To understand how they do it consider how the structure of political power affects corruption. A modern state consists of politicians at the top (the "government") and administrators below (the "civil service"). Bribery is centralized when top politicians control it, not the administrators. Conversely, bribery is decentralized when administrators control it, not top politicians. Centralization and decentralization make a big difference to corruption, as we will explain.

The top politicians who control bribes can collect them from firms by two different means. First, top politicians can take bribes directly from firms. Direct bribery works best when a few top politicians work with a few large firms. In a centralized industry with a few large firms, top politicians maximize their bribes by preventing lower level administrators from collecting bribes. Thus a large firm might have to bribe a cabinet minister, who subsequently protects it from extortion by lower officials. This is a system of political corruption and honest administration— politicians can take bribes and administrators cannot. South Korea under Park Chung-hee illustrates a strong authoritarian state with corrupt politicians at the top and mostly honest administration. Similarly, in the Soviet Union under communism, corruption was widespread but tightly controlled from above.[16]

Second, instead of collecting bribes directly, top politicians can use administrators as their agents to collect bribes. The top politicians need administrators to collect bribes when small firms produce much of the nation's wealth. In a decentralized industry with many firms, top politicians maximize their bribes by encouraging administrators to collect them and sharing the proceeds, like a large firm that maximizes its sales by employing salesmen on commission. Thus a small firm might bribe a low-level administrator who kicks back most of the bribe to the minister. The minister then protects the small firm from further extortion by others. This is a system of delegated corruption.[17]

Delegation may be necessary to harvest bribes in states where politicians require extensive support of voters.[18] In the Philippines, contractors allegedly pay up to a third of the value of the contract as a bribe to state development agencies.[19] Senior police and antinarcotics staff at the provincial level in Afghanistan are reported to pay up to US$150,000 to the politicians who appoint them.[20] Authoritarian governments require intensive loyalty by the army and police. Politicians, consequently, demand loyalty and overlook corruption, as in contemporary Russia.[21]

The top politicians may collect bribes directly and forbid civil servants from doing so, or the top politicians may use civil servants as their agents for collecting bribes. The direct approach may prevail in one country or industry, especially if the economy is centralized and direct collection is easy. The indirect approach may prevail in another country or industry, especially if the economy is decentralized and direct collection is difficult.

Whether bribe collection is direct or indirect, the burden on the economy will remain moderate if top politicians who extract bribes feel secure enough to take a long-run viewpoint. They can collect more bribes in the long run from thriving businesses than from failing ones. For businesses to thrive, the politicians must extort moderate bribes, not confiscatory bribes. Top politicians must act like godfathers, not bandits. To keep bribes moderate, top politicians must discipline civil servants so they do not compete with each other and extort too much. Business investment in a stable state with centralized corruption resembles commerce on the Rhine River in the nineteenth century. The emergence of nation-states enabled a small number of officials to replace the many barons who formerly collected tolls from passing ships, so commerce soared on the Rhine.

Conversely, when a state is unstable and politicians feel insecure, they may take a short-run viewpoint. Unstable politics shrinks the time-horizon for officials, and they extort confiscatory bribes that destroy productive firms. The state acts like a bandit, not a godfather. Thus Sege Seko in Congo and Mugabe in Zimbabwe prolonged their failing dictatorships by allowing their loyalists to steal the nation's wealth from its producers.

Similarly, weak central authority provides an opportunity for corruption to proliferate among minor officials. To operate a manufacturing business, a firm might have to bribe the officials who register companies, license production, collective taxes and tariffs, and impose environmental regulations, as well as the police officer, the electricity company, and the water supplier among others. When a firm needs help from many different officials, business activity resembles commerce on the Rhine River in medieval times when barons collected tolls from each ship that passed by. Even highly productive ventures may never launch, like the many ships that never sailed down the Rhine.[22]

Here are some contemporary examples. Silicon Valley attracts engineers from many countries, and they often outsource production to their homelands, especially China and India. An Egyptian engineer whom we know manages an investment fund for other Egyptians in Silicon Valley. He is unwilling to outsource to Egypt for fear that Egyptian officials would demand confiscatory bribes. African nations provide more examples of weak states with decentralized corruption. In Kenya businesses were regulated by a multiple licensing system that required separate approval for each line of business.[23] Similarly, India requires a license to run a small business like a tea stall, hawk goods on the street, pedal a cycle-rickshaw, or work as a railway porter. Shah and Sane found that, even after liberalization, more than 80 percent of the approximately 500,000 cycle-rickshaws in Delhi are illegal. Licensing requirements are so difficult to meet that their only rationale seems to be the extraction of bribes for inspectors and the police.[24]

Modern countries obtained honest administration partly by developing the civil service system. The civil service guards the state administration from improper influence within (cronyism), above (political interference), or outside (firms and citizens). To avoid improper influence, the civil service substitutes bureaucracy for personal relations. In hiring and promotions, the civil service relies maximally on exams, seniority, and performance ratings. This practice makes detecting improper influence easier for outside observers. Thus when promotion follows the principle of seniority, a political crony is easily detected if he gets promoted ahead of his time.

Besides general rules, the civil service has other methods to reduce corruption. Bribes require trust that often develops through enduring relationships. To undermine trust, the civil service often rotates civil servants in and out of sensitive positions. Or civil servants must act in teams whose members can monitor each other. High salaries for civil servants also increase leverage against bribery. Some states like Singapore have wiped out bribes almost completely among judges by paying them princely wages.[25]

How did high pay eliminate judicial corruption in Singapore? Not because rich people are less corrupt than poor people. Rather, high pay makes an official hesitate to take a bribe that might cause him to lose his job. Dismissing a civil servant for suspicion of accepting a bribe is much easier than convicting him of the crime. The combination of high wages in the civil service and dismissal for impropriety provides a powerful deterrent against accepting bribes. However, increasing the wages of judges does not reduce bribery when they have no fear of being fired for impropriety, as experience in Indonesia suggests.[26]

A stable group of top politicians who collect bribes (directly or indirectly) have an interest in keeping exactions moderate so that business flourishes. To keep bribes moderate, they must suppress competition for bribes and discipline lower officials. Conversely, unstable politics at the top or undisciplined officials at the bottom cause destructive competition and confiscatory bribes that destroy businesses.

In some circumstances, however, competition for bribes reduces the burden on business, instead of increasing it. To understand the difference, we must distinguish conjunctive and disjunctive licenses. Permission to act is *conjunctive* when licenses must come from officials A and B and C and D . . . With conjunctive permission, acting requires the consent of many officials. Any one of them can hold up the entire project, so each one of them can demand a bribe. Also, firms that want to stop competitors from entering the market only need to bribe one official. These conditions will paralyze business activity unless central authorities discipline lower officials to assure that bribes remains moderate rather than confiscatory.

Alternatively, permission to act is *disjunctive* when permission can come from officials A or B or C or D . . . With disjunctive permission, acting requires only one of many officials to consent, whereas stopping someone from acting requires bribing many officials not to consent. Thus an investor might have to bribe an official to register his firm, but he can choose the official who demands the lowest bribe.[27] In the disjunctive case, competition among officials drives down the cost of bribes and unburdens business.[28] Federal systems of government like Brazil,

Canada, or India create regulatory competition, which allows a firm to locate in a relatively low-bribe state. As more firms locate in low-bribe states, the overall level of corruption declines in the nation. Thus a cross-country study found that corruption correlates negatively with a proxy for regulatory competition.[29] Similarly, international competition pressures national governments to hold down bribes. Thus cross-country analysis shows that the level of corruption decreases significantly with imported goods as percent of GNP,[30] and small countries tend to be less corrupt than big countries because they have more open economies.[31]

The distinction between conjunctive and disjunctive permissions suggests a strategy for suppressing corruption. Create competition among officials to license beneficial acts, as with the chartering of corporations by states in the United States and the EU,[32] or the creation of trusts in London.[33] Conversely, require permission from multiple officials to engage in harmful acts, as with environmentally damaging practices.

Unfortunately, most regulated activities can be beneficial or harmful. To illustrate, issuing a passport is beneficial when the traveler is a legitimate businessman and harmful when the traveler is an arms dealer. Approving a new medicine is beneficial if it is properly tested and harmful if it is untested. When an activity can be beneficial or harmful, regulatory competition can be good or bad. Adequate exploration of this problem requires a more detailed theory of centralization and decentralization than we can develop here.[34]

Optimal Corruption?

How should the state target efforts to reduce corruption? Consider some of corruption's costs and benefits. Many laws and policies support business such as property, contracts, and corporate law, or provide infrastructure like airports and harbors, or supply social goods like health, education, security, and environmental protection. Effective administration of these laws increases the nation's wealth, whereas corruption has the opposite effect. The state should use its resources to prevent the corruption of good laws and policies.

However, the state also makes bad laws that impede the economy. Laws that retard business include restrictive licenses to suppress competition, noncompetitive bidding for state contracts, most cross-subsidies, and confiscatory taxes. Ideally, the state should repeal or reform bad laws that retard the economy. After repeal or reform, people no longer need to bribe officials for permits, licenses, exemptions, cross-subsidies, and other state-provided goods. However, repeal is often politically impossible. Politicians create bad laws to reward loyalty by redistributing wealth to their followers.[35] To reward their friends, politicians impose restraints on competition, enact subsidies, restrict supply below demand so that buying is a privilege, and create queues to jump, among other things.[36] Also, officials create bad laws to make productive businesses pay bribes in order to get things done. Bad law is good politics in many countries.[37]

Absent repeal, a bribe to subvert a bad law can help to get things done. Such bribes are sometimes called "speed money" because they allow business to go faster. In a study by the team of Hernando de Soto in Lima, the researchers tried to open a garment factory legally in Peru without paying bribes. They found that "a person of modest means must spend 289 days on bureaucratic procedures."[38] In general, data shows that the regulatory hurdles for doing business vary greatly from one country to another.[39] Bribes are part of legitimate business in many countries.

In addition, a substantial proportion of production occurs in gray markets that survive by bribing officials to overlook their existence. Taxes, labor law, health and safety regulations, corporate law, and banking law are ineffective in gray markets such as unlicensed street vending. Because these producers have no legal existence, they belong to the "informal sector," which occupies a larger fraction of the economy in poor countries than in rich countries.[40] According to one estimate, the informal section produces less than 17 percent of GDP in the richest countries, and it produces between 25 percent and 40 percent in poorer countries. The gray market's share of total employment is even higher than its share of GDP. The informal sector apparently employs three-quarters of the nonagricultural labor force in sub-Saharan Africa, and two-thirds in a selection of important Asian countries.[41]

In the informal sector, freedom from regulation comes at a high price: the actors hesitate to draw the state's attention to themselves by seeking its protection. They must use private means to protect property, enforce contracts, and collect debts. Organized crime protects and preys on them. Thus the Sicilian mafias originated partly to protect small farmers from crime;[42] drug cartels in Columbia protect small farmers who grow coca illegally; criminal gangs are heavily involved in debt collection in many countries, including Russia,[43] Indonesia,[44] and Ghana;[45] and Japan's bankruptcy law prescribes sufficiently unworkable procedures that gangsters play a role in the resolution of financial distress.[46] Criminal enforcement substitutes for legal enforcement in weak states, but it is an ugly substitute.[47] Productivity in the informal sector would increase sharply if the state recognized the firms in it, protected their property, and enforced their contracts. However, luring firms out of the gray market and into the white market requires reducing burdensome taxes and regulations.

As a firm gets larger, hiding from the law gets harder. Most large firms, consequently, belong to the formal sector, which is expensive. They must pay taxes and conform to regulations such as licensing laws and labor laws. In return, firms in the formal sector enjoy more advantages of law such as protection of property, enforcement of contracts, and banking services. The following table summarizes the characteristics of the formal and informal sectors.

The division between small firms in the informal sector, and large firms in the formal sector, changes the pattern of growth in poor countries as compared to rich countries. In Western countries a firm often starts as a small business and fails within a few years, but a few grow to be very large firms like Google. In developing countries, however, small firms have difficulty crossing from the informal to the formal sector. Informality reduces the access of small firms to credit that they need to invest and grow. Instead of starting as small firms in the informal sector, most large firms in poor countries start as relatively large firms in the formal sector,[48] especially in sub-Saharan Africa.[49]

We have explained that bribes destroy wealth by subverting good laws (harm). Bribes also create wealth by subverting bad laws that resist repeal (benefit), and preventing bribes is costly (prevention includes the salaries

Table 11.4 Characteristics of Formal and Informal Firms

	Formal sector	*Informal sector*
Firm size	Large	Small
Legal status	Registered	Unregistered
Ownership	Corporate	Family, partnership
Government role	Promote, protect	Unprotected

of guards, accountants, police, prosecutors, judges, reform commissions, and ombudsmen).[50] Combining these three elements provides a simple measure of corruption's net cost to society:

(net social cost of corruption) = (harm) + (prevention) − (benefit).

When laws and public policies minimize this sum, economists say that corruption is "optimal." This odd-sounding phrase draws attention to the cost of preventing corruption and the benefit of circumventing bad laws.

Efforts to combat corruption should be targeted where they will reduce social costs the most as defined by this formula. Expenditures on preventing bribes should focus on improving administration of laws that promote economic growth (e.g., registering property, enforcing contracts, collecting debts, incorporating businesses, liquidating bankrupt firms, and inviting competitive bids on government contracts) and retard harmful activities, (e.g., preventing theft, prosecuting fraud, enforcing safety regulations, undermining cartels, seizing illegal drugs, and taxing polluters).

Conversely, expenditures on preventing bribes should *not* focus on improving administration of bad laws that resist repeal, such as laws granting exclusive licenses that restrict competition, or regulations that help cartels to coordinate their prices. Also, expenditures on preventing bribes should *not* focus on improving the administration of laws that promote harmful activities such as subsidies for strip mines, logging of ancient forests, or payments to farmers for not growing wheat. It is better to administer a bad law inefficiently than efficiently, so the law falls short of its harmful aim.

Should authorities go further and tolerate bribes that undermine harmful regulations and activities? Is the legal system worse if you can pay a bribe to compete with the friend of a politician, or if you cannot compete with the friend of a politician no matter how much you pay? Tolerating bribes brings the law into disrepute, and so does enforcing bad laws. We cannot say which is worse in general. Repeal or reform is best, and any other policy is problematic, like suppressing a black market for penicillin.

Sowing Distrust

Most contracts involve exchange that is consecutive, not simultaneous. Perhaps the buyer pays now for the seller's promise of future performance, or perhaps the seller performs now for the buyer's promise of future payment. With consecutive exchange, the parties need to trust each other. Contract law enables people to make legal commitments to do what they say, which provides a basis for trust. Like contracts, many bribes are consecutive and not simultaneous. Perhaps a builder pays now for promise of a future permit, or perhaps an official delivers a permit now for promise of future payment. Bribes, however, are illegal, so the state will not enforce the promises that the parties make. Furthermore, bribes provide opportunities for the parties to abuse each other—perhaps an official extorts a bribe for a building permit and later extorts another bribe for an occupancy permit, or perhaps one of the parties extorts the other with the threat of going to the police.

States mostly deter bribery by punishing it.[51] An alternative strategy is to disrupt bribery by aggravating distrust.[52] Distrust between criminals is the subject of the "prisoner's dilemma," one of the first and most famous applications of game theory. Two people who jointly commit a crime are arrested and interrogated separately. Each one knows that if neither of them confesses, they cannot be convicted. Each one also knows that if only one of them confesses, he will receive a lenient punishment and the other one will receive a severe punishment. Thus the separate interrogation of the prisoners creates a dilemma of trust. If they trust each other sufficiently, neither will confess. If they distrust each other, both will confess.

This logic applies to bribes. The citizen who gives a bribe and the official who receives it both benefit from the bribe, provided that neither of them reports it. Like the prisoners, each one must trust the other not to confess. Since paying and receiving a bribe are both illegal, bribery involves a double trust problem. If the law of contracts, corporations, labor, and crimes can solve the double trust problem of business ventures, reversing the incentives provided by these laws can sew distrust that precludes many bribes.[53]

To disrupt bribery, the state can reward officials for reporting attempted bribery. To get incentives right, the reward should exceed the official's gain from accepting the bribe. Thus an official might receive a reward of $125 for a report that convicts a citizen who offered to pay the official $100 for an illegal driving license. Foreseeing such incentives, not many citizens will attempt to bribe officials. Recently Kaushik Basu, chief advisor of the Indian minister of finance has made a very similar proposal. He suggested that to bribe an official for a legitimate and required service should not be a criminal offence in India any more. On the contrary the briber should receive a refund of the bribe from the government after reporting the bribe.[54]

To strengthen this approach, the law can give immunity and a reward to the first person who reports the giving or receiving of a bribe. The citizen giving a bribe and the official receiving it would fear that the other one would sprint to the police with a report as soon as the bribe is paid. Faced with such incentives, few people will give or receive bribes.[55]

Actual legal systems use such rewards to combat corruption by sewing distrust. An especially interesting example is an old legal institution called "qui tam." The United States revitalized and extended this institution during the Civil War of 1861–65 to reduce rampant corruption in provisioning its army. Qui tam allows a private person to initiate a lawsuit to recover damages against someone who defrauded the government. If the suit succeeds, the government pays part of the recovery to the private person who initiated the suit. Thus an employee of a contractor who defrauded the government of $10 million might initiate a successful suit against his employer and receive $2 million from the recovery of $10 million.[56]

Qui tam induces disgruntled employees to provide a lot of information on wrongdoing in firms. The inducement is even stronger when a "whistle-blower" statute protects the accuser from retaliation. Protections from retaliation can include anonymity, immunity, job security, and the right to disclose government information to the media. Similarly, the police often reward a gangster who reports on his criminal organization by giving him immunity or reducing his prison sentence. The police sometimes protect an informer against retaliation by relocating his residence and changing his identity. Introducing an accomplice-witness program helped to increase the number of prosecutions and to reduce the number of Mafia killings in Italy from approximately seven hundred in 1991 to approximately two hundred in 2007.[57]

Chapter 7 explained that ineffective contract law channels transactions into repeat dealing among people with enduring relationships. Similarly, illegality channels bribery into relational transactions. Within small groups, people can establish the trust necessary to give and receive bribes. Suppressing bribery by sowing distrust is much harder for the state to accomplish among people with enduring ties. Besides establishing trust, relationships bring the immorality of bribes into question. Assume that a policeman stops a speeding car and the driver presents his license to the policeman with a $20 bill under it. This is clearly a bribe. Instead of attaching $20 to his license, assume the driver proposes to donate $20 to the policeman's church. Or the driver asks how the policeman enjoyed his Christmas gift of a bottle of wine. Or the driver says that he recently obtained a building permit for the policeman's cousin. Or the driver remarks that they served together in the same army unit. People can agree about the immorality of sharp-edged bribes, but donations, favors, gifts, and appeals to solidarity dull a bribe's sharp edge. With kinship, caste, ethnicity, and friendship, reciprocal obligations trump the duty not to give or receive bribes or change its moral significance.[58] Thus American businessmen sometimes see the giving of gifts as bribery, whereas Japanese see the same acts as cementing loyalty.

Other Remedies

Like termites, bribery withers in daylight, so shining a light on corruption can end it. The media profit from reporting on corruption because people love to read about it. An independent media will spotlight corruption, especially if it can protect its sources by not divulging them.[59]

According to our calculations, the corruption perception index (Transparency International) for countries has a strong negative correlation (-0.72) with the freedom of the press rating.[60]

Corrupt officials modify their tasks to make them less visible. In public procurement, kickbacks are easier to disguise for specialized goods without market prices than for standardized goods with market prices. Corrupt officials, consequently, prefer an irrigation project involving a gigantic dam rather than many small wells, or a school project involving a new building rather than uniforms for the children, or a military project requiring a battleship instead of more rifles.

To stay in the dark, corrupt officials also prefer vague legal principles rather than precise rules. The statutory qualification for appointment as a judge might be "a diploma in law from an accredited college," or the statutory qualification might be "adequate legal experience." When a politician appoints a judge, the media can easily find out whether the appointee has a diploma in law from an accredited college, but observers will disagree about whether the appointee's legal experience is "adequate." Similarly, tort law may stipulate an award of a thousand dollars for loss of a finger, or the law may stipulate "reasonable compensation." Ascertaining whether a court awarded a thousand dollars is much easier than determining whether the court's award was "reasonable." To expose corruption, laws should rely more on precise standards and less on vague principles.

Sweden suppresses all corruption among its civil servants who are as clean as the voice of its celebrated soprano Anne Sofie von Otter, whereas India has widespread corruption. Some observers think that differences in culture cause differences in corruption among nations. Prior to 2002, diplomatic immunity protected United Nations officials from parking enforcement in New York City. Although every diplomat was equally immune, a survey found that diplomats from high-corruption countries accumulated significantly more unpaid parking violations than those from low-corruption countries.[61] Old habits migrated to a new place.

Is corruption a recalcitrant cultural trait or a malleable practice? Perceived corruption has a remarkably jagged distribution across countries and sectors—high in one country or sector, and low in another. Thus Jordan, unlike other Arab countries, has a corruption rate similar to France.

Similarly, perceived corruption in Botswana is dramatically lower than in the rest of Africa, and perceived corruption in Chile is dramatically lower than in the rest of the Latin America. Protestant Latvia has corruption similar to Catholic Poland and Muslim Turkey. Recently Singapore overcame its history and became one of the world's "cleanest" states, comparable to the Scandinavian countries.

We know of no theory that completely explains these ups and downs, but the economic analysis of social norms provides a fundamental insight. Assume that most civil servants in country A expect other civil servants to be honest. To gain approval from their peers, they will shame and report those who extort bribes. Foreseeing this fact, fear stops civil servants from extorting bribes and bribery disappears. Thus country A has an honest civil service because its officials expect each other to be honest. When honesty persists, it is viewed as a cultural trait.

Conversely, assume that most civil servants in country B expect other civil servants to be dishonest. To gain the approval of their peers, they will *not* shame or report those who extort bribes. Foreseeing this fact, civil servants do not fear punishment, so they extort bribes and bribery proliferates. Thus country B has a dishonest civil service because its officials expect each other to be dishonest. When dishonesty persists, it is viewed as a cultural trait.

Corruption disappears or persists depending on the willingness of people to help the state to punish bribery, and the willingness of people to do so depends on what each person expects others to do. In economic jargon, this situation has *multiple equilibria*, some with low corruption as in country A and some with high corruption as in country B.

Besides predicting the jagged distribution of corruption across countries, the economic analysis of social norms also predicts when reforms will succeed or fail to reduce corruption. When an expectation fulfills itself, a change in behavior requires a change in expectations that proves accurate. Reducing corruption requires changing the expectations of people about whether or not others will report bribes. The previous section explained how qui tam and whistle-blower statutes reward officials who report bribes. With such rewards, reporting wrongdoing is in the self-interest of people, so everyone correctly expects that others will report wrongdoing. Singapore's dramatic elimination of corruption involved creating expectations among civil servants that others will not take bribes.

A small change in effort to suppress corruption sometimes has a large effect. Assume that so many officials take bribes that each of them feels safe enough to continue doing so. To everyone's surprise, the police announce a new goal of detecting and prosecuting one bribe per month. In the first month, someone reports a bribe to the police, and the official who extorted it gets fired. Each official now concludes that extorting a bribe is more dangerous than he thought. Furthermore, each official knows that every other official is thinking the same way. If many officials stop taking bribes, then taking a bribe will become very dangerous. Because of interdependent expectations, everyone might abruptly stop taking bribes.[62]

Conversely, a large change in effort to suppress corruption sometimes has a small effect. Assume that so many officials take bribes that each of them feels safe enough to continue doing so. To everyone's surprise, the police announce the goal of detecting and prosecuting twenty-five bribes per month. To reach this goal, the police need many civil servants to cooperate. Each civil servant does not believe that other civil servants will cooperate, so each one does not cooperate and the police fail as expected. The failure of the police convinces everyone that taking bribes is safe enough to be advantageous, just as in the past. Thus the police put large efforts into stopping corruption and obtain small results. Campaigns against corruption seldom succeed unless each official has reason to believe that many others will cooperate with the campaign.

Can prosecuting a person for breaking a window or jumping the turnstile at the subway prevent muggings or burglaries? Perhaps minor and major crimes connect through expectations. When criminals observe that they cannot get away with minor crimes, they may conclude that that they cannot get away with major crimes. Informants can sometimes help authorities to end the more serious crimes by prosecuting the less serious ones such as tax evasion and money laundering.[63] New York City followed this philosophy and dramatically reduced its crime rate after 1990.

Conclusion

Bribes are termites in the foundation that weaken an economy. Corruption slows economic growth, and slow growth lowers expenditures to combat corruption. This vicious circle, however, is not so tight as to prevent escape: some poor countries have corruption comparable to rich countries, and vice versa. Efforts to combat corruption should focus on improving administration of laws that promote economic growth, not on improving administration of laws that retard economic growth. When top politicians are secure, they may take a long run view toward corruption and extract moderate bribes that allow firms to flourish. They must, however, discipline lower officials from competing to extract bribes. When top politicians are insecure, or when they cannot discipline lower officials, confiscatory bribes may stifle the economy. To discipline officials, modern states rely on a civil service that follows bureaucratic rules, which make corruption harder to hide. Corruption often requires trust between the giver and taker of bribes. To prevent corruption, law and policy should aggravate the natural distrust between the giver and taker of bribes, especially by rewarding either one for information that convicts the other one.

Chapter 12
Poverty Is Dangerous—Accidents and Liability

Steel nets protect the road against rockslides from Torino to Basel in the Alps, but not from Kabul to Peshawar in the Hindu Kush. Compared to rich countries, poor countries are relatively dangerous places to drive a car, work in a factory, plug in a refrigerator, drink milk, check into a hospital, or live near something that is heavy, fast, volatile, or caustic. Statistics prove that poverty is dangerous. Road fatalities per 10,000 motor vehicles are much higher in developing and transition countries than in developed countries—around 17 per 10,000 motor vehicles in Asian countries, as high as 26 in Latin American countries, and only 2 in Western Europe.[1] Work accidents also occur more frequently in developing and transition countries.[2] According to one estimate, developing and transition countries suffered more than 95 percent of the 351,000 fatal work accidents that occurred in the world in 2002, and Western industrialized countries suffered less than 5 percent.[3] The same conclusion applies to fatal man-made disasters. Between 2000 and 2004, the world experienced an estimated 1,725 disastrous man-made accidents, mostly in industry and transportation, such as leaks of poisonous gas, train derailments, and collapsed buildings. Developing countries and transition countries apparently suffered 90 percent of the resulting fatalities.[4]

Why do people in poor countries have more accidents? Poor people have less money to spend on safety, just as they have less to spend on vegetables, insurance, furniture, and everything else. An economically rational individual balances the harm from accidents against the cost of avoiding them. When poor people strike the balance, accidents are relatively numerous and expenditures on precaution are relatively low.

Income is part of the answer to why people in poor countries have more accidents, but not all of it. Self-interest prompts people to buy safety for themselves and their families, but not for others. Many people weigh costs to themselves more than risks to others. Separation by class, religion, ethnicity, race, or gender aggravates the problem. Besides morality, many people need material incentives to protect others from accidents, including the incentives from liability law. Fear of liability causes many people to increase the safety of their homes, vehicles, offices, factories, and products. After income effects, the effects of liability law are the second reason for why poverty is dangerous.

Your Money or Your Life

The American comedian Jack Benny portrayed himself as a stingy tight-wad. In a famous routine, Benny is walking home at night when a man steps from the alley with a gun and says, "Your money or your life!" Most of us would immediately give up our money. Benny hesitates and says, "I'm thinking, I'm thinking."

Like Jack Benny, economists have thought about the value that people put on their lives. Economists impute such a value by an ingenious and controversial logic concerning safety expenditures. To illustrate, assume that I want to buy an alarm to protect my antique car against theft. The more I spend for an alarm, the higher my level of security. Assume that I spend US$100, which reduces the probability of theft by 1 percent. From these facts an observer can estimate my subjective valuation of the car. If I am economically rational, my valuation of the car multiplied by the reduced probability of theft roughly equals my expenditure on security:

(my valuation of car) x (.01) = $100.

This equation implies that my valuation of the car equals $10,000.[5]

Applying this logic, economists impute the subjective value of a fatal risk based on the amount that people will spend to reduce it.[6] Thus a homeowner can reduce the probability of a fatal accident by moving to a safer house, or by installing costly smoke detectors, breaker boxes, and safety cables. A worker can reduce the probability of a fatal injury on the job by quitting and looking for a safer job. The market price of safer houses, the expenditures homeowners to make houses safer, and the wage-premium paid for more dangerous work reveals the subjective cost of fatal risks.[7] Thus assume that I spend $10,000 to reduce the probability of my death by 0.001. Economists reason that my implicit valuation of my life multiplied by the reduced probability of death roughly equals my expenditure on safety:

(my valuation of my life) x (.001) = $10,000.

This equation implies that my implicit valuation of my life when buying security equals $10 million. We refer to this value as the "subject cost of a fatal risk."

Estimates of the subjective cost of a fatal risk are suggestive, even though they are imprecise and disparate. For rich countries with a GNP per capita between $25,000 and $30,000, typical numbers are $3–9 million. In other words, people in rich countries spend $3–$9 million on safety to avoid one statistical death. Relatively rich people in a country will spend more to reduce fatal risks than relatively poor people. Thus Viscusi estimated that an increase in income of 1 percent causes individuals to increase their expenditure on safety against fatal risks by roughly 0.5 percent.[8] Such estimates find higher values for a fatal risk in relatively rich countries. For Taiwan the estimated value was $0.43 million in the 1980s;[9] for South Korea, the estimate was $0.8 million; for India, some estimates vary between $1 million and $4 million.[10] If we turn from fatal risks to work-related diseases, much the same is true about the relationship between income and expenditures.[11]

The preceding numbers concern the subjective values that individuals place on risks to themselves, including the risk of death. Earlier we observed that self-interested people buy safety for their families and themselves, but not for strangers. Many people need material incentives to protect others adequately from accidents, which liability law can provide. The material incentives from liability law should ideally cause individuals to take the same care toward strangers as they take toward themselves. If this ideal were realized, liability law would cause people to spend less on the safety of others in poor countries than in rich countries. Regulatory safety standards, environmental standards, standards against workplace accidents, workplace diseases, and levels of due care would be substantially lower in poor countries as compared to rich countries.

This conclusion is consistent with the difference between roads in the Swiss Alps and Afghan roads in the Hindu Kush. Afghanistan would badly misallocate the state's revenues by spending as much money as the Swiss spend on protecting roads against rockslides. If the state in developing countries tried to imitate safety levels of rich countries, their citizens would object, because they have more urgent uses for their taxes.

This proposition about state expenditures also applies to private businesses. When developing countries impose unrealistically high standards of health and safety on businesses, the effects are all too predictable: production shifts to the gray market where regulations are ineffective.[12] Many consumers prefer cheaper and more dangerous goods produced by the informal sector, rather than more costly and safer goods produced by the formal sector. Thus much of the food and water consumed in developing countries comes from gray market producers. Egypt, for example, imposes unrealistic health standards on food products that results in more than 80 percent of the food being produced informally by low productivity small-scale providers."[13] Enforcing moderate standards improves safety more than proclaiming unrealistically high ones.

We explained that when regulators apply the same safety standards to firms in poor countries as in rich countries, markets in poor countries divert business into unregulated firms. This proposition about regulations applies to standards of care in the private law of accidents. Courts hold injurers liable for accidents caused by their negligence. If courts apply the same standards of negligence in poor countries as in rich countries, markets in poor countries divert business to firms that escape liability. Thus if courts require the maintenance of trucks in a poor country at the same level as in a rich country, trucking shifts to firms in the informal sector.

This argument about level of care in private law also applies to the level of damages. Computing compensation requires estimating the harm caused by the accident. When courts apply the same levels of compensation for accidents in poor countries as in rich countries, markets in poor countries divert business to firms in the gray sector that escape liability.

Multinational firms pose an emotionally painful form of these facts. Assume that an Indonesian employee is injured while working in the Jakarta subsidiary of a Japanese firm. The victim sues the firm. The average level of safety is higher in factories in Osaka than Jakarta. Which safety standard should the courts apply to the case? Should the court require the Japanese firm to provide the same level of safety to its Indonesian workers in Jakarta as to its Japanese workers in Osaka? Or should the court require the Japanese firm to provide the same level of safety to its Indonesian workers in Jakarta subsidiary as comparable Indonesian factories in Jakarta provide to their workers? Indonesians will sharply resent a foreign employer who treats an Indonesian life as less valuable than a foreigner's life, and a foreign firm will resent being held to higher standards in Jakarta than comparable Indonesian firms.[14]

The same dilemma arises for damages: should the court award the same damages for the same injury regardless of whether the victim works in the firm's factory in Jakarta or Osaka, or should damages be different in different places?

Transnational suits also pose this dilemma. The Indonesian worker injured in the Japanese firm in Jakarta may want to sue the firm in Osaka. Perhaps the Indonesian worker hopes that a Japanese court will apply higher standards and award larger damages than an Indonesian court. This same logic applies with much greater force to the Jakarta subsidiary of an American firm, because American courts are more generous than Japanese courts toward accident victims. In general, workers and consumers in developing countries who are injured by multinational firms may want to sue in a foreign court in the hope of getting higher safety standards and damages applied to the case.[15]

Judges in developed countries should understand that accepting such cases puts multinational firms at a competitive disadvantage relative to comparable domestic firms in the developing country.[16] Put differently, applying the tort law of the home country to cases arising in foreign subsidiaries of a firm conveys a competitive advantage to investors whose home country has the weakest tort standards and the smallest damage awards. As a result, foreign investment is distorted and reduced in developing countries. This fact may partly explain why courts are reluctant to take such transnational suits, although some courts do take them.[17]

Judgment Proof versus Trial Proof

Before the industrial revolution, accident law and safety regulations played a minor role in European law.[18] The modern law of accidents grew in Europe with industrialization, expanding markets, the welfare state, and rising living standards. These changes strengthened responsibilities for accidents that people cause to strangers. Developing countries "transplanted" much of their accident law from European civil codes, common law, and regulations. Laws are easily written down, but institutions that make them effective must develop through time. Instead of "transplanting," a better metaphor is "grafting" law, like attaching a limb from a peach tree to a plum tree's trunk. The written law from a foreign country is grafted onto existing legal institutions. To succeed, a graft must overcome resistance from its host. When relatively poor countries graft accident law from relatively rich countries, the rules must adjust to the underlying institutions.

The greater demand for safety in relatively rich countries partly explains why relatively poor countries are more dangerous. The second explanation concerns the legal incentives to take precautions against injuring others. Compared to rich countries, many more people in poor countries cannot afford to pay a liability judgment or buy liability insurance. Accident victims, whether poor or rich, cannot collect damages from people who cannot pay for the harm that they cause. With nothing to lose, poor defendants have nothing to fear from liability suits.

Liability law is ineffective for deterring very poor defendants, and poor countries have many such people. "Absolute poverty" is often defined as purchasing power of less than a dollar a day. The World Bank estimated in 2001 that 22 percent of the population in developing countries lived on less than a dollar a day, and 54 percent lived on less than two dollars a day.[19] These people obviously cannot pay compensation to their victims when they cause personal injury or death.

In rich countries like those belonging to the OECD, hardly anyone lives in *absolute* poverty as defined above. The more relevant concept is *relative* poverty. The proportion of people living in relative poverty— defined as an income less than half of the average income—was about 10 percent in the year 2000.[20] In OECD countries, courts award high damages for injury or death. Consequently, people living in relative poverty in OECD countries often cannot pay liability judgments when they accidentally injure or kill someone else. The judgment-proof problem is much smaller in rich countries than in poor countries, even though liability judgments are much larger.[21]

Instead of liability, safety regulations can alleviate the judgment-proof problem. To impose a fine, a state official must first detect the violation of a safety regulation. The sanction's trigger is a violation of the regulation, not an accident. A small fine imposed with high probability can provide effective incentives for safety by someone who is judgment proof. Thus assume that safety precautions costing $1 completely eliminate the possibility of an accident. Also assume that regulators impose a fine of $3 for violating the safety regulation, and regulators detect violations with probability 0.5. The injurer who fails to spend $1 on precaution expects to pay $1.50 in fines. A rational injurer will respond to this threat of a fine by taking the safety precaution that costs $1. Alternatively, instead of a fine, assume that the court threatens the potential injurer with liability. Failure to take precaution causes an accident with probability 0.1 and harm of $200. A rational injurer will respond to this threat of liability by taking safety precautions if he has enough wealth to pay damages of $200, but not if his wealth equals $5.[22]

As explained, a poor person who is undeterred by the threat of liability can be deterred by regulations backed by fines for violations. Therefore the scope of liability is smaller in poor countries, and the scope of regulation is larger. In general, as a country eradicates poverty, it can rely more on liability and less on fines to deter people from exposing others to unreasonable risks. (The threat of imprisonment is another form of deterrence that we will not discuss here.)

Administrative capabilities limit the extent to which a developing country can rely on safety regulations. In developing countries, the informal sector, or gray market, employs around 70 percent of the workforce on average and produces 38 percent of the national income.[23] In the best circumstances, regulations are hard to enforce in the informal sector, which avoids most taxes, labor laws, as well as health and safety regulations. More efficient administration and more realistic regulations shift production from the informal sector to the formal sector.

Another limitation of safety regulations relative to liability is that regulators may be more susceptible to corruption than judges. The legislators who enact laws and the civil servants who apply them may have more scope than judges to extract money from special interests in exchange for favors. The best balance between regulations and liability law depends on the institutional strengths and weaknesses of regulators and the judiciary in the country in question.

While poverty can make poor people judgment proof, wealth can make rich people trial proof. If a rich person can afford to defend a suit, and a poor person cannot afford to bring a suit, then the rich person is trial proof against the poor person. This situation often arises in poor countries for some kinds of accidents, such as motor vehicle accidents (richer people drive) and workplace accidents (employers are richer than their employees).

Legal aid from state bureaucracies and nonprofit organizations can reduce the trial-proof problem. However, legal aid often does not reach people outside urban areas, and legal aid suffers from other weaknesses that generally afflict public services. Alternatively, contingent fees can give poor accident victims access to courts. A plaintiff's attorney who works for a contingent fee gets paid a portion of the settlement or judgment if the plaintiff wins the case, and nothing otherwise. Contingency fees shift the financial burden of initiating litigation to the plaintiff's lawyer. The lawyer takes a case on a contingency because of its monetary value, not because of the plaintiff's wealth. Indeed, the lawyer who works on a contingency wants to sue a wealthy *defendant*, and he is often indifferent about whether the plaintiff whom he represents is wealthy or poor.

Contingency fees were traditionally prohibited in England and in most civil law countries. However, contingency fees appear to be spreading in developing countries. Thus poor plaintiffs in India rely heavily on lawyers who work for contingent fees. Contingency fees create incentive problems between client and attorney,[24] but contingency fees are the only key that will unlock the door of the courtroom for the poor in many countries.

Insurance

We have been discussing incentives to prevent accidents. Many accidents, however, are unpreventable. Now we turn from preventing accidents to spreading risk. When accidents occur, they can cause hardship. Avoiding hardship involves spreading the cost of accidental harm across people, rather than concentrating it on the accident's victim. In rich countries, social insurance by the state or private insurance purchased by victims or injurers covers most accidents. Insurance spreads the cost of accidents from the victims to all policyholders or taxpayers. In poor countries, however, insurance is often confined in practice to government workers, military personnel, civil servants, employees of large private or state-owned companies, and rich people. Poor people, especially in rural areas, mostly lack insurance.

"Uninsured out-of-pocket costs" refer to the victim's expenditures caused by an accident, minus compensation from insurance. Thus the uninsured out-of-pocket costs of a personal injury include unreimbursed medical expenditures by the victim. In low-income countries the average out-of-pocket share of injury costs is high and variable. Poor people in developing countries pay a large fraction of accident costs out of their pockets, or so we think.

Table 12.1 Out-of-Pocket Medical Expenditures as a Percentage of Total Medical Expenses in Selected Countries (1997)

Country	Expenditure	Country	Expenditure
UK	3.1%	South Africa	46.3%
Germany	11.3	Indonesia	47.4
USA	16.6	Philippines	49.1
Canada	17.0	Mexico	52.9
Japan	19.9	Brazil	54.6
France	20.4	Nigeria	71.8
Russia	23.2	China	75.1
Italy	41.8	India	84.6

We have no data to prove this fact for accidents, but we do have related data for all health expenditures. Table 12.1 gives out-of-pocket expenditures as a percentage of national health expenditures for selected countries. These are the health costs that the sick person pays himself, rather than insurance or the state paying. The percentage measures the level of risk spreading in the medical sector in any country. The numbers vary from less than 5 percent to more than 80 percent. Out-of-pocket costs are a much higher percentage in poor countries than in rich countries, because of less insurance and less state health care.[25]

Chapter 7 on contracts explained that relationships substitute for state enforcement of promises. Relationships also substitute for private or public insurance. Family, friends, and clans help someone who suffers an accident. Economic growth and urbanization change social relations in ways that increase the need for insurance. While relationships are strong in the countryside, urbanization attenuates the ties among relatives and diminishes their willingness to help each other. At the same time, markets and the state provide insurance to substitute for attenuated relationships. However, gaps persist in the institutions for spreading risk, which leaves poor people vulnerable to accidents. For example, the father of a poor Indian family may become ill, forcing the family to depend on the eldest son's income. If an accident should kill the eldest son, relatives may not provide the needed help for long enough to keep the family off the street. Thus a panel study in Indian villages determined that high out-of-pocket expenditures for illnesses and accidents are a principal cause for collapsing into absolute poverty.[26]

Everyone living moderately above absolute poverty fears collapsing into it. Why don't insurance companies sell policies to most of these people? Insurance companies must base policies on information that is cheap to collect. This information is notoriously susceptible to manipulation and fraud, as V. S. Naipaul vividly describes in his novel *A House for Mr. Biswas*. An Indian merchant in the Caribbean staves off bankruptcy by resorting to "insure-and-burn." The insurance company in the novel suspects, but cannot prove, the truth—the merchant bought an insurance policy and then burned down his own store.

To reduce fraud, a profitable insurance business usually depends on its customers generating written records in their daily lives. The formal sector of the economy generates such records and the informal sector does not generate them. Thus businesses in the formal sector use banks that document transactions, whereas businesses in the informal sector seldom use banks. Record keeping is one important reason why relatively rich individuals and firms in the formal sector have insurance, and poor victims of accidents in the informal sector have no insurance.

Perhaps liability law in developing countries should shift accident costs to the party with most access to insurance, regardless of fault. To offset the lack of insurance among relatively poor people, the state could hold individuals and firms with access to insurance strictly liable for the harm that they cause to people without access to insurance. For many transport and industrial accidents, the injurers are insured firms and the victims are uninsured individuals in the informal sector. Holding these injurers liable spreads the accident's cost through insurance, whereas a rule of no liability concentrates the accident's cost on the victim. This prescription makes the most sense where the injurer and the victim have no contract (think "automobile accidents"), so the rich cannot avoid liability by not dealing with the poor.

This prescription, however, encounters an obvious limit. Earlier we explained that manipulation and fraud raise the cost of insurance to unreachable levels for part of the population. The same forces that obstruct accident insurance also obstruct liability law. Like private insurance companies, the courts in civil liability cases can be fooled and manipulated. Thus a bankrupt shopkeeper who burns down his own store can make a false insurance claim, or alternatively, the shopkeeper could retain a lawyer on a contingency fee to bring a false liability suit against the manufacturer of the store's stove.

Standards in Accident Law

We have discussed how regulations can ameliorate the judgment-proof problem and contingent fees can ameliorate the trial-proof problem. Another general prescription concerns the form of accident law in poor countries. Accident law can rely on clear standards or vague principles. An example of a clear standard is a speed limit for cars or a weight limit for trucks. An example of a vague principle is the requirement that cars drive at a reasonable speed and trucks weigh a reasonable amount. Another example of a clear standard is stipulating the dollar value of compensation for different kinds of accidents (e.g., five thousand dollars for loss of a finger, thirty-five thousand dollars for loss of a hand), whereas a vague principle awards "income foregone plus pain and suffering."

Clear standards allow for swift decisions without collecting much information, thus reducing endemic court delays. Clear standards also make the law easier for administrators and judges to apply who have low education and little training. Also, when standards are clear, corruption and fraud is harder to hide and easier to detect. For these reasons, accident law in developing countries should rely more on clear standards and less on vague principles.

To illustrate, consider the difference between the rules of strict liability and negligence. Under a negligence rule, the court must collect information about what the defendant did to avoid the accident and then compare these efforts to the care required by law. These facts, however, are unnecessary for applying a rule of strict liability. Under this rule, liability depends on whether the injurer caused the accident, not whether the injurer was negligent. The difference between strict liability and negligence illustrates the general principle that fewer defenses simplify the application of liability law. We explained that, compared to developed countries, accident law in developing countries should rely more on clear standards and less on vague principles. An application of this principle is accident law in developing countries should rely more on the rule of strict liability and less on the rule of negligence.

As another illustration, some developing countries have introduced flat rate compensation for certain categories of accidents. When the law stipulates flat rates of compensation, the court does not have to hear arguments about damages. To illustrate, the Indian Motor Vehicle Act of 1998 replaces vague principles of the common law with clear standards. The act (articles 140–142) grants flat rates of compensation in case of death and permanent disablement, provides a comprehensive list of injuries leading to permanent disablement, and stipulates fixed sums for funeral expenses, loss of consortium, medical expenses, pain and suffering, and loss of income. The Indian Motor Vehicle Act was explicitly introduced to shorten litigation and reduce delay in compensating victims and their heirs. The law also reduced the training required for judges to decide liability cases. And the law makes corruption harder to hide. A disadvantage is that statutory damages tend to lag behind changes in the economy. To avoid lags, a panel of experts should regularly revisit the numbers and update them.

Conclusion

Life is more dangerous in poor countries because people spend less on safety for themselves and others. Conversely, people spend more on safety for themselves as their incomes rise, and they spend more on safety of others as their expected liability increases. Liability law, however, is a less effective deterrent of accidents in developing countries for two primary reasons: injurers in the informal sector cannot pay liability judgments ("liability proof"), and poor accident victims cannot pay lawyers to sue their injurers ("trial proof"). To ameliorate these problems, poor countries should control accidents by relying more on regulations and less on liability law, compared to rich countries. Also, accident law should rely more on clear standards of care and statutory stipulation of damages, rather than vague rules. In order to extend insurance to uninsured accident victims, strict liability should apply more widely to actors in the formal sector who harm people in the informal sector. And to increase access to courts, countries should allow accident victims to pay their lawyers with contingent fees.

How much protection of workers and consumers is best for industrializing countries? Similar to European nations in the nineteenth century, developing countries today want to industrialize quickly, so they encourage economic growth partly by making workers bear much of the cost of on-the-job accidents and making consumers bear much of the cost of injuries from defective products. This is a mistake. People who impose risks on others should bear the cost of the resulting harm. Otherwise the price of risk is distorted, which distorts the pattern of growth. If firms pay less than the cost of the accidents that they cause, they have too little incentive to reduce the cost of accidents by precaution and innovation. However, poor countries spend less on preventing accidents than rich countries, and they have good reasons for doing so. The liability for an accident in a poor country is lower than the liability for the same accident in a rich country, and it should be. Injurers in developing countries should bear the cost of the accidents that they cause, but the standards of care and the amount of damages for liability are, and should be, lower for equivalent injuries or death in poor countries than in rich countries.

Chapter 13
Academic Scribblers and Defunct Economists

Physicians in the eighteenth century thought that an imbalance in the blood caused disease. To restore the balance, doctors used leaches to suck blood from weak people. This treatment apparently hastened the death of the ailing composer Mozart.[1] Similarly, false theories of development weaken economies and sometimes kill people. As noted earlier, the worst example of death from bad economics was the collectivization of agriculture, which contributed to starvation and disease that killed up to 40 million Russians and Chinese in the twentieth century.[2] Bad economics also causes poverty, which is unhealthy—life expectancy today is eighty-two years in Japan and thirty-nine years in Zambia.[3]

To what extent do economic ideas, bad or good, affect economic policies? Keynes, the great theorist of the 1930s depression, thought that little else matters:

The ideas of economists and political philosophers, both when they are right and when they are wrong, are more powerful than is commonly understood. Indeed, the world is ruled by little else. Practical men, who believe themselves to be quite exempt from any intellectual influence, are usually the slaves of some defunct economist. Madmen in authority, who hear voices in the air, are distilling their frenzy from some academic scribbler of a few years back.[4]

A brief history of development economics shows how the ideas of economists, both good and bad, affected economic growth in poor countries.

Schematic Theories of Economic Development

We will distill three broad theoretical approaches from the history of development economics and stylize their claims about the causes of growth. The first approach emphasizes state leadership in the economy. The state can lead through central planning as in communism, ownership of the key industries as in socialism, or through pervasive regulation of markets in capitalism. The theory of state-led growth dominated development economics from the 1930s until roughly 1980. According to this theory, free markets result in insufficient capital accumulation and slow growth in developing countries. Administrators and politicians in developing countries should choose promising industries and direct capital to them through state ownership, subsidies, and regulations.

A hypothetical construction site in Sri Lanka illustrates the logic of state-led growth. The site has one hundred workers, ninety-nine of whom use hand shovels to excavate the same amount of dirt as one worker excavates by using a power shovel. If a second power shovel were available, production would rise by almost 50 percent. According to the theory of state-led growth, free markets underinvest in machines such as power shovels, whereas state planners can invest optimally for society.

Alternatively, the second broad approach to development economics emphasizes market liberalization as growth's cause. Liberalization theory, which is associated with neoclassical economics, favors the allocation of capital by markets. To allocate resources efficiently, liberalization theory holds that developing countries must eliminate distortions resulting from subsidies, regulations, and trade barriers. Developing countries should privatize, deregulate, and adopt free trade—the opposite prescription of state-led growth. Liberalization displaced state-led growth as the dominant theory of development in the 1980s, especially under the influence of the World Bank and the International Monetary Fund. The location of these two organizations gave liberalization theory its name—the "Washington Consensus."

Liberalization theory makes optimistic predictions about capital markets. According to this approach, local, national, and global markets channel capital to where it earns the highest rate of return. The rate of return is presumably higher in poor countries where capital is scarce relative to labor. So capital markets will cause poor countries to gain capital faster than rich countries, and living standards will converge in different nations.[5] To illustrate by the preceding example, free capital markets will cause the construction firm in Sri Lanka to buy additional power shovels so long as their productivity exceeds their cost. Construction companies in Sri Lanka will continue buying additional power shovels and the like until the ratio of capital per worker resembles countries like France or Korea.

Instead of emphasizing state leadership or liberalization, the third approach focuses on "institutions." This vague term usually refers to enduring practices that constrain policies. In the language of Douglas North, institutional constraints are the "rules of the game" for policymakers.[6] Thus "institutions" include social and legal norms that sanction rule breakers, as well as the organizations sustaining them. According to this approach, institutions determine the actual consequences of an economic policy. The same policy—say, an industrial subsidy or the regulation of a market—can have different consequences depending on the institutional setting. Thus regulations that restrict logging can stop deforestation or merely provide forestry officials with a new source of bribes.

Which institutions matter most to economic growth? We could look in many places for institutions that matter—government organizations such as ministries, civil service, courts, police, and political parties; economic organizations such as trade associations, exchanges, guilds, labor unions, ethnic trading networks, and organized crime; religious institutions such as churches, mosques, temples, and charities; educational organizations such as schools, universities, and research organizations; and social organizations such as the family, marriage, communities.

Or perhaps the institutions that matter most are legal. The contemporary turn to law began when economists looked carefully at law's role in

finance and compared the performance of different countries economet-
rically.[7] In the last decade, development scholars increasingly focused on
the legal institutions that support markets, especially property, contracts,
and business law. When effective, these laws protect property rights,
enforce promises, and assure the integrity of business organizations.

Unlike most previous writing on law and economic development,
this book concerns legal institutions that support innovation. Developing countries mostly innovate by discovering new markets and adapting
organizations, not by inventing new technologies. Innovation in markets and organizations, like any innovation, is risky. A risky venture that
unites capital and new ideas poses a problem of trust. The best solutions
to this double trust problem emerge from a framework of private law and
business law.

The approaches that preceded institutionalism neglected law or
focused on the wrong law. The theory of state-led growth favors policy
over law, because policies give officials more flexibility than laws in dealing with the economy. State-led growth also rejects private law (property, contracts) and business law (corporations, finance, bankruptcy) in
favor of public law (administrative law, regulations). Liberalization theory
neglected the role of law in creating markets and emphasized repealing
public laws that impede markets (deregulation). Thus the historical turn
toward private law and business law recalls the Psalm: "The stone the
builders rejected has become the capstone."[8] Table 13.1 summarizes this
schematic history of development economics.

Table 13.1 Schematic History of Development Economics

Name	Dates	Failure	Fix
State-led growth	1930–1975	Insufficient capital	Directed investment
Washington Consensus	1975–1990	Wrong prices	Liberalization
Institutionalism	1990–2000	Bad institutions	Market-supporting institutions
Legal	2000–present	Bad law	Laws supporting markets and organizations

State-led Growth?

Why did state-led growth originally dominate development economics? Two historical developments answer this question. First, almost a century of economic growth ended in the Great Depression of the 1930s, which crippled the world's capitalist economies and prompted skepticism about free markets and free trade. Second, as capitalism sputtered, many people thought they saw vibrant economic growth in communist Russia and Nazi Germany. The Soviet Union achieved high growth with state enforced industrialization and with little international trade. After World War II ended, other countries tried their own version of Soviet socialism. Communism triumphed in China and part of Southeast Asia. The newly independent countries of Africa and Asia implemented socialism to various degrees, as illustrated by Nehru's India and Nkrumah's Ghana. In South America, Juan Peron restructured Argentina's economy through government planning, and Francisco Franco pursued a similar policy in Spain.

In this political environment, development economics emerged as an academic discipline. In the 1940s and 1950s, many of its prominent scholars taught that developing countries need state leadership of the economy.[9] In 1957 Nobel Prize winner Gunnar Myrdal succinctly summarized the wisdom of the age:

> The most important change in state policies in underdeveloped countries is the common understanding that they should each and all have a national economic development policy. . . . Indeed it is also universally urged that each of them should have an overall, integrated national plan. All underdeveloped countries are now attempting to provide themselves with such a plan, except a few that have not yet been reached by the Great Awakening.[10]

Was state-led growth the great awakening? To answer this question, we will briefly review and critique its major schools of thought. Any introductory textbook on microeconomics explains the fundamental idea behind state-led growth. Students first learn the model of perfect competition, which textbooks describe as a self-regulating system. Next students learn about departures from perfect competition that cause markets to fail, beginning with monopoly. Monopoly occurs naturally when increasing returns to the scale of production cause the largest firm to have the lowest production costs. With natural monopoly, only one firm can survive in free competition. Similarly, oligopoly occurs naturally when the minimum efficient scale of production is large relative to the market. With natural oligopoly, only a few large firms can survive in free competition. Unlike self-regulating competition, natural monopoly and oligopoly may require regulation or other forms of state control, although economists disagree about how much they require.

If natural monopoly and oligopoly occur equally in developed and developing countries, then managing them presumably requires similar amounts of government control of the economy. However, if natural monopoly and oligopoly pervade developing countries more than developed countries, then developing countries require more government control of the economy than developed countries.

Pursuing different aspects of this idea produced several schools of thought in development economics that all favor state economic leadership. The school of "unbalanced growth," which is associated with Paul Rosenstein-Rodan, held that firms have increasing returns to scale. Starting with a very small firm, the average cost of production usually falls as the firm's size increases. When this is true, a company loses money until it reaches the "minimum efficient scale," after which it turns profitable. To be viable, each firm in the modern sector must reach a minimum size. The minimum scale for selling fruit from a cart on the street is small, and the minimum scale for refining oil is large. In the modern economy, according to this theory, the minimum scale is large like an oil refinery, not small like a fruit cart.

Private firms in developed countries already exceed the minimum efficient scale, according to this theory, whereas firms in developing countries remain below it. Unprofitable companies in developing countries would allegedly turn profitable if they got bigger. Private capital markets in developing countries would not finance the growth of firms sufficiently to make them big and profitable. The state, consequently, should subsidize domestic companies and protect them from foreign competition until they reach the minimum efficient scale to compete internationally, at which point subsidies and protection can be removed, or so the theory goes.[11]

An influential idea that complemented "unbalanced growth" is the "big push." A cluster of interdependent firms must reach the minimum efficient scale all at once to make an industry viable. For example, an automobile manufacturer and its supplier of tires may need to reach minimum efficient scale at the same time in order for either of them to compete in the world market for cars. Linkages among firms require all of them to get big at once. The required amount of capital is too large for capital markets. Instead, the state should create an investment board or a state monopoly to direct capital to promising industries. Government investment in many industries all at once is the "big push."[12]

Like the big bang in physics, the big push in development reverberates to this day. The contemporary United Nations Millennium Project presumes that African nations south of the Sahara need to stand on massive foreign investments in order to reach the first rung on the growth ladder and begin their ascent. The project calls for doubling or tripling foreign development assistance to Africa and foresees eventually wiping out poverty.[13] This rationale contradicts statistical studies that find little or no effect of development assistance on economic growth.[14] Also, instead of being trapped, some very poor countries in Africa and elsewhere have enjoyed periods of fast and sustained growth.[15]

Like the "big push," the school of "balanced growth" associated with A. O. Hirschman and G. Myrdal starts by observing that economies of scale in developing countries produce spillovers up and down the chain of supply, so each firm that buys inputs or sell outputs conveys benefits to other firms. The market prices at which the firms trade with each other undervalue these "forward and backward linkages."[16] The private benefits of production in linked industries fall short of their social value, so industries in free markets will not expand enough. To solve the problem, the state should choose promising industries and favor them with subsidies and regulations that shield them from competition. Subsidies and regulations are necessary to balance growth, but a big push is unnecessary.

Economies of scale and scope were also applied to international trade. Given scale economies, the largest firm or firms in international trade enjoy a natural monopoly because they can produce at lower costs than their competitors. This natural advantage comes from the historical accident of getting big first, not from the inherent strength of these firms. The largest firms in international trade in the 1930s and 1940s were ones in the rich countries that industrialized first. This accident of history has given these firms monopoly power in international trade.

With free trade, the large firms in developed countries will drive out the small firms in developing countries. If developing countries allow free trade, their domestic firms will never become big enough to compete internationally. To catch up, according to this argument, developing countries should reject free trade and protect their "infant industries" while their firms grow big and strong. Thus many authors writing on international trade and development advised poor countries to use tariffs to block imports.[17] As domestic industries grow behind the tariff wall, consumers will substitute domestic goods for imported goods, which allows domestic firms to grow bigger and causes their costs of production to fall. This process should proceed until domestic industries reach an efficient scale where they can compete internationally, at which point the state can remove international trade protection.[18]

Singer and Prebisch also thought exporting raw materials keeps poor countries poor. Exporting raw materials is a poverty trap because the prices of raw materials will always fall relative to manufactured goods.[19] As these prices fall with time, the poor countries that mostly export raw materials will get poorer. (Modern ecologists usually believe the contrary—that prices of raw materials will rise sharply through resource exhaustion.)

While Prebisch favored temporary tariff protection against international competition, radical trade skeptics favored permanent protection. Radical skeptics held that poor countries with small industries could never compete in international trade. By trying to do so, they will become the poor "periphery" far from the rich "center." Even worse, if poor countries allow direct foreign investment, international firms will exploit them. Exploitation of poor countries by rich countries was central to Lenin's theory of imperialism.[20] To avoid exploitation by imperialists, some contemporary critics of globalization believe that poor countries should curtail participation in the international economy.

Besides spillovers and trade skepticism, another reason for developing countries to subsidize domestic firms comes from a different strand of thought in development economics. According to Arthur Lewis's "dual economy" theory, developing economies have two distinct sectors— modern and traditional.[21] Each worker in the traditional sector produces little because he has so little to work with, like digging with a hand shovel. In contrast, each worker in the modern sector produces a lot because he has much to work with, like digging with a power shovel. According to this view, when workers move from the traditional to the modern sector, production falls a little in the traditional sector and increases a lot in the modern sector.

To illustrate concretely, a farmer employs his son to work the family's small plot of land. There are so many workers and so little land that the son's labor does not produce much. The father pays his son a subsistence wage that exceeds his son's production. The son's wage thus includes a subsidy or gift from his father. In these circumstances, if the son leaves the farm, moves to the city, gets a factory job, and supports himself, the son's income will increase and so will the father's income.[22] (This claim can be formulated more precisely in the technical language of economics.)[23]

The most important policy implication of dual market theory is that society benefits when employment shrinks in the traditional sector and increases in the modern sector.[24] Free markets will not capture this benefit, so the traditional sector tends to be too large and the modern sector tends to be too small. To correct this distortion, the state should tax the traditional sector and subsidize the modern sector, thus transferring money from poor workers in agriculture to relatively rich workers in industry. In the 1980s, many developing countries discriminated against agriculture by using regulatory price ceilings, export restrictions, and multiple exchange rates. As a result, farmers in developing countries received less than the world price for their crops.[25]

Table 13.2 Some Theories of State-Led Growth

Name	Proponent	Policy
Big push	Rosenstein-Rodan	State mobilizes capital & labor
Balanced growth	A.O. Hirschman & G. Myrdal	State subsidizes promising industries
Import substitution	Prebisch	Tariffs against imports
Imperialism	Lenin	Withdraw from world trade
Dual economy theory	W.A. Lewis	Subsidize industry & tax farms

This is a recent episode in the ancient history of towns taxing farmers.[26] (In rich democracies today, the situation usually reverses itself: towns subsidize farmers.)[27]

Table 13.2 summarizes these theories. Responding to them, the state in many developing countries led their economies through licenses, subsidies, tariffs, loans, manipulated exchange rates, and official prices. State-led growth produced impressive results in the 1950s, but its failure became obvious in many countries by the 1970s.[28] Lack of competition raised prices and lowered the quality of goods, overregulation stifled innovation and promoted corruption, and state domination of the economy channeled effort into gaining political influence rather than creating wealth. To illustrate, when Juan Peron achieved power in 1946 in Argentina, he taxed agriculture, subsidized industry, and erected tariff barriers against foreign goods. Consequently he weakened agriculture and created industries that could not compete in world markets.[29] In Ghana during the reign of Kwame Nkrumah (1957–66), a similar policy redistributed wealth and power from cocoa farmers to urban elites.[30] Tanzania under Julius Nyerere (1960–86) also pursued this strategy.

Besides affecting economic organization and performance, state-led growth impacts class and ideology. In past centuries, aristocrats in Europe looked down on businessmen. For aristocrats, "bourgeois" was a pejorative term. Much the same was true among the higher castes in India. In the twentieth century, aristocratic snobbery toward bourgeois culture transmuted into intellectual anger against capitalism. Anticapitalist anger among intellectuals has a foundation in material self-interest. Before the twentieth century, many intellectuals lived off the largess of aristocrats and shared their conservative views. Building modern states in the twentieth century, however, required developing a civil service that hires and promotes on relatively objective grounds, including education. Intellectuals perform well in school and on written exams that the civil service uses for hiring and promoting. By providing jobs, the civil service broke the dependence of intellectuals on aristocratic largess. For instance, the great sixteenth-century Danish astronomer Tycho Brahe was the imperial astronomer for the Holy Roman emperor Rudolph II, whereas the twentieth-century physicist Albert Einstein first developed his revolutionary ideas while working as an examiner in the Swiss patent office in Berne.

Intellectuals were naturally attracted to the belief that the state should lead economic growth. Shouldn't the smartest people be in charge? Leading the economy created more state jobs with higher pay for intellectuals. Left ideology made state officials confident that they could successfully lead the economy. Thus material interests and ideas converged to promote state-led growth.

Why Liberalization?

We have explained that state-led growth relied on planners to direct capital to the most promising industries and protect them from foreign competition. In the last half of the twentieth century many developing countries pursued industrial policies that favored capital accumulation over consumption, manufacturing over agriculture, heavy industry over light industry, dirty industry over clean industry, fishing and cutting wood over sustainable production, and import substitution over exports. Import-substitution in Africa and South America produced worse results than export-led growth that succeeded dramatically Japan, Korea, and Taiwan. From Poland to India, state-led growth nurtured firms that were too clumsy to survive. With subsidies and protection, helpless infant industries grew into flabby adolescents. Most economists now view these policies as mistakes that retarded economic growth.

The failure of state-led growth has three general causes. The first is motivation. By leading development, public officials increase their responsibilities, which increases their salaries and their opportunities for bribes. Public officials can keep the wealth that they receive in salaries and bribes, but not the nation's wealth from doing their jobs the right way. Industrial policy is rife with political favoritism, chicanery, cronyism, and corruption. Politicians and officials have strong incentives to invest the state's money less productively than businessmen who invest their own money.

The second cause of failure is information. Those officials are motivated to make wealth for the nation do not have the information needed to guide industrial development. An economy produces everything from pins to power plants. State officials cannot centralize enough information to manage this complexity. People in firms distort or withhold information from officials for strategic reasons—to avoid taxes, attract subsidies, or gain political influence. This strategic resistance makes economic leadership by officials intractable. Economists made these arguments against state-led growth based on information and motivation in the 1940s,[31] but they appreciated the problem of information more fully in the 1980s.[32]

The third cause of failure is the impotence of capital accumulation. On its face, capital accumulation may seem like the key to unlock the treasure chest of national wealth. On construction sites in Germany, machines resembling dental drills for dinosaurs bore the foundations of buildings, and other machines carry away the dirt without human hands touching it. With so much capital per worker, the productivity of German labor is high. In contrast, on construction sites in India, laborers with picks and shovels dig the foundations of some buildings and women remove the dirt in baskets balanced on their heads. With so little capital per worker, the productivity of Indian labor is low.

Why do Indian workers have less capital? In a market economy, households decide how much money to save and businesses decide how many machines to buy. People in poor countries voluntarily save a lot of money.[33] Could a country like India grow faster and become rich like Germany by forcing people to save and invest more? Russia tried to speed development in the 1940s and 1950s by forcing people to save more and investing their savings in machines and other capital goods. Growth rates were spectacular in the 1950s, but they proved unsustainable.[34] The facts about Russia are consistent with the *law of diminishing marginal productivity*, which predicts that total production increases at a decreasing rate as capital increases relative to other factors of production.

In general, economists who examine the data find a weaker connection between growth and capital accumulation than theories of state-led growth assumed. To illustrate, in 1960 capital per capita in the relatively rich UK was three times higher than in relatively poor Algeria. Over the next twenty-eight years, capital increased by roughly 240 percent in the UK and real income per capita increased by more than 80 percent, whereas capital per capita increased by roughly 300 percent in Algeria and income per capita stagnated. Capital accumulation brought higher incomes to Britain and not to Algeria.[35] (Algeria is not the only example of capital accumulation without growth.)[36]

According to the law of diminishing marginal productivity, capital accumulation in the UK should have caused capital's productivity to fall, but it did not.[37] How did the UK defy the law of diminishing marginal productivity? While capital accumulation proved less important to growth than many supposed, innovation proved more important.[38] Innovation in UK firms apparently increased the productivity of capital enough to offset the decrease caused by having more of it. Conversely, bad organization and leadership of Algerian firms apparently caused them to waste increasing amounts of capital. Developing countries cannot accelerate growth by importing modern machines and placing them in inefficient organizations. The state can make people accumulate more easily than it can make them innovate.

Development economics turned away from state-led growth and toward liberalization when the "Washington Consensus" emerged in roughly 1980.[39] This theory of development economics favored a retreat of state ownership, which occurred in fact. Table 13.3 distinguishes four groups of countries by income level, from low to high. In each group of countries, the percentage of GDP supplied by state-owned enterprises declined between 1980 and 1999, which indicates a worldwide trend

Table 13.3 Share of State Owned Enterprises in Gross Domestic Product

Countries (by income group)	1980	1999	Change
Low income countries	15%	2.5%	–12.5%
Lower middle income countries	11%	4%	–7%
Upper middle income countries	10.5%	4%	–6.5%
High income countries	6%	4%	–2%

Source: E. Sheshinski and L. F. Lopez-Calva, 'Privatization and Its Benefits: Theory and Evidence," CESifo Economic Studies (2003). Estimations based on World Development Indicators (Washington, DC: World Bank).

toward privatization. However, the percentage declined most in low-income countries. In 1980 low-income countries produced relatively *more* in state-owned enterprises than high-income countries, and in 1999 low-income countries produced relatively *less* in state-owned enterprises than high-income countries.[40]

Another indicator of state leadership's decline and liberalization's ascent is the shift from government development assistance to private investment in developing countries. In 1950, private direct investment in developing countries (credits and equity) was much smaller than government development assistance ("foreign aid"). In 1970, they were approximately equal—around $10 billion. Today the former is much larger than the latter. Unfortunately, international investments in stocks still concentrate in a few countries, especially shares purchased by outsiders who do not participate in managing the company ("portfolio investment"). In the developing world, more than 80 percent of all net portfolio investment went to five countries: China, India, Turkey, Brazil, and South Africa.[41] In some of the poorest countries, more capital flows out than in, because fear makes people place their money with the best protector, not the best investor.

Institutions and Law

We can compare the history of liberalization to actual growth rates as summarized in chapter 2.[42] Liberalization and growth correlated positively in some countries. Thus the pace of economic growth quickened with liberalization in East and South Asia in the 1980s, and in Central Europe in the 1990s. Liberalization and growth correlated negatively in other countries. Thus production plummeted after 1990 when liberal reforms demolished planning in Eastern Europe, Russia, and other countries of the former Soviet Union. In the 1980s, Latin America liberalized and stagnated, compared to modest growth in previous years of state activism.[43] Table 13.4 summarizes this schema.

Why did the same liberalization policy have different consequences from one country to another? The same policy gets different results when implemented with different institutions in the background, like proposing a toast with wine in Catholic Spain or Muslim Iran.[44] To succeed, liberalization requires background institutions that secure property for the makers of wealth, enforce promises in business, and distribute the profits of firms predictably. These institutions are what we mean by effective property, contract, and corporate law, as represented in table 13.5.[45]

Property, contract, and corporate law become effective through the interaction of social norms, courts, the civil service, and politics. Different countries combine these elements in different proportions.[46] Courts, state law, and constrained government provided protection in some

Table 13.4 Liberalization Experience Schematized

Positive
China
India
Central European countries that joined the EU

Negative
Africa
Latin America (excluding Chile)
Eastern European countries not joining the EU (Russia, etc.)

Table 13.5 Institutional Prerequisites for Liberalization to Cause Growth

Secure property for makers of wealth ⇔ Property law
Enforce promises ⇔ Contract law
Distribute profits of firms ⇔ Corporate law

countries in Central and Eastern Europe, such as Poland and the Baltic states after 1990. These countries dramatically improved their legal institutions in an effort to join the European Union. In other countries, the state bureaucracy, intermediate institutions, and authoritarian leaders provided protection of property, contracts, and business organizations, as in Taiwan, South Korea, China, and Vietnam.[47] In China, state-protected growth succeeded spectacularly where state-led growth failed. In the 1990s, India relaxed state planning and liberalized cautiously in phases. Growth accelerated as stagnant state industries made way for vibrant, new businesses like computer software and outsourced services. Indian state planners, who failed to foresee the success of these businesses, did little to inhibit or stimulate their development, rather like U.S. government officials did little to inhibit or stimulate Silicon Valley.

Conversely, liberalization succeeded less in countries without effective private and business law. Big-bang liberalization in Russia in the early 1990s caused gangster capitalism and economic decline. In sub-Saharan Africa, lawlessness devastated economies and shrank economies. In Latin America, liberal reforms without institutional improvements caused economic stagnation. In these countries, liberalization showed better results after institutions strengthened for private and business law.

Conclusion

To unite ideas with capital and produce growth, business needs freedom through law.[48] Recent history suggests that freeing markets caused growth in states with effective private and business law. This fact leads to our prescription for growth as depicted in figure 13.1.

According to this prescription, the state's first role in economic development is to build the legal foundations for markets. With the legal foundations in place, liberalization will promote innovation. The state should take this indirect approach to promoting growth, not the direct approach of choosing firms and industries for subsidies and special privileges.

In making economic policy, the state should mostly rely on public information. When officials decide by using public information, they

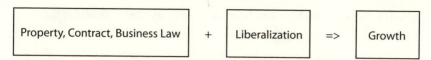

Figure 13.1: Institutional Prescription for Growth

can explain and justify their policies to the citizens. Public discussion, debate, and criticism create a basis for accountability that dampens nepotism, favoritism, and corruption. Conversely, state officials can easily divert secret investments to their cronies. Politicians mostly direct public money to their supporters in order to build loyalty, however much they may talk about economic growth.[49] Citizens in most democracies are right to demand that officials defend their economic policies publicly.

When using public information, state officials cannot predict the surge of a particular firm or industry. People who invest in innovative ideas keep many secrets in order to earn extraordinary profits. Like football teams, firms surprise outsiders by pursuing unforeseen strategies. Thus economists did not predict the invention of the "personal computer" by IBM in 1981, the explosive growth of this industry subsequently, and IBM's exit from personal computers in 2005 by selling this business to the Chinese firm Lenovo. Similarly, Japanese planners did not predict the surge of automobile manufacturers after 1960, and Indian planners did not predict the surge of computer firms in Bangalore after 1990. Most state officials cannot accelerate growth by investing public funds in particular firms except by chance, just as most private investors cannot profit by trading on public information except by chance.[50] Industrial policies that allegedly redirect capital to growth industries mostly waste resources without increasing growth rates.[51]

Developing a legal framework for competition and innovation is not the state's only role. In addition, the state must stabilize money and banking, supply public goods (defense, education, public health, social security, poverty relief, environmental protection, and so forth), and build infrastructure (roads, water, electricity, telephone lines, airports, harbors, industrial parks, and so forth).[52] By building infrastructure, the state channels and coordinates the expansion of business, without picking which firms or industries will succeed or fail. Instead of leading, the state has successfully coordinated economic growth in modest ways.[53]

Since the state has so many roles, the reader may wonder, "Why do you emphasize the institutions of private and business law?" No camera can focus on everything in the picture. Law belongs in the foreground because of its central role in economic growth. Sustained growth comes from economic innovation. Combining capital and new ideas requires solving the double trust dilemma, and the best solutions involve legal institutions, especially private and business law. If economic theories have power as Keynes believed, then understanding the double trust dilemma should help lawmakers to accelerate growth and alleviate the poverty of nations.

Chapter 14
How the Many Overcome the Few

Mary Shelley, the author of *Frankenstein*, was born August 30, 1797, and her mother died from puerperal fever ten days later. At the time, some physicians believed correctly that doctors transmitted the disease by delivering one baby after another in hospitals without washing their hands. Other doctors resisted the evidence, even after Pasteur identified the culpable bacteria in 1879.[1] Puerperal fever killed many people who could have been saved merely by washing hands. In development economics as in medicine, error resists truths that challenge interests.[2] Economic growth benefits many people and harms a few, but the few people harmed sometimes command the heights of society, like billionaires, bankers, bureaucrats, and union leaders. From the heights, a few can hold back many like sharpshooters in a mountain pass.[3]

Since the 1990s governments have spent a lot of money on "rule-of-law projects" to train judges and administrators, promote judicial independence, reduce court delays, improve law enforcement, curb corruption, solve corporate governance problems, and redraft laws and regulations.[4] If poor countries have weak legal systems because people don't know better, then better results should have come from spending all this money. The deeper problem is material self-interests, not ignorance. Reforms often do not serve the interest of those who have the power to carry them out, so the powerful few obstruct growth-promoting reforms that benefit the many. Even so, strategies of reform can overcome growth-retarding elites.

Three Types of Reforms

When communism collapsed, ownership of most state enterprises passed into private hands.[5] Konstantin Magin divided the complicated process of privatization into stages.[6] In the first stage, roughly from 1990 to 1994, managers became owners by grabbing state assets, especially in small and medium firms.[7] Restaurants, clothiers, grocers, and other small state businesses were given away or sold cheaply to their managers. Approximately fourteen thousand Russian enterprises of medium size or larger (at least fifty employees), and many more small firms, passed from state to private ownership.[8]

Privatizing small and medium firms benefitted far more people than it harmed in Russia, and the process generated more political support than opposition. In reorganizing these businesses, some employees were promoted and others were fired. The new owner-managers increased efficiency and profited personally. Competition among small businesses benefitted consumers through lower prices and higher quality.

The story is different when we turn from small to large enterprises. Like other centrally planned economies, Russia created industrial giants. State ministries controlled unprofitable conglomerates making steel, automobiles, refrigerators, ships, and other capital goods and consumer durables. In the 1990s after communism's collapse, the industrial ministries sought vast state subsidies to keep these conglomerates operating. The Russian state subsidized them by printing money, not by collecting taxes, which caused hyperinflation in 1994–95.

Despite resistance from the industrial ministries, the managers and reformers in government privatized many large enterprises.[9] In Magin's second stage, the state created private companies from large enterprises and distributed stock options to employees and other citizens ("voucher privatization"). The privatization process, however, included fraud, intimidation, and political chicanery. Given ineffective laws, insiders expropriated the holdings of outsiders.[10] Foreseeing this result, outsiders who owned a few vouchers in large firms sold them to insiders at trivial prices. What began as dispersed ownership of options ended in concentrated ownership of stock.[11]

Many scholars believed that rapid privatization of socialist firms and dispersed ownership of shares would stimulate legal reform to protect property rights. They were mostly wrong. Former managers and tycoons with access to finance bought underpriced firms and took control. Their political influence was so great that protecting property rights seemed unnecessary for them. Instead they blocked the development of laws for capital markets, as well as laws against self-dealing and stripping a firm of its assets. The private owners of large enterprises, who were called the "oligarchs," demanded property rights only after the Russian state regained power and used it against some of them.[12]

The economic effects of privatizing large enterprises were mixed. Some industries modernized, ended dependence on subsidies, and sold goods at competitive prices. In other industries, closing unprofitable plants caused local unemployment that harmed whole communities, and buyers faced high prices from private firms with monopoly power. Privatizing large enterprises probably benefitted more Russians than it harmed, but harm was widespread and the process generated controversy, not consensus.

Magin's next stage, 1998–2001, represents the response to this controversy and disagreement. In this period, Boris Yeltzin yielded the presidency of Russia to Vladimir Putin, who vigorously reasserted central authority and brought the oligarchs under government control.[13] With more centralized power, the government slowed runaway inflation by resisting the demands of industries for state subsidies.

In this stage, however, politicization replaced privatization as the dynamic of change for large enterprises. Successful operation of large enterprises now required the protection and participation of politicians. Unrealistic tax laws in Russia created tax liabilities on paper that few firms could pay. Given this fact, politicians could threaten the owners of firms with prosecution for tax evasion, fraud, and other crimes. To settle their tax arrears and avoid criminal prosecution, owners were sometimes pressed to transfer their firms or its assets to another firm controlled by politicians.[14]

In Russia's recent history, reforms moved from privatizing small firms and large enterprises to politicizing large firms. Concepts from welfare economics explain the essential difference in these three examples.[15] In the first example of privatizing small firms, many gain and a few lose. Following this logic to its conclusion leads to changes that benefit some people without harming *anyone*. A "Pareto gain"—to use the technical term for this concept—has winners and no losers.[16] No legal reforms are strictly Pareto gains, because all have some losers, but some legal reforms approximate Pareto gains, such as privatizing small enterprises in Russia.[17]

The second example, privatizing large enterprises, has many winners and many losers. Judging from experience around the world, the firms in most industries will ultimately perform better under private ownership than state control. Almost everywhere, the economy has benefitted from private ownership in such industries as steel, automobiles, refrigerators, and ships. When a legal change benefits the winners more than it harms the losers, the change is a net gain by the standard of cost-benefit analysis.[18]

In the third example of politicizing large firms, a few politicians gain a lot and the economy suffers as a whole. Politicization disrupts property law and capital markets, which deflects the pursuit of wealth into taking instead of making. When the sum of the costs exceeds the sum of the benefits, the change is a net loss by the cost-benefit standard.[19]

Table 14.1 depicts the three types of Russian legal reforms: Pareto gains, net gains, and net losses. They evoke different levels of political support and opposition. Most people favor reforms when they expect to gain from them, and conversely, they oppose reforms when they expect to lose. Because few lose from reforms that approximate Pareto gains, this type of reform provokes the fewest opponents, and reformers can often proceed by consensus, like privatizing small Russian firms. In contrast, reforms with net gains divide people into winners and losers, and the former usually outnumber the latter, as happened when the large Russian firms were privatized. A majority usually (but not always) favors reforms with net gains. Finally, when legal changes cause net losses, the losers usually outnumber the winners, as occurred when the large Russian firms were politicized. A minority usually (but not always) favors legal changes with net losses.

Table 14.1 Three Types of Reforms

Technical term	Welfare effects	Political support
Pareto gain	All win	Consensus
Net gain	More win than lose	Majority
Net loss	More lose than win	Minority

Even in democracy and other forms of polyarchy,[20] sheer numbers do not determine political outcomes. An active minority often prevails against a passive majority. Economists have analyzed conditions under which politics activates or pacifies people. A person acts when the law's effects concentrate on him. Conversely, people hold back and wait for others to act when the law's effects are diffuse.[21] Thus interest groups will form and influence laws whose benefits concentrate on a small group of people and whose costs fall on the general public. This is true regardless of whether the laws create a net gain or a net loss for society.[22]

Applying this logic to development, some causes of sustained growth benefit almost everyone and few people have reason to resist such reforms. More often, however, innovation disrupts technologies, organizations, and markets. Concentrated costs provoke active opposition by the losers from growth. Prussian industrial reforms in the first half of the nineteenth century illustrate the political problem of net gains with concentrated costs. In the feudal system of industry, manufacturers and guilds enjoyed exclusive licenses that limited competition. By restricting competition, these rights inhibited innovation and restrained production. The Prussian government eliminated these exclusive rights in 1810. All commentators agree that the move toward free markets for labor, capital, and land contributed to the economic rise of Prussia and Germany in the nineteenth century. However, the reform of 1810 was a net gain, not a Pareto gain. By abolishing monopoly rights, these reforms harmed the guilds and exclusive licensees. Consequently, the losers found ways to undermine the law and delay the effects of the reform for decades.[23]

Another historical example of net gains that provoke opposition comes from ending public access to natural resources such as grazing land, forests, and fishing grounds. Closing access to the public can stop depletion from overuse, at the cost of blocking some traditional users. Thus enclosures of common land provoked peasant revolts in Britain in the sixteenth century and the winners suppressed the losers by force.[24] Similarly, closing fishing zones in Indonesia in 1982 harmed ethnic and religious minorities.[25]

How can proponents of growth overcome opposition from concentrated losers other than by force?[26] The art of legal reform is to undermine opposition, especially by three strategies. First, buy off the losers through a more inclusive political bargain that gives them a share of the surplus from growth. Buy off might consist in subsidies, tax concessions, loans, or privileges. Giving everyone a share of the surplus transforms net gains into Pareto gains.[27]

Second, in an open economy, the winners and losers from disruptive innovation are unpredictable. A "veil of ignorance" descends when randomizing obscures the identity of future winners.[28] Growth with random winners and losers is like a game where two players each pay a dollar to draw straws and the winner gets five dollars. The game creates an *expected* gain for everyone in the statistical sense,[29] or an "expected Pareto gain," although someone will actually lose. To overcome opposition, allow more classes of people to compete in the innovation game, so more people expect to win. Sometimes a deep historical crisis can spread a veil of ignorance about who will benefit from fundamental reforms. Certainty about widespread benefits and uncertainty about the beneficiaries' identity can soften opposition to fundamental reforms.

Third, diffuse the costs of growth. When many people each bear a little of the costs of growth, their opposition will probably remain passive. Passing costs on to taxpayers or consumers pacifies opponents by diffusing the costs.[30]

Table 14.2 summarizes the three reform policies, which often combine and interact. Thus joining the World Trade Organization requires a country to lower its tariffs, which stimulates the economy as a whole and depresses some industries. To overcome opposition, the government may retrain impacted workers (buy off), pay for retraining with taxes (diffused costs), and increase uncertainty by lowering many tariffs all at once (randomize).

Table 14.2 Circumventing Opposition to Growth-Promoting Reforms

Policy	Consequence
Buy-off / Pareto gain	Convert opponents to supporters
Randomize /expected Pareto gain	Convert opponents to supporters
Concentrate benefits & diffuse costs	Activate supporters & pacify opponents

Logic of Reform in China

Some important historical examples illustrate growth-promoting reforms overcoming opposition. As described in chapter 2, Chinese reforms generated economic growth rates of roughly 9 percent per year for more than twenty-five years, reduced absolute poverty from 25 percent to less than 5 percent of the population, and increased life expectancy from sixty-four to more than seventy years.[31] This is a great historical achievement, in spite of environmental degradation and an authoritarian Chinese political system.[32] China proceeded by "dual-track development," which means a different approach for the traditional socialist sector of heavy industry and the free sector of light industry.[33] The socialist sector mostly continued under state planning in its traditional way. As socialist industries stagnated, workers, directors, and party members kept their jobs. Meanwhile China unleashed the free sector, especially in light industries. The free sector escaped bureaucratic controls and retained most of its profits. Under the dual-track system, the socialist sector remains shielded from competition and declines gradually, while the free sector grows quickly, raises national income, and creates better jobs for the young and adventurous.[34]

The dual-track system can be viewed as a political deal between the socialist and free sectors to share the benefits of growth. Instead of abruptly privatizing the socialist sector, the state gradually shrinks its size. Meanwhile, incomes increase rapidly for entrepreneurs and successful employees in the free sector. The Communist Party and the state bureaucracy keep taxes and bribes low enough so the people in the free sector who make the new wealth can keep most of it, as required by the property principle of innovation in chapter 5.

In the free sector, individuals often share ownership of firms with local and regional governments. Entrepreneurs thus include some state officials and officials in the Communist Party. People who acquire political power in the Communist Party and the state also have opportunities to acquire wealth. Communist and state officials support the free sector because they benefit from its growth. As mentioned in chapter 5, party chairman Deng Xiao Ping promoted reforms with the slogan, "For everyone to get rich, some must get rich first." This aphorism suggests that reforms will benefit everyone at uneven rates. Everyone gets a little richer as entrepreneurs get a lot richer first, including some state and communist officials. Since innovation is unpredictable, open competition among entrepreneurs naturally randomizes the winners and losers from growth. China offers its people an economic lottery with good odds for winning, so they are eager to play.

Like China, Pareto growth was the development strategy in Japan, Republic of Korea, Taiwan, Hong Kong, and Singapore. As they opened their markets to domestic and international competition in the 1950s, these countries spread the surplus so almost everyone gained. Instruments to spread wealth included pubic services such as schools, hospitals, and rural infrastructure; legal changes such as land reform and judicial independence; and opportunities open to talent. Many people in East Asia could start new businesses and rise in the social hierarchy. The state protected new wealth from predation and encouraged economic transformation without political disruption. The result approximates a Pareto gain with unequal distribution of the surplus.[35]

The Loser's Dilemma in Economic Growth

We explained how the Chinese government overcame opposition to growth-promoting reforms by using the three strategies shown in table 14.1. Why isn't every country like China? Why do governments reject growth-promoting reforms with Pareto gains or expected Pareto gains?[36] Reforms usually require a political bargain with an inherent obstacle that we call the "dictator's dilemma."

The general Augusto Pinochet staged a military coup against the elected government of Chile in 1973. He imprisoned and killed some of his opponents. After ruling the country as dictator for more than a decade, he eventually returned political offices to civilians in a process ending with his resignation as head of state in 1990. He remained head of the army until he stepped down from that position in 1998. In 2004 he was arrested and charged with various crimes. He died of natural causes in 2006 before courts resolved most criminal charges.

This story depicts a dilemma: an aging dictator wants to resign from power, but he fears prosecution for crimes. His only effective guarantee against prosecution is to retain the power that he wants to relinquish. The dictator's dilemma exemplifies a general problem of trust in politics. The proponents of growth-promoting reforms may want to buy off the opposition, but the winners may be unable to commit to paying off the losers. The winners cannot guarantee that the losers will continue to receive subsidies, retraining, tax breaks, and protection against competition, because the law preserves the right of politicians to change their minds. A future government can legally repeal almost any policy or law made by the current government.[37] The many who benefit from growth may want to buy off the few who oppose it, but the political bargain is not legally enforceable.

A historical example from India illustrates this problem. Before independence, India contained many small states where maharajas ruled and owned much of the land. Societies in which a small minority owns land and capital often have difficulties establishing legal rules that trigger entrepreneurial innovations broadly. Abolishing these small states had many advantages for India, including removing impediments to development. As compensation for the transfer of their states into the Union of India and their loss of tax income in 1947, the maharajas were granted a subsidy called the "Privy Purse." However, the subsidy was revoked in 1975.[38] In general, political commitment is especially problematic when the bargain extends for years, as with the Privy Purse. "Grandfather clauses" that preserve minority privileges look worse to the majority as memory fades of the bargain that created them.

Quieting Disagreements about Redistribution

Like the double trust dilemma of innovation, the dictator's dilemma is a problem of trust with no perfect solution.[39] The best solution aligns the interests of the reformers and the groups harmed by growth-promoting reforms. To align interests, the parties bargain and make agreements, but they are seldom enforceable legally. Political deals often need to encompass groups with a history of confrontation, not cooperation. The dictator's dilemma is more severe than the innovator's dilemma because politics involves more confrontation and less cooperation than business.[40] To avoid prosecution, Pinochet needed political cooperation from families whose members he had imprisoned and killed.

Trust has no magic solution, but a general strategy for building it in business also applies to politics. Two business executives agree to meet for lunch each Tuesday in order to discuss the possibility of merging their companies. Should they take turns paying the bill for lunch, or should each one buy his own lunch? Behavior at lunch may reveal something about their traits that predicts their behavior in a merger. By taking turns paying, each one will get to see whether the other party orders inexpensive wine when he pays and expensive wine the other party pays. As discussed in chapter 7, reciprocity requires commensurability of benefits given and received. After reciprocity in a lot of lunches, they may start to trust each other. The general strategy for building trust is to break reliance down into many small steps and spread them over time.

Like building trust over many lunches, security in property builds gradually over years. Thus judges in common law countries such as Canada and India create property law through the gradual accretion of precedents. Securing property requires quieting redistributive disputes. Quiet falls when most people accept the broad division of wealth that property law yields. As explained in chapter 5, entrepreneurs innovate when they believe that they will be able to keep much of what they make, so property law for growth must provide them with this security.

Once citizens feel secure against others taking their property, they can accept moderately adverse redistributions of wealth by taxes, government expenditures, statutes, and regulations. Conversely, a political agenda that redistributes too fast might destroy the trust necessary to secure property, and the reform might collapse like a sprinter who leans too far forward in the starting blocks. An historical contrast illustrates the difference. The French national assembly abolished feudalism in a sweeping reform in 1789. The peasants ceased to be serfs, and the reforms redistributed aristocrat lands among the peasants, which impoverished aristocrats. (Besides losing their wealth, many lost their heads.) The reforms created the framework for markets in land and also disrupted property rights and unleashed redistributive disputes. Production grew in the long run, but slowly. In 1851, agricultural productivity per worker in France still amounted only to 44 percent of the British level.[41]

In contrast, Prussia wanted modernization without revolution, so it crafted reforms that benefited both peasants and aristocrats. Under the feudal system serfs kept part of the harvest and gave the rest to their lords. Furthermore, each side was tied to the other by feudal bonds that restricted freedom of contract. To modernize the system, reforms from 1807 to 1822 applied a simple formula: the peasants had to buy themselves out of serfdom by transferring up to half of the land to the lords. Both sides were freed from feudal restrictions, including compulsory labor. Like France, Prussian land reform created a framework for markets in agricultural land and labor, but unlike France, Prussian reforms enlisted support of landlords and peasants by benefiting both of them. As a result, the transition was relatively smooth and production rose. Between 1800 and 1850, production per agricultural worker increased by 60 percent, and production per unit of arable farm land increased by 44 percent. In contrast, during the four previous centuries, agricultural productivity had barely advanced.[42]

The United States had a revolution like France and subsequent economic success like Prussia. Uncertainties created by revolution were quieted in the United States by a constitution that secured property through dividing political power.[43] As constitutional protection proved effective, redistributive disputes quieted and economic growth soared.

Conclusion

In 1513, Machiavelli wrote, "The reformer has enemies in all those who profit by the old order, and only lukewarm defenders in all those who would profit by the new."[44] Yet Central Europe, South Asia, and East Asia provide recent examples where legal reforms triggered spectacular economic results. Contrary to Machiavelli, the many who win from economic growth can often overcome the few who lose, and economic analysis shows how. Three principles provide a guide for activating support and pacifying opposition to progrowth reforms. First, a more comprehensive political bargain that uses subsidies, taxes, and privileges turns losers from economic growth into winners (Pareto gain), so opponents become supporters. Second, opening competition among entrepreneurs gives more people the possibility to win the innovation lottery (expected Pareto gain). Third, a more comprehensive bargain spreads losses, which pacifies opponents. Conversely, concentrating losses from economic growth on a small group of people activates their opposition. If they are powerful, they may prove Machiavelli right by frustrating policies that benefit the nation.

Spreading the gains to erode opposition to economic growth often requires future payoffs. In politics, future payoffs mostly rest on counterveiling power, not on legal guarantees. The loser's dilemma is that economic growth erodes the power by which he secures his share of future gains.

While this dilemma has no perfect solution, something can be done. Doing something requires evolving institutions, not just enacting laws. Laws and social norms must braid into institutions that strengthen each other like the strands in a rope. Trust develops from a history of cooperation and fair competition. By solving trust problems, law provides the framework for economic innovation to end the poverty of nations.

Chapter 15
Legalize Freedom—Conclusion

Sustained growth occurs through business ventures that innovate. Launching a venture poses a problem of trust between innovators with new ideas and financiers with capital (the double trust dilemma of development). To create trust, an effective legal framework insures that the creators of wealth can keep much of it (the property principle for innovation), people can commit to keeping their promises (the contract principle for coordination), and entrepreneurs can enter most lines of business and choose their firm's organization from a menu of legal templates (principle of organizational liberty). Property, contracts, and corporate law provide the legal framework to overcome distrust and launch innovative business ventures.

An old disagreement between right and left animates debate about the economy's legal framework: to what extent should the state regulate markets? This debate misses the main point about growth in developing countries. Successful deregulation presupposes effective property, contract, and corporate law. Without this legal framework, deregulation causes disarray and violence. With this legal framework, many regulations are unnecessary and repealing them unburdens business transactions. Economic freedom consists in the legal framework for markets and the absence of unnecessary regulatory burdens. The first cause of economic growth is *legalizing* economic freedom—that is, creating effective property, contract, and corporate law, and repealing unnecessary regulations.

Legalizing freedom releases the energies of entrepreneurs and allows innovation to take its creative, unpredictable path. Each innovation creates business secrets, private information brings extraordinary profits to the innovator, extraordinary profits attract imitators, imitators decipher the secrets, and the innovator's profits return to ordinary. At the end, when the innovation disseminates, the nation is more productive and wealthier, and the stage is set for the next innovation. By this process, nations become rich.

Another disagreement between right and left concerns the state's ability to promote economic growth. This debate confuses leadership and competition. Innovators with novel ideas disclose them to a few investors in order to finance their development. Private investors decide which innovations to finance based on *private* information, so their plans remain secret from competitors. In contrast, state officials using public funds should ideally decide which innovations to finance based on *public* information, so they can explain and defend their decisions to the citizens. Private investors who use private information to pick winning firms in the growth race can do better on average than state officials who pick winning firms based on public information. When state officials try to speed growth by reallocating capital among firms, they usually slow it down. Instead of picking winners, the state should provide equal opportunity for firms to compete in the growth race, like FIFA provides equal opportunity for football teams to compete in the World Cup. To promote economic growth, the state should provide the rules for competition, not pick the winners.

Besides legalizing freedom, much remains for the state to do, such as supplying domestic and international security (police and military), infrastructure and town planning (roads, harbors, airports, electricity, telecommunications, industrial zones), education (primary schools, secondary schools, universities), basic research (scientific laboratories, research grants), environmental protection (pollution taxes, marketable pollution rights, restrictions on hazardous chemicals), and poverty relief (social security, unemployment benefits, medical care). In addition, the state should use rising tax revenues from economic growth to benefit the residual poor whose incomes lag behind rising wages.

Another political disagreement between right and left concerns fairness and equality: how much inequality is fair? This debate misses the main point about the welfare of people in developing countries. A growing economy lifts workers out of poverty by increasing wages. Wages are higher in wealthy countries primarily because people are more productive, not because they are more equal. The first justification of inequality is to increase the welfare of people by making them more productive. Theories of fairness must build on this fact, not disregard it.

The social justification of inequality resembles patents. A patent creates a temporary monopoly that raises the price paid by consumers. Consumers lose by paying more for a good while its patent lasts, but they gain from new inventions stimulated by patents. The permanent gain in welfare from faster innovation overtakes the temporary loss from higher prices. Similarly, when less equality temporarily lowers the wealth of the poorer classes in society, it is easily justifiable if they gain even more from faster innovation (overtaking theorem). Thus the Chinese economy surged after 1980 when entrepreneurs were allowed to keep more of the wealth that they created. Conversely, if more equality increases consumption by the poorer classes and also increases the rate of innovation, then equality is doubly justified. More equality apparently increased economic growth in northern Europe in the twentieth century when better education and health raised the productivity of workers. To improve human welfare, law and policy should decrease or increase equality as required to maximize growth in wealth and productivity.

Is more wealth an appropriate goal for society? This question also divides left and right. "Wealth" is *in*appropriate as a social goal if it excludes public goods, nonmaterial goods, and a better environment. In focusing on growth, the state must not fetishize partial measures of wealth like gross national product (GDP). Also, good growth is long run. Temporary growth that collapses from resource exhaustion is tragic, not merely inappropriate. With these qualifications, the hard question remains: is maximizing the rate of sustained growth in a comprehensive measure of wealth an appropriate social goal?

Wealth, which almost everyone craves, is a means, not an end like happiness, goodness, holiness, beauty, love, knowledge, or self-fulfillment. Wealth is a means to ends that include education, recreation, self-cultivation, and psychological health. We read a novel, we play football, we listen to opera, and we participate in psychotherapy. However,

economics refers to expenditures on a novel, football, opera, or psychotherapy as *consumption*, as if all these activities resemble eating food.
Food is important—people were hungry in China during the Cultural
Revolution but the recovery of law and the economy after 1980 restored
China's status as a culinary superpower. However, people do more than
eat. The language of consumption falsely suggests that growth is a pie-
eating contest whose prize is another pie.

Economics has a good reason for applying "consumption" to household
expenditures on different kinds of things. Each person usually thinks that
he knows best how to spend his own money to achieve his ends, just like
he knows best how to drive. People do not welcome unsolicited advice on
what to buy or how to drive. (In Berkeley, where health food is a religion,
a stranger standing in line at the grocery store once critiqued the items in
Mrs. Cooter's shopping basket.) Freedom to spend your money as you see
fit is a basic liberty. Out of respect for individual liberty, many economists
feel that they should tell people how to make wealth, not how to spend it.

A long tradition in economics limits its claims to expertise about
what people ought to buy. Besides respect for individual liberty, this tradition has several other strands. Some economists think that values are
personal tastes like hating mustard and loving ketchup. Similarly, some
economists think that satisfying one want is as good as another, rather
like some utilitarians think that one pleasure is as good as another.[1] If
values reduce to personal tastes, wants, or pleasures, there is not much
to debate about values.

By explaining how to increase a nation's wealth, economists advise
a nation on how to get what its citizens want, without discussing what
people ought to want. Not all economists agree with this approach. Some
economists think that their subject should advise people on the uses of
wealth. People often buy the wrong thing, like uncomfortable shoes, and
regret it later. Many people use wealth in ways that defeat their own ends,
like buying love. A few people fetishize wealth, like craving gold's glitter.
Nations pursue destructive policies, like leveling beautiful mountains in
West Virginia to rip out the coal. Given the likelihood of error and weakness, citizens must struggle to make good choices. To guide choice, intellectuals should debate about how to spend money. This is part of the larger
debate about what is truly valuable. Economists disagree about whether

debate about values belongs inside or outside of their subject. Some economists enter the fray and others observe coolly from a distance.

An older generation of economists approached the problem of values differently from modern economists.[2] "Material welfare" refers to the benefits of food, clothing, shelter, and health. Once material needs are met, most people turn to higher needs such as education, recreation, and cultivation. More wealth enables people to progress up a scale of values. In this older understanding, the economic critique of values especially concerns the lower levels of the hierarchy of wants. Economists can know a lot about material needs that everyone has. Thus the cost-benefit techniques that economists use to critique public expenditures work well for basic goods like food, shelter, health, and primary education. Disagreements about values seldom vitiate the conclusions. Economists can know a lot less about immaterial needs, which pose many interesting value questions that economists do not address. Thus cost-benefit techniques provoke more disagreements about value that vitiate their conclusions when applied to public expenditures on haute cuisine, luxury condominiums, cosmetic surgery, higher education, culture, or religion. Cost-benefit techniques do not displace humanistic traditions in disputes about sophisticated food, tasteful architecture, liberal education, support for the opera, or maintenance of cathedrals.

This book follows the long tradition of dividing intellectual labor between making wealth and spending it. It concerns how a nation can get wealthy, not the uses it should make of its wealth. Enthusiasm for increasing the sustained rate of growth in a comprehensive measure of wealth, however, does not imply approval of all of its uses. Many uses of wealth are mistaken, callous, crude, degraded, irresponsible, or destructive, but the critique of the uses of wealth is not a subject of this book.

Does democracy cause economic growth? Again, the debate is confused. Democracy's effect on economic growth depends on an intervening variable—the strength of private and business law. Democracy can cause political instability that disrupts the economy by weakening private and business law. In these circumstances, a dictator can sometimes increase economic growth by increasing political stability. That is what happened in Chile after 1973 when a bloody coup by General Pinochet overthrew the democratically elected socialist President Allende. South Korea and

Taiwan also achieved high growth rates under dictatorship. Reversing the direction of change, a transition from dictatorship to democracy promotes economic growth when it strengthens private and business law. This happened in Chile after 1990 when Pinochet transferred power to a democratically elected government that Chileans thought would last. South Korea and Taiwan also followed the pattern of growth under dictatorship that was extended after transitioning to democracy.

What about reversed causation? Does economic growth cause democracy? Economic innovation requires developing new ideas that especially come from educated people. Economic freedom and educated workers create a cascade of innovations that sustain growth. The experience of economic freedom and the advantages of competition in business create a demand for it in politics. As education improves and people experience economic freedom, governments may need competitive elections to sustain belief in their legitimacy. This fact partly explains why Taiwan and South Korea transitioned from dictatorship to democracy.

Almost everyone benefits from growth, but some lose relative to others, and a few lose absolutely. The losers may be strategically placed to obstruct reforms. Pacifying them requires credible political deals to pay them off by redistributing wealth. With redistribution, everyone can share in the gains from growth (Pareto gain). Credibility is hard to achieve in politics because governments are so free to change their minds. As a group loses relative wealth, it also loses political power, which diminishes its ability to protect its wealth. The loser's dilemma in economic growth is a trust problem that law can ameliorate.

We have sketched law's role in ending the poverty of nations. If the obstacles seem overwhelming, the benefits are more so. Relative to sustained growth, nothing else is significant for lifting nations out of poverty. If most people appreciated that 2 percent growth for a century increases wealth by seven times, and 10 percent increases wealth by almost fourteen thousand times, their desire to make laws for growth would be irresistible.

Notes

Preface

1. Coase arguably inaugurated modern law and economics by providing the first demonstration that economic theory, as opposed to economic thought, was useful for analyzing property and contract law, not just for analyzing, say, antitrust or tax law. See R. Coase, "The Problem of Social Cost," *Journal of Law and Economics* 3 (1960): 1–44. Law and economics subsequently emerged as a specialization with its own university courses in the 1980s in the top U.S. law schools. It now possesses good textbooks, monographs, and specialized journals.

2. The tradition of growth theory represented by Solow (1969) contains no institutions and says nothing about the causes of innovation. Consequently, it is not useful for law and development economics. Newer and relatively undeveloped theories of endogenous growth are useful to law and economic development.

Chapter 1: It's about the Economy

1. Angus Maddison, *The World Economy: A Millennial Perspective* (Paris: Development Center of OECD. He used 1990 dollars as the base. See further discussion of his findings in chapter 2.

2. "Perhaps the eradication of poverty—underway for the first time in history, and when only two countries on earth are formally committed to socialism—will serve to confirm his [Schumpeter's] theory that growth happens at the hands of individual, risk-taking entrepreneurs, unmolested and lightly taxed by government, and that the more of them we have the better off everyone will be." Carl

229

J. Schramm, "Economics and the Entrepreneur," *Claremont Review of Books* 8.2 (2008): 1–7, at 7.

3. This account is based on R. Harris, "Law, Finance and the First Corporations," in *Global Perspectives on the Rule of Law*, ed. James Heckman, Robert L. Nelson, and Lee Cabatingan (London: Routledge, 2009).

4. The joint stock company has earlier origins. In the Middle Ages, the republic of Venice monopolized trade with Alexandria, through which the products of Asia flowed. The Venetians improved a legal form from classical Roman times (*fraterna compagnia*). In case of a loss of a ship, every merchant lost a share instead of one merchant losing everything. Commercial risk spreading was a crucial condition for the rise of capitalism. See H. W. Sinn, "Social Insurance, Incentives, and Risk-taking," *International Tax and Public Finance* 3 (1996): 259–280. In the seventeenth century, the English and Dutch greatly improved this form by allowing different parties to have different numbers of shares and allowing the owner of a share to sell it to others. Marketable shares are very different from earlier forms like partnerships, as explained in chapter 7.

5. We distinguish innovations into technology, organization, and markets. Joseph Schumpeter distinguished a new good, a new method of production, a new organization, and a new market. Since technological innovations yield new goods and methods, his categories resemble ours. However, he adds a fifth type: new sources of raw materials. We omit his fifth type because, unlike ideas, resources are exhaustible. In general, our theory of innovation draws heavily on Schumpeter, especially his idea of entrepreneurs creatively disrupting equilibria. See Joseph A. Schumpeter, *The Theory of Economic Development: An Inquiry into Profits, Capital, Credit, Interest, and the Business Cycle*, translated from the German by Redvers Opie (Cambridge, MA: Harvard University Press, 1936).

6. William Easterly, *The Elusive Quest for Growth: Economists' Adventures and Misadventures in the Tropics* (Cambridge, MA: MIT Press, 2001).

7. These are hypothetical examples inspired by real cases known to the authors.

8. As chief executive of the investment banking firm Goldman Sachs, Paulson advocated "self-regulation" to comply with international banking protocols known as "Basel II." Self-regulation allowed investment banks to sharply increase their ratio of debt to equity ("leverage"). The result was extreme risk taking, which yielded vast bonuses to executives in the short run and the collapse of the investment banks in the long run. Banks like Goldman Sachs, however, profited from the bailout directly by holding bonds and stocks in companies receiving bailout funds, and also indirectly by using their intimate knowledge of government officials to predict the firms that the government would bail out so that they could invest in them.

9. The champion of this view in development economics is Amartya Sen, as two quotes suggest. "Economic growth cannot be sensibly treated as an end in itself. Development has to be more concerned with enhancing the lives we lead and the freedoms we enjoy." *Development as Freedom* (New York: Knopf, 1999), 14. "The challenge of development . . . is to improve the quality of life. Especially in the world's poor countries, a better quality of life generally calls for higher incomes— but it involves much more. It encompasses as ends in themselves better education,

higher standards of health and nutrition, less poverty, a cleaner environment, more quality of opportunity, greater individual freedom, and a richer cultural life." World Bank, *World Development Report 1991* (New York: Oxford University Press, 1991).

10. More strictly speaking, "income" is a flow and "wealth" is a stock. Thus wealth accumulates by earning more income than is consumed.

11. Note that governments supply many nonmarket goods, and GDP measures their value by their cost (e.g., salaries paid to civil servants), not by their benefits to the citizens. Cost-benefit analysis can measure some of these nonmarket values more convincingly. To measure the value of nonmarket goods, economists try to find out how much people would pay for them if they had to pay, given that they don't have to pay. This can cause a measurement maelstrom, so national accounting limits its use of cost-benefit analysis.

12. From Barrett Strong's hit song "Money (That's What I Want)" of 1959, and the Beatles' "Money Can't Buy Me Love" of 1964.

13. B. S. Frey and A. Stutter, "What Can Economists Learn from Happiness Research?" *Journal of Economic Literature* 40 (2002): 402–435.

Chapter 2: The Economic Future of the World

1. A. Maddison, *Monitoring the World Economy, 1820–1992* (Paris: OECD, 1995), *The World Economy: A Millennial Perspective* (Paris: OECD Development Centre, 2001), and *The World Economy: Historical Statistics* (Paris: OECD Development Centre, 2003).

2. Data for 1870, Felipe A.M de La Balze, *Remaking the Argentine Economy* (New York: Council on Foreign Relations Press, 1995). Data for 2004, A. Heston, R. Summers, and B. Aten, *Penn World Table Version 6.2* (Philadelphia: Center for International Comparisons of Production, Income and Prices, University of Pennsylvania, September 2006).

3. Some low- and high-growth countries are depicted in the following table.

Accumulated Growth of Per Capita GDP in Percent for Selected Countries from 1993 to 2003*

Low growth		High growth	
Congo, Rep.of	−32.5	China	133.2
Sierra Leone	−21.6	Ireland	97.8
Zimbabwe	−20.7	India	55.4
Ukraine	−11.8	Korea, Rep. of	54.4
Uganda	−11.8	Poland	50.3
Paraguay	−9.9	Taiwan	46.9
Niger	−4.2	Malaysia	46.6
Argentina	−3.5	Finland	41.6

(*continued*)

Accumulated Growth of Per Capita GDP in Percent for Selected Countries from 1993 to 2003* (continued)

Low growth		High growth	
Cote D'Ivoir	−3.2	Chile	38.9
Ecuador	−2.6	Hungary	36.4
Honduras	−1.3	Botswana	38.1

*Calculated from Alan Heston, Robert Summers, and Bettina Aten, Penn World Tables, Center for International Comparisons of Production, Income, and Prices (Philadelphia: University of Pennsylvania, 2006), table 6.2.

4. In economic jargon, cultures are equilibria that separate when wealth diverges.

5. GDP per capita is the most common measure of income per capita used by economists, but not the only one.

6. GDP per capita in sub-Saharan Africa has declined since 1974, roughly by the order of 20 percent. In 1974 it was US$600 (at constant prices of 2000) per capita. It declined to US$470 in 1994 and since then increased slowly to US$510 in 2003. See World Bank, *World Development Indicators 2005* (Washington, DC: World Bank, 2005).

7. Thus Botswana's income per capita grew 38 percent in the decade between 1993 and 2003. Calculated from Heston, Summers, and Aten, *Penn World Tables 6.2, 2006.*

8. These are brilliantly depicted in Chinua Achebe's novels, *Things Fall Apart* and *No Longer at Ease.*

9. After 1989, some of the formerly communist countries—Poland, the Czech Republic, Slovakia, Slovenia, Hungary, Latvia, Estonia, and Lithuania—committed to a path resulting in full membership in the European Union in 2004. More recently, Bulgaria and Rumania completed a similar process and joined the EU. Russia, Belarus, Georgia, Moldova, and Ukraine did not commit to a path leading to EU membership.

10. This estimate in the World Bank Development Indicators attempts to encompass the illegal, underground economy, which is large and hard to measure. Subsequently, Russia has somewhat, presumably because the country is more lawful and international prices of minerals have increased.

11. The pattern in figure 2.3 is presumably correct, but the numbers require cautious interpretation. Under communism, producers overstated production in order to meet the targets set for them by the state. Under capitalism, producers understate production in order to avoid paying taxes.

12. "The peculiar problem of eastern Europe is that the state of its capital stock by far exceeds the development of its institutional environment." A. Rapaczynski, "The Roles of the State and the Market in Establishing Property Rights," *Journal of Economic Perspectives* 10 (1996): 87–103, at 91.

13. A more accurate term than *property rights* is *use rights*. Soviet officials had stable, predictable powers to use particular resources in particular ways, including

socialist firms, although not necessarily the right to sell them. See A. Sajo, "Diffuse Rights in Search of an Agent: A Property Rights Analysis of the Firm in the Socialist Market Economy," *International Review of Law and Economics* 10 (1990): 41–60. In Russia, contracts between enterprises were enforced through "arbitration courts." For a series of empirical papers on them, see Kathryn Henley's publications at http://law.wisc.edu/profiles/pubs.php?iEmployeeID=143.

14. Poland, the Czech Republic, Slovakia, Slovenia, Hungary, Latvia, Estonia, and Lithuania joined in 2004. More recently, Bulgaria and Rumania completed a similar process and joined the EU.

15. Russia, Belarus, Georgia, Moldova, and Ukraine.

16. Azerbaijan, Kazakhstan, Kyrgyzstan, Tajikistan, Turkmenistan, and Uzbekistan.

17. Rising world oil prices were probably the most important factor in Russia, but not in Belarus, Georgia, Moldova, and Ukraine.

18. We discuss the "Washington Consensus" and privatization in chapter 11.

19. Yingyi Qian, "How Reform Worked in China," University of California, Berkeley, Discussion paper, 2001, 1–63.

20. C. J. Dahlman, Luce Professor of International Affairs and Information of Georgetown University, predicted that China would catch up with the United States in national income in 2014. The prediction was made at the Chinese Reform Summit, National Development and Reform Commission (NDRC), Beijing Diaoyutai State Guesthouse, July 12–13, 2005. Dahlman extended existing trends, allowed for a modest slowing of Chinese growth rates. This prediction compares income of the two nations based on purchasing power parity, not exchange rates, which makes a significant difference.

21. George T. Abed, "Unfulfilled Promise, Why the Middle East and North Africa Region Has Lagged in Growth and Globalization," *Finance and Development* 40 (2003): 1.

22. The task is to estimate simultaneous equations in several variables. Determining causation requires breaking down aggregate variables like GDP and the Rule of Law Index into smaller components, notably the protection of property, enforcement of contracts, and effective business law. Given small units, the next step is to examine the timing of events and exploit statistically the fact that causes precede their effects in time. For example, one could compare the dates for the dissolution of communes in different regions of China and the increase in agricultural production. If the former is the cause of the latter, then the former should precede the latter in each region.

Chapter 3: The Double Trust Dilemma of Development

1. Economists call this fact "Arrow's paradox of information." A central insight of the economics of information is that one party to a transaction often knows more than the other but cannot authenticate this fact. Thus the seller may

know that a good is high quality but proving this fact to the buyer can be problematic. For an early exploration of this problem of asymmetric information, see Kenneth J. Arrow, "The Value of and Demand for Information," in *Decision and Organization*, ed. C. B. McGuire and R. Radner (New York: North-Holland, 1972), chapter 6.

2. How can an investor, who puts his money under the control of a manager, write a contract so that the manager profits most when the investor profits most? This is the "principal-agent problem." Much contemporary research in finance builds on an earlier literature addressing this problem. The "double trust dilemma" is a "principal-agent game with double sided moral hazard." For a general discussion of legal incentive involving asymmetrical information, see Edmund W. Kitch, "The Law and Economics of Rights in Valuable Information," *Journal of Legal Studies* 9 (1980): 683–723.

3. The son and daughter were to marry if peace were preserved. Alas, Theoderich allegedly plotted against Geiserich, so Theoderich's daughter was mutilated and sent back to her father.

4. Lance Williams, "How a 'Visionary' Raised—and Lost—a Fortune," *San Francisco Chronicle*, December 7, 2008, available at http://www.sfgate.com/cgi-bin/article.cgi?f=/c/a/2008/12/07/MNIK147QU3.DTL.

5. For a recent application, see Bernard Black and Ronald Gilson, "Does Venture Capital Require an Active Stock Market?" *Journal of Applied Corporate Finance* 11 (winter 1999): 36–48.

6. Beyond contracts, flourishing private finance leads to specialized laws for debt collection, bonds, and banking.

7. Each animal begins life as a single cell containing genetic instructions for how to grow into a complex organism. For animals in different species with a common evolutionary ancestor, the path of individual growth suggests the older, evolutionary forms found in the fossil record. While the pattern of individual growth does not strictly recapitulate the evolution of the species, comparing them provides useful clues about the genes that control the development of individuals and species. For a book that finds the origin of the human fetus in fish, see Neil Shubin, *Your Inner Fish: A Journey into the 3.5-Billion-Year History of the Human Body* (New York: Pantheon Books, 2008).

8. See P. M. Deane, *The First Industrial Revolution* (Cambridge: Cambridge University Press, 1965), summary on 166–167. For financing of key eighteenth-century inventions by name, see 165.

9. See chapter 8 for details on finance in different countries.

10. To deter a rational person from doing wrong, the expected sanction should equal or exceed the person's gain from wrongdoing. The expected sanction equals the probability of the sanction times its magnitude. A sanction worth $100 applied with probability ½ will deter wrongdoing by a rational person whose gain does not exceed $50 (assuming risk neutrality). Applying the sanction is seldom necessary.

11. B. Malinowski, *Crime and Custom in Savage Society* (New York: Harcourt Brace, 1926).

12. Lisa Bernstein, "Opting Out of the Legal System: Extralegal Contractual Relations in the Diamond Industry," *Journal of Legal Studies* 21 (1992): 115–157.

13. China has a dual system of government. For each office in the state—mayor, legislator, judge, administrator—there is a parallel office in the Communist Party. State officials have discretion in routine affairs, but the Communist Party official has final say in important matters.

Chapter 4: Make or Take

1. A. O. Hirschman argues that intellectuals in the eighteenth century developed and promoted the ideal of capitalism so that trade might pacify the fierce aristocratic virtue of honor and save the nations from war. In this chapter's language, extolling making might cause less taking. See *The Passions and the Interests* (Princeton: Princeton University Press, 1977).

2. Mikhail Khodorkovsky, the richest of the gangster capitalists, was arrested in 2005, sentenced to nine years in prison, and the Russian state expropriated his company. Khodorkovsky's opponents believe that he was guilty of criminal actions related to the privatization of state assets during the 1990s. Khodorkovsky's supporters, however, believe that Vladimir Putin, the Russian president, retaliated against Khodorkovsky for his support of political groups that opposed the government.

3. But not all—the 2006 list includes the Queen of England and Fidel Castro.

4. The Zimbabwe constitution prohibited the state from taking land without compensation, so Mugabe amended the constitution. The amendment shifted the responsibility for compensating white farmers from Zimbabwe to its former colonial power, Britain. In the end, no one compensated the white farmers, most of them were robbed and exiled, and some of them were murdered. For a popular memoir of these events, see Peter Godwin, *When a Crocodile Eats the Sun: A Memoir of Africa* (New York: Little, Brown, 2007). For facts about compensation, see E. Pan, *Africa: Mugabe's Zimbabwe* (New York: Council on Foreign Relations, 2005), available at http://www.cfr.org/publication/7723/africa.html.

5. The same rationales are given for tariffs. For a survey with examples of goods assembled in developing countries whose imported components cost more than importing the assembled good, see Henry J. Bruton, "A Reconsideration of Import Substitution," *Journal of Economic Literature* 36 (1998): 903–936. Also see our discussion in chapter 13.

6. For an international audience like the readers of this book, prices in U.S. dollars are more transparent than local currency. To compare living standards, however, wages should be compared according to their local purchasing power.

7. This is the "emiseration hypothesis." Besides declining wages, Marx also predicted declining profits and rising production. If the workers and the capitalists

are getting poorer, where is rising production going? Noting the problem, Robert Solow remarked dryly that Marx made one prediction too many.

8. Here is how it works. The employer pays the seamstress her wage and sells her product. If her product exceeds her wage, the employer earns a profit from her labor. Competition will prevent him from doing so. If her employer pays her a wage that is below the value of her product, another employer can profit by inducing her to change jobs at a slightly higher wage. Competition among employers should bid up her wage until it approaches her marginal value product, which is $10 per week.

9. For a Marxist theory that focuses on monopoly power, see P. A. Baran and P. M. Sweezy, *Monopoly Capital: An Essay on the American Economic and Social Order* (New York: Monthly Review Press, 1966).

10. UN Subcommission on the Promotion and Protection of Human Rights, "The Enslavement of Dalit and Indigenous Communities in India, Nepal, and Pakistan through Bondage," February 2001.

11. For an summary of economic theories of discrimination as market imperfections, see chapter 14 of Robert Cooter's *The Strategic Constitution* (Princeton: Princeton University Press, 2000),

12. The increase in production from hiring additional labor or renting additional capital has a determinant answer expressed by the "production function" in microeconomics, which is often written $y = f(l, c)$. In contrast, investing resources in innovation yields an increase in production that is imperfectly predictable.

13. Forty-four percent of U.S. businesses started in the 1990s still existed four years afterward. See A. E. Knap, "Survival and Longevity in the Business Employment Dynamics Data," U.S. Department of Labor, Bureau of Labor Statistics, 2005. The number given by Dun and Bradstreet is 37% as cited in "Some of the Reasons Why Business Fail and How to Avoid Them," *Entrepreneur Weekly* 36, March 10, 1996.

14. Technically minded readers will recognize that a new product creates a surplus for consumers on the inframarginal purchases, but not on the marginal purchase.

15. Forbes magazine annually estimates the wealth of the world's richest people and ranks them.

16. A fund of $50 billion, if managed conservatively like a university endowment, might yield 4 percent per year, or $2 billion. You need to spend $3,815 per minute to use it up in a year.

17. Three of the five started life relatively poor and made all of their wealth. Two of the five started life with modest wealth and then added vastly to it. Forbes magazine's list of people with at least $1 billion in personal wealth in 2006 consisted of 746 people, most of whom made their money through business.

18. All the world's fisheries are beyond the maximum sustainable yield. For theory and data, see Tom Tietenberg, *Environmental and Natural Resource Economics*, 3d ed. (New York: Harper Collins, 1992).

Chapter 5: The Property Principle for Innovation

1. OECD, *China in the Global Economy; Income Disparities in China: An OECD Perspective* (Paris: OECD, 2004).

2. *World Development Indicators 2008* (Washington, DC: World Bank, 2008); and B. Milanovic, "Explaining the Increase in Inequality during Transition," *Economics of Transition* 7.2 (1999): 299–341, esp. 319.

3. P. Krugman, "The Myth of Asia's Miracle," *Foreign Affairs* 73.6 (Nov./Dec. 1994): 62 –78.

4. For a survey P. Honohan, "Financial Development, Growth, and Poverty: How Close Are the Links?" Development Research Group and Financial Sector Operations and Policy Department, World Bank Working Paper No. 3203, World Bank, Washington, DC, 2004. Also see S. Claessens and E. Perotti, "Finance and Inequality: Channels and Evidence," *Journal of Comparative Economics* 35 (2007): 748–773.

5. Empirical studies have borne out negative correlations between growth and inequality. See cross-country studies by A. Alesina and D. Rodrik, "Distribution Politics and Economic Growth," *Quarterly Journal of Economics* 109 (1994): 465–490; Torsten Persson and Guido Tabellini, "Is Inequality Harmful for Growth?" *American Economic Review* (June 1994), 84.3: 600–621; R. Perotti, "Growth, Income Distribution, and Democracy: What the Data Say," *Journal of Economic Growth* 1 (1996): 149–187; and Ricardo Hausmann and Michael Gavin, "Securing Stability and Growth in a Shock-Prone Region: The Policy Challenges for Latin America," in *Securing Stability and Growth in Latin America,* ed. R. Hausmann and Helmut Reisen (Paris: OECD, 1996), 23–64. In contrast to these studies, a positive impact of inequality on growth was found by K. J. Forbes, "A Reassessment of the Relationship between Inequality and Growth," *AER* 90.4 (2000): 869–887.

6. The next chapter has more on dissolving China's communes.

7. Given weak capital markets, Chinese farmers had to invest in their farms from retained earnings. Some economic theory suggests that an equal division of land probably enabled the best farmers to earn and invest more than an unequal division. For the proposition that an equal initial division of property is efficient in the presence of weak capital markets, see Yeon-Koo Che and Ian Gale, "Market versus Non-Market Assignment of Initial Ownership," Berkeley Law and Economics Workshop, 2007.

8. "Inequality of wealth leads to the inequality of influence, which in turn subverts the impartiality of institutions, weakens property rights, and leads finally to reduced growth." Hilton Root, *Capital and Collusion: Political Logic of Global Economic Development* (Princeton: Princeton University Press, 2006), 33.

9. The average value for the rule-of-law index (a number between -2 and 2) is –0.46 for the 24 counties with the highest income inequality (Gini coefficient higher than 0.5). In contrast, it is 0.1 for all other 100 countries in the sample. There are only some rare countries, which have combined extreme income inequality

with the rule of law, namely, Botswana, Namibia, South Africa, and Chile. For information about the rule-of-law index, see D. Kaufmann, A. Kraay, and M. Mastruzzi, "Governance Matters III: Governance Indicators for 1996–2002," World Bank Policy Research Working Paper 3106, World Bank, Washington, DC, 2003; for information about the Gini coefficient, see *Human Development Report* various years, 1983–2003 (New York: UN Development Program, 2005). For a valuable analysis of the rule of law in development, see Michael J. Trebilcock and Ronald J. Daniels, *Rule of Law Reform and Development: Charting the Fragile Path of Progress* (Cheltenham, UK: Edward Elgar, 2008).

10. K. Hoff and Joseph Stiglitz, "After the Big Bang? Obstacles to the Emergence of the Rule of Law in Post-Communist Societies," NBER Working Paper No. 9282, National Bureau of Economic Research, Cambridge, MA, 2002.

11. T. Eggertssen, *Imperfect Institutions, Possibilities, and Limits to Reform* (Ann Arbor: University of Michigan Press, 2005), see chapter 7, "Why Iceland Starved," esp. 99.

12. D. Acemoglu and J. A. Robinson, "Persistence of Power, Elites, and Institutions," NBER Working Paper No. 12108, National Bureau of Economic Research, Cambridge, MA, 2006; Stanley L. Engerman and Kenneth L. Sokoloff, "Factor Endowments, Institutions, and Differential Growth Paths among New World Economies," in *How Latin America Fell Behind*, ed. Stephen Haber (Stanford: Stanford University Press, 1997), 260–296. D. Acemoglu, S. Johnson, and J. A. Robinson, "The Colonial Origins of Comparative Development: An Empirical Investigation," *American Economic Review* 91.5 (2001), 1369–1401. See also F. Bourguignon and T. Verdier," Oligarchy, Democracy, Inequality, and Growth," *Journal of Development Economics* 62 (2000): 285–313. Theses authors model individual political power as a function of individual wealth and education variables.

13. To be precise, he first calculates wages in terms of grams of silver per day, and then deflates by prices of a basket of consumer goods with roughly 70 percent food (mostly food). He used this consumer basket in 1820 to define the poverty line. Naturally, the data gets much better in the nineteenth and twentieth centuries, so we have more confidence in the more recent results.

14. R. Allen, "The Great Divergence in European Wages," available at www .economics.ox.ac.uk/Members/robert.allen/WagesFiles/wagesnew2.pdf.

15. Ibid.

16. For example, when the business cycle turns down and causes unemployment, the ratio of capital to employed workers rises, so labor productivity can rise. From the three Latin American countries shown in figure 4.3, slow growth in the region seems to have affected wages more negatively than other sources of income.

17. This section is based on a book manuscript on law and growth economics by Robert Cooter and Erin Edlin, parts of which can be read at "Overtaking," in *The American Illness: Essays on the Rule of Law*, ed. Frank Buckley (Yale University Press, forthcoming), and "Maximizing Growth vs. Static Efficiency or Redistribution," *Berkeley Law and Economics Working Paper* (Spring 2011).

18. Robert Nozick, *Anarchy, State, and Utopia* (New York: Basic Books, 1974).

19. L. B. Murphy and T. Nagel, *The Myth of Ownership: Taxes and Justice* (New York: Oxford University Press, 2002). While we do not agree with the thesis that ownership is a myth, we commend this book for a remarkable interweaving of philosophy and economics. They write

> Individual citizens don't own anything except through laws that are enacted and enforced by the state. Therefore, the issues of taxation are not about how the state should appropriate and distribute what its citizens already own, but about how it should allow ownership to be determined.

20. John Rawls, *A Theory of Justice* (Cambridge, MA: Harvard University Press, 1971).

21. This formulation of the motto, which is distilled from a longer paragraph, is from Robert Elegant, *Pacific Destiny: Inside Asia Today* (New York: Crown, 1990), 309.

22. Albert Hirschman formulated the "tunnel effect" in "The Changing Tolerance for Income Inequality in the Course of Economic Development," in *Essays in Trespassing* (Cambridge: Cambridge University Press, 1981).

23. T. Smeeding, "Poor People in Rich Nations: The United States in Comparative Perspective," *Journal of Economic Perspectives* 20.1 (2006): 69–90.

24. See table 4.1, "Poverty Headcount: Percentage of Population Living from Less than 2 Dollars a Day, 2001," *World Development Indicators* (Washington DC: World Bank, 2005).

25. Social justice theories focus on the state's role in redistribution, not the powerful role of family and charity in alleviating human suffering. Transfers within families, including bequests, exceed all other forms of transfers. In 2006 Warren Buffett committed to giving 85 percent of his wealth—roughly $37 billion—to the charity established by Bill Gates, whose mission is "bringing innovations in health and learning to the global community." This fact inspires a thought experiment: suppose that you wanted to find a cure for malaria, one of the world's great killers. You could either tax 100 percent of Buffett's $37 billion and give all of it to a government ministry to search for a cure, or you could allow Warren Buffet to organize the search for the cure by donating 85 percent of his wealth and keeping 15 percent for himself. Which alternative is more likely to find a cure for malaria?

26. Smeeding, "Poor People in Rich Nations."

27. We say "might" because economic growth extends across generations and the theory of Rawls does not encompass justice between different generations of people. Thus theorists quickly realized that innovation creates problems for the maximin principle. With innovation, future generations have an advantage over the present generation. If the present generation is worse off than future generations, the maximin principle authorizes the present generation to consume enough capital to exactly offset the advantage of innovation to future generations. Thus every generation is equal and society never gets richer. For various essays reconsidering Rawls, see E. S. Phelps, ed., *Economic Justice: Selected Readings* (Baltimore: Penguin Education, 1973).

Chapter 6: Keeping What You Make—Property Law

1. See Henk Hogeboom van Buggenum, Reviewing Hernando de Soto, *The Mystery of Capital—Why Capitalism Triumphs in the West and Fails Everywhere Else,* Foundation Teilhard De Chardin, Netherlands, 2005, available at http://www.teilhard dechardin.nl/book_soto.htm.

2. "Source List and Detailed Death Tolls for the Twentieth Century Hemoclysm," available at http://users.erols.com/mwhite28/warstat1.htm. For the history of the communes, see Justin Yifu Lin, "Collectivization and China's Agricultural Crisis, 1959–1961," *Journal of Political Economy* 98 (1961): 1228–1252.

3. For economic statistics on the collapse of the economy, see David Coltart, "A Decade of Suffering in Zimbabwe: Economic Collapse and Political Repression under Robert Mugabe," Center for Global Liberty and Prosperity, Cato Institute, Washington, DC, March 24, 2008.

4. See S. Berry, "Debating the Land Question in Africa," *Comparative Studies in Society and History* 44.4 (October 2002): 638–668. "Specific legislative instruments varied from one colony to another, but they conveyed a common message. From Senegal to Malawi, French and British authorities claimed that 'by right of conquest,' all 'vacant and ownerless land' belonged to the colonial state. Vast tracts of land were often judged 'vacant and ownerless' on the basis of cursory inspection or none at all, and then sold to European buyers."

5. This is an application of the general principle that market transactions move resources to the parties who value them the most.

6. Li Ping et al., "Land Reform and Tenure Security in China: History and Current Challenges," in *Legalising Land Rights,* ed. Janine M. Ubink, Andre J. Hoekema, and Willem J. Assies (Leiden, Netherlands: Leiden University Press, 2009), 409–434.

7. The Seven Years' War of 1756–63 left many Prussian provinces in ruins, especially Silesia. To hasten reconstruction, Silesia repealed prohibitions against the nobility mortgaging land, and an active credit market quickly emerged. As a result, Silesian agriculture reconstructed quickly, whereas other areas of Germany that retained feudal prohibitions reconstructed slowly. French intellectuals called the "Physiocrats" provided the intellectual basis for the Silesian reforms. In the eighteenth century, productivity gains in English agriculture outstripped French agriculture, and the Physiocrats explained the difference by better-developed agricultural markets in England compared to France. They attributed the difference in marketization partly to the law—England swept aside feudal constraints and state regulations that kept productivity low in France. For example, the traditional practice of dividing the crop between landlord and tenant according to a fixed percentage ("sharecropping") did not allow the party who invested in new capital to receive more of the increase in production. The Physiocrats prescribed a remedy: create free markets in rural land, labor, and agricultural products by ending state intervention and removing feudal constraints. (Besides favoring markets,

the Physiocrats believed in some oddly metaphysical theories about economic growth coming from agriculture and not industry.)

8. Japan's Land Revision Act of 1873 gave customary owners a secure legal title to land, replaced rice taxes owed to feudal lords with money taxes owed to the central government, and permitted sale, division, annexation, mortgage, and lease of land. Marketizing agriculture caused a surge in productivity that was part of the nineteenth century "Japanese miracle." Unfortunately, absentee landlords paid lower taxes than independent farmers, so ownership shifted from the latter to the former. See Y. Yamasaki and R. V. Andelson, *American Journal of Economics and Sociology* 59.5 (2000): 353–363, available at http://www.findarticles.com/p/articles/mi_m0254/is_5_59/ai_70738933.

9. Alain de Janvry, "The Role of Land Reform in Economic Development: Policies and Politics," *American Journal of Agricultural Economics* 63 (1981): 384–392. See table 2 for characteristics of land reform in twenty countries.

10. Table 2 in Csaba Csaki and Zvi Lerman, "Structural Change in the Farming Sectors in Central and Eastern Europe: Lessons for the EU Accession," Second World Bank/FAO Workshop, June 27–29, 1999, World Bank Technical Paper No. 465, World Bank, Washington, DC.

11. For example, consider this common sequence of events: a Jewish family owned property in Poland; the Nazis invaded and murdered the owners; after the defeat of the Nazis, non-Jews claimed the property; the communists subsequently took the property for the state. After the collapse of communism, the descendants of the Jewish and non-Jewish owners dispute about who is the rightful heir.

12. With a discount rate of 5 percent, the present value of $100 to be paid in 100 years is less than a dollar. So the present value of a 100-year lease on land is almost the same as the value of owning the land. Thus a person with a 100-year lease will make almost identical investment decisions as a land owner. However, to retain equivalence, the lease must be renewed frequently, so that each new buyer of the lease still has close to 100 years of rights to it. Use rights are often complex and change over time. Thus in 2007 China farmers were allowed to sublease, exchange, or transfer their land use rights, but only for agricultural uses and for no longer than 30 years. Thanks to Zhang Wei for providing these details.

13. "Successful programmes of property rights reform recognise the complexity and uniqueness of existing property environments." Karol Boudreaux and Paul Dragos Aligica, *Paths to Property: Approaches to Institutional Change in International Development* (London: Institute of Economic Affairs, 2007), 15.

14. Note that Papua New Guinea has a special class of land courts that may modernize customary ownership much like English common law evolved from family ownership of property in medieval times to individual ownership. As cited above, see R. Cooter, "Inventing Market Property: The Land Courts of Papua New Guinea," *Law and Society Review* 25 (1991): 759–801, and also R. Cooter, *Issues in Customary Land Law: Port Moresby, Papua New Guinea* (Canberra, Australia: Institute of National Affairs, 1989).

15. See Ibid.

16. T. N. Madan, *The Householder Tradition in Hindu Society: The Blackwell Companion to Hinduism* (New Delhi: Wiley-India, 2008). R. Mearns, "Access to Land in Rural India, Policy Issues and Options," World Bank Policy Research Working Paper 2123, World Bank, Washington, DC, 1999. Tribal land in India is often organized as a common and is difficult to sell and transfer but is often subject to illegal encroachment.

17. Throughout India a couple that marries can choose whether or not to apply to the state for the law of the "undivided Hindu family" for their property. The undivided Hindu family consists in all living members of the husband's bloodline. Opting into the law has tax advantages. However, all members of the undivided Hindu family must agree in order to pledge real estate as security for a loan, so mortgages are rare.

18. Interestingly, the study also found the converse—that more investment on the land causes more individual property rights. Individuals who want to invest in the land apparently influence government to strengthen their ownership rights. See T. Besley, "Property Rights and Investment Incentives: Theory and Evidence from Ghana," *Journal of Political Economy* 5 (1995): 903–937. For more evidence on this point, see Lee J. Alston, Gary D. Libecap, and Bernardo Mueller, *Titles, Conflict, and Land Use: The Development of Property Rights and Land Reform on the Brazilian Amazon Frontier* (Ann Arbor: University of Michigan Press, 1999).

19. When kinsmen help each other, each one needs to save less to protect against misfortune. Kinship acts like insurance, which reduces the need for a financial cushion.

20. In 1862 Congress gave railway companies ten square miles of land for every mile of track built on the transcontinental railway. Squatters often established homesteads before acquiring title, which created an economy outside the law's control. American law eventually imposed secure title and effective markets on all of the land, but the long process involved constant tension, occasional violence, spasmodic reversals, and many compromises. See D. de Soto, "Citadels of Dead Capital: What the Third World Must Learn from U.S. History," *Reason* (May 2001), available at http://reason.com/archives/2001/05/01/citadels-of-dead-capital. For an excellent comparison of how squatters became owners in the United States, Australia, and Brazil, see Lee J. Alston, Edwyna Harris, and Bernardo Mueller, "De Facto and De Jure Property Rights: Settlement and Land Conflict on the Australian, Brazilian, and U.S. Frontiers," Working paper presented at the The Ratio Research Colloquium on Property Rights, the Conditions for Enterprise and Economic Growth, Stockholm, Sweden, 2011.

21. Most seizures are by the poor, but wealthy people have also seized land in Latin America, such as the beaches of southern Peru and ranches in the Amazon.

22. F. Santinoni Vera, "The Social Function of Property Rights in Brazil," Latin American and Caribbean Law and Economics Association, Annual Meeting, Buenos Aires, May 19, 2006. Vera Nascimento, "Property Rights and Land Conflicts in

Brazil: The Case of the Mongangua's Growers Association," *Latin American Law and Caribbean Law and Economics Association*, Interlegis, Brasilia, May 25, 2007.

23. We are grateful to Luciano Benetti Timm, a Brazilian law and economics scholar, for information on land seizures, leases, and mortgages in Brazil.

24. Belgium has more than 70 percent. Thanks to Bruno Salama who found these numbers in the following sources: for countries other than Brazil: J. J. Swinnen, "Private Enforcement Capital and Contract Enforcement in Transition Countries," *American Journal of Agricultural Economics* 83.3: 686–690. For Brazil, Brazilian Institute of Geography and Statistics, "Census of 1996." Rental markets in Brazil cover 2.43 percent of land that is suitable for farming and 7.13 percent of all rural properties.

25. Workers with secure salaries such as state employees can obtain mortgages because a debtor's future income is the lender's primary security, not the value of the property purchased with the loan.

26. J. Saddi, "Creditor-Debtor Law in Brazil," Latin American and Caribbean Law and Economics Association, Annual Conference, Interlegis, Brasilia, Brazil, June 2007.

27. Sharecropping is a legal alternative. However, labor courts in Brazil may recharacterize sharecropping as an employment contract, which dramatically increases the taxes and social security payments due from the property's owner. Gabriel Buchmann, "Determinantes do Mau Funcionamento do Mercado de Arrendamento de Terras no Brasil," Applied Economics Research Institute, Catalogue No. 001.44 I59 06 IPEA 159-06, Brasilia, Brazil: IPEA, 2007. In addition, legal caps on the amount payable by sharecroppers create uncertainty over whether or not a state official will adjust the terms of the contract after it is made. The remaining alternative for a poor farmer is to sell his labor. Unfortunately, employment contracts in agriculture often do not work as well as sharecropping.

28. Cooter, "Inventing Market Property."

29. Thanks to Dr. Gesner Oliveira and Companhia de Saneamento Básico do Estado de São Paulo S.A (SABESP) for organizing Cooter's visit to the "Integrative Park" that SABESP is building on cleared land over the aqueduct.

30. Even with active real estate markets, however, housing the poor remains problematic. For analysis of housing the residual poor, see K. Deininger, "Land Policies for Growth and Poverty Reduction," World Bank Policy Research Report No. 26384, Washington, DC, World Bank, 2003.

31. The creditor wants the collateral's value to stay as high as the remaining debt. "Basically, the bank wants to ensure a rough balance between the value of the debt outstanding and the value remaining in the project, including the value of the collateral, at all times." O. Hart, *Firms, Contracts, and Financial Structure* (New York: Oxford University Press, 1995), 8–9. With liquid real estate markets, an entrepreneur can mortgage her house or apartment to invest in her business. Or she can borrow money to buy an apartment or house, which frees other funds to invest in her business.

32. The "spread" refers to the difference between the interest rate on a mortgage and the interest rate on bonds issued by stable companies or governments. When a creditor can easily seize and resell the real estate of a defaulting debtor, the creditor is secure and the spread is small. When seizing the real estate of a defaulting debtor is difficult and expensive, the creditor is insecure and the spread is large. Graphing the spread on the vertical axis for countries of the world and gross domestic product per capita shows an unmistakable downward slope, which indicates a smaller spread in richer countries.

33. Many poor countries do not have registries for ownership of real estate, or the registries are defective due to incompetence or corruption. Land registries for Peru are organized by owner's name and not by location of property, so it is difficult for a potential buyer to find out whether or not more than one person claims the same property. R. Ravina, "Costos de transacción en la transferencia de bienes inmuebles," Latin American and Caribbean Law and Economics Association, Lima, Peru, 2004. For evidence that land registration can increase land prices and economic growth, see Frank F. K. Byamugisha, "How Land Registration Affects Financial Development and Economic Growth in Thailand," Policy Research Working Paper No. 2241, World Bank, East Asia and Pacific Region, Rural Development and Natural Resources Sector Unit, 1999.

34. A. Kim, "North versus South: Politics and Social Norms in the Evolution of Private Property Rights in Vietnam," Comparative Law and Economics Forum, Chicago, 2005.

35. When the plaintiff's burden of going forward exceeds the stakes in the case, a rational person does not bother to file a legal complaint.

36. To illustrate, most U.S. states allow a fast procedure called a "nonjudicial foreclosure" or "summary judgment." It avoids a trial and gives the creditor immediate control over the property.

While the creditor gets immediate control, the creditor may still lose a lot of money.

To illustrate numerically, assume the creditor loaned $100,000, the borrower repaid $10,000, and then the borrower stopped paying. The creditor gets a summary judgment, seizes the property, and sells it for $50,000. Thus the creditor loses $40,000, which is called the "deficiency. To address the deficiency, the creditor must follow a slower procedure called "judicial foreclosure," which allows the creditor to obtain a "deficiency judgment." In the preceding example, the creditor can sell the property for $50,000 and then collect $40,000 from the debtor, assuming the debtor has the ability to pay. However, judicial foreclosure also gives the debtor the right to delay resale of the property by the creditor while the debtor tries to find the money to buy it. This right of the debtor is called "equity of redemption."

37. This is true, even though the study found that land counts for only 22 percent of the value of corporate assets. Mehnaz Safavian, Heywood Fleisig, Jevgeniji Steinbucks, "Unlocking Dead Capita: How Reforming Collateral Laws Improves

Access to Finance," *Viewpoint* 307, The World Bank, Washington, DC, 2006, available at http://rru.worldbank.org/PublicPolicyJournal/Summary.aspx?id=307.

38. Stephen Greenblatt, *Will in the World: How Shakespeare Became Shakespeare* (New York: W. W. Norton, 2004)

39. Motoko Rich, "Record First-Day Sales for Last 'Harry Potter' Book," *New York Times*," July 22, 2007, available at http://www.nytimes.com/2007/07/22/books/22cnd-potter.html?_r=1&oref=slogin.

40. In the United States, patents have been extended to some types of innovations in business organization, which are called "business method patents." For a proposal to increase the first-mover advantage by extending intellectual property rights to entrepreneurial innovators, see J. F. Duffy and M. Abramawitz, "Intellectual Property for Market Innovation," Berkeley Law and Economics Seminar, Berkeley, CA, 2006.

41. Innovation builds on prior innovation, so innovators need free access to some prior innovations.

Excessive intellectual property laws slow innovation by raising the cost of access to common resources needed by innovators. In the United States, excessive legal restrictions on copying apparently slow creativity, whereas socially optimal intellectual property law maximizes the rate of innovation. In various papers and books, Larry Lessig and Mark Lemley have developed this important theme in U.S. scholarship on intellectual property laws. Also see Michael Heller, *The Gridlock Economy: How Too Much Ownership Wrecks Markets, Stops Innovation, and Costs Lives* (New York: Basic Books, 2008).

42. If Brazil had no compulsory licensing law for pharmaceutical patents, or if the law were clearer and more favorable to patent owners, then Brazil would have to pay significantly more for AIDS drugs. The Brazilian government distributed the drugs to AIDS victims for free. Thus a vague law for compulsory licensing of a patent advantaged AIDS victims and taxpayers in Brazil. Bruno Salama and Daniel Benoliel, "Patent Bargains in Newly Industrialized Countries (NICs): The Case of Brazil," Latin American and Caribbean Law and Economics Association, Annual Conference, Mexico City, May 2008.

43. The scope and breadth of intellectual property laws differ from one country to another. For example, U.S. patents endure for 20 years from the date of the application's filing, whereas "petty patents" in Japan, China, South Korea, Taiwan, and other countries last from 4 to 10 years. However, the difference in effective law between the United States and these countries concerns enforcement of laws, not their drafting.

44. For the argument that developing countries should not have intellectual property laws, see E. Pasquel, "¿No era la necesidad la madre de la inventiva? Por qué eliminar las patentes y los derechos de autor" (Wasn't necessity the mother of invention? Why should we eliminate patents or copyright?), Latin American and Caribbean Law and Economics Association's Annual Meeting, Lima, Peru, 2004. For empirical evidence that India benefits from manufacturing cheap generic drugs

without recognizing the patent or paying royalties to the inventor, see P.K.G. Shubham Chaudhuri and Panle Jia, "Estimating the Effects of Global Patent Protection in Pharmaceuticals: A Case Study of Quinolones in India," Bureau for Research in Economic Analysis of Development, Working Paper No. 125, New Delhi, 2006.

45. *San Francisco Chronicle*, August 12, 2003.

46. In 1999 the United States granted nearly 150,000 patents of which 2,160 applicants were from India and 7,737 were from China. Patents granted to applicants from China increased by almost 300 percent from 1999 to 2002. World Intellectual Property Organization, IP/STAT/1981–2002.

47. *Arab Human Development Report 2003* (New York:.UN Development Programme, 2003).

48. Their success is much more likely in computer programming, where development costs are relatively low, as compared to pharmaceuticals, where development costs are very high. With existing technology, proving the safety of a new drug is prohibitively expensive, and only the most advanced companies can afford to do this.

49. This essential reputation for cold drinks was however badly undermined. "Tests conducted by a variety of agencies, including the government of India, confirmed that Coca-Cola products contained high levels of pesticides, and as a result, the Parliament of India has banned the sale of Coca-Cola in its cafeteria." Available at http://www.indiaresource.org/campaigns/coke/index.html.

50. A full discussion of values and legal policy with respect to fashion is in Scott Hemphill and Jeannie Suk, "The Law, Culture, and Economics of Fashion," *Stanford Law Review* 61 (2009): 1147.

51. When several people act like one rational person, we describe their behavior as "corporate." Thus we define an organization as *a structure of offices and roles capable of corporate action*. Conversely, when several people are incapable of acting like one rational person, we describe their behavior as "individual rather than corporate.

52. Henry Manne is especially responsible for developing the argument that the market for corporations will keep them focused on maximizing the value of the firm's stock. Henry Manne, "Mergers and the Market for Corporate Control," *Journal of Political Economy* 73.2 (1965): 110–120.

53. Firms should focus on nothing but making money, according to Milton Friedman's essay, "The Social Responsibility of Business Is to Increase Its Profits," *New York Times Magazine*, September 13, 1970. Frank Easterbrook and Daniel Fischel agree with Friedman in their influential book, *The Economic Structure of Corporate Law* (Cambridge, MA: Harvard University Press, 1991). From this viewpoint, corporations should advance the interest of shareholders maximally and not concern themselves with the interests of stakeholders such as employees, the local community, or charities.

54. Privatizing either involves the sale of a state firm to private buyers, or when the state enterprise is not organized as a firm, the sale of state assets.

55. A. Kramer and H. Timmons, "Mittal Wins Bidding for Ukraine's Top Steel Maker," *International Herald Tribune*, October 25, 2005.

Chapter 7: Doing What You Say—Contracts

1. Sun Tzu, *The Art of War* (Project Gutenberg, 1910), section XI, part 3. Destroying your own ability to retreat is a tactic used by the Greek general Xenophon, the Vandal king Geiseric, and the Mexican conqueror Cortez.

2. In the language of game theory, an effective commitment transforms the payoff matrix of a game with a noncooperation equilibrium into a game with a cooperative equilibrium that is more productive. See R. Cooter and T. Ulen, *Law and Economics*, 5th ed. (Boston: Pearson Addison Wesley, 2007), chapter 6. See H.-B. Schäfer and C. Ott, *The Economic Analysis of Civil Law*, 4th ed. (London: Edward Elgar, 2005), chapter 13.

3. "Relational contracts" and "private contracts" are standard terms in legal scholarship that we use in the conventional way. "Public contracts" has no single, standardized meaning. We use the term for contracts with essential terms that the state prescribes and enforces by regulations. In contrast, another possible meaning for the term is a contract in which the state is a party, such as a procurement contract by the military.

4. Another usage of "private" and "public" contrasts nonstate and state activity. Thus a "public contract" might refer to a procurement contract with the government. In Germany the phrase "public contract" also refers to a very special kind of contract in which an official government body contracts with a private person on a subject of public law, such as relaxing a regulation. The German phrase is "oeffentlich-rechtlicher Vertrag."

5. For a related theory of how contracts evolve, see Marcel Fafchamps, "Spontaneous Market Emergence," *Topics in Theoretical Economics* 2.1 (2002): 1–35, available at http://www.bepress.com/bejte/topics/vol2/iss1/art2Markets, Trust and Reputation.

6. A. Greif, P. Milgrom, and B. Weingast, "Coordination, Commitment, and Enforcement: The Case of the Merchant Guild," *Journal of Political Economy* 102.3 (1994): 745–76; A. Greif, "Microtheory and Recent Developments in the Study of Economic Institutions through Economic History," in *Advances in Economics and Econometrics: Theory and Applications, Seventh World Congress*, ed. D. M. Kreps and K. F. Wallis (Cambridge: Cambridge University, 1997), vol. 2, 79–113.

7. Avner Greif, "Contract Enforceability and Economic Institutions in Early Trade: The Maghribi Traders' Coalition," *American Economic Review* 83 (1993): 525–548.

8. D. MacMillan and W. Woodruff , "Dispute Prevention without Courts in Vietnam," *Journal of Law and Economic Organization* 15 (1999): 637–658.

9. In the strategy of "tit-for-tat," a player responds to cooperation with cooperation, and she responds to defection with defection. See A. K. Dixit and B. J. Nalebuff, *Thinking Strategically* (London: Norton, 1991).

10. The classic paper on relational contracting is S. Macaulay, "Non-contractual Relations in Business: A Preliminary Study," *American Sociological Review* 28 (1963): 55–69. To see where the study of relational contracts has gone, look at V. Goldberg, *Framing Contract Law* (Cambridge, MA: Harvard University Press, 2007).

11. Lisa Bernstein, "Private Commercial Law in the Cotton Industry: Creating Cooperation Through Rules, Norms, and Institutions," *Michigan Law Review* 99 (2001): 1724–1790.

12. Max Weber noted this fact in his classic on the ethical foundation of the industrial revolution, called *The Protestant Ethic and the Spirit of Capitalism.*

13. A. Greif, "Reputation and Coalitions in Medieval Trade: Evidence on the Maghribi Traders," *Journal of Economic History* 49.4 (1989): 857–882.

14. Self-enforcing mechanisms analyzed by economists have exotic names such as hostage exchange, bonding, vertical integration, efficiency wages, coownership, and franchising. Self-enforcing devices for markets and hierarchies are discussed in O. Williamson, *The Economic Institutions of Capitalism: Firms, Markets, Relational Contracting* (New York: Free Press, 1985), and O. Williamson, "Comparative Economic Organization: The Analysis of Discrete Structural Alternatives," *Administrative Science Quarterly* 36.2 (June 1991): 269–296.

15. The dispute often concerns what to do when an explicit contract term violates a custom in trade. To illustrate, contracts in the Memphis cotton exchange specify that the buyer must weigh cotton when taking delivery from a seller, but the usual custom is for the buyer to accept the seller's representation of the weight. Lisa Bernstein argued that the custom in the trade applies to successful relationships, whereas the contract refers to failing relationships—the buyer stops accepting the seller's reputation of the weight when their relationship is failing. So she favors enforcing such terms as written. See Lisa Bernstein, "Private Commercial Law in the Cotton Industry: Creating Cooperation through Rules, Norms, and Institutions," *Michigan Law Review* 99 (2001): 1724–1790, at 1724. Robert Scott has extended these arguments in a series of papers, including Robert Scott and Alan Schwartz, "Contract Theory and the Limits of Contract Law," *Yale Law Journal* 113 (2004): 541. In contrast, Mel Eisenberg stresses that enforcing written terms that violate generally accepted ideas of fairness can increase distrust in business relations and make contracting more difficult. See Melvin Eisenberg, "Why There Is No Law of Relational Contracts," *Northwestern University Law Review* 94 (2000): 805–822. The alternative dispute resolution movement stresses that resolving a dispute in a relationship requires repairing it, not merely remedying the breach that is the cause of legal action. This approach was taken by early feminist scholars, including Laura Nader.

16. Schäfer observed this tea cooperative.

17. Schäfer's observation of the tea factory at Palampur prompted statistical research that proved this result. See A. Raja and H.-B. Schäfer, "Are Inventories a Buffer against Weak Legal Systems? A Cross-Country Study," *Kyklos* 60.3 (2007): 415–439. Fafchamps et al. show firms in Zimbabwe reduce contract risk by increased inventory holdings; see M. Fafchamps, J. W. Gunning, and R. Oostendorp, "Inventories and Risk in African Manufacturing," *Economic Journal* 110 (2000): 861–893

18. H. Eyzaguirre, "El impacto del Poder Judicial en la inversión privada" (Impact of Power of Judiciary in Private Investment), University of California, Berkeley Berkeley Program in Law & Economics, Annual Papers to Latin American and Caribbean Law and Economics Association, Lima, Peru, 2004.

19. Thanks to Kenneth Leonard for this example, which is inspired by Marcel Fafchamps, *Market Institutions in Sub-Saharan Africa: Theory and Evidence* (Cambridge, MA: MIT Press, 2005), esp. 59.

20. Thus local business flourishes, national business stagnates, and international business flourishes. See A. K. Dixit, *Lawlessness and Society: Alternative Modes of Government*, (Princeton: Princeton University Press, 2004), 125. Also, the World Summit 2005, High-level plenary meeting of Building Momentum to End Poverty, Tunis, September 14–16, 2005, characterizes developing countries as being "crippled by weak internal markets."

21. E. Z. Gabre-Madhin, "Of Markets and Middlemen: The Role of Brokers in Ethiopia," MSSD Discussion Paper No. 39, International Food Policy Research Institute, Washington, DC.

22. F. Fafchamps, "The Enforcement of Commercial Contracts in Ghana," *World Development* 24.3 (1996): 427–448.

23. G. Redding, *The Spirit of Chinese Capitalism* (Berlin: de Gruyter, 1990).

24. M. Fafchamps, J. W. Gunning, and R.Oostendorp, "Inventories and Risk in African Manufacturing," *Economic Journal* 110.466 (2000): 863–891; J. T. Landa, "A Theory of the Ethnically Homogenous Middleman Group: An Institutional Alternative to Contract Law," *Journal of Legal Studies* 10.2 (1981): 349.

25. Here's an example: Li, who lives in a small town near Wuhan, has a Xiali automobile in good repair. The pleasure of owning and driving the car is worth $3,000 to Li. Wu, who has been coveting the car, inherits some money and decides to try to buy the car from Li. After inspecting the car, Wu decides that the pleasure of owning and driving it is worth $4,000 to her. A sale will transfer the automobile from Li who values it at $3,000 to Wu who values it at $4,000. The gain of $1,000 is surplus from the exchange. In general, voluntary exchange creates a surplus by moving a resource from a lower valued use to a higher valued use.

26. This is a central theme in Douglas North's many influential writings on the development of economics and institutions. For example, see Douglas North, *Structure and Change in Economic History* (New York: Norton, 1981); Douglas North, *Institutions, Institutional Change, and Economic Performance* (Cambridge: Cambridge University Press, 1990).

27. Our usages is consistent with the meaning of "private law," which traditionally refers to those bodies of law that enable individuals who suffer harm to obtain a remedy from the injurer in a state court or similar body.

28. See S. Djankow and M. U. Klein, *Doing Business* (New York: Oxford University Press and World Bank, 2004), 65.

29. Debt collection was the first topic of discussion raised by members of the Mexican Supreme Court with Cooter in 2002.

30. The first reason for caution is that the measure of speed in the survey is imperfect. Some countries such as the United States or the United Kingdom have small claims courts with a streamlined and swift procedure, and only large claims go to the ordinary courts. The second reason is that speed of resolution says nothing about its quality. A court can decide a case in no time by flipping a coin.

31. The misleading cases are China, Vietnam, Russia, and Belarus. These cases are misleading because central planning traditionally required courts to meet their quota of decisions, just like farms and factories had to meet their production quotas. Because of this tradition, cases are decided quickly in these countries, which is admirable. However, the quality of the decisions is allegedly low, much like the quality of goods supplied to meet production quotas.

32. See *Pratapchand Nopaji v. Kotrike Venkatta Setty & Sons and Ors*, Civil Appeal Nos. 2382–2384 of 1968, decided on 12.12. 1974. Note that this is consistent with the common law tradition of courts refusing to enforce promises to perform criminal acts or promises by a citizen to pay a state official for performing his official duties.

33. The "good faith" principle is part of the new Dutch Civil Code of 1992. It was also introduced in Canada: see M. Ejan, V. Leblanc, N. Kost-de Sèvres, and E. Darankoum, "L'économie de la bonne foi contractuelle," in *Mélanges Jean Pineau*, ed. J. Pineau and B. Moore (Montréal: Éditions Thémis, 2003), 421–459. The so-called Lando Principles, a European model contract law, include "good faith." The United States included "good faith" in the Uniform Commercial Code in 1981 and in the Restatement of Contracts (second). The United Nations Convention on Contracts for the International Sale of Goods (CISG) of 1980 introduced it in article 7. The same applies for the private international law of merchants, the UNIDROIT principles. Brazil included it into contract law in a legal reform of 1990.

34. See examples in R. Zimmermann and S. Whittaker, ed., *Surveying the Legal Landscape in Good Faith in European Contract Law* (Cambridge: Cambridge University Press, 2000).

35. Note, however, that "good faith" was introduced in Britain through the back door by the European directive on unfair terms in consumer contracts.

36. In *Walford v. Miles*, the British House of Lords rejected the principle as being inconsistent with the adversarial position of the parties Miles, W. v. (1992), 2 W.L.R. 174, at 181 (H.L.). English judges favor more specific rules like "implied terms," "misrepresentation," "fraud," "custom," and "usage. The difference

between German and English interpretation of contracts affect their length. Frankfurt bankers write short contracts that refer to the principle of good faith. Longer contracts are unnecessary because German judges interpret the terms flexibly. In contrast, London bankers write long contracts because English judges interpret the terms literally, so the contract must provide explicitly for all contingencies.

37. R. La Porta, A. Shleifer, R. W. Vishny, and F. Lopez De Silames, "Law and Finance," NBER Working Paper No. 5661, National Bureau of Economic Research, Cambridge, MA, July 1996.

38. The Russian Supreme Court seems reluctant to develop civil law along general principles of fairness. See V. B. Kozlov, "The New Russian Civil Code of 1994," Rome, 1996, 1–30, available at http://w3.uniroma1.it/idc/centro/publications/21kozlov.pdf. Kozlow writes about abstract principles of justice: "These principles are not expressly mentioned in the Civil Code and the Russian judiciary has in a great many cases demonstrated its unwillingness to apply and develop them in Russia" (25).

In contrast, the Chinese Contract Law of 1999 recognizes the "good faith" principle, but Chinese courts have not yet applied this new principle. Q. Zheng, Q., "A Comparative Study on the Good Faith Principle of Contract Law," *Unusuniversus* (2000), 38–65, available at http://www.iolaw.org.cn/en/art2.asp.

Brazil adopted "good faith" in a reform of 1990, but a survey for Brazil indicates "excessive formalism" as one of the main causes for distrust in courts, which suggests that the principle of good faith has not been used very well. M. Dakolias, "Court Performance around the World," World Bank Technical Paper, Washington, DC, World Bank, 1999, 1–72.

In India, the Supreme Court used the good faith principle 731 times from 1950 to March 2007, according to the Manupatra data base.

39. Article 141 of the Constitution of India says that "the law declared by the Supreme Court shall be binding on all courts within the territory of India." A similar solution giving more but not full authority to lower courts could allow a lower court judge to present the case to the Supreme Court, if the judge believes that the law contradicts the principle of good faith. Referral is the procedure in the European Union where every national court can refer a case to the European Court of Justice.

40. The economic analysis of contract law has taken great pains to work out differences in the incentive effects of alternative measures of damages. For an overview, see Cooter and Ulen, *Law and Economics*, chapters 6 and 7, or see Schäfer and Ott, *Economic Analysis of Civil Law*, chapter 13

41. In rich OECD countries 11 percent can be regarded as judgment proof because they receive an income that is half the median income or lower. M. Förster and M. M. d'Ercole, "Income Distribution and Poverty in OECD Countries in the Second Half of the 1990s," OECD Social Employment and Migration Working Paper No. 22, OECD Directorate for Employment, Labour and Social Affairs,

Paris, 2005. The proportion of people living in absolute poverty, defined as less than US$1.25 a day, averaged 23 percent in low- and middle-income countries (in 2005), and these people are certainly judgment proof. World Bank, *World Development Indicators 2009* (Washington, DC: World Bank, 2010).

42. Luciano Benetti Timm, "The Social Function of Contract Law in Brazilian Civil Code: Distributive Justice Versus Efficiency," presentation at the Annual Meeting, Latin American and Caribbean Law and Economics Association, Pompeu Fabra University, Spain, June 16, 2009.

43. Another problem concerns corruption. The judge can vary damages continuously, which helps to disguise corruption and bribes. Thus the defendant might pay the judge a bribe equal to 10 percent of the stakes in the case and the judge might reduce damages by 20 percent. In general, money damages facilitate corruption of courts. Compared to money damages, specific performance makes disguising corruption harder. We thank Henrik Lando for this insight.

44. According to legal theory, the basic remedy in civil law countries for breach of contracts is specific performance, and the basic remedy in common law countries is expectation damages, but one legal system almost always applies the same remedy as the other in the same circumstances.

45. In the planned economies of socialist countries, stores sold goods at official prices, but the goods were in short supply. A person with money might not be able to find anyone willing to sell a good at its official price. People got into the end of a line to buy things in Soviet Russia, according to many jokes, without knowing what was for sale at the front of the line. Little wonder that, instead of compensation at official prices, communist enterprises preferred specific performance as the remedy for broken contracts. Y. Yu, "The Evolution of Contract Law in China: Comparisons with the West and the Soviet Union," *Studies In Comparative Communism* 19.3–4 (1986): 193–212.

46. The traditional rule was specific performance. The contract law reform of 1999 includes damages and specific performance and leaves the choice at the discretion of the plaintiff. N. Zhu, "A Case Study of Legal Transplant: The Possibility of Efficient Breach in China," *Georgetown Journal of International Law* 36 (2005): 1145.

47. See www.msnbc.msn.com/id/26901721.

48. The Nobel Prize committee acknowledged this fact in 2001 by awarding the prize jointly to three pioneers of information economics—George A. Akerlof, A. Michael Spence, and Joseph E. Stiglitz.

49. For access to health insurance see WHO, *World Health Report 2005*, Statistical appendix. Access to banking data is scattered and depend on household surveys. For access to formal banking, see S. Claessens, "Access to Financial Services: A Review of the Issues and Public Policy Objectives," World Bank Policy Research Working Paper No. 3589, World Bank, Washington, DC, 2005, 1–38. In the United States, this quota of banked persons was 91 percent (2001), in India 47 percent (2003), in China 42 percent (1997), in Brazil (urban areas) 43 percent

(2003), and in Pakistan 12 percent (1991). See Claessens, "Access to Financial Services," Statistical appendix, table 1.

50. F. Schneider, "The Size of Shadow Economies in 145 Countries from 1999 to 2003," Discussion Paper No. 1431, Forschungsinstitut zur Zukunft der Arbeit (IZA), Bonn, Germany, 2005.

51. This follows from the fact that the informal sector produces less per worker than the formal sector.

52. One such doctrine is the principle of void for illegality. See See J. R. Hay, A. Shleifer, and R. W. Vishny, "Toward a Theory of Legal Reform," available at http://post.economics.harvard.edu/faculty/shleifer/papers/TheoryLegalReform.pdf, 1995, 1–13. Another such doctrine is "ultra vires"—e.g., the doctrine is void unless a firm's corporate charter authorizes the activity in question. In the gray market, the firm has no charter, or it has a charter that deliberately makes no reference to its gray market activities, or the state deliberately issues charters that do not encompass all of the company's foreseeable activities. Thus the manufacturer of a cement mixer may be unable to enforce a sales contract with a fitness studio because the latter's charter does not encompass mixing cement.

53. Hay, Shleifer, and Vishny, "Toward a Theory of Legal Reform," 1–13.

54. Uncertainty was defined as immeasurable risk in F. Knight's classic, *Risk, Uncertainty, and Profit* (New York: Houghton-Mifflin, 1921).

Chapter 8: Giving Credit to Credit—Finance and Banking

1. In economic jargon, this is a "Pareto improvement."

2. For a review, see R. Levine, "Financial Development and Economic Growth," *Journal of Economic Literature* 35.2 (1997): 688–726. Also see R. Rajan and L. Zingales, "Financial Dependence and Growth," *American Economic Review* 88 (1998): 559–586; R. Rajan and L. Zingales, "Financial Systems, Industrial Structure, and Growth," *Oxford Review of Economic Policy* 17 (2001): 457–466; Mark J. Manning, "Finance Causes Growth: Can We Be So Sure?" *Contributions to Macroeconomics* 3 (2003): 1–22.

3. Bank development and stock market liquidity are good predictors of future economic growth in a developing country. See Robert King and Ross Levine, "Finance and Growth: Schumpeter Might Be Right," *Quarterly Journal of Economics* 108 (1993): 717–737; Rajan and Zingales, "Financial Dependence and Growth."

4. World Bank, *World Development Indicators 2005*, table 2.5.

5. Empirical evidence on the rate of return for credits given to the poor is still scanty, but shows high average rates. A field survey based on 133 credits to small peasants in the Philippines found an average rate of return of 117 percent. Financing of mobile phones yields a very high return. M. Hossain and C. P. Diaz, "Reaching the Poor with Effective Microcredit: Evaluation of a Grameen Bank

Replication in the Philippines," Working paper, Social Sciences Division, International Rice Research Institute (IRRI), Los Baños, Laguna, Philippines, 1999. Investment in schooling in poor countries yields a higher private rate of return than the historical average for investment in the stock market.

6. "Money says the proverb, makes money. When you have got a little, it is often easy to get more. The great difficulty is to get that little." Adam Smith, *The Wealth of Nations* (1776; Safari Books online, 2009), chap. 20, p. 41.

7. Figures for the quota of unbanked adults at the turn of the century were Brazil 57.2 percent, Colombia 58.8 percent, Ecuador 66 percent, México 75 percent, Perú 80 percent, F. P. Sanz, "Expanding Financial Services in Latin America, Banking the Unbanked," Summit of the Americas Center, Florida International University, 2007, available at http://www.frbatlanta.org/news/CONFEREN/07ConsumerBanking/prior.pdf.

8. A general name for these organizations is "rotating savings and credit associations" or "roscas." Specific names vary from one country to another. For example, for Palestinians the name is "jam'eyah" (جمعية), and for Koreans the name is "gae."

9. As they grew, chit funds adopted a better method than a random draw to choose the winner of the pot to buy cars and houses. Some chit funds auction the pot, like a bank offering a loan to the person who pays the highest rate of interest. To illustrate, if the pot is $120 in January, members can bid for it by offering to take less than $120, and the lowest bidder wins. The winner in January might offer to take $108, in which case $12 remains in the pot, which can be divided among the members with each receiving $1, like interest on a loan. India's Chit Fund Act of 1982 set a limit of 30 percent on the amount that could be bid for the pot, like a prohibition on usury. See J. Eeckhout and K. Munshi, "Institutional Change in the Non-Market Economy: Endogenous Matching in Chennai's Chit Fund Auctions," Working paper, University Pennsylvania, Department of Economics, Philadelphia, 2002.

10. India nationalized many of its banks in 1969 and 1980, which caused a surge in nonbank financial institutions like chit funds. In recent years, banking activity has shifted from nonbanks to banks in response to less regulation and more privatization of banks. Reserve Bank of India, "Non-Banking Financial Institutions," part 1, 2005, available at http://www.rbi.org.in/scripts/PublicationsView.

11. A. Hollis and A. Sweetman, "Microcredit: What Can We Learn from the Past," *World Development* 26.10 (1989): 1875–1891, esp. 1882.

12. Specifically, each member's liability to a multiple of his share value. Thus a member's liability depended on how much he invested in the bank, not on the total amount of his wealth.

13. M. Ghatak and T. W. Guinnane, "The Economics of Lending with Joint Liability: Theory and Practice," *Journal of Development Economics* 60 (1999): 195–221.

14. We owe this information to Klaus Glaubitt, director at the Kreditanstalt fuer Wiederaufbau, and in charge of microfinance, the German development agency for capital transfers.

15. These problems have been extensively discussed in the Narashimham report. This report shows how gradual improvement is possible. It proposes to restrict obligatory lending to rural development banks to a fixed and moderate quota of total saving accounts of commercial banks and to end the political influence to finance sick corporations.

16. Grameen Bank of Bangladesh, report available at http://www.grameen-info.org/bank/index.html, 2006.

17. M. Hossain, "Credit for Alleviation of Rural Poverty: The Grameen Bank in Bangladesh," Research Report 65, International Food Policy Research Institute and the Bangladesh Institute of Development Studies, Dhaka, Bangladesh, 1988.

18. J. Morduch, "The Microfinance Promise," *Journal of Economic Literature* 37.4 (1999): 1569–1615.

19. Two massive quasi-government banks (Fannie Mae and Freddy Mac) bought mortgages from private banks. During the 1990s, politicians pressured them to buy mortgages made to poor people who could not qualify by commercial standards of credit. In October 2008, these two quasi-government banks failed because too many poor people defaulted on their mortgages.

20. A recent study concluded dryly that, for Grameen Bank lending, "the consumer surplus probably exceeds the subsidy . . . [so Grameen Bank subsidies are] probably a worthwhile social investment." M. Schreiner, "A Cost-Effectiveness Analysis of the Grameen Bank of Bangladesh," *Development Policy Review* 21.3 (2003): 357–382.

21. In Sweden the proportion of the self-employed to all working people declined from 26 percent in the year 1850 to 12 percent in the year 2000 (R. Edvinsson, "Growth, Accumulation, Crisis: With New Macroeconomic Data for Sweden 1800–2000," Ph.D. diss, University of Stockholm, 2005). In the Netherlands the proportion fell from more than 20 to less than 10 percent over roughly the same period (F. de Goey, "Economic Structure and Self Employment in the 20th Century," Working paper, Faculty of History and Arts, Erasmus University, Rotterdam, The Netherlands, 2004, fig. 6). Today, self-employment is 7.3 percent in the United States, 10.9 percent in Germany, 23.5 percent in Portugal, and 27.8 percent in Turkey (data of 2007, *Eurostat 2008*, available at http://www.lex.unict.it/eurolabor/documentazione/altrestat/eurostat051006.pdf). The data also show a slight increase in self-employment for OECD countries since the 1980s. The causes are still much debated.

22. D. Gollin, "Getting Income Shares Right," *Journal of Political Economy* 110.2 (April 2002): 458–474, figures are for the 1990s.

23. S. Claessens and E. Perotti, "Finance and Inequality: Channels and Evidence," *Journal of Comparative Economics* 35 (2007): 748–773, 756; and J. Morduch, "The Microfinance Promise," *Journal of Economic Literature* 37.4 (1999): 1569–1615. "It is hard to maintain hope that chronic poverty can be reduced appreciably by credit-based interventions. Chronic poverty is not typically due to 'market failure' in credit or other markets, but to low factor productivity, and

to low endowments-per-person of non-labor factors. If these conditions prevail, even perfect responses of all factor, product and credit markets may leave substantial chronic poverty." Michael Lipton maintains that absolute poverty declines if wages rise for unskilled workers, landless laborers get land as property, and children of poor people get access to school. M. Lipton and M. Ravaillon, "Poverty and Policy," in *Handbook of Development Economics,* vol. 3, ed. J. Behrman and T. N. Srinivasan (Amsterdam: North-Holland, 1995): 2553–2657, esp. 2630.

24. Compare *World Bank Development Indicators 2007* (Washington, DC: World Bank, 2007). More recent figures from *World Bank Development Indicators 2009* maintain that poverty actually decreased during the same period.

25. See *World Development Indicators 2007.*

26. C. Bruck, "Millions for Millions," *New Yorker Magazine,* October 30, 2006: 62–73.

27. For a model of immiseration by moneylenders, see E. Ligon, "Formal Markets and Informal Insurance," *International Review of Law and Economics* 25 (2004): 75–88.

28. The bank credit card was an innovation by the Bank of America. Its inventor told Cooter that bankers were amazed to discover that, instead of paying promptly, consumers would carry credit card balances month after month and pay the maximum legal interest rate. Even bankers did not anticipate that so many people could be that foolish.

29. For a survey of the literature, see A. K. Garg and N. Pandey, "Making Money Work for the Poor in India: Inclusive Finance through Bank-Moneylender Linkages," Working paper, University of Indiana, Bloomington, 2006, 1–38, available at dlc.dlib.indiana.edu. See also K. Hoff and J. E. Stiglitz, "Moneylenders and Bankers: Price-increasing Subsidies in a Monopolistically Competitive Market," *Journal of Development Economics* 55.2 (1998): 485–518.

30. Beside banking and brokerage, financial services also include insurance and payments instruments (credit cards, checks, electronic funds transfers, notes). In recent years, the financial services industry has found lucrative new ways to package risk, such as derivatives, swaps, letters of credit, and mortgage-backed securities.

31. The U.S. enacted regulations in the 1930s, notably the Glass-Steagall Act, that confined commercial and investment activities to separate firms, and other countries like Japan adopted this model. The separation has eroded in small ways by new laws and court decisions in the United States. The financial collapse of 2008 has renewed pressure to separate commercial and investment banking.

32. To assure that the borrower is not diminishing the collateral's value, the bank may require an annual audit of the borrower by an independent accountant. The loan agreement may also require the borrower to open a checking account with the bank for its everyday transactions and to maintain a stipulated balance. The bank stays informed about the borrower's financial health by monitoring the transactions in its checking account.

33. N. Ferguson, "Wars, Revolutions, and the International Bond Market from the Napoleonic Wars to the First World War," Discussion Paper, Yale University, New Haven, 1999, available at http://icf.som.yale.edu/pdf/NF.pdf, 13; and F. McDonald, "Is Public Indebtedness Essential to Democracy and Freedom?" GMU History News Network, January 19, 2004.

34. World Bank, *Doing Business around the World* (Washington, DC: World Bank, 2005), 44. India has revised its law to accept credit agreements on the repossession of movable collateral without court involvement. The Securitization and Reconstruction of Financial Assets and Enforcement of Security Interest Act (SARFAESI Act, 2002).

35. F. C. Salaverry, "Accesso al credito mediante la reforma de la legislacion sobre garantias reales," Latin American and Caribbean Law and Economics Association, Lima, Peru, 2004.

36. Assume that a farmer wants to offer a herd of 100 cattle worth $100,000 as collateral for a loan. In Uruguay the court will refuse the pledge as collateral unless the farmer lists each of the cows and the list is continuously updated. In Kansas, in contrast, the rancher can pledge a herd of cattle worth $100,000, even though the identity of the cows changes continuously. Similarly, in Uruguay a dealer in wool can only pledge the particular wool in the warehouse, so the collateral will dissipate as the wool in the warehouse turns over through sales. In Wyoming a dealer in wool can pledge wool worth $100,000 in a warehouse, and the pledge remains good as the particular wool in the warehouse turns over through sales. "The fallacy of concreteness" is the name given to the impractical requirements for offering movables as collateral in some civil law countries like Uruguay. See H. Fleisig, "Secured Transactions: The Power of Collateral," *Finance and Development* 33.2 (1996): 44–46. Similarly, according to a civil law tradition, the pledge of a movable good requires the creditor to take possession of it. If a shop in Germany sells a television on credit and lets the buyer take it home with him, the shop cannot have the television as collateral for the loan. (To circumvent this problem, the shop in Germany would retain title of the television until the debt is paid.)

37. Ricardo Salinas explained these facts to Cooter.

38. Marcel Fafchamps, "The Enforcement of Commercial Contracts in Ghana," *World Development* 24.3 (1996): 427–448.

39. L. Rochas-Suarez, "Rating Banks in Emerging Markets," Working Paper 01/6, Institute for International Economics, 2001, available at http.iie.com/publications/wp/01-6.pdf. Note, however, that low spreads do not necessarily reflect low risk and a better institutional environment. They can be found in banks in crisis, in politically influenced banks, and in banks that can count on a bailout from the state. And high spreads can reflect monopoly power of banks rather than undeveloped creditor's rights.

40. Ejecutoria de la Contradiccion de Tesis 31/ 98 and Ejecutoria de la Contradiccion de Tesis 32/98 (October 7, 1998).

41. J. T. Noonan, *The Scholastic Analysis of Usury* (Cambridge, MA: Harvard University Press, 1957).

42. Person A wants to borrow $1 from person B and repay $1.5 in one year. Here is how they can disguise the interest of 0.5 on the loan. A has goods that he is sure not to use until next year. A sells the goods to B for $1, and they agree that A will repurchase the goods from B for $1.5 in one year. During the year, B agrees to leave the goods in A's possession. The net result is that A receives $1 immediately from B and A promises to pay $1.5 to B in one year, just as with the loan. To make the disguise less transparent, the two parties often involve a third party in the transaction. This ploy was explained by H. Hamidi in a lecture, "You Say You Want a Revolution: Deviationist Doctrine, Interpretive Communities, and the Origins of Islamic Finance," Berkeley Faculty Seminar, University of California, Berkeley, 2007.

43. "Investment bank" refers to a narrower group of organizations in New York than in Frankfurt. New Yorkers said that the United States had only five "investment banks" (Goldman-Sachs, Morgan Stanley, Lehman Brothers, Bear Stearns, and Merrill Lynch), and all of which were transformed or disappeared in the financial meltdown of 2008. The activity of investment banking did not disappear forever, so the future of the phrase "investment bank" is uncertain in New York.

44. Thus if a firm secures a commercial loan by the value of its inventory, the lender may monitor to make sure that the firm does not deplete its inventory, but the lender does not have to know the borrower's business plan or its other secrets.

45. The firm's market value is measured by how much a buyer will pay for it, including its name, reputation, good will, contracts, roles, and relationships. In contrast, the market value of its assets equals the sum of its parts when sold piecemeal, such as machines, buildings, materials, and accounts receivable.

46. D. Cobham, and R. A. J. Subramaniam, "Corporate Finance in Developing Countries: New Evidence for India," CRIEFF Discussion paper 9512, University of St Andrews, St. Andrews, UK, 1995.

47. A friend of Cooter's consulted on an aviation deal in which Europeans invested more than $40 million, their Chinese partners took all of it, and the Europeans eventually wrote off the loss and abandoned the project.

48. A. Demirguc-Kunt and V. Maksimovic, "Law, Finance, and Firm Growth," *Journal of Finance* 53 (1998): 2107–2137.

49. Bernard Black et al., "How Does Law Affect Finance? An Examination of Financial Tunneling in an Emerging Market," Berkeley Law and Economics Workshop, Berkeley, CA, 2007.

50. These companies currently have four classes of stock:

1) Nontradable shares held owned by the state.
2) Nontradable shares with nonstate owners (e.g., state officials in their capacity as private persons).
3) Tradable shares on domestic exchanges. (Chinese citizens can own them.)
4) Tradable shares on foreign exchanges. (Chinese citizens cannot own them.)

51. To hasten the end, the government could make the subsidies overt instead of covert. If the subsidies appeared in the state budget as expenditures, people would recognize them more easily and weigh the alternatives. This was the theme of a speech by Raghuram Rajan, economic counselor and director of research of the International Monetary Fund, and also a speech by Charles Goodhart of the London School of Economic. Proceeding of the NDRC Economic Summit, Beijing, China, July 11, 2005.

52. Econometrics from survey data has proved what people know intuitively: Unemployment makes people very unhappy and damages their self-esteem. B. S. Frey and A. Stutzer, "Happiness, Economy, and Institutions," *Economic Journal* 110 (2000): 918–938. B. S. Frey and A. Stutzer, "What Can Economists Learn from Happiness Research?" *Journal of Economic Literature* 40 (2002): 402–435.

53. Here are three steps to harden the bankruptcy constraint:

1) Prohibit state banks from making loans to failing enterprises. Put state banks on a commercial basis.

2) If the state bank stops loaning to state-owned enterprise, central or local officials can decide to pay the subsidies

3) Create a reorganization procedure for failing state enterprises that is similar to bankruptcy under chapter 11 in the United States.

C. Goodhart, "Remarks on Chinese Bank Debt," China Reform Summit: Promoting Further Economic Restructuring by Focusing on Administrative Reform, Organized by National Development and Reform Commission, P.R. China, Assisted by USB, July 12–13, 2005, Beijing, China.

54. The proposition that weak legal systems tilt finance away from stocks and toward bank bonds seems to contradict an important theorem in finance whose discovery won Nobel prizes for Modigliani and Miller. This theorem asserts that changing the proportion of stocks and bonds used to finance a firm cannot change its value. To understand their theorem, assume that a firm issues additional stock and uses all of the money to pay back some of its bonds. The amount of capital available for the firm to invest in developing its business remains unchanged. If the firm's investment remains unchanged, its stream of future profits is also unchanged. Under certain assumptions (e.g., tax neutrality and risk discounting), the firm's stream of future profits equals the firm's value as measured by the market value of its stocks. The Modigliani and Miller theory implicitly assumes that a strong legal system stops insiders from making profits disappear from the firm and reappear in their pockets. An analysis of developing countries cannot assume a strong legal system for finance.

55. A. Demirguc-Kunt and R. Levine, "Bank-Based and Market-Based Financial Systems: Cross-Country Comparisons," World Bank Policy Research Working Paper No. 2143, World Bank, Washington, DC, 1999. Data available for 57 countries.

56. La Porta et al., "Corporate Ownership around the World," *Journal of Finance* 54 (1999): 471–517.

57. Demirguz-Kunt and Levin have constructed an index to measure the extent to which bank loans or capital markets provides more finance. Their analysis

shows a tendency for more market- based systems in richer countries. In the sample of fifty-seven countries, seven out of seventeen countries with a GNP per capita of more than $10,000 dollars are more market based than bank based. In countries with GNP per capita of less than $10,000, only eleven of forty counties are more market based than bank based. See Demirgüc-Kunt and Levine, "Bank-Based and Market-Based Financial System."

58. Alexander Gerschenkron drew this conclusion in a 1962 book comparing these three countries. During Germany's rapid industrialization from 1895 to 1913, the ratio of bank deposits to shares of stock increased in value from 1.5 to 3.4. His explanation, however, was not based on law, but rather on differences in human capital. He thought that a few large banks could economize better on scarce expertise in the area of finance, whereas markets would require more people with expertise. Gerschenkron, *Economic Backwardness in Historical Perspective* (Cambridge, MA: Harvard University Press, 1962).

59. Public firms sell stock in markets where prices are recorded publicly, whereas private firms often sell stock privately to selected individuals in transactions at undisclosed prices.

60. Takeo Hoshi and Anil Kashyap, *Corporate Financing and Governance in Japan* (Cambridge, MA: MIT Press, 2001).

61. Ironically, an international agreement ("Basel II") that intended to increase the stability of banks actually contributed to the financial disaster of 2008. To implement the international agreement in 2002, the administration of President Bush repealed a mandatory cap on the ratio of bonds to stock ("leverage") and allowed the five American investment banks to "self-regulate" by judging their own stability. The banks judged themselves very stable and sharply increased their leverage. These events remind Cooter of a headline he saw in a newspaper called the *Sacramento Bee* that read: "How Good Are Sacramento Doctors? Local Physicians Rate Them Highly."

62. Breaking a loan into its parts and selling the parts separately "derives" new securities from the original loan. Thus a lender receives a stream of interest payments from the borrower unless the borrower defaults. The lender can sell the rights to the stream of interest payments to one party, and also pay an insurer to bear the risk of default, thus deriving two kinds of financial securities from one. Derivatives are written in nonstandard contracts, which increase the risk of cash-flow bankruptcy by making them hard to sell quickly for cash. Insuring against default was how the American Insurance Group (AIG) accumulated the largest losses in the history of any financial institution in 2009, which the American taxpayers assumed. Banks also divide their loans into groups and resell them as securities. With securitization, bank assets become liquid, so a bank can quickly sell its portfolio of loans and obtain cash when depositors want to withdraw their funds. In the financial crisis of 2008, however, bank sold their low-risk loans as securities, but they often continued holding their high-risk securities. Selling low-risk loans and holding high-risk loans caused many bank failures.

63. Market value of the portfolio of loans held by a bank can rise or fall with market conditions. A bank whose portfolio of loans is worth less than its deposits has negative net value at market rates. It is "balance sheet bankrupt." Banks increase this risk by increasing the proportion of their risky loans.

64. As explained, commercial banking obtains its funds from depositors and loans the money to borrowers. Depositors can usually withdraw their funds freely at any time, whereas the bank receives interest payments from its borrowers according to a fixed schedule that often extends over years, such as a fifteen-year mortgage on a house. If a large fraction of depositors abruptly wants to withdraw their money, a commercial bank needs a lot of cash. This is a bank run, usually caused by panic. To raise cash to pay back depositors, the bank may try to sell its portfolio of loans. A bank that cannot liquidate its loan portfolio fast enough cannot satisfy its legal obligation to allow depositors to withdraw their money. It is "cash-flow bankrupt."

65. Ordinary households that deposit money in commercial banks cannot assess the bank's risk of bankruptcy. This failure assures that the market for commercial banking cannot regulate itself. The state often corrects the failure by supplying deposit insurance or guarantees similar to it. State regulators need to police commercial banks for the risk of bankruptcy. Unfortunately, the state often aggravates the risk. Thus part of the mortgage crisis in U.S. banking in 2008 was caused by unsound state operation of two massive state-owned banks known as "fannie mae" and "freddie mac" that repurchased bank mortgages, especially for loans made to relatively poor borrowers.

66. Here are some examples that involve central bank mismanagement: in Argentina in the 1980s, inflation undermined the economy. Conversely, in Argentina in the 1990s, a stable but overvalued currency destroyed exports and caused unemployment. Mishandling of exchange rates in Thailand in 1997 caused an economic slump that spread throughout East Asia. Abrupt devaluation of the Mexican peso in 1994 caused an economic downturn that affected most Latin American countries ("peso crisis"). Russia defaulted on its debts in 1998 and the ruble plummeted, which increased the country's economic distress. If the central bank must finance excessive government deficits, the sale of government bonds can crowd out private credits, so growth slows in the private sector.

67. The Asian crisis of 1997 led to the Basel core principles of banking and credit regulation proposed by the World Bank and the IMF. These principles emphasize minimal capital requirements and risk assessment of credits. Under the "Basel II agreements," banks should retain capital equal to 8 percent of liabilities or else submit to an "internal rating basis" that requires disclosing their credit evaluations of their debtors to bank regulators. See G. Hertig, "Basel II to Facilitate Access to Finance: Fostering the Disclosure of Internal Credit Ratings," Law and Economic Workshop, Hamburg University Law and Economics Center, 2005. The Basel Committee on Banking Supervision is an arm of the Bank for

International Settlements whose rules apply to the banking regulators in each of thirteen participating countries. Additional countries may voluntarily sign on. Implementation of Basel II for U.S. investment banks allowed them to increase their leverage through self-regulation. In October 2008, all five of the major US investment banks reorganized or went bankrupt.

Chapter 9: Financing Secrets—Corporations

1. Theorists who want to efface the difference between markets and firms say that firms are a nexus of contracts. But this fact cannot define a firm, since most large organizations that are not firms are also a nexus of contracts (e.g., a university, a symphony orchestra, or the department of highways). Also, some nonorganizations form a nexus of contracts such as a Middle Eastern bazaar or the California bar. For the firm as a nexus of contracts, see Michael C. Jensen and William H. Meckling, "Theory of the Firm: Managerial Behavior, Agency Costs, and Ownership Structure," *Journal of Financial Economy* 3 (1976): 305–360; Frank Easterbrook and William Fischel, *The Economic Structure of Corporate Law* (Cambridge, MA: Harvard University Press, 1991).

2. Some organizations, such as a partnership, church, club, or family, have an existence apart from the state. They exist in fact, whether or not the state recognizes them in law. Other organizations. such as a corporation, trust, the bar, or the Department of Commerce, come into existence through law. Without going through steps prescribed in law, a corporation seldom exists in fact. (There are some exceptions, notably informal investment schemes that look a lot like a corporation without having a legal existence.)

3. Connaught Place is publically owned, so mergers and acquisitions by its leasees would have political implications.

4. Other types of transactions costs analyzed by economists include agency problems, risk spreading, hold up, flexibility, and tax avoidance. The "agency problem" refers to the problem of managers controlling employees when contracts are incomplete. See Margret Blair and Lynn Stout, "A Team Production Theory of Corporate Law," *Virginia Law Review* 85.247 (1999): 247–311, on team production. Risk spreading refers to such things as avoiding liability in tort. Richard R. W. Brooks, "Liability and Organizational Choice," *Journal of Law and Economics* 45 (2002): 91–121. Hold up involves specific capital investment. See Oliver E. Williamson, "Hierarchies, Markets, and Power in the Economy: An Economic Perspective," Business and Public Policy Working Paper BPP-59, Center for Research in Management, Berkeley, CA, 1994. Flexibility involves the relative ease of ending a contract and the legal difficulties of firing an employee. Tax avoidance involves various techniques to allocate profits among associated corporations.

5. A. Sajo, "Diffuse Rights in Search of an Agent: A Property Rights Analysis of the Firm in the Socialist Market Economy," *International Review of Law and Economics* 10 (1990): 41–60. In general, large firms can overcome the free-rider problem of political lobbying, as explained by Mancur Olson in his classic, *The Logic of Collective Action: Public Goods and the Theory of Groups* (Cambridge, MA: Harvard University Press, 1965).

6. Mitu Gulati provided this information in a personal communication, based on his research into contract practices in India. However, international technology firms operating in India apparently use nondisclosure agreements.

7. We explain the boundaries of the firm by the need to protect market power by keeping innovations secret. In contrast, a celebrated analysis by Oliver Hart explains the boundaries of the firm as conserving decision-making power. He writes:

> Firm boundaries are chosen to allocate power optimally among the various parties to a transaction. I argue that power is a scarce resource that should never be wasted. One implication of the theory is that a merger between firms with highly complementary assets is value-enhancing, and a merger between firms with independent assets is value-reducing. The reason is as follows. If two highly complementary firms have *different* owners, then neither owner has real power since neither can do anything without the other. It is then better to give all the power to one of the owners through a merger. On the other hand, if two firms with independent assets merge, then the acquiring firm's owner gains little useful power, since the acquired firm's assets do not enhance his activities, but the acquired firm's owner loses useful power, since she no longer has authority over the assets she works with. In this case, it is better to divide the power between the owners by keeping the firms separate.

Firms, Contracts, and Financial Structure (New York: Oxford University Press, 1995), 8.

8. A joke nicely illustrates this:

> *Board member:* "Why did you fire our accountant?"
>
> *CEO:* "He called me an idiot."
>
> *Board member:* "He should be fired. Employees can't disclose company secrets."

9. Other studies confirm the general pattern of table 9.3. Erica Gorga cites data that 90 percent of the firms in a large sample from the Brazilian stock exchange have a single stockholder owning more that 50 percent of shares. Only a few companies are controlled by a coalition of blockholders. See E. Gorga, "Analysis of the Efficiency of Corporate Law," Latin American Law and Caribbean Law and Economics Association, Interlegis, Brasilia, Brazil, 2007.

10. Konstantin Magin, "Reforms with No Place to Stand" (Ph.D. diss., University of California, 2003).

11. The exception is a growth firm whose owners expect it to be acquired before it ever pays dividends. Here the price of stocks is determined by the expected future sale price of the firm, not by the present value of the stream of future dividends.

12. Other empirical evidence also supports the conclusion that the control premium falls when outside investors enjoy better legal protection. Thus Nenova obtained the same negative correlation using a more specific index of minority protection of shareholders, instead of the rule-of-law index. Also see Dyck and Zingales as discussed in Erica Gorga, "Analysis of the Efficiency of Corporate Law." A. Dyck and L. Zingales. "Benefits of Private Control," NBER Working Paper No. 8711, National Bureau of Economic Research, Cambridge, MA, 2004.

13. Improved investor protection causes an increase in total market capitalization in two distinct ways. First, outside investors bid the stock price up. Second, some strictly private firms offer shares to the public for the first time.

14. Note that market capitalization as a percentage of GDP increases with an index of public disclosure of company news, as shown by the *World Bank Development Indicators 2005* (Washington, DC: World Bank, 2006).

15. In OECD countries the number of procedures to register property was 4.7 on average in 2004, whereas it was 6.6 in middle- and low-income countries (*World Bank Development Indicators 2005* [Washington, DC: World Bank, 2006]). Also see Enterprise Directorate General of the European Commission, "Benchmarking the Administration of Business Startups," Centre for Strategy and Evaluation Services, January 2002. This study found that setting up a new company took seven days in the UK and thirty-five days in Italy.

16. Henry Hansmann and Reinier H. Kraakman, "The End of History for Corporate Law," *Georgetown Law Journal* 89.439 (2001): 439–468.

17. Deane's pioneering economic history lists seven "changes in the methods and characteristics of economic organization which, taken together, constitute a development of the kind which we would describe as an industrial revolution." The modern corporate form, or the extension of the joint stock company to manufacturing, is not among them. See Phyllis Deane, *The First Industrial Revolution* (Cambridge: Cambridge University Press, 1965), 1.

18. The faster growing, midsize firms benefited most. The increase in stock prices was especially due to an increase in investment by foreigners. B. S. Black and V. Khanna, "Can Corporate Governance Reform Increase Firms' Market Values? Evidence from India," American Law and Economics Association, Annual Meeting, Harvard Law School, 2007.

19. B. S. Black and W. Kim, "The Effect of Board Structure on Firm Value in an Emerging Market: IV, DiD, and Firm Fixed Effects Evidence from Korea," American Law and Economics Association, Annual Meeting, Harvard Law School, 2007.

20. F. Lopez de Silanes, "Legal Origins and Corporate Finance," Annual Meeting of Latin American and Caribbean Law and Economics Association, Interlegis, Brasilia, Brazil, 2007.

21. W. A. Reese, and M. S. Weisbach, "Protection of Minority Shareholder Interests, Cross-listing in the United States and Subsequent Equity Offerings,"

mimeo, University of Illinois, January, 2000; S. Claessens, D. Klingebiel, and S. Schmukler, "Explaining the Migration of Stocks from Exchanges in Emerging Economies to International Centers," World Bank Discussion Paper No. 3301, World Bank, Washington, DC, 2002; A. Karolyi, "Why Do Companies List Shares Abroad?" *NYU Salomon Brothers Center Monograph Series* 7.1 (1998): 1–60.

22. The rules include Generally Accepted Accounting Procedures (GAAP) and reporting rules. Pavel Didenko, "Compliance with the Sarbanes-Oxley Act of 2002: Challenges for Russian Corporate Governance," Discussion paper, *Corporate Governance eJournal* (2005), available at http://epublications.bond.edu.au/cgej/1/. Short of listing its stock, a foreign company can gain indirect access to the New York Stock Exchange or other American capital markets by using an "American Depository Receipt," or ADR. In effect, the company deposits stock with an American bank that then sells certificates (ADRs) entitling the owner to most of the benefits of a stockholder. The ADRs are traded in American capital markets. The foreign firm can choose the extent to which it will conform to American securities regulation. The level of conformity determines the breadth of the markets in which American law allows the ADRs to be sold.

23. Stulz, Doidge, and Karolyi.examined stock prices for 712 cross-listed firms and 4,078 that were not cross-listed in 1997. They found that "cross-listed stocks were worth 16.5 percent more on average than comparable firms that were not cross-listed. This cross-listing premium was even more dramatic for firms listed on NYSE, where it was 37 percent on average." R. M. Stulz, C. Doidge, and G. A. Karolyi, "Why Are Foreign Firms Listed in the U.S. Worth More?" NBER Working Paper No. 8538, National Bureau of Economic Research, Cambridge, MA, October 2001, and *Journal of Financial Economics* 71.2 (2004): 205–238.

24. Roberta Romano, "The State Competition Debate in Corporate Law," *Cardozo Law Review* 8.4 (1987): 709–757; Lucian Arye Bebchuk, "Federalism and the Corporation: The Desirable Limits on State Competition in Corporate Law," *Harvard Law Review* 105 (1992): 1437–1510; Oren Bar-Gill, Michal Barzuza, and Lucian Bebchuk, "The Market for Corporate Law," *Journal of Institutional and Theoretical Economics* 134 (2006): 162.

25. Cross-listing and foreign chartering lead to disputes that domestic courts should decide by using foreign laws. Also, cross-listing and foreign chartering lead to damage awards by foreign courts against domestic firms that domestic courts should enforce. By enforcing foreign laws and damage awards, domestic courts maintain the credibility of the firm's submission to foreign laws, which attracts more investments in domestic firms.

Chapter 10: Hold or Fold—Financial Distress

1. For the full lyrics to this riveting song, browse the internet for Kenny Rogers, "The Gambler."

2. In a world without transactions costs, a state bankruptcy procedure would not be necessary. Corporations would conclude fully specified credit contracts with clauses for the assignment of rights and duties to creditors, owners, and managers in case of financial distress. This is an application of the "Coase Theorem," which is fundamental for law and economics. In a world with transactions costs, however, bankruptcy law can help to verify assets and liabilities, improve coordination among claimholders, protect third-party claimants, maintain the asset value and remove liquidity constraints during the procedure. D. C. Smith and P. Strömberg, "Maximizing the Value of Distressed Assets, Bankruptcy and the Reorganisation of Firms," Discussion Paper, *World Bank Conference on Systematic Financial Distress*, 2004, 42.

3. In the recent past, scholars believed that chapter 11 bankruptcy reorganization allowed failed management to retain control over U.S. firm for too long and deplete its capital. To illustrate, when Eastern Airlines filed for bankruptcy under chapter 11, the company lost a billion dollars as its managers and trustees attempted to reorganize it. Success would have repaid creditors in full, but delays from reorganizing caused many creditors to receive nothing. However, better contracts for refinancing have mostly solved this problem. See Jagdeep Bhandari, S. Lawrence, and A. Weiss, "The Untenable Case for Chapter 11: A Review of the Evidence," *American Bankruptcy Journal* 67 (1993): 131.

4. A spectacular example is the bankruptcy of Borgward, one of the most successful producers of motor vehicles in its time. After a liquidity crisis in 1963, large banks succeeded in liquidating the company and recovering their loans to it. Liquidation revealed that the market value of the firm's assets exceeded the total value of its bank loans. The banks apparently wanted to take no risks when it came to repaying themselves. They also wanted to tilt competition in favor of other automobile manufacturers. See Giacinta Cestone and Lucy White, "Anticompetitive Financial Contracting: The Design of Financial Claims," *Journal of Finance* 58.5 (October 2003): 2109–2142.

5. Swedish laws apparently use market prices more fully than other legal systems. In Sweden the bankruptcy trustee must offer the whole firm for sale, and he also must offer to sell its assets separately. If the bids for the firm are higher than the bids for its assets, the trustee sells the firm to the highest bidder. Conversely, if the bids for the firm are smaller than the bids for its assets, the trustee liquidates the firm and sells its assets to the highest bidders. Thus the bankruptcy trustee must compare the sale and liquidation value of the firm. When applying these rules, the Swedish trustee uses market values. He does not have to use valuations by stakeholders to make his own valuation of the firm. Most economists believe that prices in competitive markets value assets more accurately than state officials. Note that the Swedish system cannot work without a robust market for firms to generate bids for the distressed company.

Scholars have proposed visionary legal reforms to improve the bankruptcy process that go beyond the Swedish model in using market valuations. Thus

Bebchuk proposed that courts organize an auction for a distressed firm, in which groups of people could present plans to repay the firm's creditors. The highest bidder would win the firm, unless no one bid enough to repay the creditors, in which case the firm would be liquidated.

6. To illustrate numerically, assume that A loans 10 to a firm and secures the loan by the firm's cement truck. B loans 15 to the firm without security. C loans 5 without security. The firm goes bankrupt and defaults on its loans. Its net assets consist of 6 in cash and a cement truck worth 12. Firm A seized and sells the cement truck for 12 to satisfy its debt of 10, and returns 2 to the firm. Now the firm has a total of 8 in cash, but it owes 20. B and C will each get repaid 8/20 = 40 percent of what they are owed. Specifically, B gets 6 and C gets 2.

7. To illustrate, assume that a firm buys a store for 100 by using a first mortgage of 60 and a second mortgage of 40. The mortgage documents stipulate that the first creditor has priority over the second creditor. The firm goes bankrupt, the store is its only asset, and the store sells for 80. The holder of the first mortgage gets repaid 60 and the holder of the second mortgage gets repaid 20.

8. A real estate registry answers the question, "How does the buyer know that the seller of a house actually owns it?" The real estate registry also includes liens on the house created by giving it as security for a loan.

9. *Par condicio omnium creditorum.*

10. The first lender fears that the court might give equality to the second lender. Consequently, the contract with the original lender will preclude a second mortgage. Some numbers clarify the point. Assume that person with 15 of his own money needs to borrow 85 in order to buy a house costing 100. In the United States, a bank might offer a first mortgage of 80. In addition, the buyer might borrow 5 by using a second mortgage. If the buyer defaults and the house is worth 50, a U.S. court gives the bank 50 and the second lender gets 0. If, however, an Italian court applied principle of equality, the bank gets repaid $50/85 \times 80$, and the second lender gets $50/85 \times 5$.

11. In numbers, assume that A loans 10 to a firm secured by the firm's cement truck, and B loans 20 to the firm without security. The firm goes bankrupt and its only asset is the cement truck, which sells for 12. If the court enforces the security term in the financial contract, then A gets repaid 10 and B gets repaid 2. Alternatively, if the court applies a mandatory law guaranteeing the unsecured creditors at least 1/3 of the bankrupt firm's liquidation value then, A gets repaid 8 and B gets repaid 4.

12. To illustrate, the pyramiding of loans through second mortgages, or even third mortgages, contributed to the financial disaster in the United States in 2008. With equality among creditors, the contract with lenders for the first mortgage will preclude a second mortgage. Thus equality among creditors sometimes suppresses high-risk chicanery in lending as occurred in the U.S. housing markets after 2000.

Note another advantage of equality: the interests of lenders converge, so they can agree more easily on how to resolve a firm's financial distress. Conversely, distinctions among creditors by security and priority cause their interests to diverge, so they disagree over how to resolve the firm's financial distress. Thus secured creditors want the firm to maintain the value of the specific assets securing the loan, and unsecured creditors want the firm to preserve the assets of the firm as a whole.

13. Here is a numerical example: A firm wants to buy a new cement truck for 10. The firm would like to pay 2 of its own money and borrow 8 from a bank. The cement truck's resale value is 8, so the truck can fully secure the loan. The bank, however, will not make the loan unless the law will fully enforce the security term. In contrast, assume that the law contains a mandatory rule that, in the event of bankruptcy, only half of the cement truck's resale value can go to the bank and the other half must go to unsecured lenders. As a result of this mandatory rule, the bank may to refuse the loan, or demand more burdensome terms.

14. The terms may be worse in several ways: smaller loan, more security, higher interest, or more costly disclosure. Note that banks frequently require a borrower to conduct its daily transactions through an account at the bank. By monitoring the transaction account, the bank can obtain advanced warning if the firm descends into financial distress, in which case the bank can demand immediate repayment of its loan in full ("acceleration") before the other creditors appreciate the danger.

15. Stijn Claessens, Simeon Djankov, Leora Klapper, "Resolution of Corporate Distress, Evidence from East Asia's Financial Crisis," World Bank Policy Research Working Paper No..2133, World Bank, Washington, DC, 1999.

16. William Pyle, "Resolutions, Recoveries and Relationships: The Evolution of Payment Disputes in Central and Eastern Europe," *Journal of Comparative Economics* 34.2 (June 2006): 317–337.

17. Ibid.

18. A takeover is friendly or hostile depending on whether or not the management of the firm being bought agrees to be acquired. In a hostile takeover, an outsider buys enough of a firm's stock to gain control over the board of directors and fire the managers. To succeed, hostile takeovers require background laws. Instead of supporting takeovers, most countries suppress them by law and tradition. Consequently, hostile takeovers are common in the United States and United Kingdom, and rare in other countries.

19. J. Armour and S. Deakin, "Norms in Private Insolvency Procedures: The 'London Approach' to Financial Distress," University of Cambridge, ESRC, Center for Business Research, Working Paper No. 173, 1999, 2.

20. When a U.S. firm applies for bankruptcy reorganization under chapter 11 of the Uniform Commercial Code, the judge must approve its plans and assure fair treatment for each class of creditors. Managers and large creditors generally know a lot more about a distressed firm than a judge or trustee. By requiring stakeholders to propose plans for the distressed firm, the legal process allows them to apply their superior knowledge. By requiring approval of the judge, the court tries to assure fairness toward the parties.

21. Private workouts dominate in Bangladesh, Ghana, Mauritania, Belarus, Guatemala, Mozambique, Bolivia, Indonesia, Pakistan, Brazil, Iran, Panama, Costa Rica, Jamaica, Portugal, Egypt, Malaysia, Turkey, Georgia, Mali, and Uruguay; see World Bank, *Doing Business around the World* (Washington, DC: World Bank, 2004), 79. Also see Stijn Claessens and Leora F. Klapper, "Bankruptcy around the World: Explanations of its Relative Use," *American Law and Economics Review* 7.1 (2005): 253–283.

22. This phrase is attributed to William Gladstone, nineteenth-century British prime minister.

23. *Doing Business* (2010), available at http://www.doingbusiness.org/Explore Topics/ClosingBusiness/.

24. C. Wihlborg and S. Gangopadhyay, "Infrastructure Requirements in the Area of Bankruptcy Law," Wharton School Center for Financial Institutions, University of Pennsylvania, Center for Financial Institutions, Working Papers No. 01-09, 2001, 50. Also see Philip R. Wood, *Principles of International Insolvency* (London: Sweet & Maxwell, 1995). The following table summarizes the results:

Ranking	*Countries*
1 = most pro-creditor	Former British colonies except S. Africa and Zimbabwe
2	England, Australia, Ireland
3	Germany, Netherlands, Indonesia, Sweden, Switzerland, Poland
4	Scotland, Japan, Korea, New Zealand, Norway
5	United States, Canada except Quebec
6	Austria, Denmark, Czech and Slovak Republics, S. Africa, Botswana; Zimbabwe (last three Dutch-based)
7	Italy
8	Greece, Portugal, Spain, most Latin American countries
9	Former French colonies, Egypt, Belgium and Zaire
10 = most pro-debtor	France
No insolvency law	Liberia, many Arab countries
Unclassified	Russia, Belarus, Ukraine, Kazakhstan

25. Oliver Hart, Tatiana Nenova, and Andrei Shleifer, "Efficiency in Bankruptcy," *Working paper*, Department of Economics, Harvard University, 2003.

26. K. Pistor, "Who Is Tolling the Bells to Firms? Tales from Transition Economies," Paper given at the Comparative Law and Economics Forum conference, 2005.

27. Political clout may come from interdependencies that ripple through industries and endanger the economy, as happened in the financial meltdown in New York in 2008. Or political clout may come because the firm employs many workers and provides them with social services such as health, schooling, and housing. When such a firm goes bankrupt, its workers lose more than their jobs.

In this respect, gigantic socialist firms resemble the "company towns" built by private firms in the early stages of the industrial revolution in the United States and elsewhere. Under socialism or capitalism, company towns have a gigantic disadvantage for workers: failure in the core industrial enterprise endangers a worker's job and his housing, health, and schooling. In contrast, failure of a small firm endangers a worker's job but not necessarily his social support system. In company towns, loss of employment correlates with loss of social services, which is very risky in a dynamic, changing society. (A similar disability characterizes worker-owned firms.) The correlation of employment and social services increases the motivation of employees in gigantic firms to mobilize politically and protect themselves from disruptive innovations.

28. Political agitation for debt relief has a long history in the United States. In the early part of the nineteenth century, debtors tried to block the creation of a national bank, and in the later part of the nineteenth century debtors wanted the paper dollar backed by silver as well as gold ("bimetalism"), not just gold ("gold standard").

29. This happened in the aftermath of the Asian crisis in Indonesia. In some of the largest Indonesian firms with outstanding debts into the billions of dollars, managers and blockholders still controlled the firm at the expense of outsiders after years of bankruptcy procedure. See R. Tomasic, "Some Challenges of Indonesian Bankruptcy Reform in Indonesia," Forum for Asian Insolvency Reform, Bali, Indonesia, February 7–8, 2001, 19.

30. To solve this problem some developing countries enacted investor-friendly laws in the 1990s, but defects in legal institutions frustrated their application. See K. Pistor, G. Raiser, and S. Gelfer, "Law and Finance in Transition Countries," *Economics of Transition* 8(2) (2000): 325–368.

31. We know of no country whose national accounts include the cost of risk from government guarantees of private loan repayment. Potential liability can mount with no effect on the budget until the risk materializes.

32. For a survey of this research, see Boileau Loko, Montfort Mlachila, Raj Nallari, and Kadima D. Kalonji, "The Impact of External Indebtedness on Poverty in Low-Income Countries," IMF Working Paper 03/61, Washington, DC, International Monetary Fund, 2003.

33. An example is the London debt contract of 1953, in which the Allied countries excused 50 percent of Germany's international prewar debt.

34. The Paris Club is a small group of rich OECD countries that lends to other states. Its members are officials who represent their national governments and take orders from them. The loans include public and publicly guaranteed debts.

35. Present evidence suggests that the severity of financial crises has changed little in emerging markets from the pre-1914 era to the present. A with-without comparison of countries receiving IMF assistance during crises in the period 1973–98 with countries in the same region not receiving assistance suggests that the real performance of the former group was possibly worse than the latter.

M. D. Bordo and A. J. Schwartz, "Measuring Real Economic Effects of Bailouts: Historical Perspectives on How Countries in Financial Distress Have Fared with and without Bailouts," *Carnegie-Rochester Conference Series on Public Policy* 53.1 (2000): 81–160. Also see See J. Frankel and N. Roubini, "The Role of Industrial Country Policies in Emerging Market Crisis," NBER Working Paper No. 8634, National Bureau of Economic Research, Cambridge, MA, 2001.

36. Available at www.spiegel.de/wirtschaft/soziales/0,1518,691847,00.html.

37. A. Meltzer, "Asian Problems and the IMF," Testimony Prepared for the Joint Economic Committee, U.S. Congress, 1998.

38. One proposal would restrict IMF loans to a level where the debt is sustainable. Implementing this proposal requires defining benchmarks for unsustainable debt. See International Monetary Fund and International Development Association, "Debt Sustainability in Low-Income Countries—Proposal for an Operational Framework and Policy Implications," Prepared by the Staffs of the IMF and the World Bank, Approved by M. Allen and G. Nankani, February 3, 2004.

A second proposal advocates a formal bankruptcy procedure for sovereign credits. In 2001, Anne Krueger, the first deputy managing director of the International Monetary Fund, proposed a statutory bankruptcy procedure for sovereign debt. The IMF has not accepted this proposal as yet. However, sovereign bankruptcy law continues to develop through standardized terms in financing contracts such as the London Approach. A current debate concerns whether nations need statutory bankruptcy provisions from the IMF articles or whether a procedure should evolve by market forces and private contracts.

A third proposal, discussed briefly in this chapter, would make IMF loans contingent on the state rescheduling its debts to private creditors. Under this proposal, private banks would help the IMF to save distressed states, instead of the IMF helping the distressed states to save private banks.

See M. White, "Sovereigns in Distress: Do They Need Bankruptcy?" *Brookings Papers on Economic Activity* 1 (2002): 287–319.

39. We benefitted from reading Yvonne Wong's Berkeley Ph.D. dissertation on odious debt and Stefanie Bonilla's Hamburg doctoral thesis, later published as *Odious Debt: Law-and-Economics Perspectives* (Wiesbaden: Gabler Verlag, 2011).

40. Although not required by law, the Paris Club canceled most debts that Iraq owed to its members in November 2004, which amounted to 80 percent of Iraq's state-to-state debts of $37 billion. The IMF report for the Paris Club says that it cancelled Iraq's debts for concern about their long-term sustainability, not their odiousness. This rationale is not credible for a country with the second highest oil reserves in the world.

41. P. Adams, *Odious Debts: Loose Lending, Corruption, and the Third World's Environmental Legacy* (London: Earthscan, 1991).

42. The United States used these ideas to cancel debts contracted by the slaveholding states that attempted to secede in its Civil War. The 14th Amendment to the U.S. Constitution states that "neither the United States nor any State shall

assume or pay any debt or obligation incurred in aid of insurrection or rebellion against the United States . . . all such debts, obligations and claims shall be held illegal and void." After the war against Spain (1898), the United States employed the doctrine of Unconscionability to cancel Cuba's debts owed to Spain, because "they were imposed upon the people of Cuba without their consent and by force of arms." The treaty of Versailles (1919) used the same principle to relieve Poland from all debts owed to Germany and Russia, who had divided and occupied Poland for more than a century. In the 1920s an arbitration court repudiated Costa Rica's debt because its dictator had used the loan for private purposes and the lender had not acted in good faith. Chief Justice Taft of the U.S. Supreme Court used two tests when he arbitrated a dispute over Costa Rica's debts in 1923: exploitation and good faith. He used the exploitative test to determine the percentage of the debts that were squandered or used for illegal purpose. He used the good faith test to check whether or not the creditor knew this. In the 1920s Alexander Sack, professor in Paris and a former czarist minister, developed the concept of "dettes odieuses" to justify the cancellation of Russia's foreign debts after the Russian Revolution.

The principle of odious debt could be grounded in contract principles such as unconscionability, good faith, free consent, fair dealing, and "exceptio doli generalis." However, any definition is fraught with difficulties. To illustrate, following Chief Justice Taft, international law might focus on an exploitation test: "Did international borrowing benefit the citizens of the debtor nation?" However, the exploitation test seems unworkable because *many* governments squander money without benefitting their citizens, including democratic governments.

43. Two alternative implementations are a sanctions approach and a contract approach. See S. Jayachandran and M. Kremer, "Odious Debts," Discussion Paper," Conference on Macroeconomic Policies and Poverty Reduction, IMF, Washington, DC, 2005. Under a sanctions approach, an international authority could declare contracts void that provide *future* loans to a particular country. Under this approach, creditors know for certain whether or not a government is odious when they loan it money. Alternatively, under a contract law approach, a new government can ask a court to determine whether or not the previous government's debts are odious. Under this approach, creditors do not know for certain whether or not international law will enforce a government's debt until after a new government succeeds it and brings suit. Either approach should sharply curtail lending to governments that are odious. In 1997 the International Monetary Fund as well as Western countries broke off economic relations with Croatia, but banks continued lending $2 billion. A declaration that this government was odious might have curtailed such loans.

44. Thus a recent study on the International Court of Justice concluded:

The data suggest that national bias has an important influence on the decision making of the I.C.J. Judges vote for their home states about 90 percent of the time. When their home states are not involved, judges vote for states that are similar to their home states—along the dimensions of wealth, culture, and political regime.

See E. A. Posner, "Is the International Court of Justice Biased?" John M. Olin Law and Economics Working Paper No. 234 (2D Series), Chicago, 2004.

45. Winston Churchill allegedly said, "The U.N. was set up not to get us to Heaven but only to save us from Hell."

46. Did he say this? We could not find out for sure. Nelson Polsby stated the general difficulty: "Great sayings migrate to the mouths of great people."

47. Minimizing the loss from noncooperation is called the "normative Hobbes theorem" in Robert Cooter and Thomas Ulen, *Law and Economics,* 6th ed. (Saddle River, NJ: Prentice Hall, 2011), chapter 4.

Chapter 11: Termites in the Foundation—Corruption

1. These facts are vividly detailed in D. Levy, "Price Adjustment under the Table: Evidence on Efficiency-enhancing Corruption," *European Journal of Political Economy* 23.2 (June 2007): 423–447. A famous American comedian, Will Rogers, said, "It's easy being a humorist when you've got the whole government working for you."

2. Cited in J. Svensson, "Eight Questions about Corruption," *Journal of Economic Perspectives* 19.3 (2005): 19–42.

3. John Cassidy, "The Next Crusade: Paul Wolfowitz at the World Bank," *The New Yorker,* April 9, 2007, 36–51. Jan van Dijk finds a substantial negative effect of corruption on nation wealth. Jan van Dijk, *The World of Crime: Breaking the Silence on Problems of Security, Justice, and Development Across the World* (Newberry Park, CA: Pine Forge Press, 2007), chapter 12.

4. In a remarkable break with past practice, the U.S. president Barak Obama visited Ghana in 2009 and said in a speech that good governance "has been missing in far too many places for far too long. . . . That is the change that can unlock Africa's potential and that is a responsibility that can be met only by Africans." Speech in Ghana, July 11, 2009, as reported by Peter Baker, "In Ghana, Obama Preaches Tough Love," NYTimes.com, July 2009, available at http://www .nytimes.com/2009/07/12/world/africa/12prexy.html?_r=1&hp.

5. For surveys on corruption and economics, see Toke S. Aidt, "Economic Analysis of Corruption: A Survey," *The Economic Journal* 113 (2003): F632–F652; J. C. Andvig, "The Economics of Corruption: A Survey," *Studi Economici* 43 (1991): 57–94; P. Bardhan "Corruption and Development: A Review of Issues," *Journal of Economic Literature* 35 (1997): 1320–1346; S. Rose-Ackerman *Corruption and Government: Causes, Consequences, and Reform* (Cambridge: Cambridge University Press, 1999); and Arvind K. Jain, "Corruption: A Review," in *Issues in New Political Economy* (*Surveys of Recent Research in Economics*), ed. S. Sayer (Cambridge: Blackwell, 2001), 241–292.

6. Spearman rank correlation, 175 countries, 2 tailed critical value, 1 percent: 0.81.

7. E. Luce, *In Spite of the Gods: The Strange Rise of Modern India* (London: Abacus, 2006), 87

8. Transparency International also publishes a "bribe payer's index," which ranks the world's wealthiest and economically dominant countries by the likelihood of their firms to bribe abroad. It is based on the informed observations of several thousand senior business executives in developing and developed countries. In Germany bribes were tax deductible until this practice was abolished after protests from developing countries like India. V. von Nell (2006), "Korruption: Individuelles Handeln im Zeichen der Globalisierung," in *Korruption im Internationalen Vergleich,* ed. von Nell, Schwitzgebel, and Vollet (Weisbaden, Germany: Deutscher Universitätsverlag, 2006), 17. The Organization for Economic Cooperation and Development (OECD) has issued a code of conduct, but it has no teeth. K. Gordon, "The OECD Guidelines and Other Corporate Responsibility Instruments: A Comparison," OECD Working Papers on International Investment No. 2001/5, Paris, 2001. Real progress has occurred in the UNAC (United Nations Convention against Corruption) of 2005, which obliges all signatory states to punish bribery of "foreign public officials" as a criminal offense. In 2009 about 135 states had ratified this convention. United Nations Convention against Corruption, available at http.unodc.org/pdf/crime/convention_corruption/signing/Convention-e.pdf.

9. The currency approach provides an example of an indirect measure: if we know the quantity of money and its rate of circulation, then we can calculate the total monetary value of all transactions. Subtracting from it the value of taxed transactions, we have an estimate of the size of the untaxed transactions. In many tax systems, the untaxed transactions are black market or gray market activities. For estimates using Swiss and international data, see B. Torgler and F. Schneider, "Shadow Economy: Tax Morale, Governance, and Institutional Quality—A Panel Analysis," Berkeley Law and Economic Workshop, Berkeley, CA, 2007.

10. United Nations Surveys on Crime Trends and the Operations of Criminal Justice Systems.

11. Data collection begins with victim's reports to the police. However, people in different countries have different attitudes about the advantages and disadvantages of reporting a crime. Where police are dishonest, a crime report can cause trouble for the victim. Where police are incompetent or overburdened, a crime report is a waste of time. In addition, the police have administrative and political incentives to distort the reports to make them look better than they appear, or to disguise the fact that they are worse than they appear.

12. This crime is usually reported to the authorities. Even so, authorities differ in how they classify the causes of death, especially in countries with domestic uprisings or civil wars.

13. Pearson rank correlation, 133 countries, 2 tailed critical value, 1 percent: 0.232

14. Pearson rank correlation, 112 countries, 2 tailed critical value, 1 percent: 0.232.

15. Our brief discussion omits many important variables affecting the relationship between national wealth and corruption. Wealth increases the opportunities and rewards for corruption, so corruption may increase in spite of spending more to prevent it. This situation is analogous to industrialization causing pollution to increase in spite of rising expenditures on abatement. People have more to steal and rich owners may be less vigilant about losing small amounts. However, the opportunity cost of becoming a criminal is higher in countries with greater rewards for legitimate work. Wealth distribution also plays a role. If a very poor country starts to grow, growth often concentrates in particular regions and sectors. That makes some people very rich very quickly and leaves the incomes of many others unaffected. This concentration of wealth also attracts more crimes. As you can see, the argument gets complicated fast.

16. A. Shleiffer and R. W. Vishny, "Corruption," *Quarterly Journal of Economics* 108 (1993): 599–617. The collapse of communism in the 1990s caused decentralization of corruption in Russia and led to the redistribution of the country's wealth to managers and oligarchs. Other possible Asian cases include the Philippines under Marcos and Indonesia under Suharto, although the top politicians in these countries also tolerated lower-level corruption.

17. In game theory, this is a "principal-agent problem." James Cohen, *The Application of Principal-Agent Theory to Security Sector Reform in Fragile States* (Geneva: IUHEID, 2008).

18. Root argues that democracy requires more extensive support than dictatorship, so democratic politicians will spread largess broadly to gain a lot of votes, whereas dictators will focus largess more intensively to gain greater loyalty from fewer people. See Hilton Root, *Capital and Collusion: The Political Logic of Global Economic Development* (Princeton: Princeton University Press, 2005).

19. See inquirer.net, available at http://opinion.inquirer.net/inquireropinion/columns/view/20090522-206417/Pork-barrel-is-root-cause-of-corruption.

20. Anthony Loyd, 'Corruption, Bribes, and Trafficking: A Cancer that Is Engulfing Afghanistan," *The Times*, November 24, 2007.

21. "International research organizations rank Russia as having the world's most corrupt large economy, in part because of bribery linked to law enforcement personnel. But senior Russian officials have long seemed to view the loyalty of police officers as more important than their integrity." Clifford Levy, "Videos Rouse Russian Anger toward Police," *New York Times*, July 28, 2010, sec. Europe.

22. See Michael Heller, *The Gridlock Economy: How Too Much Ownership Wrecks Markets, Stops Innovation, and Costs Lives* (New York: Basic Books, 2008).

23. C. Abuodha and R. Bowles, "Business License Reform in Kenya and Its Impact on Small Enterprises," *Small Enterprise Development* 11.3 (September 2000): 16–24.

24. Parth J. Shah and Renuka Sane, 2008. "India: The Elephant in the Age of Liberation," in *Making Poor Countries Rich: Entrepreneurship and the Process of Economic Development*, ed. Benjamin W. Powell (Stanford: Independent Institute, 2008), 309–341, at 324.

25. The Judges Remuneration Act of 1994 fixed the yearly salary of a judge of appeal at 253,000 Singapore dollars, which was then US$166,000. In 1997, "high court judges [received] A$835,020, besides other perks and privileges, like a motor car, a government bungalow at economic rent. The chief justice received A$1,260,000 [equivalent to US$700,000] per annum, besides an official residence [or a housing allowance in lieu thereof], a chauffeur-driven car, among other handsome perks and privileges of office. Indeed, he received more than the combined stipends of the Lord Chancellor of England, the Chief Justices of the United States, Canada and Australia." F. T. Seow, former solicitor general of Singapore, "The Politics of Judicial Institutions in Singapore," lecture given in Sydney, Australia, 1997. While judges do not take bribes, they allegedly take instruction from politicians in some cases.

26. Thus Indonesia reformed bankruptcy law and introduced special commercial courts in 1998. The newly appointed judges received special training and improved pay, but accusations of incompetency and corruption persist. Romas Tomasic, "Some Challenges for Insolvency System Reform in Indonesia," Forum for Asian Insolvency Reform in Asia, An Assessment of the recent Developments and the Role oft the Judiciary, Bali, Indonesia, 7–8 February 2001.

27. Bardhan, "Corruption and Development."

28. Several authors have proposed to eliminate some types of corruption by allowing competition between offices. See Rose-Ackerman, *Corruption and Government*.

29. The proxy for federalism is the fraction of government expenditures made by state and local governments. R. Fizman and R.Gatti, "Decentralization and Corruption: A Cross-Country Analysis," *Journal of Public Economics* 83 (2002): 325–345.

30. A. Ades and R. Di Tella, "Rents, Competition, and Corruption," *American Economic Review* 89.4 (1999): 982–993

31. Transparency International data for 2008.

32. A firm can incorporate in any state in the United States, regardless of the location of its headquarters or business activity. This fact created a chartering competition mostly won by Delaware. Many scholars believe the competition was benign on the whole. See Roberta Romano, "The State Competition Debate in Corporate Law," Faculty Scholarship Series, Paper No. 1947, 1987. Available at http://digitalcommons.law.yale.edu/fss_papers/1947.

33. The trust exists in common law but not in civil law. With the creation of the European Union, many Europeans in civil law countries have gone to London to create trusts, which has put pressure on bankers in Frankfurt and Paris to develop instruments under civil that substitute for the trust. See Henry Hansmann and Hogo Mattei, "The Functions of Trust Law: A Comparative Legal and Economic Analysis," *NYU Law Review* 73 (1998): 434–479.

34. For a more complete sketch of the theory of centralization and decentralization of the state, see Robert Cooter, "Part III: The Optimal Number of Governments," *The Strategic Constitution* (Princeton: Princeton University Press, 2000); and Robert Inman and Daniel L. Rubinfeld, "Rethinking Federalism," *Journal of Economic Perspectives* 11 (1997): 43–64.

35. "Bad policy is good politics for the incumbent if it frees resources to invest in loyalty." Hilton Root, *Capital and Collusion*, 36.

36. V. Tanzi, "Corruption around the World: Causes, Consequences, Scope, and Cures," *IMF Staff Papers* 95.4 (1998): 559.

37. This phrase is from Hilton Root, *Capital and Collusion*. Root argues that redistribution to political allies builds committed loyalists.

38. Hernando de Soto, *The Other Path* (New York: Basic Books, 1989), 151.

39. The following table uses data from the World Bank, *Doing Business* (Washington, DC: World Bank, 2010), to show the differences in the number of procedures and costs across regions for opening a business for up to fifty employees. The data should be treated skeptically because of high aggregation and unclear definitions.

Region or economy	Procedures (number)	Cost (% of income per capita)
East Asia & Pacific	8.2	25.8
Eastern Europe & Central Asia	6.7	8.3
Latin America & Caribbean	9.5	36.6
Middle East & North Africa	7.9	34.1
OECD*	5.7	4.7
South Asia	7.3	27.0
Sub-Saharan Africa	9.4	99.7

*The Organization for Economic Cooperation and Development (OECD).

40. See Delhi Group on Informal Sector Statistics, "The Contribution of Informal Sector to GDP in Developing Countries: Assessment, Estimates, Methods, Orientations for the Future," Geneva, August 28–30, 2000. Also see Edgar L. Feige, "Defining and Estimating Underground and Informal Economies: The New Institutional Economics Approach," *World Development* 18.7 (July 1990): 989–1002.

41. William E. Cole and Bichaka Fayissa, "The Urban Subsistence Labor Force: Toward a Policy-Oriented and Empirically Accessible Taxonomy," *World Development* 19.7 (July 1991): 779–789.

42. Bandiera has shown this for the rise of the Sicilian mafia. During Napoleonic times the kingdom of Naples abolished the feudal system and distributed land to small famers. Stealing and robbery during harvest times became a much bigger problem than before, as the large farm holdings required less policing. As the police force was not increased with the land reform the small farmers took refuge in the evolving mafia, which assessed fees to protect their property.

See O. Bandiera, "Land Reform, the Market of Protection, and the Origins of the Sicilian Mafia," *Journal of Law, Economics, and Organization* 19.1 (2003): 218–244.

43. J. O. Finckenauer and Y. A.Voronin, "The Threat of Russian Organized Crime," U.S. Department of Justice, National Institute of Justice, 2001, available at http://www.ojp.usdoj.gov/nij.

44. S. Christiansen, "Violent Youth Groups in Indonesia: The Cases of Yogyakarta and Nusa Tenggara Barat," *Journal of Social Issues in Southeast Asia* 18 (2003): 110–138.

45. M. Fafchamps, "The Enforcement of Commercial Contract in Ghana," *World Development* 34.3 (1996): 427–448.

46. The Japanese Bar association estimated that more than a thousand illegal "fixers" provided their services in bankruptcy procedures in 1995. "Fixers" (*seiriya*) can paralyze or speed up foreclosure, intimidate debtor or debt collectors, or evict tenants whom the law tries to protect. See C. J. Milhaupt and M. D. West, "The Dark Side of Private Ordering: An Institutional and Empirical Analysis of Organized Crime," *University of Chicago Law Review* 67 (2000): 41.

47. See Geneva Declaration, "The Global Burden of Armed Violence," Geneva, September 2008. The underlying theoretical problem concerns natural monopoly and public goods. Effective protection of property and enforcement of contracts requires an organization with more power than any competing organization. Thus a gang cannot protect property effectively unless it is more powerful than any rival within its territory. Instead of diminishing returns, there are increasing returns to power in protecting property and enforcing contracts. Besides the characteristics of a natural monopoly, these enforcement activities also have the characteristics of a public good. To illustrate, the police who make a street safe protect everyone on it, regardless of whether or not they have paid their taxes. Since people benefit without paying, protection activities are difficult to finance voluntarily. The state finances protection activities through taxes, whereas the mafia finances protection activities by extortion. Extortion and gang warfare are much cruder than courts and taxes as ways to capture economies of scale and solve the public goods problem of protecting property and enforcing contracts.

48. See J. van Biesebroeck, "Growth and Productivity Growth in African Manufacturing," *Economic Development and Cultural Change* 53.3 (2005): 545–583, 546; and G. Ranis, "Analytics of Development: Dualism," in *Handbook of Development Economics*, ed. H. Chenery and T. Srinivasan, vol. 1 (New York: North-Holland, 1988), chapter 4. Also note that large companies seldom go public.

49. van Biesebroeck, "Growth and Productivity Growth in African Manufacturing." Remarkable counterexamples do exist for some family enterprises. Thus the Ndegwa Group in Kenya and the Mukwano Group in Uganda developed out of tiny enterprises. Also, the number of stock-listed companies in Africa (except South Africa) is extremely low compared to other regions in the world. In 2004 the number of listed firms per million of population was 1.2 in Ghana, 1.8 in Kenya, 1.5 in Nigeria, 0.1 in Uganda, and 12.0 in South Africa. The world average

was 27.7. See S. Djankow, "The Law and Economics of Self Dealing," World Bank Research Papers 1-80, World Bank, Washington, DC, 2005.

50. Osterfeld distinguishes between corruption that increases output and corruption that decreases it. D. Osterfeld, *Prosperity versus Planning: How Government Stifles Economics Growth* (New York: Oxford University Press, 1992). For empirical application of this distinction, see Douglas A. Houston, "Can Corruption Ever Improve an Economy," *Cato Journal* 27 (2007): 325; and Mushfiq us Swaleheen and Dean Stansel, "Economic Freedom, Corruption, and Growth," *Cato Journal* 27 (2007): 343. Ineffective administration of laws that retard business increase the nation's wealth. To illustrate, the International Trade Commission allows the state to subsidize domestic producers facing unfair competition from foreigners. Sykes argues that the law should be repealed. If not repealed, then he favors an incoherent test for unfair competition in order to make the law ineffective. See Alan O. Sykes, "The Economics of Injury in Antidumping and Countervailing Duty Cases," *International Review of Law and Economics* 16.1 (March 1996): 5–26.

51. For an overview, see Johann Graf Lambsdorff, *The Institutional Economics of Corruption and Reform: Theory, Evidence, and Policy* (Cambridge: Cambridge University Press, 2007).

52. Our discussion of aggravating distrust to prevent bribes is based on a working paper by Robert *Cooter and Nuno Garoupa*, "The Virtuous Circle of Distrust: A Mechanism to Deter Bribes and Other Cooperative Games," Berkley Olin Program in Law and Economics, Working Paper Series, 2000, available at http://repostitories.cdlib.org/blewp/32.

53. See especially G. Fiorentini and S. Peltzman, *The Economics of Organized Crime* (Cambridge: Cambridge University Press, 1995), 1–30; C. Aubert, W. Kovacic, and P. Rey, "The Impact of Leniency and Whistleblowing Programs on Cartels," *International Journal of Industrial Organization* 24 (2006): 1241–1266; G. Spagnolo, "Optimal Deterrence Mechanisms against Cartels and Organized Crime," mimeo, Mannheim University, 2003. We cannot discuss other reasons for organized crimes. For instance, criminal organizations can reduce aggregate punishments by assigning crimes to the member of the gang who expects the most lenient treatment. Besides reducing aggregate punishment, criminal organizations can spread it among the members, rather like insurance spreads the costs of accidents. See N. Garoupa, "The Economics of Organized Crime and Optimal Law Enforcement," *Economic Inquiry* 38 (2000): 278–288.

54. *The Wall Street Journal*, 30 March 2011.

55. To illustrate numerically, a citizen who pays an official $100 for an illegal driving permit should be able to report the crime, hand over the illegal permit and other evidence to convict the official, and receive immunity plus a reward of $125. Similarly, the official who received the bribe should be able to report the crime, hand over the money and other evidence to convict the citizen, and receive immunity plus a reward of $125. The first one to file a successful report would receive immunity and the reward, and the other one would get prosecuted and

convicted. Besides severely disrupting trust, this approach reduces the problem of proof. A report of an attempted bribe will often lack adequate proof. Tangible proof often comes from completing the attempt. The law overcomes this problem by giving immunity and a reward to the first party who reports that he gave or received a bribe.

56. David Kwok, a student of Robert Cooter, is currently writing a Ph.D. dissertation on qui tam. For preliminary results, see David Kwok, "Coordinated Private and Public Enforcement of Law: Deterrence under Qui Tam," Annual Meeting, American Law and Economics Association, May 7–8, 2010.

57. Antonio Acconciay, Giovanni Immordinoz, Salvatore Piccolo, and Patrick Rey, "Accomplice-Witnesses and Organized Crime: Theory and Evidence from Italy," Discussion paper, Center for Studies in Economics and Finance, Naples University Frederico II, 2009.

58. Christopher Kingston, "Parochial Corruption," *Journal of Economic Behavior and Organization* 63.1 (2007): 73–87.

59. A. Brunetti and B. Weder, "A Free Press Is Bad News for Corruption," *Journal of Public Economics* 87.7–8 (August 2003): 1801–1824.

60. This result was calculated with logarithmic values. As usual, there are outliers, such as Singapore, that has no perceived corruption and limited freedom of press.

61. Raymond Fisman and Edward Miguel, "Corruption, Norms, and Legal Enforcement: Evidence from Diplomatic Parking Tickets," *Journal of Political Economy* 115 (2007): 1020.

62. Multiple equilibria characterize models of social norms. See R. Cooter, "Three Effects of Social Norms on Law: Expression, Deterrence, and Internalization," *Oregon Law Review* 79 (2000): 1–22. For the application of this idea to corruption, see P. Bardhan, "Corruption and Development."

63. A jurimetric study of 107 countries show the effectiveness of assets forfeiture programs for combating organized crime. Edgardo Buscaglia, "The Paradox of Expected Punishment: Legal and Economic Factors Determining Success and Failure in the Fight against Organized Crime," *Review of Law and Economics* 4.1 (2008): 290–317, available at http://www.bepress.com/rle/vol4/iss1/art14.

Chapter 12: Poverty Is Dangerous—Accidents and Liability

1. The total number of road fatalities worldwide was estimated at 543,000 in 1999, of which 99,000 occurred in highly motorized rich countries and all others in developing and transition countries. If we considered injuries, the gap would widen many times, because 30 to 45 injuries occur for every fatality. These numbers are estimates that combine data of uneven quality. All figures are from G. Jacobs, A. Aeron-Thomas, and A. Astrop, *Estimating Global Road Fatalities* (London: Department for International Development, 2000), available at http://www

.esafetysupport.org/download/eSafety_Activities/Related_Studies_and_Reports/
Estimating%20Global%20Road%20Fatalities%20report,%20TRL.pdf; WHO, *World Health Statistics*, various issues (New York: WHO). If one corrects these figures for the underreporting bias, they increase insignificantly for Western countries but on the order of 200,000 to 300,000 for developing countries. The *World Health Report 2000* arrives at a much higher number of fatal road traffic accidents (1.23 million for the world and 129,000 for Europe (see statistical appendix, table 3, 168).

2. International Labor Organization, "World Day for Safety and Health at Work: A Background Paper," ILO, Geneva, 2005, available at http://www.ilo.org/public/english/bureau/inf/download/sh _background.pdf.

3. Ibid.

4. Calculated from EM-DAT: The OFDA/CRED International Disaster Database, Université Catholique de Louvain, Brussels, Belgium, available at http.em-dat.net. For a disaster to be entered into the database at least one of the following criteria must be fulfilled: ten or more people reported killed, one hundred or more people reported affected, declaration of a state of emergency, call for international assistance. The following table shows some countries with a large number of fatalities from man-made disasters per 10 million inhabitants during the period 2000–2004:

Country	Fatalities per 10 million inhabitants	Country	Fatalities per 10 million inhabitants
Nigeria	10.76	Thailand	2.65
Iran	9.23	Bangladesh	2.60
Egypt	6.96	Indonesia	2.30
Turkey	5.14	China	2.24
Zaire	4.42	Pakistan	2.19
Russia	3.53	Brazil	2.09
Philippines	2.72		

Source: Calculated from EM-DAT: The OFDA/CRED International Disaster Database, Université Catholique de Louvain, Brussels, Belgium, available at http.em-dat.net.

5. Solving the equation, the value of the car equals $100/.01 or $10,000.

6. In the simplest form of reasoning, if a person will spend $100 to reduce the risk of a fatal accident by 0.001, then value of a fatal risk is $1,000,000. Economists' phrase for the subjective cost of a fatal risk is the "value of a statistical life."

7. W. K.Viscusi and J. E. Aldy, "The Value of a Statistical Life: A Critical Review of Market Estimates throughout the World," *Journal of Risk and Uncertainty* 27.1 (2003): 5–76.

8. Ibid. The income elasticity for the optimal investment to save statistically one life is estimated at 0.5–0.6. The related function between optimal safety investment (I) and per capita income (y) would then be $I = 725y^{0.6}$.

9. J. Liu, J. K. Hammit, J. Liu, "Estimated Hedonic Wage Function and Value of Life in a Developing Country," *Economic Letters* 57.3 (1979): 353–358. Data from 1980s, expressed in 1990 dollars.

10. See W. K.Viscusi and J. E. Aldy, "The Value of a Statistical Life: A Critical Review of Market Estimates throughout the World," *Journal of Risk and Uncertainty* 27.1 (2003): 5–76, 27–28, table 4.

11. Statistics on health tell a similar story to accidents. Work-related diseases kill four times more people than work-related accidents, and these deaths also concentrate in developing and transition countries. The World Health Report of 2005 shows that in 2002 the United States spent 14.6 percent of the GDP on health, and GDP per capita exceeded $27,000. Note that combining accidents and disease puts the total number of work-related fatalities at 2.2 million per year worldwide. Asbestos kills around 100,000, chemical fertilizer and pesticides killed another 70,000, and the hazards of construction work killed approximately 60,000 people. The numbers are far higher for injuries. The number of work accidents causing three or more days of absence is estimated at 268,000,000 for 2001. Of those only 5 percent occur in Western industrialized countries. These numbers increase in most developing countries, especially those with high industrial growth rates. India is a noticeable exception to these results, presumably because of its superior legal and regulatory system relative to many developing countries. Turning to health expenditures, the United States spent roughly $4,000 per capita on health in 2002, which was more than the gross domestic product per capita in many Asian and African countries. World Health Organization, *World Health Report 2005*, Statistical Annex 5, 198.

12. Chapter 11 explains in detail that gray markets operate outside of state regulations.

13. V. Palmade, "Why Worry About Rising Informality? The Biggest and Least Well Understood Impediment to Economic Development," mimeo, The World Bank, Washington, DC, 2005.

14. In principle, a foreign court can accept a tort case and decide it according to the law of the country where the accident occurred, but this is difficult in fact. International law has not resolved this problem. The UN or the ILO set international codes of conduct for multinational firms with respect to safety, health, and the environment. However, international codes are soft law and have no binding force. See K. Tapiola, *UN Global Compact and Other ILO Instruments* (Paris: OECD, 2001); R. Blanpain and M. Colucci, *The Globalization of Labour Standards: The Soft Law Track* (Leiden: Kluwer Law International, 2004.

15. When a court in a developed country applies the same law to resolve a case as a domestic court in a developing country, the injured worker may still want to bring the case in a foreign court because it may be more honest and efficient than the domestic court. Competition for jurisdiction can improve the efficiency of courts, just as competition for markets improves the efficiency of firms. Almost everyone benefits from more efficient courts. In general, if international firms operate in a country with corrupt and inefficient courts, courts in developed countries should hear cases involving torts committed in foreign countries, but the courts should apply standards, care levels, and damages appropriate for low-income countries. In our example, the Japanese court should apply the accident

law of Indonesia, not Japan. Indonesian standards of safety and levels of damages will produce better incentives for plants operating in Jakarta than Japanese standards and damages.

16. Sykes develops this argument in detail in analyzing the effects of the Alien Torts Claim Act (ATCA) of 1789, which regulates access of foreigners to American courts. Alan O. Sykes, "Transnational Forum Shopping as a Trade and Investment Issue," *Law & Economics Colloquium,*.April 21, 2008, Northwestern University, Chicago, Searle Center on Law, Regulation and Economic Growth.

17. Thus English courts have opened the forum to plaintiffs from developing countries in damage claims against multinational firms. See *Lubbe and Others v. Cape Plc.* [2000] 4 All ER 268, in an asbestos case with an English mother company as defendant and citizens from Namibia as plaintiffs.

18. The Code Civil, which France enacted in 1804, devoted only two sections to the law of torts.

19. World Bank, *World Development Indicators* (Washington, DC: World Bank 2005), table 2.5.

20. See M. Förster and M-M. D'Ercole, *Income Distribution and Poverty in OECD Countries in the Second Half of the 1990s* (Paris: OECD, 2005), table 7.4, 74.

21. S. Rose-Ackerman, "Establishing the Rule of Law," in *When States Fail: Causes and Consequences*, ed. R. Rotberg (Princeton: Princeton University Press, 2003), 182–221.

22. If the injurer's wealth only equals $5, then he is almost judgment proof. If he fails to take precaution, his expected liability is .1x$5, which equals $0.50. He saves money by facing expected liability of $0.5 rather than taking precaution that costs $1. Consequently, liability law will not cause a rational injurer with wealth of $5 to take safety precautions in our example.

23. For a comprehensive study see F. Schneider, "Shadow Economies and Corruption All over the World: New Estimates for 145 Countries," *Open-Assessment E-Journal* 1.9 (2007): 1–66. These show estimation results for the period 1999–2005.

24. Roughly speaking, a lawyer working by the hour gains from working more hours than benefit the client, whereas a lawyer who works for a contingency gains by working fewer hours than benefit the client. The attorney working for a contingent fee might put little effort into a case and agree on a settlement with a low recovery for the client, thus yielding a high income per hour worked. For an explanation of these incentives, see Robert Cooter and Tom Ulen, *Law and Economics*, 6th ed. (Saddle River, NJ: Prentice Hall, 2011), chapter 10. Also see A. M. Polinski and D. L. Rubinfeld, "A Note on Settlements under the Contingent Fee Method of Compensating Lawyers," *International Review of Law and Economics* 22.2 (2002): 217–225. Available at http://www.sciencedirect.com/science?_ob=JournalURL&_cdi=5846&_auth=y&_acct=C000047720&_version=1&_urlVersion=0&_userid=10 93976&md5=30359928f2da6a4287539ded6222850f.

25. P. Musgrove, R. Zeramdini, and G. Carrin, (2002) "Basic Patterns in National Health Expenditure," *Bulletin of the World Health Organization* 80.2 (2002): 134–146; also see *World Health Report 2000* (New York: WHO, 2001), 93.

26. A. Krishna, "Escaping Poverty and Becoming Poor: Who Gains, Who Loses, and Why?" *World Development* 32.1 (2004): 121–136.

Chapter 13: Academic Scribblers and Defunct Economists

1. Ralph DePalma, Virginia Hayes, and Leo Zacharski, "Bloodletting: Past and Present," *Journal of the American College of Surgeons* 205 (2007): 132.

2. The Soviet Union apparently suffered approximately 10 million military deaths and 12 million civilian deaths in WWII. World War II killed approximately 4 million Chinese military and 6 million Chinese civilians. So the combined total of war deaths is around 30 million. Robert Conquest estimates famine deaths in the Soviet Union as 11 million from 1926 to 1937. China's Great Leap Forward apparently resulted in around 30 million deaths. So the combined total of famine deaths is over 40 million. Estimates of deaths vary significantly by source. Collectivization of agriculture occurred in a context of other disastrous policies that contributed to the deaths, such as forcing farmers to neglect agriculture and work in village industries in China. For a website that compares estimates, see "Source List and Detailed Death Tolls for the Twentieth Century Hemoclysm," available at http://users .erols.com/mwhite28/warstat1.htm. For a list of casualties by country in World War II, see "World War II casualties," Wikipedia, available at http://en.wikipedia .org/wiki/List_of_World_War_II_casualties_by_country#Casualties_by_country.

3. Data for 2009 from Central Intelligence Agency, *The World Factbook*, available at https://www.cia.gov/library/publications/the-world-factbook/rankorder/ 2102rank.html.

4. John Maynard Keynes, *The General Theory of Employment, Interest, and Money* (London: Macmillan, 1936), 383.

5. The marginal benefit of capital declines with the amount of it, so countries with the least capital benefit the most from getting more of it. Furthermore, the marginal benefit measures the amount that borrowers will pay for capital in a competitive market. Capital markets will lend where borrowers pay the most, which is in poor countries where the marginal benefit of capital is greatest.

6. D. C. North, *Institutions, Institutional Change, and Economic Performance* (Cambridge: Cambridge University Press, 1990), 3; North, "Institutions and Economic Growth: An Historical Introduction," *World Development* 17.9 (1989): 1319, 1321; North and R. P Thomas, *The Rise of the Western World: A New Economic History* (Cambridge: Cambridge University Press, 1973); Barry R. Weingast, "The Economic Role of Political Institutions: Market-Preserving Federalism and Economic Development," *Journal of Law, Economics, and Organization* 11.1 (1995): 1–31.

7. The leading figure in this movement is Andrei Shleifer, and his coauthors E. Glaeser, R. La Porta, F. Lopez-de-Silanes, and R. Vishny. They use cross-country econometrics to conclude that common law tends to evolve toward greater

efficiency than civil law, but this claim has not withstood econometric scrutiny. See Daniel Klerman et al., "Legal Origin and Economic Growth," Working Paper 03-07, Georgia State University School of Policy Analysis, 2009. However, their work can be mined for evidence on growth-increasing differences in the legal basis for financial markets.

We draw on their work here, but, compared to them, we emphasize innovation and deemphasize the common law or civil law origins of different legal systems. Note that an earlier law and development movement in the 1960s flourished briefly and then fizzled out. See D. M. Trubek, "Toward a Social Theory of Law: An Essay on the Study of Law and Development," *Yale Law Journal* 82 (1972): 1; D. M. Trubek and M. Galanter, "Scholars in Self-estrangement: Some Reflections on the Crisis in Law and Development Studies in the United States," *Wisconsin Law Review* 4 (1974): 1062. In contrast, the contemporary economic analysis of law rose like a solid building—excavated tentatively in 1960s, as, e.g., by Ronald Coase, "The Problem of Social Cost," *Journal of Law and Economics* 3 (1960): 1–44; foundations laid in the 1970s, by Guido Calabresi, *The Costs of Accidents* (New Haven, CT: Yale University Press, 1970) and Richard Posner, *Economic Analysis of Law* (Boston: Little, Brown, 1973), and rising dramatically in the 1980s.

8. Psalm 118:22.

9. See P. Krugman, "Complex Landscapes in Economic Geography," *American Economic Review* 84.2 (1994): 412.

10. Gunnar Myrdal, *Economic Theory and Under-Developed Regions* (London: Duckworth, 1957), 79.

11. This claim about developing countries is much like the European claim that Airbus Industrie needed government financing to reach the scale necessary to compete with the Boeing Corporation in building commercial airplanes. Designing large commercial airplanes is so expensive that the world probably has room only for a few manufacturers. In the 1970s the Boeing Corporation dominated the world market, and the Europe Union formed Airbus Industrie to challenge Boeing. European governments heavily subsidized the creation of Airbus, but once it achieved a prominent position in world markets, the consortium was privatized and the subsidies were allegedly removed. (Airbus and Boeing often trade accusations that governments clandestinely subsidize the other firm in violation of the World Trade Organization's rules.) Private capital markets allegedly did not have enough funds to finance Airbus at the scale needed for profitability.

Was the European Union prudent to use state funds? Commentators disagree. Perhaps Airbus is one of those exceptional cases of a good investment that is too large for the private market to finance. Or perhaps Airbus is an uneconomic folly, like the supersonic passenger airplane named the Concorde, which was built using British and French subsidies. The Concorde, whose commercial service began in 1976 and effectively ended with a deadly crash in Paris in 2000, set speed records and never came close to recouping the massive government investments in it. Travelers preferred cheap fares.

12. See P. N. Rosenstein-Rodan, "Problems of Industrialization of Eastern and Southeastern Europe," *Economic Journal* 53.210/211 (1943): 202–211. Leibenstein took a similar view, when he asserted that self-sustained industrial growth first requires state assistance to assure "critical minimum effort." Harvey Leibenstein, *Economic Backwardness and Economic Growth* (New York: Wiley, 1957). Note that big push theory resembles Marx's concept of "primitive accumulation," which played an important role in debate over industrialization in the Soviet Union. The modern industrial sector, according to Marx, *Capital: A Critique of Political Economy* (1867), must achieve a minimum size before it can exist on its own. Capitalists financed the original accumulation of machines, buildings, railroads, and other capital goods by stealing wealth from the guilds, peasants, and others in the traditional sector, not by retaining profits from their own production. To achieve "primitive accumulation," the Soviet state extracted resources from the agricultural sector to finance the industrial sector.

13. See goal 8 of the United National Millennium Project, available at http://www.unmillenniumproject.org/goals/gti.htm#goal8.

14. William Easterly, *The White Man's Burden: Why the West's Efforts to Aid the Rest Have Done So Much Ill and So Little Good* (New York: Penguin Press, 2006).

15. D. Rodrik, "Goodbye Washington Consensus, Hello Washington Confusion? A Review of the World Bank's Economic Growth in the 1990s: Learning from a Decade of Reform," *Journal of Economic Literature* 44.4 (2006): 973.

16. See A. O. Hirschman, *The Strategy of Economic Development* (New Haven: Yale University Press, 1958); and G. Myrdal, *Economic Theory and Underdeveloped Regions* (London: Gerald Duckworth, 1957).

17. See H. J. Bruton, "A Reconsideration of Import Substitution," *Journal of Economic Literature* 36.2 (1998): 903.

18. Raul Prebisch, *The Economic Development of Latin America and Its Principal Problems*, UN document No. E/CN.12/89/Rev.1 (Lake Success, NY: United Nations, 1950).

19. Specifically, demand for raw materials is inelastic, according to Prebisch, so an increase in their supply from developing countries would cause a decline in their world prices. Thus the terms of international trade always turn against exporters of raw materials. So don't focus your economy on exporting raw materials. In addition, random shocks in supply combined with price inelasticity causes large price fluctuations, which disrupt economies. So create a government board to smooth out world price fluctuations. Ibid.; also see H. W. Singer, "The Distribution of Gains between Investing and Borrowing Countries," *American Economic Review: Papers and Proceedings* 40 (1950): 473.

20. Lenin, the leader of Russia's communist revolution that began in 1917, argued that the rich and poor countries stand in the same relationship to each other as the capitalists and the workers in Marx's theory—the former exploit the latter. V. I. Lenin, *Imperialism: The Highest Stage of Capitalism* (New York: International Publishers, 1984).

21. W. A. Lewis, "Economic Development with Unlimited Supplies of Labor," *Manchester School of Economic and Social Studies* 22.2 (1954): 139; J. C. H. Fei and G. Ranis, *Development of the Labor Surplus Economy: Theory and Policy* (Homewood, IL: R. D. Irwin, 1964); D. W. Jorgenson, "The Development of a Dual Economy," *Economic Journal* 71 (1961): 309–334; A. K. Sen, "Peasants and Dualism with and without Surplus Labor," *Journal of Political Economy* 74 (1966): 425–450.

22. The same argument held when a precapitalist feudal landlord under the "noblesse oblige" rule guaranteed a subsistence income to his serf independent of the serf's marginal productivity of labor.

23. Generalizing, dual economy theory holds that the traditional sector sets wages more like a family than a market. Each worker in the traditional sector receives a subsistence wage that depends on the average product per worker, not the marginal product. When a worker moves from the traditional sector to the modern sector, the remaining workers in the traditional sector benefit. Specifically, they benefit by the difference between the traditional worker's average and marginal product. In contrast, competition in the modern sector causes a worker's wage to equal his marginal product.

24. Another policy implication that we do not discuss concerns evaluating investment projects. The World Bank and national development agencies often apply cost-benefit analysis to investment projects in poor countries. According to dual economy theory, cost-benefit analysis should assign little cost to labor drawn from the traditional sector. This accounting practice prices labor below prevailing wages, which makes projects undertaken by the World Bank and national development agencies seem more valuable. In reality, migration from the traditional to the modern sector depends on wage differentials between them. With free migration, the shadow wage in the traditional sector approximately equals the market wage in the market sector. See Raaj Kumar Sah and Joseph E. Stiglitz, "The Social Cost of Labor and Project Evaluation: A General Approach," *Journal of Public Economics* 28 (1985): 135.

25. For a table showing the depression of prices paid to farmers relative to world prices for the main staples in fifty developing countries, see Daphne S. Taylor and Truman P. Phillips, "Food-Pricing Policy in Developing Countries: Further Evidence on Cereal Producer Prices," *American Journal of Agricultural Economics* 73.4 (1991): 1036.

26. In 1756 in the famous Diderot Encyclopedia, Francois Quesnay criticized this feature of mercantilist France as follows: "Wrong promises have drawn people from the countryside into the cities, where the necessity to offer cheap labor led to political pressure on the price for wheat. . . . [This has]has knocked down agriculture into a miserable state of subsistence." F. Quesnay, "Grains," *Encyclopedie de Diderot et d'Alambert* (1757), authors' translation from French.

27. A possible explanation is that farm subsidies in rich countries, where farmers are few, benefit relatively few people, so they can overcome free-riding and devote resources to influencing politicians. Conversely, farm taxes in poor

countries, where farmers are numerous, impose small costs on many people, so they cannot overcome free-riding and devote resources to influencing politicians.

28. An important book that demonstrates the failure and its causes was Bela Balassa and Associates, *The Structure of Protection in Developing Countries* (Baltimore: Johns Hopkins University Press, 1971); also see H. J. Bruton, "A Reconsideration of Import Substitution," *Journal of Economic Literature* 36 (1998): 903.

29. Note that Peron's policies in Argentina and their consequences resemble the mercantilists in France in the eighteenth century, which Adam Smith had criticized.

30. Daron Acemoglu, Simon Johnson, James Robinson, and Yunyong Thaicharoen, "Institutional Causes, Macroeconomic Symptoms: Volatility, Crises, and Growth," *Journal of Monetary Economics* 50 (2003): 49.

31. Two of the seminal works were published in 1944: Abba Lerner, *The Economics of Control* (New York: Macmillan, 1944), and Friedrich A. Hayek, *The Road to Serfdom* (Chicago: University of Chicago Press, 1944).

32. In 2001 the Nobel Prize was awarded to Michael Spence, George Akerlof, and Joseph Stiglitz for contributions to information economics.

33. In recent years, people in low-income countries voluntarily save a larger fraction of their income than people in high-income countries. In general, people save more when they have to pay for their own retirement and medical treatment, rather than the state providing social security and medical care. See *World Development Indicators* (Washington, DC: World Bank, 2007).

34. After the 1950s, capital kept accumulating, but productivity stopped rising and growth rates began a long decline that contributed to the downfall of communism in 1991. M. Harrison and K. B. Ye, "Plans, Prices, and Corruption: The Soviet Firm under Partial Centralization, 1930 to 1990," *Journal of Economic History* 66.1 (2006): 1.

35. All data are from R. G. King and R. Levine, "Capital Fundamentalism, Economic Development, and Economic Growth," Carnegie-Rochester Conference Series on Public Policy 40, 1994.

36. From 1980 to 1992, capital per capita increased by more than 1 percent per year in Costa Rica, Ecuador, Peru, and Syria, and per capita GDP decreased. W. Easterly and R. Levine, "It's not Factor Accumulation: Stylized Facts and Growth Models," Central Bank of Chile Working Paper No. 164, Central Bank of Chile, Santiago, 2002, 10. Between 1980 and 2004, average per capita growth rates in high-income countries were 1.93 per cent per annum, compared to 1.97 percent per annum in low- and middle-income countries.

Note, however, that the experience of Tunisia in this period resembles Britain more than it resembled its neighbor, Algeria. In Tunisia the capital output ratio was slightly higher than in Algeria in 1960 and the capital stock per capita was then about half of what it was in Algeria. Between 1960 and 1988 the per capita capital stock in Tunisia increased by around 70 percent. Tunisia experienced a real per capita growth of about 40 percent over the period of twenty-eight years.

The capital output ratio decreased substantially during the same period. Easterly and Levine, "It's not Factor Accumulation."

37. The ratio of output to capital measures capital's productivity. The capital-output ratio changed little in the UK as capital accumulated and income increased. Easterly and Levine, "It's not Factor Accumulation."

38. In general, an increase in an economy's output per worker can be subdivided into the amount caused by increases in capital per worker, more education of workers, and a residual that represents better organization and other unmeasured changes. Thus Easterly and Levine analyzed the growth of income per capita for sixty countries between 1960 and 1992. They found more capital and education explained roughly 40 percent, leaving 60 percent unexplained. In their study, immeasurable variables like better organization cause most growth. Ibid.

39. J. Williamson, "Democracy and the 'Washington Consensus,'" *World Development* 21.8 (1993): 1329.

40. For privatization by sector in developing countries, see table 2 in Pierre Guislain, "The Privatization Challenge: A Strategic, Legal, and Institutional Analysis of International Experience," *World Bank and Regional and Sectoral Studies* (Washington, DC: World Bank, 1997).

41. Also, of all net private direct investments (equity capital investment of inside investors) into developing countries in 2005, 78 percent went to only twenty-three countries. World Bank, *Global Development Finance* (Washington, DC: World Bank, 2006), statistical appendix.

42. For data on growth rates by region and country, see A. Maddison *Monitoring the World Economy, 1820–1992* (Paris: OECD, 1995), *The World Economy: A Millennial Perspective* (Paris: OECD Development Centre, 2001), *The World Economy: Historical Statistics* (Paris: OECD Development Centre, 2003).

43. Hugo A. Hopenhayn and Pablo A. Neumeyer, "Latin America in the XXth Century: Stagnation, then Collapse," Department of Economics Working Papers No. 028, Discussion paper 2004, Universidad Torcuato Di Tella, Buenos Aires, Argentine, 1–28.

44. D. Rodrik, A. Subramanian, and F. Trebbi, "Institutions Rule: The Primacy of Institutions over Geography and Integration in Economic Development," *Journal of Economic Growth* 9 (2004): 131.

45. The ideal index for testing a legal theory of economic growth would measure *effective* law as distinguished into three components: property, contracts, and business law. For an attempt to measure the effective law of property and contracts, and to use the index in cross-country regressions, see Bernhard Heitger, "Property Rights and Their Impact on the Wealth of Nations—A Cross-Country Study," Kiel Working Paper No. 1163, Kiel Institute for World Economics, Keil, Germany, 2003. His simultaneous regression model indicates that doubling the index of the quality of property rights leads to a more than doubling in per capita incomes.

46. Rodrik, "Goodbye Washington Consensus, Hello Washington Confusion?" 979, summarized his research results with the following words:

The cross-national literature has been unable to establish a strong causal link between any particular design feature of institutions and economic growth. We know that growth happens when investors feel secure, but we have no idea what specific institutional blueprints will make them feel more secure in a given context. The literature gives us no hint as to what the right levers are. Institutional function does not uniquely determine institutional form.

47. E. L. Glaeser, R. la Porta, F. Lopez-De-Silanes, and A. Shleifer, "Do Institutions Cause Growth?" *Journal of Economic Growth* 9 (2004): 271. Democracy and constrained government cannot explain growth. But as growth occurs it generates better institutions according to their findings. They also find human capital to be a strong determinant of growth, contrary to findings by other authors such as Robert E. Hall and Charles I. Jones, "Levels of Economic Activities across Countries," *American Economic Review* 87.2 (1997): 173–177; and Easterly, who point to institutions and social capital.

48. An insightful book with a similar conclusion about economic development is William Baumol, Robert Litan, and Carl J. Schramm, *Good Capitalism, Bad Capitalism, and the Economics of Growth and Prosperity* (New Haven: Yale University Press, 2007).

49. To illustrate, inflation-adjusted oil prices increased sharply from the mid 1970s until 1980, and then fell back to the previous low levels where they remained until turning up again in 2002. Whereas public officials predicted a sharp rise in oil prices, they remained stable for twenty years. Politicians in the United States, however, used the prediction of rising oil prices to justify subsidies for private companies to construct and operate plants to extract oil from shale. The plants were uneconomic at current prices, but politicians and state officials predicted that prices would rise enough to justify the investment. In fact, these plants never became economic and they closed down after the subsidies expired. U.S. taxpayers lost a massive amount of money and some very large energy companies profited handsomely.

50. The technical name for this proposition is the "efficient market hypothesis." According to the efficient market hypothesis, market prices incorporate all public information, so no one investor can do better than chance when relying on public information. This is the "semistrong" form of the efficient market hypothesis. You don't have to accept the semistrong form of the efficient market hypothesis in order to accept that much business innovation is unpredictable from public information. Consequently, if private investors cannot profit by trading on public information except by chance, then public officials are unlikely to do better.

51. As clearly seen in the example of the U.S. oil shale boondoggle mentioned in note 50 of this chapter.

52. Infrastructure projects often face obstacles that only the state can overcome. To illustrate, developing infrastructure often requires assembling large tracts of land from fragmented private owners. Thus a proposed road may cross

land owned by many different people. Voluntary purchase of land to construct the road encounters a fatal problem: owners who holdout by refusing to sell their land can command a higher price. To avoid holdouts, most legal systems allow the state to compel owners of land to sell it. Also, some forms of infrastructure are natural monopolies. For example, most towns do best with a single grid of electricity wires connecting homes and businesses, a single superhighway system to connect towns, and a few cable systems for Internet and television. Natural monopoly, especially for infrastructure, often requires state participation as owner or, if not as owner, then as regulator of the private owner.

53. Milhaupt and Pistor regard coordination as an important role of the state in promoting economic development. See C. J. Milhaupt and K. Pistor, *Law and Capitalism: What Corporate Crises Reveal about Legal Systems and Economic Development around the World* (Chicago: University of Chicago Press, 2008). Thus the best and brightest staff Korea's Ministry of Finance and Japan's MITI. In the 1950s and 1960s, MITI coordinated miraculous economic growth in Japan by such methods as pressuring companies to share technological innovations through cross-licensing. Similarly, Zenishi Shishido told Cooter that MITI did not choose industrial winners so much as mediate industrial conflicts. Thus MITI arranged for a gradual rundown of the coal mining industry in the 1950s and 1960s to get workers out of this uneconomical business. More recently, MITI in cooperation with the Ministry of Justice adopted a rule for administrative guidance on hostile takeovers similar to Delaware. This has opened the market for hostile acquisitions. Economic experts dispute whether MITI *caused* rapid growth, or other forces caused growth and MITI merely *participated* in it. See M. Yishiro and J. M. Ramseyer, "Capitalist Politicians, Socialist Bureaucrats? Legends of Government Planning from Japan," Discussion Paper No. 385, Harvard John M. Olin Center for Law, Economics, and Business Discussion Paper Series, Cambridge, MA, 2002. In any case, investment bankers agree that the period of MITI's guidance of the economy diminished with time until it ended around 1990. A similar history applies to Korea. In contrast, since 1990 Taiwan has grown at about the same rate as Korea and faster than Japan, although Taiwan has no equivalent of Japan's MITI or Korea's Ministry of Finance.

Chapter 14: How the Many Overcome the Few

1. Another curious fact: for more than a millennium, until the seventeenth century, science regarded children as having a biological bond only with their fathers and not with their mothers, in spite of the obvious fact that children often resembled their mother.

2. A party to a legal dispute, say, the plaintiff in an antitrust case, interviews experts to find someone to present testimony in court. You can be sure that the

plaintiff will select an expert whose testimony will be favorable to the plaintiff. Selection for a favorable expert is just as rigorous when a minister or similar political official hires an economist to give expert advice. The economic expert is selected to give the sanction of science to the economic policies of the politician or party that hires him. Politicians mostly select economic ideas for political usefulness, not for inherent truth.

3. Omar Azfar remarked, "Politics makes economists seem optimistic."

4. R. J. Daniels and M. J. Trebilcock, "The Political Economy of Rule of Law Reform in Developing Countries," Manuscript 1-44 (2004), which in revised form later was published as *Rule of Law Reform and Development: Charting the Fragile Path of Progress* (London: Elgar Press, 2008). Believing that the problem was ignorance was also an error of the law and development movement in the 1970s. See David M. Trubeck and Marc Galanter, "Scholars in Self-Estrangement: Some Reflections on the Crisis in Law and Development," *Wisconsin Law Review* 4 (1974): 1062–1101.

5. Paul Stephan argues that Gorbachev abandoned central planning with the aim of supporting the Communist Party's power by taxing a market economy, but he could not retain political control for the Communist Party as the economy privatized. See "The Fall—Understanding the Collapse of the Soviet System," *Suffolk University Law Review* 29 (1996): 17–49. Also see "Privatization after Perestroika: The Impact of State Structure," *Whittier Law Rev.* 14 (1993): 403.

6. Kondtatine Magin, "Corruption in Russia in the 1990s: A Time Bomb and a Necessity of Business," Ph.D. diss., University of California at Berkeley, 2003.

7. This is called "spontaneous nomenklatura privatization."

8. Andrei Shleifer and Daniel Treisman, *Without a Map: Political Tactics and Economic Reform in Russia* (Cambridge, MA: MIT Press, 2001), 9. This figure covers the years 1991–95, whereas Magin's characterizes the first state of privatization as the years 1990–94.

9. See Shleifer and Treisman, *Without a Map*, 13.

10. Chapter 9 discusses the "control premium"—the difference in the price per share when someone buys a few shares of stock, and the price per share when someone buys a controlling block of shares.

11. Magin's Ph.D. dissertation describes several causes of concentrations. The banks that organized auctioning of shares were also buyers, so they manipulated the process to direct shares to themselves or to associated companies. Inflation pauperized workers and caused them to sell their shares to wealthy people. Inflation also caused the state to borrow money from 1995 to 1998. The lenders were the oligarchs who got shares as collateral. When the state defaulted, the oligarchs kept the shares.

12. K. Hoff and Joseph Stiglitz, "After the Big Bang? Obstacles to the Emergence of the Rule of Law in Post-Communist Societies," National Bureau of Economic Research Working Paper No. 9282, NBER, Cambridge, MA, 2002.

13. The holdings of some oligarchs were expropriated under threat of imprisonment. Others were bought, notably by giving them the privilege of buying high-yielding government bonds. See Shleifer and Treisman, *Without a Map*, 13.

14. Roman Frydman, Katharina Pistor, and Andrzej Rapaczynski, "Investing in Insider-Dominated Firms: A Study of Russian Voucher Privatization Funds," in *Corporate Governance in Central Europe and Russia,* vol. 1, *Banks, Funds, and Foreign Investors,* ed. Roman Frydman, Cheryl W. Gray, and Andrzej Rapaczynski (Budapest: Central European University Press, 1996); and Roman Frydman, Katharina Pistor, and Andrzej Rapaczynski, "Exit and Voice after Mass Privatization: The Case of Russia," *European Economic Review* 40.3–5 (April 1996): 581–588.

15. A. Dixit, "On Pareto-Improving Distributions of Aggregate Economic Gains," *Journal of Economic Theory* 41.1 (1987): 133–153; D. Acemoglu and J. A. Robinson, "Political Losers as a Barrier to Economic Development," *American Economic Review* 90 (2000): 126–130.

16. Vilfredo Pareto was a nineteenth-century Italian economist who first recognized the centrality of these changes to economic analysis.

17. The paradigm in economic theory for Pareto gains is exchange in free markets. In the absence of coercion or misinformation, exchange creates a surplus that the parties share to their mutual benefit.

18. The paradigm for a net gain is state provision of a local public good such as a road. Commuters ideally gain from driving on the road, much more than taxpayers lose from paying for it. Those taxpayers lose who pay for the road without using it, such as pedestrians who do not drive. There is a net gain for society but some individuals lose.

19. The paradigm for a net loss is a cartel. The members of the cartel gain less in monopoly profits than the consumers lose from higher prices.

20. Polyarchy is government by many persons, of whatever order or class. "We may be able to loosen the grip of a few organized interests on power by forcing them to share political leverage with a variety of other groups. This is polyarchie; it is also rough justice, the only kind human beings will ever experience.".S. Holmes, "Lineages of the Rule of Law," in *Democracy and the Rule of Law,* ed. J. M. Maravall and A. Przeworski (Cambridge: Cambridge University Press, 2003), 19–60.

21. For economists, this is the problem of "free riding," which arises wherever results require "collective action" (people must act jointly in order to produce a result.)

22. This view is especially associated with the Chicago school in economics, for example, see George Stigler, *The Citizen and the State* (Chicago: University of Chicago Press, 1975); and Sam Peltzman, "Towards a More General Theory of Regulation," *Journal of Law and Economics* 19 (1976): 211–240. This view is also identified with the concept of "rent seeking" as that term is used in public choice theory. An early work that remains a classic is Mancur Olson's *The Logic of Collective Action: Public Goods and the Theory of Groups* (Cambridge, MA.: Harvard University Press, 1965). Conventional examples of such laws that usually cause a net loss to society include tariffs on imported goods, regulations restricting entry into a business, and most industrial subsidies. Our discussion of loans in chapters 4 and 6 describe an unconventional example. The borrowers who default on current loans receive a large benefit from actively resisting the seizure of their

collateral by the lender. Laws and policies that prevent creditors from seizing the collateral of defaulting debtors cause lenders to deny many future applications for loans, but the future borrowers are a diffuse group who may respond passively.

23. B. Vogel, "Introduction," in *Preussische Reformen, 1807–1820*, ed. B. Vogel (Berlin: Verlagsgruppe Athenäum, 1980), 1–29; H. Bleiber, "Die Preußischen Agrarreformen in der Geschichtsschreibung der DDR, " in *Gemeingeist und Bürgersinn, die Preußischen Reformen*, ed. B. Sösemann (Berlin: Duncker and Humblot, 1993), 109–125.

24. P. K. Bardhan, *Scarcity, Conflicts, and Cooperation: Essays in Political and Institutional Economics of Development* (Cambridge, MA: MIT Press, 2004). Also, for a good discussion of obstacles to institutional development in poor countries, see P. K. Bardhan, "Understanding Underdevelopment: Challenges for Institutional Economics from the Point of View of Poor Countries," *Journal of Institutional and Theoretical Economics* 156: 216–235.

25. J. M. Baland and J. P. Platteau, "Wealth Inequality and Efficiency in the Commons, Part II," *Oxford Economic Papers* 50 (1998): 1–22

26. "Governments seeking supports for policies to open the economy face the challenge of making the policies credible (anticipation). To be credible, however, the policies must enjoy the support of large numbers of diverse social groups (cohesion). Cohesion is unlikely unless the benefits are perceived to be widely distributed (inclusion). Without these elements in place, market-friendly regimes will have difficulty establishing themselves and surviving." Hilton Root, *Capital and Collusion: Political Logic of Global Economic Development* (Princeton: Princeton University Press, 2006), 18.

27. Every net gain can be turned into a Pareto gain by appropriate redistribution of the surplus. If political powerbrokers detect a net gain in society, then they can propose a bargain that makes everyone better off. This proposition extends the Coase theorem from law to politics. Various obstacles, notably transaction costs and strategic behavior, can obstruct such bargains. In addition, every bargain poses a problem of distributing the surplus between the parties. Economists have proposed axiomatic, rational solutions to the division of the surplus, most famously Nash and Rubinstein. See Ariel Rubinstein, "Perfect Equilibrium in a Bargaining Game," *Econometrica* 50 (1982): 97–109; and M. J. Osborn and A. Rubinstein, *Bargaining and Markets*, (Leiden: Elsevier, 1990). These models, however, fail to predict the frequency with which parties fail to cooperate because they cannot agree on how to divide the surplus.

28. The "veil of ignorance" is the famous phrase used by John Rawls in his magisterial book, *A Theory of Justice* (1971). Rawls connects ignorance with fairness, because people are more nearly impartial about a law when they do not know who will win and lose. Ackerman suggests that the veil of ignorance can descend historically when a society faces a large constitutional crisis and everyone is uncertain about the future. This is one kind of "constitutions moment." See B. Ackerman, *The Future of Liberal Revolution* (New Haven: Yale University Press, 1992).

29. In statistical terms, each player expects to win 1.5, so playing the game makes everyone better off ex ante than not playing the game. Ex post, however, one person wins 4 and the other loses 1.

30. Note that diffuse costs pacify opponents and diffuse benefits pacify proponents. When diffuse benefits pacify proponents, we have a "free rider problems": everyone waits for someone else to take the initiative of enacting the growth-promoting reform.

31. Yingyi Qian, "How Reform Worked in China," University of California, Berkeley, Discussion paper, 2001, 1–63

32. Authoritarian governments that lack legitimacy from democratic elections often seek legitimacy in economic growth and welfare.

33. Lawrence J. Lau, Yingyi Qian, and Gérard Roland, "Pareto-Improving Economic Reforms through Dual-Track Liberalization," *Economics Letters* 55.2 (1997): 285–292. In July 2005, Cooter had the privilege of a brief conversation with China's premier, Wen Jiabao, who is regarded as the leading figure behind China's economic policy. Cooter asked, "What is the difference between a social market economy and a capitalist market economy?" The premier replied, "The difference is historical." In the present, there is apparently little difference.

34. In a private e-mail to Cooter on April 7, 2008, Xu Guangdong provides a more nuanced view that distinguishes Chinese economic reforms into two phases.

> Generally speaking, the overall process of China's economic reform may be interpreted as consisting of two main phases. The first phase, from 1979 to 1992, was known for the famous dual-track system, which refers to the coexistence of a traditional plan and a market channel for the allocation of a given good. The market track improved efficiency while the plan track achieved Pareto-improvement by providing implicit transfers to compensate potential losers from market liberalization. As a result, it was very rare for a major social group to suffer significant economic losses and this phase has been labeled "reform without losers." During this period, rural incomes grew 15% per year from 1978 to 1985, and 2.8% per year from 1985 to 1991. Urban incomes increased 7% per year from 1978 to 1985, and 4.8% per year from 1985 to 1991. At the same time, the economic reform narrowed the urban-rural gap and led China's overall Gini coefficiency to 0.28 in 1983, which made China one of the most equal countries in the world. Besides, the proportion of the population living in poverty fell dramatically from 53% in 1981 to 17% in 1987.
>
> The second phase, which greatly changed the regulatory and administrative framework in the key market sectors including banking system, tax system, the system of corporate governance, and so on, did impose significant losses on substantial social groups and lead to a "reform with losers." First, due to state-owned enterprise restructuring, millions of workers were laid off with limited compensation and insufficient social security. Second, more and more

rural lands were taken by local governments to support urban projects, to finance the operation of local governments, or even serve the private interests of officials. Furthermore, government shirked its responsibility to provide education, healthcare, and housing, which have become the biggest outlays in household expenditure. During this period, rural incomes grew 4.9% per year from 1991 to 2004, while urban incomes increased 7.7% per year. However, at the same time, the fiscal revenues increased 16% per year from 1995 to 2007, which means that government became the main beneficiary of economic reform. Meanwhile, inequality has been rising. The Gini coefficiency increased to 0.447 in 2001, which made China similar to the most unequal Asian developing countries such as Thailand (0.43) or the Philippines (0.46). Furthermore, from 2001 to 2003, the income of people [in poverty] decreased 2.4% per year.

Xu Guangdong's views were influenced by Barry Naughton, *The Chinese Economy: Transitions and Growth* (Cambridge, MA: MIT Press, 2007), chapter 4. Also see Martin Ravallion and Shaohua Chen, "China's (uneven) Progress against Poverty," *Journal of Development Economics* 82 (2007): 1–42.

35. In the language of Campos and Root, these countries made "credible commitments" to property owners that secured "the political foundation of economic rights." J. E. Campos and H. Root, *The Key to the Asian Miracle: Making Shared Growth Credible* (Washington, DC: Brookings Institutions Press, 1996), 175. Campos and Root stress the advantages of policies that not only cause Pareto gains but also convince the public of the state's commitment to such policies. Their account of Asia's success is very similar to ours.

36. Economists sometimes summarize these facts by saying "there is no political Coase theorem." The Coase theorem is the proposition that people can always achieve the surplus from bargains when the transaction costs are not too high. This proposition is more true of individual choices than collective choices.

37. A legislature sometimes enacts a statute forbidding its repeal by a future legislature, but most constitutions give the legislature broad powers that effectively preclude such "entrenchment."

38. The government tried to abolish the privy purse by an executive order, which the Supreme Court ruled unconstitutional in 1971. Parliament subsequently abolished it by an amendment of the Indian constitution in 1975. S. J. Sorabjee, "Palkhivala and the Constitution of India," in *Nani Plakhivala: A Role Model for India,* ed. M.G.N. Kuma (Delhi: Universal Law Publications, 2006), 46–61.

39. The dictator's dilemma is a single-trust problem: the dictator gives up power first and trusts the civilian government not to prosecute him. In contrast, innovation is a double trust problem.

40. In terms of game theory, politics has relatively more zero sum games (redistribution), and business has more positive sum games (production). The political philosopher Carl Schmitt famously defined the political as the sphere of conflict in which people confront each other as enemies.

41. G. Clark, "Labour Productivity in English Agriculture: 1300–1860," in *Agricultural Productivity in the European Past*, ed. B.M.S. Campbell and M. Overton (Manchester, UK: Manchester University Press, 1991), 211–235.

42. Figures taken from Gertrud Helling, "Die Entwicklung der Agrarproduktivität in der deutschen Landwirtschaft im 19. Jahrhundert," *Jahrbuch für wirtschaftsgeschichte* 1 (1966): 129–141, 134, 139. The latter figure refers to the whole of Germany and cereal products only. A debate remains about the extent to which reforms contributed to these productivity gains.

43. See Federalist Papers 10 and 51.

44. *The Prince* (1513), chapter 6.

Chapter 15: Legalize Freedom—Conclusion

1. In his essay "Utilitarianism," John Stuart Mill broke with the utilitarian tradition by arguing that pleasures differ in quality, and some are better than others. See *Utilitarianism, Liberty and Representative Government* (New York: Dutton, 1951).

2. Robert Cooter and Peter Rappoport, "Were the Ordinalists Wrong about Welfare Economics?" *J. Economic Literature* 22 (1984): 507.

Bibliography

Acemoglu, Daron, and James Robinson. 2001. Inefficient Redistribution. *American Political Science Review* 95: 649–661.

———. 2006. Economic Backwardness in Political Perspective. *American Political Science Review* 100: 115.

Adelman, I. 1999. Fallacies in Development Theory and their Implications for Policy. CUDARE Working Paper Series No 887, University of California at Berkeley, Department of Agricultural and Resource Economics and Policy.

Adelman, I., and C. Taft Morris. 1997. Development History and Its Implications for Development Theory. *World Development* 25.6: 831–840.

Adelman, Irma, and Erinc Yeldan. 2000. Is This the End of Economic Development? *Structural Change and Economic Dynamics* 11.2 (July): 95–109.

Agrawal, Arun. 2001. Common Property Institutions and Sustainable Governance of Resources. *World Development* 29.10 (October): 1649–1672.

Allen, Franklin, and Jun Qian. 2008. China's Financial System: Past, Present and Future. In *China's Great Economic Transformation*, edited by L. Brandt and T. Rawski, 506–568. Cambridge: Cambridge University Press.

Allen, Robert C. 2005. Real Wages in Europe and Asia: A First Look at the Long-term Patterns. In *Living Standards in the Past: New Perspectives on Well-Being in Asia and Europe*, edited by Robert C. Allen, Tommy Bengtsson, and Martin Dribe, chapter 5. Oxford: Oxford University Press.

Amable, Bruno, and Jean-Bernard Chatelain. 2001. Can Financial Infrastructures Foster Economic Development? *Journal of Development Economics* 64.2 (April): 481–498.

Anand, Sudhir, and Amartya Sen. 2000. Human Development and Economic Sustainability. *World Development* 28.12 (December): 2029–2049.

Anderson, Gary M., and Robert D. Tollison. 1983. The Myth of the Corporation as a Creation of the State. *International Review of Law and Economics* 3.2 (December): 107–120.

Anderson, Michael. 2002. Getting Rights Right: Is Access to Justice as Important as Access to Health or Education? *International Development 21 Insights:
Communicating Development Research* 43, available at http://www.id21.org/
insights/insights43/insights-iss43-art00.html.

Anti-Monopoly Law of the People's Republic of China (Draft). 2003.

Armour, John, and Priya Lele. 2008. Law, Finance, and Politics: The Case of India.
ECGI Law Working Paper No. 107/2008.

Baran, P. A., and P. M. Sweezy. 1966. *Monopoly Capital: An Essay on the American
Economic and Social Order.* New York: Monthly Review Press.

Bardhan, Pranab. 1990. Symposium on the State and Economic Development.
Journal of Economic Perspectives 4.3 (summer): 3–7.

———. 1993. Economics of Development and the Development of Economics.
Journal of Economic Perspectives 7.2 (spring): 129–142.

———. 1993. Symposium on Democracy and Development. *Journal of Economic
Perspectives* 7.3 (summer): 45–49.

———. 1996. Efficiency, Equity, and Poverty Alleviation: Policy Issues in Less
Developed Countries. *Economic Journal* 106.438 (September): 1344–1356.

———. 1997. Corruption and Development: A Review of Issues. *Journal of Economic Literature* 35.3 (September): 1320–1346.

Barro, R. J. 1996. Determinants of Economic Growth: A Cross-Country Empirical Study. NBER Working Paper No. 5698. National Bureau of Economic
Research, Cambridge, MA.

Barzel, Yoram. 1990. *Economic Analysis of Property Rights.* New York: Cambridge
University Press.

Baumol, William, Robert Litan, and Carl J. Schramm. 2007. *Good Capitalism, Bad
Capitalism, and the Economics of Growth and Prosperity.* New Haven: Yale University Press.

Bekaert, Geert, and Campbell R. Harvey. 2003. Emerging Markets Finance. *Journal of Empirical Finance* 10.1–2 (February): 3–56.

Berg, Sanford V. 2000. Sustainable Regulatory Systems: Laws, Resources, and
Values. *Utilities Policy* 9.4 (December): 159–170.

Berkowitz, Daniel, and Wei Li. 2000. Tax Rights in Transition Economies: A Trag-
edy of the Commons? *Journal of Public Economics* 76.3 (June): 369–397.

Black, B., R. H. Kraakman, and J. Hay. 1996. Corporate Law from Scratch. In *Corporate Governance in Central Europe and Russia*, edited by R. Frydman, C. Gray,
and A. Rapaczynski. Vol. 2. *Insiders and the State*, 247–302, esp. 257. Washington, DC: World Bank.

Bolton P, and G. Roland. 1997. The Breakup of Nations: A Political Economy Analysis. *Quarterly Journal of Economics* 112: 1057–90.

Borensztein, E., J. De Gregorioand, and J-W. Lee. 1998. How Does Foreign Direct
Investment Affect Economic Growth? *Journal of International Economics* 45.1
(June 1): 115–135.

Bosworth, Barry, and Susan M. Collins. 2008. Accounting for Growth: Comparing China and India. *Journal of Economic Perspectives* 22 (2008): 45–66.

Brander, James A. 1992. Comparative Economic Growth: Evidence and Interpretation. *Canadian Journal of Economics* 25.4 (November): 792–818.

Brautigam, Deborah. 1992. Governance, Economy and Foreign Aid. *Studies in Comparative International Development* 27.3 (fall): 3–26.

———. 1997. Substituting for the State: Institutions and Industrial Development in Eastern Nigeria. *World Development* 25.7 (July): 1063–1080.

Brinkerhoff, Derick W. 2000. Democratic Governance and Sectoral Policy Reform: Tracing Linkages and Exploring Synergies. *World Development* 28.4 (April): 601–615.

Buchanan, J. M. 1987. The Constitution of Economic Policy. *American Economic Review* 77.3: 243–250.

———. 1988. Contractarian Political Economy and Constitutional Interpretation. *American Economic Review* 78.2: 135–139.

———. 2001. Judicial Reform in the Americas. Canadian Foundation for the Americas. November. Available at http://www.focal.ca/images/pdf/Judicial.pdf.

Burg, Elliot M. 1997. Law and Development: A Review of the Literature and a Critique of "Scholars in Self-Estrangement." *American Journal of Comparative Law* 25: 492–530.

Burgess, Robin, and Nicholas Stern. 1993. Taxation and Development. *Journal of Economic Literature* 31.2 (June): 762–830.

Buscaglia, Edgardo. 2001. An Analysis of Judicial Corruption and Its Causes: An Objective Governing-based Approach. *International Review of Law and Economics* 21.2 (June): 233–249.

———. 2001. The Economic Factors behind International Legal Harmonization: A Jurimetric Analysis of the Latin American Experience. *Emerging Markets Review* 2.1 (March 1): 67–85.

Buscaglia, Edgardo, William Ratliff, and Robert Cooter, eds. 1997. *Law and Economics of Development*. Greenwich, CT: JAI Press.

Buscaglia, Edgardo, William Ratliff, and Maria Dakolias. 1995. *Judicial Reform in Latin America: A Framework for National Development. Essays in Policy Studies*. Stanford, CA: Stanford University Press.

Buscaglia, E., and T. Ulen. 1997. A Quantitative Assessment of the Efficiency of the Judicial Sector in Latin America. *International Review of Law and Economics* 17.2: 275–291.

Calderón, César, and Lin Liu. Article in press. The Direction of Causality between Financial Development and Economic Growth. *Journal of Development Economics*.

Campbell, Bruce, Alois Mandondo, Nontokozo Nemarundwe, Bevlyne Sithole, Wil De Jong, Marty Luckert, and Frank Matose. 2001. Challenges to Proponents of Common Property Resource Systems: Despairing Voices from the Social Forests of Zimbabwe. *World Development* 29.4 (April): 589–600.

Campos, J. Edgardo, Donald Lien, and Sanjay Pradhan. 1999. The Impact of Corruption on Investment: Predictability Matters. *World Development* 27.6 (June): 1059–1067.

Carino, Ledivina V., ed. 1986. *Bureaucratic Corruption in Asia: Conse-quences, and Controls.* Quezon City, Philippines: JMC Press.

Carothers, Thomas. 1998. The Rule of Law Revival. *Foreign Affairs* 77. 2 (March–April): 95–107.

Chen, Albert H. Y. 1999. Rational Law, Economic Development and the Case of China. *Social and Legal Studies* 8.1: 97–120.

Chen, Baizhu, and Yi Feng. 2000. Determinants of Economic Growth in China: Private Enterprise, Education, and Openness. *China Economic Review* 11.1 (spring): 1–15.

Chibundu, Maxwell O. 1997. Law in Development: On Tapping, Gourding, and Serv-ing Palm-wine. *Case Western Reserve Journal of International Law* 29: 167–261.

Coase, Ronald H. 1988. The Nature of the Firm. *Journal of Law, Economics, and Organization* 4: 3–47.

———. 1988. *The Firm, the Market, and the Law.* Chicago: University of Chicago Press.

Cobham, David, and Ramesh Subramaniam. 1998. Corporate Finance in Devel-oping Countries: New Evidence for India. *World Development* 26.6 (June): 1033–1047.

Cooter, Robert D. 1994. Structural Adjudication and the New Law Merchant: A Model of Decentralized Law. *International Review of Law and Economics* 14.2 (June): 215–231

———. 1996. The Theory of Market Modernization of Law. *International Review of Law and Economics* 16.2 (June): 141–172.

Cooter, Robert D., and Wolfgang Fikentscher. 1998. Indian Common Law: The Role of Custom in American Indian Tribal Courts. *American Journal of Comparative Law* 46.3: 509–580.

Cooter, Robert D., and Tom Ginsburg. 1996. Comparative Judicial Discretion: An Empirical Test of Economic Models. *International Review of Law and Economics* 16.3 (September): 295–313.

Cooter, R., and J. Gordley. 1991. Economic Analysis in Civil Law Countries: Past, Present, Future. *International Review of Law and Economics* 11.3 (December): 261–263.

Crafts, Nicholas, and Kai Kaiser. Article in press. Long-term Growth Prospects in Transition Economies: A Reappraisal. *Structural Change and Economic Dynamics.*

Cross, Frank B. 1999. The Relevance of Law in Human Rights Protection. *International Review of Law and Economics* 19.1 (March): 87–98.

———. 2002. Law and Economic Growth. Symposium: The Impact of Civil Jus-tice on the American Economy and Policy. *Texas Law Review* 80: 1737.

Dakolias, Maria. 1995. A Strategy for Judicial Reform: The Experience in Latin America. *Virginia Journal of International Law* 36.167 (fall): 167–231.

———. 1999. Court Performance around the World: A Comparative Perspective. *Yale Human Rights and Development Law Journal* 2: 87–142.

————. 1996. The Judicial Sector in Latin America and the Caribbean: Elements of Reform. World Bank Technical Paper No. 319, Washington DC.

Davis, F. E., and M. J. Trebilcock. 2001. Legal Reforms and Development. *Third World Quarterly* 22.1: 21–36.

Davis, Kevin, and Michael B. Kruse. 2007. Taking the Measure of Law: The Case of the Doing Business Project. *Law and Social Inquiry* 32.4: 1095–1119.

Demirguc-Kunt, Asli, and Vojislav Maksimovic. 1998. Law, Finance, and Firm Growth. *The Journal of Finance* 53.6 (December): 2107–2137.

De Soto, H. 2000. *The Mystery of Capital: Why Capitalism Triumphs in the West and Fails Everywhere Else.* New York: Basic Books.

————. 2002. *The Other Path.* New York: Basic Books.

Dixit, A. 2003. Some Lessons from Transaction-Cost Politics for Less-Developed Countries. *Economics and Politics* 15.2: 107–133.

Dixit, Avinash, Peter Hammond, and Michael Hoel. 1980. On Hartwick's Rule for Regular: Maximin Paths of Capital Accumulation and Resource Depletion. *Review of Economic Studies* 47.3 (April): 551–556.

Dollar, David, and Aart Kraay. 2003. Institutions, Trade, and Growth. *Journal of Monetary Economics* 50.1 (January): 133–162.

Duckett, Jane. 2001. Bureaucrats in Business, Chinese-Style: The Lessons of Market Reform and State Entrepreneurialism in the People's Republic of China. *World Development* 29.1 (January): 23–37.

Duquette, Michel. 1998. The Chilean Economic Miracle Revisited. *Journal of Socio-Economics* 27.3: 299–321.

Easterly, William. 2001. *The Elusive Quest for Growth: Economists' Adventures and Misadventures in the Tropics.* Cambridge, MA: MIT Press.

————. 2001. The Lost Decades: Developing Countries' Stagnation in Spite of Policy Reform, 1980–1998. *Journal of Economic Growth* 6.2: 135–157.

————. 2007. *The White Man's Burden: Why the West's Efforts to Aid the Rest Have Done so Much Ill and so Little Good.* New York: Penguin Press.

Eni, Fundazione. 2001. *Emerging Markets Review* 2.2 (June): 109–137.

Fei, J.C.H., and G. Ranis, 1964. *Development of the Labor Surplus Economy.* Homewood: Richard Irwin.

Fisman, Raymond, and Roberta Gatti. 2002. Decentralisation and Corruption: Evidence across Countries. *Journal of Public Economics* 83.3 (March): 325–345.

Fjeldstad, Odd-helge, and Joseph Semboja. 2001. Why People Pay Taxes: The Case of the Development Levy in Tanzania. *World Development* 29.12 (December): 2059–2074.

Foley, Duncan K., and Thomas R. Michl. 1999. *Growth and Distribution.* Cambridge, MA: Harvard University Press, 1999.

Fölster, Stefan, and Magnus Henrekson. 1999. Growth and the Public Sector: A Critique of the Critics. *European Journal of Political Economy* 15.2 (June): 337–358.

Gaddy, Clifford, and Barry Ickes. 1998. Russia's Virtual Economy. *Foreign Affairs* (September/October).

Golub, Stephen, and Kim McQuay. 2001. Manila Legal Empowerment: Advancing Good Governance and Poverty Reduction. Law and Policy Reform. Asian Development Bank. Available at http://www.adb.org/Documents/Others/Law_ADB/lpr_2001.pdf.

Gore, Charles. 2000. The Rise and Fall of the Washington Consensus as a Paradigm for Developing Countries. *World Development* 28.5 (May): 789–804.

Goudie, A., and D. Stavage. 1997. Corruption: The Issues. Research Programme on Political Economy and Development in Africa, Technical Paper No. 122. Paris: OECD.

Gould, D., and R. Ruffin. 1993. What Determines Economic Growth? Federal Reserve Bank of Dallas. *Economic Review* 2: 25–40.

Hammergren, Linn. 1998. Fifteen Years of Judicial Reform in Latin America: Where We Are and Why We Haven't Made More Progress. Democracy Fellow Draft Paper, USAID Global Center for Democracy and Governance. Available at http://www.uoregon.edu/~caguirre/hammergrenpr.html.

Hasan, Iftekhar, and Katherin Marton. Article in press. Development and Efficiency of the Banking Sector in a Transitional Economy: Hungarian Experience. *Journal of Banking & Finance.*

Hausner, Jerzy, Bob Jessop, and Klaus Nielson, eds. 1995. *Strategic Choice and Path Dependency in Post-Socialism: Institutional Dynamics in the Transformation Process.* Brookfield, VT: E. Elgar Press.

Hay, Jonathan R., and Andrei Shleifer. 1998. Private Enforcement of Public Laws: A Theory of Legal Reform. *American Economic Review* 88.2 (May): 398–404.

Helpman, Elhanan. 2004. *The Mystery of Economic Growth.* Cambridge, MA: Harvard University Press.

Hirschman A. O. 1958. *The Strategy of Economic Development.* New Haven: Yale University Press.

Hodgson, Geoffrey M. 1988. *Economics and Institutions: A Manifesto for a Modern Institutional Economics.* Philadelphia: University of Pennsylvania Press.

Hotte, Louis, Ngo Van Long, and Huilan Tian. 2000. International Trade with Endogenous Enforcement of Property Rights. *Journal of Development Economics* 62.1 (June): 25–54.

Howse, Robert, and Michael J. Trebilcock. 1996. The Fair Trade-Free Trade Debate: Trade, Labor, and the Environment. *International Review of Law and Economics* 16.1 (March): 61–79.

Iversen, Torben. 2005. *Capitalism, Democracy, and Welfare: The Changing Nature of Production, Elections, and Social Protection in Modern Capitalism,* chapters 1–2. Cambridge: Cambridge University Press.

Jensen, Robert T. Article in press. Do Private Transfers "Displace" the Benefits of Public Transfers? Evidence from South Africa. *Journal of Public Economics.*

Kanda, Hideki, and Curtis J. Milhaupt. 2003. Reexamining Legal Transplants: The Director's Fiduciary Duty in Japanese Corporate Law. *American Journal of Comparative Law* 51: 887.

Kaplow, L., 2000. General Characteristics of Rules. In *Encyclopedia of Law and Economics*, edited by G. de Geest and B. Bouckaert, 502–528. Cheltenham, UK: Edward Elgar.

Kast, Kenneth L., and Keith Rosen. 1975. *Law and Development in Latin America*. Berkeley: University of California Press.

Kauffman Task Force on Law and Growth. 2011. *Rules for Growth: Promoting Innovation and Growth through Legal Reform*. Kauffman Foundation, Kansas City, MO.

Kenny, Charles, and David Williams. 2001. What Do We Know About Economic Growth? Or, Why Don't We Know Very Much? *World Development* 29.1 (January): 1–22.

Klitgaard, Robert. 1988. *Controlling Corruption*. Berkeley: University of California Press.

———. 1991. *Adjusting to Reality: Beyond State versus Market in Economic Development*. San Francisco: ICS Press.

———. 1995. *Institutional Adjustment and Adjusting to Institutions*. Washington, DC: World Bank.

Knight, Jack. 1992. *Institutions and Social Conflict*. Cambridge: Cambridge University Press.

Krugman, P. 1994. The Fall and Rise of Development Economics. In *Rethinking the Development Experience: Essays Provoked by the Work of Albert O. Hirschman*, edited by L. Rodwin and D. A. Schön, 39–58. Washington, DC: Brookings Institution.

Kuran, Timur. 2004. Why the Middle East Is Economically Underdeveloped: Historical Mechanisms of Institutional Stagnation. *Journal of Economic Perspectives* 18: 71–90.

———. 2005. The Absence of the Corporation in Islamic Law: Origins and Persistence. *American Journal of Comparative Law* 53: 785–834.

———. 2011. *The Long Divergence: How Islamic Law Held Back the Middle East*. Princeton: Princeton University Press.

Laffont, J. J. 1999. Competition, Information, and Development. In *Proceedings of the Annual World Bank Conference on Development Economics 1998*, edited by J. Stiglitz, 237–257. Washington DC: World Bank.

Laffont, Jean-Jacques, and Tchétché N'Guessan. 1999. Competition and Corruption in an Agency Relationship. *Journal of Development Economics* 60.2 (December): 271–295.

Langlois, Richard, ed. 1986. *Economics as a Process: Essays in the New Institutional Economics*. Cambridge: Cambridge University Press.

La Porta, R., F. Lopez-de-Silanes, A. Shleifer, and R. Vishny. 1997. Legal Determinants of External Finance. *Journal of Finance* (Papers and Proceedings Fifty-Seventh Annual Meeting, American Finance Association, New Orleans, Louisiana January 4–6) 52.3 (July): 1131–1150.

———. 1999. Corporate Ownership around the World. *Journal of Finance* 54.2: 471–517.

Lau, Lawrence J., Yingyi Qian, and Gérard Roland. 1997. Pareto-Improving Economic Reforms through Dual-Track Liberalization. *Economics Letters* 55.2: 285–292.

Lee, J. A., G. D. Libecap, et al. 1999. *Titles, Conflict, and Land Use: The Development of Property Rights and Land Reform on the Brazilian Amazon Frontier.* Ann Arbor: University of Michigan Press.

Levine, Ross. 1997. Financial Development and Economic Growth: Views and Agenda. *Journal of Economic Literature* 35.2 (June): 688–726.

Lewis, W. A. 1954. Economic Development with Unlimited Supplies of Labor. *Manchester School* 22.2: 139–191.

Libecap, Gary D. 1978. Economic Variables and the Development of the Law: The Case of Western Mineral Rights. *Journal of Economic History* 38.2 (June): 338–362.

Lopez, Ramon.2003. The Policy Roots of Socioeconomic Stagnation and Environmental Implosion: Latin America 1950–2000. *World Development* 31.2 (February): 259–280.

Lucas, Robert E. 2004. *Lectures on Economic Growth.* Cambridge, MA: Harvard University Press.

Mahoney, Paul J. 2001. The Common Law and Economic Growth: Hayek Might Be Right. *Journal of Legal Studies* 30 (June): 503–525.

Maitra, Pushkar, and Ranjan Ray. 2003. The Effect of Transfers on Household Expenditure Patterns and Poverty in South Africa. *Journal of Development Economics* 71.1 (June): 23–49.

Marx. K. 1867. *Das Kapital. Kritik der politischen Oekonomie. Band 1: Buch I: Der Produktionsprocess des Kapitals.* Hamburg: Meissner.

Mattei, Ugo. 1994. Efficiency in Legal Transplants: An Essay in Comparative Law and Economics. *International Review of Law and Economics* 14.1 (March): 3–19.

Mattei, Ugo, and Roberto Pardolesi. 1991. Law and Economics in Civil Law Countries: A Comparative Approach. *International Review of Law and Economics* 11.3 (December): 265–275.

Maynard, Geoffrey, and Graham Bird. 1975. International Monetary Issues and the Developing Countries: A Survey. *World Development* 3.9 (September): 609–631.

Mazzoleni, Roberto, and Richard R. Nelson. 1998. The Benefits and Costs of Strong Patent Protection: A Contribution to the Current Debate. *Research Policy* 27.3 (July): 273–284.

McGee, Robert W. 1992. *The Market Solution to Economic Development in Eastern Europe.* New York: Edwin Mellen Press.

Mello, Luiz de, and Randa Sab. 2002. Government Spending, Rights, and Civil Liberties. *International Review of Law and Economics* 22.3 (September): 257–276.

Merryman, John. 1997. Comparative Law and Social Change: On the Origin, Style, Decline and Revival of the Law and Development Movement. *American Journal of Comparative Law* 25.3: 457–491.

Messick, Richard E. 1999. Judicial Reform and Economic Development: A Survey of the Issues. *World Bank Research Observer* 14 (1999): 117–136.

Migdal, Joel S. 1988. *Strong Societies and Weak States: State-Society Relations and State Capabilities in the Third World*. Princeton: Princeton University Press.

Milhaupt, C. 2007. Law and Capitalism: Legal Systems and Economic Development around the World. Latin American Law and Caribbean Law and Economics Association. Interlegis, Brasilia, Brazil.

———. 2009. Beyond Legal Origin: Rethinking Law's Relationship to the Economy—Implications for Policy. *American Journal of Comparative Law* 72.4: 831.

Mishkin, F. S. 1996. Understanding Financial Crises: A Developing Country Perspective. In *Annual World Bank Conference on Development Economics 1996*, edited by M. Bruno and B. Pleskovic, 29–62. Washington, DC: World Bank.

Moser, Peter. 1999. The Impact of Legislative Institutions on Public Policy: A Survey. *European Journal of Political Economy* 15.1 (March): 1–33.

Murphy, K. M., A. Shleifer, and R. W. Vishny. 1989. Industrialization and the Big Push. *Journal of Political Economy* 97.5: 1003–1026.

———. 1992. The Transition to a Market Economy: Pitfalls of Partial Reform. *Quarterly Journal of Economics* 107.3: 889–906.

Myrdal, G., 1957. *Economic Theory and Under-Developed Regions*. London: Gerald Duckworth.

Nabli, Mustapha K., and Jeffrey B. Nugent. 1989. *The New Institutional Economics and Development*. New York: Elsevier.

Nawab, Syed, and Haider Naqvi. 1995. The Nature of Economic Development. *World Development* 23.4 (April): 543–556.

Nelson, Paul. 1995. *The World Bank and Non-Governmental Organizations: The Limits of Apolitical Development*. New York: St. Martin's Press.

Nelson, Richard R. 2005. *Technology, Institutions, and Economic Growth*. Cambridge, MA: Harvard University Press.

Noorbakhsh, Farhad, Alberto Paloni, and Ali Youssef. 2001. Human Capital and FDI Inflows to Developing Countries: New Empirical Evidence. *World Development* 29.9 (September): 1593–1610.

North, Douglass C. 1989. Institutions and Economic Growth: An Historical Introduction. *World Development* 17.9 (September): 1319–1332.

———. 1990. *Institutions, Institutional Change, and Economic Performance*, New York: Cambridge University Press.

———. 1990. A Transaction Cost Theory of Politics. *Journal of Theoretical Politics* 2.4: 355–367.

———. 1993. *The Paradox of the West*. Economics Working Paper Archive. St. Louis, MO: Washington University.

———. 1995. The New Institutional Economics and Development. Economics Working Paper Archive at WUSTL, Economic History 9309002. Available at http://www.econ.iastate.edu/tesfatsi/NewInstE.North.pdf.

North, D. C., and R. P. Thomas. 1976. *The Rise of the Western World: A New Economic History*. New York: Cambridge University Press.

North, D. C., and B. Weingast. 1989. The Evolution of Institutions Governing Public Choice in 17th Century England. *Journal of Economic History* 49: 803–832.

Ofosu-Amaah, W. Paatii. 2000. *Reforming Business-Related Laws to Promote Private Sector Development: The World Bank Experience in Africa*. Washington, DC: World Bank.

Ostrom, Elnor. 1990. *Governing the Commons: The Evolution of Institutions for Collective Action*. Cambridge: Cambridge University Press.

Parchomovsky, Gideon, and Alex Stein. 2008. Torts and Information. *Michigan Law Review* 107: 285.

Pejovich, Svetozar, and Enrico Colombatto. 2008. *Law, Informal Rules, and Economic Performance: The Case for Common Law*. Cheltenham, UK: Elgar.

Picciotto, Robert, and Eduardo Wiesner, eds. 1998. *Evaluation and Development: The Institutional Dimension*. Washington, DC: World Bank.

Posner, Richard A. 1984. Wealth Maximization and Judicial Decision-making. *International Review of Law and Economics* 4.2 (December): 131–135.

———. 1999. Creating a Legal Framework for Economic Development. *World Bank Research Observer* 13.1 (February): 1–11.

Prado, Mariana, and Michael Trebilcock. 2009. Path Dependence, Development, and the Dynamics of Institutional Reform. A Special Report on Entrepreneurship. *The Economist*, March 14.

Prebisch, R. 1950. *The Economic Development of Latin America and its Principal Problems*. Lake Success, NY: United Nations Department of Social Affairs.

Prima-Braga, Carlos Alberto. 1990. The Developing Case for or against Intellectual Property Protection. In *Strengthening Protection of Intellectual Property in Developing Countries*. Washington, DC: World Bank.

Ranis, Gustav, Frances Stewart, and Alejandro Ramirez. 2000. Economic Growth and Human Development. *World Development* 28.2 (February): 197–219.

Rapaczynski, A. 1996. The Roles of the State and the Market in Establishing Property Rights. *Journal of Economic Perspectives* 10: 87–103.

Ravallion, Martin, and Gaurav Datt. 2002. Why Has Economic Growth Been More Pro-poor in Some States of India Than Others? *Journal of Development Economics* 68.2 (August): 381–400.

Rose-Ackerman, Susan. 1982. Charitable Giving and "Excessive" Fundraising. *Quarterly Journal of Economics* 97.2 (May): 193–212.

———. 1987. Ideals versus Dollars: Donors, Charity Managers, and Government Grants. *Journal of Political Economy* 95.4 (August): 810–823.

———. 1991. Tort Law as a Regulatory System Regulation and the Law of Torts. *American Economic Review* (Papers and Proceedings of the Hundred and Third Annual Meeting of the American Economic Association) 81.2 (May): 54–58.

———. 1996. Altruism, Nonprofits, and Economic Theory. *Journal of Economic Literature* 34.2 (June): 701–728.

————. 1997. Corruption and Development. In *Annual World Bank Conference on Development Economics,* edited by J. Stiglitz and B. Pleskovic, 149–171. Washington DC: World Bank 1998.

————. 1999. *Corruption and Government.* New York: Cambridge University Press.

————. 2004. Establishing the Rule of Law. In *When States Fail: Causes and Consequences,* edited by R. Rotberg, 182–222. Princeton NJ: Princeton University Press.

Rosenstein-Rodan, P. 1943. Problems of Industrialization in Eastern and South-Eastern Europe. *Economics Journal* 55: 202–211.

Sachs, Jeffrey D., Andrew Warner, Anders Aslund, and Stanley Fischer. 1995. Economic Reform and the Process of Global Integration. *Brookings Papers on Economic Activity* (25th Anniversary Issue) 1: 1–118.

Saez Garcia, Felipe. 1998. The Nature of Judicial Reform in Latin America and Some Strategic Considerations. *American University International Law Review* 13: 1267.

Schäfer, H.-B. 2000. Enforcement of Contracts. Villa Borsig Workshop Series 2000, Institutional Foundations of a Market Economy.

Schwartz, Herman M. 2000. *States versus Markets: History, Geography, and the Developments of the International Political Economy.* New York: St. Martin's Press.

Sen, A. 2000. What Is the Role of Legal and Judicial Reform in the Development Process? World Bank Legal Conference, Washington, DC.

Shapiro, Ian, ed. 1994. *Rule of Law.* New York: New York University Press.

Shavell, S. 1984. Liability for Harm versus Regulation for Safety. *Journal of Legal Studies* 13: 357–374.

Shihata, I. E. 1995. Judicial Reform in Developing Countries and the Role of the World Bank. World Bank Technical Paper No. 280. Background Paper for the World Bank Conference, Judicial Reform in Latin America and the Caribbean.

————. 1997. Corruption—A General Review with an Emphasis on the Role of the World Bank. *Dickinson Journal of International Law* 15: 451– 485.

————. 1997. The Role of Law in Business Development. *Fordham International Law Journal* 20: 1577–1588.

Shupp, Franklin R. 2002. Growth and Income Inequality in South Africa. *Journal of Economic Dynamics and Control* 26.9–10 (August): 1699–1720.

Singer, H. W. 1950. The Distribution of Gains between Investing and Borrowing Countries. *American Economic Review* 40.2: 473–485.

Solow, R. M. 1970. *Growth Theory: An Exposition.* New York: Oxford University Press.

Sullivan, John D. 1998. Institutions and Private Sector Development. *China Economic Review* 9.1 (spring): 85–95.

Symposium on Legal Origins. 2009. *American Journal of Comparative Law* 72 (fall).

Tavares, José, and Romain Wacziarg. 2001. How Democracy Affects Growth. *European Economic Review* 45.8 (August): 1341–1378.

Temple, Jonathan. 1999. The New Growth Evidence. *Journal of Economic Literature* 37.1 (March): 112–156.

Thirlwall, A. P. 2003. Book review of Jamie Ros, *Development Theory and the Economics of Growth* (Ann Arbor: University of Michigan Press). *Journal of Development Economics* 70.2: 559–562.

Thorbecke, Erik, and Chutatong Charumilind. 2002. Economic Inequality and Its Socioeconomic Impact. *World Development* 30.9 (September): 1477–1495.

Torstensson, J. 1994. Property Rights and Economic Growth: An Empirical Study. *Kyklos* 47: 231.

Trebilcock, Michael. 1984. Restrictive Covenants in the Sale of a Business: An Economic Perspective. *International Review of Law and Economics* 4.2 (December): 137–161.

———. 1997. What Makes Poor Countries Poor? The Role of Institutional Capital in Economic Development. In *The Law and Economics of Development*, edited by Edgardo Buscaglia, William Ratliff, and Robert Cooter, 3. Greenwich: JAI Press.

Trebilcock, Michael J., and Ronald J. Daniels. 2008. *Rule of Law Reform and Development: Charting the Fragile Path of Progress.* Cheltenham, UK: Edward Elgar.

Trebilcock, Michael J., and Douglas G. Hartle. 1982. The Choice of Governing Instrument. *International Review of Law and Economics* 2.1 (June): 29–46.

Trubek, D. M. 1972. Toward a Social Theory of Law: An Essay on the Study of Law and Development. *Yale Law Journal* 82: 1–50.

Trubek, D. M., and M. Galanter. 1974. Scholars in Self-Estrangement: Some Reflections on the Crisis in Law and Development Studies in the United States. *Wisconsin Law Review.* 1: 1062–1102.

Tshuma, Lawrence. 1999. The Political Economy of the World Bank's Legal Framework for Economic Development. *Social and Legal Studies: An International Journal* 8.1: 75–96.

Vinod, Hrishikesh D. 2003. Open Economy and Financial Burden of Corruption: Theory and Application to Asia. *Journal of Asian Economics* 13.6 (January): 873–890.

Waterbury, J. 1999. The Long Gestation and Brief Triumph of Import-Substituting Industrialization. *World Development* 27.2: 323–341.

Weaver, Catherine. 2000. The Discourse of Law and Economic Development in the World Bank. Available at http://polisci.wisc.edu/users/weaver/Documents/CROLpaper.pdf.

Webb, Douglas. 1999. Comments on the Role of Legal Institutions on the Economic Development of the Americas: The Law and Demands of an Interdependent Economic System: an Assessment. *Law and Policy in International Business* 30: 179.

———. 1999. Legal and Institutional Reform Strategy and Implementation: A World Bank Perspective. *Law and Policy in International Business* 30: 161–170.

Weber. M., 1922. *Wirtschaft und Gesellschaft.* Tübingen: J. C. B. Mohr.

Williamson, O. E. 1985. *The Economic Institutions of Capitalism.* New York: Free Press.

Wolfensohn, James D. 1999. A Proposal for a Comprehensive Development Framework. Available at http.worldbank.org/cdf/cdf-text.htm.

Yanikkaya, Halit. Article in press. Trade Openness and Economic Growth: A Cross-country Empirical Investigation. *Journal of Development Economics.*

Yotopoulos, Pan A. 2000. New Theories in Growth and Development: Fabrizio Coricelli, Massimo di Mateo, and Frank Hahn. *Journal of Economic Behavior and Organization* 42.1 (May): 141–143.

Zee, Howell H., Janet G. Stotsky, and Eduardo Ley. 2002. Tax Incentives for Business Investment: A Primer for Policy Makers in Developing Countries. *World Development* 30.9 (September): 1497–1516.

Index

Page numbers for entries occuring in figures are followed by an *f*, and those for entries occuring in tables by a *t*.

accidents and liability: overview, 179–80, 191–92; insurance gaps, 187–90; judgment-proof problem, 184–86, 283n22; multinational firm dilemmas, 183–84, 282nn14–15, 283nn16–17; safety spending decisions, 179–83, 281n6; standards prescription, 190–91; statistics, 179, 280n1, 281n4; trial-proof problem, 186–87; work-related disease, 181, 282n11

Ackerman, B., 294n28

Ackerman, Susan Rose, xiv

administrative sanctions, 37, 83–84, 96–99, 253n52. *See also* regulatory framework

ADRs (American Depository Receipt), 265n22

Afghanistan, corruption pattern, 164–65

African countries, generally: diamond industry example, 6; and economic development theory, 197, 199, 202; income levels, 2, 13, 16–17, 25, 232n6; informal sector statistics, 169; liberalization policy effects, 208. *See also specific countries*

AIG (American Insurance Group), 260n63

Airbus Industrie, 285n11

air fare example, 43

Akerlof, George A., 252n48, 288n32

Algeria, 205, 288n36

Alien Torts Claim Act, 283n16

Aligica, Paul Dragos, 241n13

Allen, Robert, 58, 238n13

Ambani, Mukesh, 48

American Depository Receipt (ADR), 265n22

American Insurance Group (AIG), 261n63

antitrust law, 43, 55

Arab countries, generally, 23–25, 77. *See also specific countries*

Argentina, 14, 20, 133, 202, 261n67, 288n29

aristocrats, in state leadership economic theory, 202–3

Armour, John, xiv

Arrow, Ken, xiv

Arrow's paradox of information, 233n1

Asian countries, generally: corporate ownership statistics, 55, 56t; homicide rates, 162; informal sector statistics, 169; liberalization policy effects, 207; Pareto growth strategies, 218, 296n35. *See also specific countries*

Asian crisis (1997), 262n68, 270n29

Atiah, Robert, xiv

authoritarian governments, legitimacy-seeking strategies, 295n32

balanced growth perspective, economic development theory, 199

balance sheet bankrupt, defined, 261n64
Bandiera, O., 277n42
Bangladesh, 5, 105–7, 269n21
banking systems, formal: overview, 109,
    120–22, 256nn30–31; commercial types,
    109–12, 113, 256n28, n32, 257n34, n36,
    n39, n42; financial brokers, 117–20,
    259n55, 260nn58–60; importance of,
    102–3, 253n3; investment types, 109,
    113–17, 258n43, n45, n47, 259n54; mis-
    management consequences, 260n62,
    261n63, 261nn64–68; in 2008 financial
    crisis, 121–22, 260n62, 261n63, 261n66;
    use statistics, 103, 105, 252n49, 254n7.
    See also credit systems
banking systems, relational: chit funds,
    101–2, 103–4, 105, 254nn9–10; coopera-
    tive types, 104–5, 254n12; microlending,
    105–7, 253n5, 255n20; rural develop-
    ment types, 105, 255n15; village money-
    lenders, 108–9
Bank of America, 256n28
bank run, defined, 261n65
bankruptcy proceedings: bonded labor,
    45; court role, 150, 268n20; Japan's
    illegal fixers, 170, 287n46; market-based
    valuation models, 266n5; obstacles for
    developing countries, 151–57, 270nn29–
    30; political uses, 153–55, 269n27,
    270nn29–30; public sector, 115, 155–57,
    258n50, 270n33; stakeholder control
    effects, 146–49, 266n3–4; value of,
    145–46, 266n2. See also financial dis-
    tress, resolutions
Bardhan, Pranab, xiv
bargaining processes, financially-
    distressed firms, 144–46, 266n2
Basel II agreements, 260n62, 261n68
Bebchuk, Lucian Arye, 266n5
Behrens, Gisèle, xiv
Belarus, 232n9, 233n17, 250n31, 269n21
Belgium, land ownership, 243n24
benefit concentration strategy, in growth-
    promoting reform, 216, 217–18, 295n34
Benny, Jack, 180
Bernstein, Lisa, 248n15
Bhimji Depar Shah, 4–5
big push perspective, economic develop-
    ment theory, 198, 286n12
Bigus, Jochen, xiv
Black, B. S., 139
Boeing Corporation, 285n11

Bolivia, 269n21
bonded labor, 45
Borgward, 266n4
Botswana, 16, 176, 237n9
Boudreaux, Karol, 241n13
Brazil: banked person statistics, 252n49;
    bank use statistics, 254n7; contract
    law, 94–95, 250n33, 251n38; control
    premium, 134; corporation ownership,
    263n9; debt collection law, 110; financial
    distress resolution, 152, 269n21; income
    levels, 20; intellectual property rights,
    74; land ownership, 69–71, 152–53,
    243nn24–25; pharmaceutical patents, 75,
    245n42; sharecropping, 243n27; wages-
    national income relationship, 58–59
bribe payer's index, 274n8
bribery and corruption: overview, 159–60,
    178; attitude changes, 160, 273n4, 274n8;
    benefits and costs, 168–72, 277n42,
    279n50, 287nn46–47; and civil sanc-
    tions, 252n43; contract law, 252n43;
    control strategies, 166–67, 171–77,
    276nn25–26, 279n55; and cooperative
    banking, 105; estimates of, 160–63,
    274n9; political structure correlations,
    163–68, 275nn16–18; poverty relation-
    ships, 160–61, 163, 275n15; and safety
    regulation effectiveness, 186; as wealth-
    taking, 40–41
Britain. See United Kingdom
brokers, financial, 117–20, 259n55,
    260nn58–60
Buffett, Warren, 48, 239n25
Bukhara, 39–40
Bulgaria, 115, 232n9, 233n14
Bush, George W. (and administration),
    260n62
business method patents, 245n40
business organizations, types, 126–27. See
    also corporations
Butler, Henry, xiii, xiv
buy-off strategy, in growth-promoting
    reform, 216, 217–18, 294n27, 295n34

Campos, J. E., 296n35
Canada, 134, 250n33
capital accumulation, in state-led growth
    failure, 204–5, 288n34
capital per capita statistics, 205, 288n36
car sale example, 249n25
cartels. See monopolies and cartels

cement truck example, 146–47, 267n6
centralized vs. decentralized corruption, 164–66, 275n16
charitable loans, 104–5, 106, 255n19
Charles II, 69, 135
charter location, competition effects, 140–41, 168, 276n32
chess and pennies story, 1
Chile, 20, 134, 176, 219, 227–28, 237n9
China: banked person statistics, 252n49; banking systems, 114–15, 119; contract law, 37, 92–93, 97, 250n31, 251n38, 252n46; dual-track development approach, 217–18, 295nn33–35; famine deaths, 55, 65, 193, 284n2; government system, 235n13; growth-equality relationships, 50, 52, 55, 237n7; growth rate, 1; income levels, 21–22, 233n20, 295n34; intellectual property rights, 74, 76–77; land ownership, 65, 66–67, 71, 241n12; land reform consequences, 65, 66–67; land seizure law, 71; liberalization policy effects, 208; paper company example, ix; patent filings, 246n46; soft-budget constraints, 8–9, 115–16; wages-national income relationship, 58, 107
chit funds, 101–2, 103–4, 105, 254nn9–10
Churchill, Winston, 157, 273nn45–46
civil sanctions, 36–37, 83–84, 90–96, 109–12, 234n10, 250nn29–33
civil service systems, 166–67, 176, 203
Clinton, Bill, 12
Closely held companies, international comparisons, 132–33
coal and tea example, contract enforcement, 88
Coase, Ronald, 128–29, 229n1, 296n36
Coca-Cola, 78, 246n49
Cohen, Lloyd, xiv
Colombia, 170, 254n7
commercial banking, 109–12, 113, 256n28, n32, 257n34, n36, n39, n42
common law tradition, private contracts, 93–94, 250n36
communist countries. See Eastern European countries; Russia; Soviet Union
company towns, 116, 269n27
competitive equilibrium, defined, 31
compound growth, examples, 1, 51, 63, 236n15
Concorde aircraft, 285n11
Congo, 40, 165

conjunctive vs. disjunctive licenses, 167
Connaught Place, India, 128, 262n3
Conquest, Robert, 284n2
consumer's surplus, defined, 47, 236n13
contingency fees, 186–87, 283n24
contract law: overview, 30–31, 32, 82–84, 100; economic growth benefits, 5–6; enforcement levels, 35–37; as innovation, 5; private contracts, 83–84, 90–96, 250n27, nn31–33, 251nn38–39, n41; public contracts, 37, 83–84, 96–99, 247nn3–4, 253n52; relational stage, 35–36, 83–90, 132, 248n15, 249n20
control premium, correlations, 134, 264n12
convergent vs. divergent growth, 14
cooking oil company, 4–5
cooperation banking, 104–5, 254n12
Cooter, Robert D., 236n11, 238n17, 241n14, 247n2, 251n40, 273n47, 277n34, 279n52, 280n62, 283n24, 295n33, 297n2
copyright protection, 74–78
corporate vs. individual behavior, defined, 124, 246n51
corporations: investor protection, 133–35, 137–38, 264nn12–14; organizational characteristics, 124–27, 262n2; origins, 123–24, 135–36; profit maximizing argument, 246nn52–53; secrecy preservation, 129–33, 263nn6–7; size determinants, 128–29, 262n4; value of law improvements, 135–41, 264n18, 265n23, n25
corruption. See bribery and corruption
Costa Rica, 269n21, 271n42, 288n36
cost-benefit analysis, 231n11, 287n24
cost-diffusion strategy, in growth-promoting reform, 216, 295n30
cotton exchange example, contract enforcement, 248n15
creativity protection, 74–78
credit cards, 108, 256n28
credit systems: importance of, 101–3; law's value, 8–10; legal protections, 8–9, 32; poverty-reduction limitations, 107, 255n23; real estate loans, 70, 72–73, 243n25, n31, 244nn32–33, nn35–36; return statistics, 253n5. See also banking entries
crime rates, 161–63, 274nn11–12
criminal strategies for wealth removal from others, 39–41

Croatia, odious debt, 272n43
cross-listing of stocks, benefits, 140, 265n23, n25
Cuba, odious debt, 270n42
currency approach, as corruption measure, 274n9
Czechoslovakia, privatization failure, 133–34
Czech Republic, 117, 134, 232n9, 233n14

Dahlman, C. J., 233n20
damages-proof problem, 94, 184–86, 251n41, 283n22
Dar es Salaam, contract value example, 89–90
Deane, Phyllis, 264n17
debt collection. *See banking entries;* credit systems; financial distress, resolutions
decentralized vs. centralized corruption, 164–66, 275n16
delegated corruption systems, 164–65, 275n18
Demirguz-Kunt, Asli, 259n57
democracy and economic growth, 227–28, 290n47. *See also* institutionalism approach, economic development theory
Deng Xiaoping, 21–22, 62
depletion, in sustainability arguments, 60–61
deregulation. *See* regulatory framework
derivatives, 98, 261n63
De Soto, Hernando, 65, 169
diamond production, 6, 36
dictator's dilemma, 218–20, 296nn37–40
diffusion of costs strategy, in growth-promoting reform, 216, 295n30
diminishing marginal productivity law, 205
disjunctive vs. conjunctive licenses, 167–68
distressed firms. *See* financial distress, resolutions
distrust sowing strategies, bribery control, 172–74, 279n55
divergent vs. convergent growth, 14
Doidge, C., 265n23
double trust dilemma: bribery situations, 172–74, 279n55; described, 2–3, 5, 27–28, 102, 234n2; legal protections, 31–38; party-binding solutions, 28–29, 113–14; trust-building stages, 29–31. *See also* corporations
dual economic theory, 201, 287nn22–24

Easterly, W., 289n38
Eastern Airlines, 266n3
Eastern European countries: contract law development, 96, 232n12, 252nn45–46; European Union membership, 232n9, 233n14; income levels, 13, 17–19, 25, 53; liberalization policy effects, 207–8; privatization as theft, 80; production patterns, 18, 232n12. *See also specific countries*
economic development theories: institutionalism approach, 195–96, 206–11, 284n7, 289nn45–46, 290n47; market liberalization approach, 194–95, 205–7, 284n5; policy consequences, 193–94, 202–8; reunification with law, x, 229nn1–2; state leadership approach, 194, 197–206, 285n11, 286n12, nn19–20, 287nn22–24; types of, 194–96. *See also* growth-promoting reform, opposition problem
economic growth, overview: international patterns, 1–2, 13–25, 231n3; law's value, 6–10, 31–38; legal framework correlations, 16–25, 232n12; with legalized freedom, 223–28; sources of, 2–6, 229n2 (ch2), 230n5; sustainability arguments, 59–60; value of, 10–12, 230n9. *See also specific topics, e.g., banking entries;* India; wealth acquisition
economists, role of, 226–27, 291n2
Ecuador, 9–10, 254n7, 288n36
edible oil company, 4–5
Edlin, E., 51
education: civil service development, 203; and economic growth, 50, 54–55, 57; government role, 168, 209, 224; India's judiciary, 94; production shifts with, 76, 225; return rate, 253n5, 289n38; as wealth use, 225–26, 230n9
Edwards, Paul, xiii, xiv
efficiency, growth compared, x
efficient market hypothesis, 290n50
Eger, Thomas, xiv
Egypt, 13, 65, 73, 166, 182, 269n21
Eisenberg, Mel, xiv, 248n15
emiseration hypothesis, 235n7
EndNote, 27
endowment example, 236n15
England. *See* United Kingdom
equality-growth relationships: overview, 57, 63, 224–25; international comparisons,

51–54, 295n34; and rule of law, 55–56, 237n9; social justice arguments, 61–63, 224–25; theory about, 50–51. *See also* wealth acquisition

Equatorial Guinea, 40

Estonia, 232n9, 233n14

European Union, 17–19, 140–41, 251n39, 285n11. *See also specific countries*

evolution, 33, 234n4

exploitation arguments, labor value, 43–46, 235n7, 236n8

extortion. *See* bribery and corruption

fairness arguments, 61–63, 224–25

famine deaths, 55, 56, 65, 193, 284n2

Fannie Mae, 255n19, 261n66

feudalism, 67, 221, 240n7, 241n8, 277n42, 287n22

Fiat, 84

Fikentscher, Wolfgang, xiv

finance stages, start-ups, 29–38. *See also banking entries;* credit systems

financial crisis (2008): leverage problems summarized, 98, 121–22, 260n62, 261n63, 261nn64–65; mortgage loans, 154, 255n19, 261n66; as regulation incentive, 256n31; as self-regulation problem, 9, 230n8; and world economy, 102

financial distress, resolutions: overview, 142–44, 149–50, 151*f*, 157–58; creditor treatments, 146–49, 267nn6–7, nn11–12; for government debt, 155–57, 270n33, n35, 271n38, n40, n42, 272nn43–44; obstacles for developing countries, 151–57; stakeholder perspectives, 144–49, 266nn2–5. *See also* bankruptcy proceedings

Finland, bankruptcy proceedings, 152

flat rate compensation, accidents, 191

food regulation, 96–97, 182

Forbes Magazine, richest people list, 40, 47–48, 235n3, 236nn14–15

foreign investors: and economic development theory, 200–201, 286n20; risks for, 114–15, 155, 258n47, 270nn29–30

Fox, Merritt, xiv

France: bankruptcy law, 149; closely held corporation statistics, 133; control premium, 134; corruption patterns, 175; feudalism abolishment, 221; historic mercantilist policies, 287n26, 288n29; Napoleon's debt policy, 110; Physiocrat

philosophy, 240n7; prodebtor bias, 153, 269n24; rural land rental, 70; wages-national income relationship, 58

Freddy Mac, 255n19, 261n66

free riding, defined, 293n21

free sector, in China's dual track approach, 217–18, 295n34

free trade arguments, economic development theory, 200–201, 286nn19–20

free use and innovation, 74–75, 245n41

Friedman, Milton, 246n53

Gambia, crime rates, 161, 162

game theory language, 172, 247n2, 275n17, 296n40

Gates, Bill, 48, 239n25

Gazprom, 140

GDP-market capitalization ratios, 135, 264n14

GDP measures, limitations of, 11–12, 231n11. *See also* income levels

Geiserich, King, 28, 234n3

Genghis Khan, 39–40

Georgia (country), 159, 232n9, 233n17, 269n21

Germany: bankruptcy politics example, 155; bribery law, 274n8; closely held corporation statistics, 133; contract law, 93, 99, 250n36; control premium, 134; crime rates, 161; odious debt, 270n42; public contract definition, 247n4; self-employment statistics, 255n21; war debt, 270n33

Germany, banking systems: commercial types, 109, 119, 260n59; cooperative types, 104–5, 254n12; debt collection law, 110, 257n36; investment type, 114

Gerschenkron, Alexander, 260n58

Ghana: banking systems, 111, 269n21; and economic development theory, 197, 202; land ownership correlations, 68; Obama's speech, 273n4; organized crime, 170; stock-listed companies, 278n49

Gini coefficient, defined, 52

Glaeser, E., 284n7

Glass-Steagall Act, 256n31

Goldman Sachs, 230n8

good faith principle, 93–94, 250nn33–36, 251n38

Gorbachev, M., 292n4

Gorga, Erica, 263n9

government role, efficient economic
growth, 208–10, 223–24, 290nn49–50,
n52, 291n53. *See also* growth-promoting
reform, opposition problem
Grameen Bank, 105–7, 255n20
gray markets, 98–99, 169, 182, 253n52
Greece, bailout package, 156
growth-promoting reform, opposition
problem: circumvention strategies,
216–22, 294nn26–28, 295nn29–30; as
dictator's dilemma problem, 218–20,
296nn37–40; gain-loss changes, 293n17–
19, nn21–22; natural resource restriction
example, 215–16; Prussian industrialization example, 215; in Russia's privatization stages, 212–14, 215t, 292n5, n11,
n13. *See also* government role, efficient
economic growth
Guatemala, private finance, 269n21

Hacker, Peter, xiv
Hamidi, H., 257n42
happiness, money correlations, 12
Hart, Oliver, 263n7
Häseler, Sönke, xiii
health spending, 188, 282n11
health standards, Egypt, 182
Heitger, Bernhard, 289n45
Hirschman, A. O., xiv, 235n1
Holland, 58, 70, 105, 230n4, 250n33,
255n21
Holler, Manfred, xiv
Holmes, Oliver Wendell, 48
Holmes, S., 293n20
homicide statistics, 161–62, 274n12
Hong Kong, 84, 133
hostage exchange solution, 28
hostile takeovers, 268n18, 291n53
A House for Mr. Biswas (Naipaul), 189
Hungary, 232n9, 233n14

IBM, 209
Iceland, cartel impact, 56
idea-related financial distress, resolution,
144
ideas vs. resources, sustainability arguments, 59–61
illiquid assets, defined, 72
illiquid unique goods, price effects, 98
income levels: capital accumulation
correlations, 205; China's changes,
21–22, 233n20, 295n34; as contract

enforcement problem, 94, 251n41;
contract law correlations, 91–92,
250nn30–31; corruption correlations,
160–61; crime rate correlations, 162;
and equality-growth relationships, 54–
57; international patterns, 1–2, 13–16,
231n3, 232nn10–11; legal framework
correlations, 16–25, 289n45; and relational banking, 103; safety spending,
181, 281n8; and wage-growth relationships, 58–59, 238n16. *See also* equality-
growth relationships
India: accident/illness costs study, 188–
89; accident law, 191; banked person
statistics, 252n49; banking systems,
101–2, 103–4, 105, 114, 254nn9–10;
bankruptcy procedures, 152, 154; Coca-
Cola products, 78, 246n49; contracts, 88,
93, 94, 250n32, 251nn38–39; corporate
governance effects, 138–39, 264n18;
corporation size example, 128; corruption patterns, 161, 166, 175, 279n53;
crime rates, 161; debt collection law,
257n34; as dictator's dilemma example,
219, 296n38; income levels, 22–23,
43–44, 58; income-safety expenditure
relationship, 181; intellectual property
rights, 74, 76–77; land ownership, 68, 71,
242nn16–17; liberalization policy effects,
208; nondisclosure agreements, 131,
263n6; patent filings, 246n46; pharmaceutical patents, 75, 245n44; soft-budget
constraints, 116, 154
Indonesia: Asian crisis aftermath, 270n29;
bankruptcy law, 276n26; corruption
patterns, 170, 275n16, 276n26; private
finance, 269n21; safety liability problem,
183, 282n15; textile production example,
7–8
industrial revolution, 33–34, 138, 264n17
inequality. *See* equality-growth
relationships
informal sector and corruption, 169–71
information: Arrow's paradox, 233n1; government role, 208–9, 224, 290nn49–50;
as innovation foundation, 129–33, 224,
263nn6–7; in state-led growth failure,
204. *See also* double trust dilemma
infrastructure projects, government role,
209–10, 290n52
innovations, overview: life cycle of, 29;
profit level changes, 47–48; role in

economic growth, 196, 205, 208–10, 223–24; in sustainability argument, 59–61; types of, 2–5, 230n5. *See also specific topics, e.g., contract entries;* double-trust dilemma; equality-growth relationships; property law

institutionalism approach, economic development theory, 195–96, 206–11, 284n7, 289nn45–46, 290n47

insurance, 187–90

intellectual property protection, 74–78

International Court of Justice, 272n44

International Fund for Agricultural Development, 106

International Monetary Fund, 156, 194–95, 270n35, 271n38, 272n43

International Trade Commission, 279n50

inventory levels, contract benefits, 88–89, 249n17

investment banking, 109, 113–17, 258n43, n45, n47, 259n54

Iran, 13, 269n21

Iraq, 13, 157, 271n40

Ireland, cooperative banking, 105

Italy: banking systems, 105; closely held corporation statistics, 133; control premium, 134; corruption perception, 161; crime patterns, 162, 170, 277n42; income levels, 13; mortgage law, 149, 267n10; start-up time requirements, 264n15

Jack Benny story, 180

Jamaica, private finance, 269n21

Japan: bankruptcy law, 170, 278n46; economic growth factors, 291n53; finance tradition, 85, 114, 120; land reform effects, 67, 241n8; relationship-based business pattern, 85; safety liability problem example, 183, 282n15

Johnson, D. Bruce, xiv

joint stock companies, development, 2–3, 124, 135–37, 230n4. *See also* corporations

Jordan, corruption rate, 175

judgment-proof problem, 94, 184–86, 251n41, 283n22

judicial foreclosure, United States, 244n36

Kansas, collateral procedures, 257n36

Karolyi, G. A., 265n23

Kenya, 4–5, 166, 278n49

Keynes, John Maynard, 193

Khanna, V., 139

Khodorkhovsky, Michail, 153–54, 235n2

Kia, in size decision-making example, 128

Kim, W., 139

kin groups and land ownership, 67–69, 242n19, 242nn16–17. *See also relational entries*

Kitch, Ed, xiv

Knight, F., 100

Knight, Philip, 4

Kolkata factory, 43–44

Kötz, Hein, xiv

Kozlov, V. B., 251n38

Kraus, Willy, xiv

Krueger, Anne, 271n38

Kuchma, Leonid, 80

Kuran, Timur, xiv

Lablanc, Gregory, xiv

labor value, 43–46, 58–59, 235n7, 236n8. *See also* wage levels

Lando Principles, 250n33

land ownership: creditor protections, 70, 72–73, 243n25, n31, 244n32; and infrastructure projects, 290n52; kinship-based societies, 67–69, 241n14; lease rate comparison, 241n12; productivity relationships, 55, 65–67, 237n7, 240n7; registry information, 72–73, 244n33, 267n8; squatter conflicts, 69–71, 242nn20–21. *See also mortgage entries;* property law

land theft example, 40

La Porta, R., 284n7

Latin American countries: homicide rates, 162; income inequality, 52; income levels, 13, 19–20, 25; liberalization policy effects, 207, 208; productivity-wage relationships, 58–59, 238n16. *See also specific countries*

Latvia, 232n9, 233n14

law, economic disciplines, reunification, x, 229n1

law, economic growth correlations, overview, 6–10

lease rates, land, 241n12

legalized freedom, overview, 223–28

Lemley, Mark, 245n41

Lenin, V., 286n20

Lenovo, 209

Lessig, Larry, 245n41

Levine, R., 289n38

Lewis, Arthur, 201

liability law. *See* accidents and liability
Libenstein, Harvey, 286n12
life expectancy, 21, 193, 217
Lipton, Michael, 255n23
Litan, Bob, xiii, xiv
liquid assets, defined, 72
liquidation solution, financial distress, 144,
    145, 149–50, 151*f*, 266nn4–5
Lithuania, 176, 232n9, 233n14
litigation threats, as contract enforcement,
    36–37
loan systems. *See banking entries;* credit
    systems
London Approach, 150
Lopez de Silanes, F., 139, 284n7

Machiavelli, 222
Madang, Papua New Guinea, 70–71
Maddison, Angus, 13
Magin, Konstantin, 212, 292n11
make-or-buy question, 128–29, 131–32
malaria research example, 239n25
Malaysia, private finance, 269n21
Mali, private finance, 269n21
Malinowski, Bronislaw, 35–36
management-related financial distress,
    resolution, 143–44
Manne, Henry, 246n52
marginalism theory, 44–46, 236n8
market capitalization, correlations, 134–35,
    264nn13–14
market liberalization approach, economic
    development theory, 194–95, 196, 205–7,
    284n5
Marxist theory, 44–46, 235n7, 286n12
Mauitania, private finance, 269n21
maximin principle, 61–62, 239n27
media role, bribery control, 174–75
merge-or-divest question, 128–29, 131–32,
    263n7
Mexico: bank use statistics, 254n7; closely
    held corporation statistics, 132–33;
    debt collection, 8, 91, 111, 112, 250n29;
    income levels, 14, 20; peso crisis, 261n67
microlending, 105–8, 255n20
Microsoft, 27
middlemen, relational contracts, 90
Milhaupt, C. J., xiv, 291n53
Mill, John Stuart, 297n1
Millennium Project, United Nations, 199
mineral resources, theft example, 40
minority shareholders, protection, 115

MITI, Japan's economic growth, 291n53
Mittal, Lakshmi, 48, 130
modern sector, in dual economic theory,
    201–2, 287nn22–24
Moldova, 232n9, 233n17
monopolies and cartels: British mercantil-
    ism, 135; in economic development
    theory, 198, 200; inequality relation-
    ships, 55–57; net loss paradigm, 293n19;
    wage levels, 45; for wealth removal from
    others, 40, 42–43
mortgage markets, credit obstacles, 70,
    72–73, 243n25, n31, 244nn32–33,
    nn35–36. *See also* land ownership
mortgages, second, 149, 267n10, n12
motivation cause, state-led growth failure,
    204
motor vehicle fatalities, 179, 280n1
Mozambique, private finance, 269n21
Mugabe, President, 40, 66, 165, 235n4
Müller-Langer, Frank, xiii
multinational firms, safety liability prob-
    lem, 183–84, 282n14, 283nn16–17
Mumbai, 43–44, 71, 128
Murphy, L. B., 238n19
Musgrave, Richard, xiii
Myrdal, Gunnar, 197

Nagel, T., 238n19
Naipaul, V. S., 189
Namibia, 161, 237n9
"The Nature of the Firm" (Coase), 128–29
negligence rule, 190–91. *See also* accidents
    and liability
Nenova, Tatiana, 134, 264n12
net gain, in reform policy, 214, 293n18. *See
    also* growth-promoting reform, opposi-
    tion problem
Netherlands, 58, 70, 105, 230n4, 250n33,
    255n21
net loss, in reform policy, 214, 293n19. *See
    also* growth-promoting reform, opposi-
    tion problem
New York City, crime reduction, 177
New York Stock Exchange, 55, 140,
    265n22
New Zealand, 160, 161
Ng, Ida, xiii
Nigeria, stock-listed companies, 278n49
Nike Corporation, 4
Niles, Richard, 27
Nine Dragons Paper Industries, ix

Nobel Prize winners, 252n48, 288n32
nondisclosure agreements, 131, 263n6
nonjudicial foreclosure, United States, 244n36
nonmarket economies, firm size factors, 129–30
nonrivalry, defined, 60
North, Douglas, xiv, 195
Nowa Huta plant, 129–30
Nozick, Robert, 61

Obama, Barack, 273n4
Obiang, Teodoro, 40
odious debt, 155–57, 271n40, n42, 272n43–44
oil production, 23–24, 40, 233n17, 290n49
oligarchies, equality-growth relationship, 55–56, 237n8
oligopoly, 198
Olson, Mancur, xiv
ontogeny capitulates phylogeny, 33, 234n4
opportunity costs, labor, 44–45
organization, defined, 246n51
organizational liberty, legal development, 135–37
organizations as property, 79–80
organized crime, 162, 170, 277n42
Osterfeld, D., 279n50
Ott, Claus, xiv
overtaking theorem, welfare, 51–52, 57
ownership myth, 238n19

Pakistan, 252n49, 269n21
Panama, private finance, 269n21
Papua New Guinea, 67–68, 70–71, 241n13
Pareto, Vilfredo, 293n16
Pareto gains, 214–15, 216, 218, 293n17, 294n27. See also growth-promoting reform, opposition problem
Paris Club, 156, 270n34, 271n40
Parisi, Francesco, xiv
Parker, Geoffrey, xiv
partnership, corporation compared, 126–27
patent law, 74–78, 225, 245nn40–44
Paulson, Henry, 9, 230n8
Pay By Touch, 30
Pejovich, Svetozar, xiv
Penn, William, 69
personal organization, corporation compared, 126
Peru, 89, 110, 169, 242n21, 244n33, 254n7, 288n36

pharmaceutical patents, 75, 245n42, 246n46
Phelps, Ned, xiv
Philippines, 164, 253n5, 275n16, 295n34
Physiocrats, 240n7
Pinochet, Augusto, 219, 228
Pistor, K., xiv, 291n53
Plath, Christa Randzio, xiv
Poland, 67, 129–30, 176, 232n9, 233n14, 270n42
Polsby, Nelson, 273n46
polyarch, defined, 293n20
Portugal, 255n21, 269n21
poverty reduction, credit system limitations, 255n23. See also banking systems, relational; income levels
Prada, 84
Prebisch, Raul, 200
principle-agent problem, described, 234n2
prisoner's dilemma, 172
private accumulation, in Marxism, 286n12
private contracts, 83–84, 90–96, 250n27, nn31–33, 251nn38–39, n41
private direct investment, changes, 206, 289n41
private finance, 29–31, 32, 33–35, 109–12, 149, 151, 269n21
private information and secrets, 129–33, 224, 263nn6–7. See also double trust dilemma
privatization: defined, 246n54; Gorbachev's goal, 292n4; with land reform, 66–67; Latin America's transitions, 20; legal protection requirements, 133–34; politics-based bankruptcy, 153–54; property law need, 80; Russia's stages of, 212–14, 292n11; soft-budget constraint problem, 8–9
Privy Purse, India, 219, 296n38
profit maximizing argument, 79–80, 246nn52–53
property law: copyright/patent protection, 74–78, 245nn40–44; enforcement levels, 31–38; finance stages, 31–33; and land investment, 68–69, 242n18; organization ownership, 79–80; for property principle of innovation, 64, 81; real estate loans, 70, 72–73, 243n25, n31, 244nn35–36; and redistribution acceptance, 220–21; security purpose, 6–8, 64, 80–81; squatter conflicts, 69–71, 242n20; as wealth-taking prevention, 39. See also land ownership

property principle of innovation, stated, 50, 63, 100. *See also* contract law; equality-growth relationships; property law
Prussia, 67, 221, 240n7
public contracts, 37, 83–84, 96–99, 247nn3–4, 253n52
public finance stage, innovations, 31, 32, 33–34, 35, 117–20, 259n55
public information role, economic development, 208–9, 224, 290nn49–50
puerperal fever, 211

Quesnay, Francois, 287n26
qui tam institution, 173–74

Raiffeisen, Friedrich, 104–5
Raja, Angara, xiv
randomizing strategy, in growth-promoting reform, 216, 217–18, 294n28, 295n29
Rawls, John, xiv, 61, 294n28
real estate markets. *See* land ownership
reciprocity principle, 85–87
redistribution efficiency, 62–63, 239n25
refinancing solution, financial distress, 143, 145, 149–50, 151*f*
registries: creditor, 148; land ownership, 72–73, 244n33, 267n8
regulatory framework: bribery costs and benefits, 166, 167–72, 277n42, 278nn46–47, 279n50; as business development obstacle, 136–37, 264n15, 277n39; as economic growth foundation, 223–24; for judgment-proof problem, 185–86; level of care problem, 182–83; for public contract enforcement, 37, 83–84, 96–99, 253n52; for wealth-taking, 41–42, 43
relational contracts, 31–32, 35–36, 83–90, 132, 248n15, 249n17, n20
relational finance, 29, 33–34, 103–9, 149, 254nn9–10, n12
relationship framework as insurance substitute, 188–89, 242n19
religion, as banking obstacle, 112, 258n42
rent seeking, defined, 293n22
reorganization solution: financially distressed firms, 143–44, 149–50, 151*f*, 155–57, 266n3, 268n18; for sovereign bankruptcy, 155–57, 270n33, n35, 271n38
reputational sanctions, 35–36
residual poverty, 62–63

resources vs. ideas, sustainability arguments, 59–61
retreat opportunities, tactics, 82–83, 247n1
reward strategies, bribery control, 172–74
Richardson, George, xiv
Riggs Bank, 40
risk valuations, safety spending, 180–82, 281n6. *See also* accidents and liability
Robinson, Joan, 102
Rodrik, D., 289n46
Rogers, John P., 30
Root, Hilton, 275n18, 296n35
Rose-Ackerman, Susan, 160
Rosenstein-Rodan, Paul, 198
Rowling, J. K., 74
rule-of-law index, 56, 134, 237n9
Rumania, 232n9, 233n14
rural development banks, India, 105, 255n15
Russia: contract enforcement, 232n13, 250n31; contract law, 251n38; corruption patterns, 275n16, n21; crime patterns, 161, 170; debt default impact, 261n67; European Union path, 232n9; expropriation tactics, 153–54, 292n13; gangster capitalism, 40, 56, 114, 235n2; Gazprom cross-listing, 140; Gorbachev's privatization goal, 292n4; income growth, 17–18, 232n10; investor vulnerabilities, 114, 117, 212; liberalization policy effects, 207, 208; odious debt, 270n42; oil resources, 233n17; privatization stages, 212–14; security tax example, 6–7

Sack, Alexander, 270n42
safety spending, risk valuation, 180–82, 185–86, 283n22. *See also* accidents and liability
Salama, Bruno Meyerhof, xiv
Salinas, Ricardo, 8, 111
sanctions approach, odious debt, 272n43
Sane, Renuka, 166
savings and loan crisis, U.S., 116–17
savings rate, 204–5, 288nn33–34
Scandinavian countries, 52, 62, 134, 152. *See also* Sweden
Schäfer, Hans-Bernd, 71, 247n2, 249n17, 251n40
Schmitt, Carl, 296n40
Schramm, Carl, xiii, xiv
Schumpter, Joseph, 229n2, 230n5
Schweitzer, Heike, xiv

science knowledge, 211, 291n1
secrets and private information, 129–33, 224, 263nn6–7. *See also* double trust dilemma
secured creditors, bankruptcy law, 146–49, 267n12
security tax example, 6–7
Seko, Mobutu Sese, 40, 165
self-employment, 107, 255n21
self-enforcing contracts, 87–88, 248n14
self-regulation, U.S. banking sector, 230n8
Sen, Amartya, 230n9
Senegal, income per capita, 14
Shah, Parth J., 166
Shakespeare, William, 74
Shang Yin, ix
sharecropping, 243n27
Shelley, Mary, 211
Shishido, Zenishi, 291n53
Shleifer, Andrei, 284n7
Shopper's Stopper, 128
Silesia, 67, 240n7
silver bracelets, Afghanistan, 101–2
Singapore, 133, 152, 167, 176, 276n25
Singer, H. W., 200
Slim, Carlos, 48
Slovakia, 232n9, 233n14
Slovenia, 232n9, 233n14
Smith, Adam, 135–36, 254n6, 288n29
socialist sector, in China's dual track approach, 217–18, 295n34
social justice arguments, 61–63, 224–25
social sanctions, 35–36, 83–90
soft-budget constraints, 8–9, 115–17, 154, 259n54
Solomon's knot, described, 3
Solow, Robert, 235n7
Somalia, corruption, 160
South Africa, 237n9, 278n49
South Korea: closely held corporation statistics, 133; control premium, 134; corporate governance effects, 139; corruption patterns, 164; government coordination factor, 291n53; income levels, 14; life valuation statistic, 181; patent filings, 77; political structure and economic growth, 227–28
Soviet Union: capital accumulation policy, 153–54, 288n34; corruption patterns, 164; and economic development theory, 197, 286n12; economic growth foundation, 53–54; famine statistics, 193,

284n2; property use policy, 232n13. *See also* Russia
Spain, 197, 270n42
specific performance, as civil sanction, 95–96, 252nn44–46
Spence, A. Michael, 252n48, 288n32
spice voyages, financing, 2–3, 123
spread, interest rate, 111, 112f, 244n32, 257n39
squatters, 69–71, 242nn20–21
standardization, as public contract, 97–98
standards prescription, accidents and liability, 190–91
start-ups, statistics, 47, 236n12. *See also* innovations, overview
state leadership approach, economic development theory, 194, 196, 197–206, 285n11, 286n12, nn19–20, 287nn22–24, 288n29, n34. *See also* China; Eastern European countries; Soviet Union
statistical proofs, challenges, 25–26, 233n22
steel company examples, 8–9, 80, 129–30
Stephan, Paul, 292n4
Stiglitz, Joseph, 252n48, 288n32
stock markets: ADR certificates, 265n22; cartel potential, 55; cross-listing benefits, 140, 265n23, n25; as finance system, 117–20, 259n55; law's value, 9–10, 32–33; price influences, 134–35, 139, 264nn11–14, 265n23
strict liability rule, 190–91
Strong, Barrett, 12
Stulz, R. M., 265n23
sub-Saharan Africa. *See* African countries, generally; *specific countries*
subsidies: with bankruptcy proceedings, 154–55; in economic development theory, 198–202, 209, 285n11, 287n27, 290n49; with soft budget constraints, 8–9, 115–17, 154; for wealth-taking, 40, 41–42
Sun Tzu, 83
sustainability arguments, economic growth, 59–60
Sweden, 14, 146, 175, 255n21, 266n5
Switzerland, banking systems, 105
Sykes, Alan O., 283n16
Syria, capital per capita, 288n36

Taft, Chief Justice, 270n42
Taiwan, 152, 181, 227–28, 291n53

takeovers, 268n18, 291n53
Talley, Eric, xiv
Tanzania, 89, 155, 202
tariffs, 200–201, 235n5
taxes: in corruption calculations, 274n9; in dual economy theory, 201–2, 287nn26–27; as ownership decision, 238n19; and public goods monopoly, 278n47; and residual poverty, 62–63; Russia's political uses, 154, 213; as subsidies, 41–42
textile industry examples, 5, 7–8, 43–45
Thailand, 261n67, 295n34
theft, for wealth-taking, 40–41
Theoderich, King, 28, 234n3
Thomas, Robert K., xiv
tit-for-tat strategy, 85, 248n9
Tomasic, Romas, 276n26
trademark law, 78
traditional sector, in dual economic theory, 201–2, 287nn22–24
transaction costs, in corporation size question, 128–29, 262n4
transnational suits, safety liability problem, 183–84, 282nn14–15, 283nn16–17
Transparency International, 160, 274n8
Trebilcock, Michael, xiv
trial-proof problem, accidents and liability, 186–87
Trobriand Islanders, dispute resolution, 35–36
trust creation, United Kingdom, 168, 276n33
Tunisia, capital output ratio, 288n36
Turkey, 14, 176, 255n21, 269n21

Uganda, 278n49
Ukraine, 80, 232n9, 233n17
ultra vires doctrine, 253n52
unbalanced growth perspective, economic development theory, 198–99, 285n11
undercapitalization problem, resolution, 143
uninsured out-of-pocket expenses, accidents, 187–88
United Kingdom: bankruptcy law, 150; capital per capita, 205, 289n37; civil contracts, 93; closely held corporation statistics, 132–33; colonial land claims, 240n4; commercial risk spreading, 230n4; contract law, 93, 250nn35–36; control premium, 134; historical agricultural production, 221, 240n7; liability law, 283n17; procreditor bias, 153,

269n24; regulatory restriction example, 98–99; royal monopoly transitions, 135–36; start-up time requirements, 264n15; trust creation, 168, 276n33; wages-national income relationship, 58–59; Zimbabwe's land compensation policy, 235n4
United Nations, bribery law, 274n8
United States: banked person statistics, 252n49; bankruptcy law, 266n3, 268n20; charitable mortgage loans, 255n19; closely held corporation statistics, 133; collateral procedures, 257n36; contract law, 250n33; control premium, 134; foreclosure law, 244n36; growth rate, 1; health spending, 282n11; historic income growth, 13; homicide rates, 162; income inequality, 52; land rental, 70; odious debt policies, 155–57, 270n42; patent filings, 77, 246n46; patent laws, 245n40, n43; qui tam strategy, 173–74; savings and loan crisis, 116–17; self-employment statistics, 255n21; squatters, 69, 242n20; work-related disease, 282n11
unowned organizations, 79–80, 125
unsecured creditors, bankruptcy law, 146–49, 267n6, nn11–12
Uruguay, 257n36, 269n21
utilitarianism, 226, 297n1

van Dijk, Jan, 162, 163t, 273n3
veil of ignorance, 216, 294n28
Venice, commercial risk spreading, 230n4
venture finance stage, 29–31, 32, 33–35, 109–12
Vera, Flavia Santinoni, xiv
Versaille Treaty, 270n42
Vietnam, 72–73, 250n31
village moneylenders, 108–9
Viscusi, W. K., 181
Vishny, R., 284n7
void for illegality doctrine, 253n52
Voigt, Stefan, xiv
von Wangenheim, Georg, xiv

wage levels: as bribery control, 166–67, 276n25; in dual economic theory, 201, 287nn22–24; national income relationships, 58–59, 107; productivity relationships, 58–59, 238n16. See also income levels; labor value

Washington Consensus, economic
    development theory, 194–95, 196, 205–7,
    284n5
wealth, values of, 10–12, 225–27
wealth acquisition: fairness arguments,
    61–63; innovation profits, 46–48, 50,
    236n16; labor value theories, 43–46,
    235n7, 236n8; law impact overview, 39,
    48–49; ownership myth, 238n19; taking
    strategies, 40–43, 55–56, 235n4. *See also*
    equality-growth relationships
wealth gap, 1–2, 13–16
welfare overtaking theorem, 51–52, 57
Wen Jiabao, 295n33
whistle-blower strategies, bribery control,
    173–74, 279n55

Wittes, Ben, xiii
Wolfensohn, James, 160
work-related disease, 282n11. *See also* acci-
    dents and liability
World Bank, 159–60, 194–95
World Trade Organization (WTO), 76, 216
Wyoming, collateral procedures, 257n36

Xu Guangdong, 295n34

Yukos, 153–54
Yunus, Muhammad, 105–6
Yushchenko, Viktor, 80

Zhang Wei, xiii
Zimbabwe, 40, 66, 165, 235n4, 249n17